The Future of Scholarship on Race in Organizations

A Volume in Research in Social Issues in Management

Series Editors

Eden B. King
Rice University
Quinetta M. Roberson
Michigan State University
Mikki R. Hebl
Rice University

Research in Social Issues in Management

Eden B. King, Quinetta M. Roberson, and Mikki R. Hebl, Editors

The Future of Scholarship on Race in Organizations

Edited by

Eden B. King
Rice University

Quinetta M. Roberson
Michigan State University

Mikki R. Hebl
Rice University

INFORMATION AGE PUBLISHING, INC.
Charlotte, NC • www.infoagepub.com

Library of Congress Cataloging-in-Publication Data

CIP record for this book is available from the Library of Congress
http://www.loc.gov

ISBNs: 978-1-64802-841-0 (Paperback)

   978-1-64802-842-7 (Hardcover)

   978-1-64802-843-4 (ebook)

CONTENTS

PREFACE

RESEARCH ON SOCIAL ISSUES IN MANAGEMENT

The Future of Scholarship on Race in Organizations

Quinetta M. Roberson, Eden B. King, and Mikki R. Hebl

Since the term "workforce diversity" was first coined in the 1990s, the topic has received consistent and increasing attention by researchers. Over the last 30 years, a body of theory and research has amassed which recognizes diversity as an important work unit characteristic and explored its influence on organizational functioning and performance. Some research has focused on the conceptualization and operationalization of diversity, offering insights into its complexity as a construct and the consequences of its varying types and forms. Other work has explored these consequences in greater detail, examining the value for diversity in organizations based on in terms of the individual, workgroup and organizational outcomes of heterogeneity at different places in organizations. Studies have also examined the mechanisms through which diversity effects occur, highlighting identity and information exchange processes as critical for understanding how diversity operates, as well as how features of an internal and external environments influence its operation.

The Future of Scholarship on Race in Organizations, pp. vii–ix
Copyright © 2022 by Information Age Publishing
All rights of reproduction in any form reserved.

Despite these advancements, the field is at a critical juncture where new ideas, emphases, theories, predictions and approaches are needed to propel our understanding of the meaning, import and functioning of diversity in organizations. Accordingly, we wanted to look to the future of diversity work for our third volume of this series. By future, we refer to both the content of the chapters and to the contributors. We endeavored to give a voice to emerging scholars who *are* the future of our field and can help to set a future research agenda to push our understanding of diversity in organizations. Therefore, only graduate students and post-docs were eligible to submit proposals to this volume.

The focus on a future research agenda was particularly important to us given all that was happening in the world when we sent out the call for proposals. Beyond coping with the effects of a global pandemic that altered all aspects of life and work, the world was challenged to deal with the direct and indirect effects of discord between racial and ethnic groups stemming from the murder of George Floyd, armed conflicts and attacks on nations, mass violence against people simply based on their identities, and strained international relations. Further, as society still wrestled with issues of gender parity, misleading information and censorship, and climate change, scholars were forced to defend their vocations and avocations as people debated the value of science. Given the demands and trials of that moment in time, we were thrilled to receive 33 proposals for chapters from graduate students and post-docs in the field.

To provide a space for the diversity of voices and perspectives on the future of diversity, we have separated the chapters into two volumes grouped by topic of interest. The chapters in this volume raise new and provocative questions about race in organizations that deliberate on the state of our science, our understanding of complex experiences of race, and a more nuanced view of race in terms of intersectionalities. We describe the content and contributions of the chapters in greater detail below.

In a pair of introductory chapters, Torrez and colleagues and Warren and colleagues describe and push back on the state of scholarship on race in organizations. These chapters directly confront explicit and implicit norms in management scholarship that might perpetuate oppression. These critiques focus on the notion of objectivity and the functionalist lens common in this area of work. In so doing, these chapters set the stage for deeper considerations of race.

Indeed, the next section of the volume problematizes simplistic views of race by providing rich descriptions of the complex experiences of Black people. Several of these pieces point to potential opportunities for improvement. First, Burgess and Norris take a positive lens and describe a strength-focused approach. Second, Ramirez and Walker emphasize the importance of concordance between supervisors and subordinates in terms of their viewpoints of race. Third, Kea-Edwards and Reichard propose that the narratives people use to understand their experiences—including racial microaggressions—can help in the development of leadership competencies.

Several other contributions in this section focus on the challenges experienced by Black people at work. For example, Green and colleagues discuss the consequences of racial mega-threats and racist political ideologies on the experiences of Black people at work. Moore and Phillip's chapter, as another example, presents an analysis of publicly available organizational statements about racial inequality that exemplify varying levels of authentic commitments to diversity and inclusion.

The final section of this volume considers both challenges and opportunities for change from the lens of intersections between race and gender. Summerville and Ruggs describe an authenticity paradox for Black women that is spurred by racialized and gendered work environments. Carter and Ponce de Leon integrate the potentially opposing predictions of double jeopardy and intersectional invisibility by considering moderating conditions (e.g., context) that explain how the intersection of race and gender are experienced. Lastly, Massey and Roberson's contribution tackles the emerging and futuristic question of racial and gender diversity in programming, customization, and consequences of artificial intelligence.

Overall, each of these chapters provokes the status quo and, in so doing, offers a fresh perspective on the study of diversity in general and race and racism more specifically. We believe the end result is a more comprehensive exploration of the phenomenon and the development of an exciting future research agenda. More importantly, we believe that this group of scholars helps to advance our vision for this series by inventively pushing our understanding of diversity in organizations.

CHAPTER 1

EXAMINING THE RACIALIZED CONSEQUENCES OF OBJECTIVITY IN MANAGEMENT SCHOLARSHIP

Brittany Torrez, Cydney H. Dupree, and Michael W. Kraus
Yale University

ABSTRACT

Black, Latinx, and Indigenous scholars remain severely underrepresented in the academy of management, as does racial scholarship. In this chapter, we will discuss one factor that contributes to the continued marginalization of historically underrepresented scholars of color: the scientific method's commitment to traditional notions of objectivity. We argue that objectivity—defined as practices and policies rooted in the heightened value placed on research methodology that is ostensibly free from bias—is central to the founding of primarily White scholarship in management and remains central to knowledge production within the field. We contend that racial scholarship is perceived as less aligned with these traditional standards of objectivity. Moreover, the insistence on objectivity in its current form advantages White scholars and their perspectives on race relations while simultaneously marginalizing underrepresented racial minorities as they attempt to integrate their own lived experiences with the methods and practices of racial

The Future of Scholarship on Race in Organizations, pp. 1–27
Copyright © 2022 by Information Age Publishing
All rights of reproduction in any form reserved.

scholarship. Ultimately, objectivity norms exist in every evaluative sphere of academia and, without careful attention to the downstream consequences, they can reproduce the exact kinds of racial inequality scholars seek to remedy.

A Latina graduate student enters her doctoral program in management to pursue a scientific understanding of diversity and inclusion. Like other graduate students of color, her primary motivation is to rigorously investigate how her and other marginalized people's lived experiences can be utilized to expand and challenge management theory with the goal of better understanding and, ultimately, improving the lives of underrepresented minorities in the workplace. Her department seminar is a sea of White faces. Her classes review all of the management classics—another deluge of Whiteness taught by a continuous stream of White men. Aside from her conspicuousness as the only Latina in the room, she starts to stick out as the only one challenging problematic, and often racially ignorant, assumptions in management literature. When she does, she is actively interrogated, discredited, and her lived experiences are minimized. Her excitement wanes as she finds herself constrained in her ability to fully express herself, let alone her research ideas, in this environment. Her initial research momentum stalls, or disappears altogether, as she navigates academia.

The overrepresentation of White scholars and the marginalization of racial minority scholars—both generally and specifically scholars who study explicitly racialized topics—is a notable and persistent feature of academia (Armstrong, 1979; Blackwell, 1988). This includes management and organizational behavior. Today, Black, Latinx, and Indigenous scholars remain severely underrepresented in the academy of management, especially among senior leadership positions (Minefee et al., 2018). In this chapter, we will discuss one factor that contributes to the continued marginalization of historically underrepresented scholars of color: the scientific method's commitment to traditional notions of objectivity. We argue that objectivity—defined as practices and policies rooted in the heightened value placed on research methodology that is ostensibly free from bias—is central to the founding of primarily White scholarship in management and remains central to knowledge production within the field. We contend that racial scholarship is perceived as less aligned with these traditional standards of objectivity. Moreover, the insistence on objectivity in its current form advantages White scholars in their pursuit of research while simultaneously marginalizing underrepresented racial minorities (URMs) as they attempt to integrate their own lived experiences into racial scholarship.

The Racialized Function of Objectivity

Objectivity, defined as the "extent to which a researcher's methods are free from prejudice," is typically upheld across the social sciences as a norm indicating scientific rigor, personal detachment, and a lack of bias (Armstrong, 1979, p. 423; Zuberi & Bonilla-Silva, 2008). Detachment and disinvestment are purportedly key to rigorous and high-quality scholarship, a crucial imperative in organizational research (Anteby, 2013; Greenberg et al., 2019). Studying topics that are personally relevant to researchers is therefore considered taboo. Personal attachment to one's work—for example, the idea that your research could inform changes to improve your own experience and that of others like you—introduces the researcher's stake in the research process and thus runs counter to this predominant norm of objectivity. With regards to racial scholarship, this precedent is echoed in the words of sociologist Robert Park: "The world was full of crusaders. [One's] role instead was to be that of the calm, detached scientist who investigates race relations with the same objectivity and detachment with which the zoologist dissects the potato bug" (Morris & Ghaziani, 2005, p. 52).

Applying traditional standards of objectivity to the study of an undeniably subjective topic, such as race, has many costs for researchers and their scholarship. In the realm of publication, topics like race are likely to run afoul of objectivity norms because of their inherently perceived subjectivity (e.g., the conclusions were predetermined, the researchers brought their own experiences into the research process). As a result, race scholarship is likely to be underrepresented fieldwide. For example, in separate scoping reviews of the literature in psychology and management over four decades, only 17% of publications in the *Journal of Applied Psychology* were about demographics (e.g., race and ethnicity; Cascio & Aguinis, 2008) and only 5% of the publications across six of the top journals in psychology were about race (Roberts et al., 2020). Investigations of publications in management and psychology reveal that diversity scholarship generally—and race scholarship in particular—remains underrepresented across the literature. Moreover, existing diversity scholarship is largely dominated by White scholars (Cascio & Aguinis, 2008; Chugh & Brief, 2008; Konrad, 2003; Roberts et al., 2020).

To better understand the impact of objectivity norms on the fieldwide outcomes mentioned above, this chapter meets four broad goals. First, we theorize the process through which racial minority scholars who study race-related topics may be more likely to incur threats to their objectivity and scientific rigor. Second, we use examples to review how objectivity interrogation is directed toward research on race. Third, we consider the downstream consequences of such threats and objectivity interrogations for the long-term success and retention of URM scholars in academia (e.g., Syed, 2017), whose sense of well-being and self-presentation may be shaped by these dynamics. Finally, we turn to solutions, drawing on insights from other disciplines, such as sociology, and qualitative methodologies to guide our understanding of these contextual issues. We hope that this work will inspire current and future scholars to value, rather than problematize, the lived experiences of URM scholars in the domain of race scholarship, recognizing and alleviating the impact of traditional objectivity norms on the most underrepresented scholars and the insights they bring to the field.

HOW OBJECTIVITY THREATENS AND SHAPES RACIAL SCHOLARSHIP

Perceived objectivity, defined as a lack of bias or subjectivity, is a highly valued component of management scholarship (Amabile & Hall, 2018; Anteby, 2013; Armstrong, 1979; Greenberg et al., 2019). However, traditional norms of objectivity make racialized topics more prone to undervaluation, stigmatization, and marginalization. Racial scholarship is thought to lack objectivity for three reasons: (1) the typical methodology runs counter to dominant modes of quantification, (2) the topic itself is considered subjective, or (3) the identity of the scholar conducting this research herself invites concern about detachment from racialized topics (Cha & Roberts, 2019; Jané et al., 2018; Torrez et al., 2021). In this section, we map out how perceptions of qualitative methods—historically associated with critical race theory—delegitimize its position in a field historically focused on ostensibly objective metrics of performance and efficiency. In addition, we review evidence demonstrating how critical racial scholarship, in particular, challenges this historical focus and, in doing so, disrupts the status quo and threatens perceived objectivity. Lastly, we discuss how this disruption elicits criticism directed, in particular, toward URM scholars, whose personal attachment to their work violates norms about objectivity, therefore imbuing additional rigor and detachment onto White perspectives of racial issues. Such dynamics can inhibit the development and publication of needed scholarship in management.

Positivism and Profit in Management Scholarship

At this moment, racial scholarship faces predominant norms in management scholarship that threaten to devalue racial justice as a research topic and the methodologies that race scholars may employ. Almost all social scientific fields, including management and related disciplines, have attempted to assimilate to dominant modes of quantification in an effort to gain the same legitimacy as natural sciences (Pfeffer & Fong, 2002). Statistics and quantitative data are thought to lend credibility to rigorous and testable theoretical models. Endeavors to pursue such paradigms and methodology decrease the philosophical chasm between the social and natural sciences, therefore increasing the status and legitimacy of social science research. Such endeavors are widespread in historical accounts of social scientific development and scholarship (Hempel & Oppenheim, 1948; Lieberson & Lynn, 2002). These attempts culminated in a focus on objectivity and positivism in management and psychological scholarship (Hassard, 1995; Katyal, 2009; Salter & Adams, 2013). Inversely, qualitative methodologies have become and continue to be stigmatized as lacking the appropriate empirical rigor expected in management scholarship; such methodologies are often underutilized as a result (Bluhm et al., 2011; Colella et al., 2017; Jané et al., 2018).

Positivism is a philosophical theory that posits that all truth is verifiable, and that scientific evidence exactly reflects the reality of the world—completely free of values (Katyal, 2009). Race scholars move toward objectivity by adopting field standards for rigor and quantification which are central elements of a positivist approach to management science. One natural conclusion of this historical focus on rigor and quantification? The prevailing assumption that what can be measured and quantified about a firm is what should be the focus of management scholarship (Katyal, 2009). Diversity and race were thus primarily conceptualized in the management literature as variables to be quantified and understood instrumentally in relation to organizational efficiency and effectiveness (Konrad, 2003). The business case for diversity became a substantial motivation for both workplace scholarship on diversity and workplace programs on diversity. By the end of the 20th century nearly all Fortune 500 companies had created diversity management programs; many of these programs currently advocate for this instrumental case for diversity (Georgeac & Rattan, 2021). Race and diversity would come to be measured and contextualized within the framework of quantitative methods toward better understanding organizational performance and profits (Colella et al., 2017; Katyal, 2009; Konrad, 2003). This approach constrains the types of questions that management scholars might ask about race and the operationalization of organizational experiences that are shaped by race—narrowly focusing on what furthers organizational goals. Perspectives that are more openly critical of the central organizing principles of profit and performance, particularly in the domain of race, that would require deeper analysis of individual lived experiences (e.g., organizational practices that increase belonging for minoritized colleagues but at a cost to productivity) have been less likely to emerge in management scholarship.

Conversely, qualitative methods—including storytelling, ethnography, and participatory action research—are at the forefront of the research paradigms of critical race theory. Critical race theory is an area of scholarship that has transformed the scholarly study of race and activism to attenuate racial hierarchy (Carbado & Roithmayr, 2014; Delgado & Stefancic, 2017; Parker & Lynn, 2002; Sablan, 2019). In contrast to the methods of positivism, qualitative methods can more directly center the lived experiences of marginalized voices. Analyses using these methods or even simply informed by them have a greater capacity to place racial issues in a broader historical and societal context—bringing issues of race and power into the spaces where they are likely to be best understood (Kraus & Torrez, 2020). Qualitative methods give voice to the lived experiences of marginalized groups. Such groups are ultimately one of the most critical sources of information on race and racism (Adams et al., 2018). Adams and colleagues (2018) highlight this truth by recalling Dr. Martin Luther King, Jr.'s address to the American Psychological Association in 1968:

> One reason some advances were made in the South during the past decade was the discovery by northern whites of the brutal facts of southern segregated life. It was the Negro who educated the nation by dramatizing the evils through nonviolent protest. The social scientist played little or no role in disclosing truth. The Negro action movement with raw courage did it virtually alone. (Adams et al., 2018, p. 339)

The lived experiences of racial minorities in organizations, though they may not prioritize an understanding of organizational performance, are key to our understanding of racial justice. However, the inevitable outcome of a tension between the methods and discoveries brought about by these methods is that race scholarship in management seeks legitimation and objectivity through positivism, quantification, and performance-oriented outcomes. Most race scholarship in management, therefore, tends to ignore the lived contexts of the very people who are likely best positioned to bring novelty to the scholarship around race and racism in the workplace—those most affected by it. Overall, there is a hesitance to merge critical race perspectives with organizational theory and related management disciplines (Adams et al., 2015; Salter & Adams, 2013). Such merging would better inform organizational research and social science (Ray, 2019; Ray et al., 2017; Sablan, 2019) by contributing novel insights. This is a point we return to in the conclusion section of our chapter.

Research Standards and the Status Quo

Because management research has foundations in efficiency and performance, many programs of research develop that investigate similar outcomes (e.g., firm performance, worker productivity) with respondents whose perspectives are seen as more generalizable (e.g., White employees) and who primarily provide a complimentary view of organizations (Katyal, 2009). Therefore, research that attempts to complicate this conventional paradigm or challenge these core ideas will naturally violate the status quo. Scholars of color, who wish to study race in the context of management, must contend with these norms and the constraints on scholarship that they produce.

Scholarship focused on racial justice violates traditional norms in each of the aforementioned ways. Therefore, such work is likely to engender heightened interrogations of objectivity as it is conducted, communicated, and published. When people confront bias or challenge the status quo, they are more likely to be discredited by others (Ashburn-Nardo et al., 2008; Kaiser & Miller, 2001) and perceived as self-interested (O'Brien & Crandall, 2005). Academics conducting racial scholarship, advocating for racial justice, or encouraging the application of science to activism may therefore be perceived as less objective (Richter et al., 2020). Our research supports this argument by exploring journalism, another domain wherein objectivity is a key occupational feature. In our research we find that White evaluators rated journalists covering racial issues (e.g., racial disparities) as less objective and more biased than those covering less explicitly racialized issues (e.g., technology; Torrez et al., 2021). Applying this finding to publication and science communication, strong negative reactions to researchers who challenge the status quo can contribute to the objectivity interrogation we review here, prompting a more skeptical review process whereby ordinary claims require more evidence.

To understand objectivity interrogation of racial scholarship in management, we draw on prior work evaluating the legitimacy of another marginalized research topic: gender. A recent study examining journal submissions to the *Journal of Management* demonstrated this relative devaluation of gender equity research. The study found that research about gender diversity must reach a much higher caliber for publication compared to non-diversity-related work (King et al., 2018). Moreover, when female authors conduct research on gender equity, male evaluators respond negatively, discrediting the author and her work. Anecdotally and empirically, there is evidence of these shifting standards toward gender scholarship (Bell et al., 2020; Jané et al., 2018). In comparing gender scholarship to more mainstream scholarship in management, one academic said:

> People doing gender research will have to justify themselves more. If you want to publish about gender in a more general journal you will need to have an editor who sees something in this topic, right? Whereas if you do, let's say strategy research or cross-cultural communication, you have to explain much less.... It's not so easily challenged. (Jané et al., 2018, p. 415)

These higher standards increase the barriers to publication in top-tier, mainstream venues, potentially stalling programs of research, promotions, and careers. Race scholarship in management is up against these same forces, requiring higher standards, increased quantification, and more normative paradigms to be seen as objective, aligned with the status quo, and thus worthy of academic success.

Racial Identity and Objectivity

A scholar's racial identity may also influence the perceived objectivity of racial scholarship. As previously noted, in management scholarship and academia, shedding one's personal biases is perceived as the pathway to objectivity (Anteby, 2013; Nzinga et al., 2018; Porter, 1996). For racial minority academics attempting to bring their lived experiences to their work, acknowledgment of their racial identity might influence their perceived ability to shed personal biases—and therefore, their perceived objectivity. In contrast, due to historical power dynamics, White scholars' personal biases and lived experiences are perceived as default, neutral, and therefore, more easily adhere to traditional notions of objectivity. The link between racial identity and perceived objectivity can sabotage efforts to create a more realistic and complex picture of race scholarship.

Such sabotage is evident when we examine the literature on bias confrontation. Minority groups who confront bias are met with skepticism (Czopp & Monteith, 2003; Drury & Kaiser, 2014; Rasinski & Czopp, 2010). Indeed, Black people who confront racial bias face more backlash compared to White confronters (Schultz & Maddox, 2013). Relatedly, Black employees who engage in diversity-promoting initiatives are viewed as more self-interested compared to White employees who do the same (Gardner & Ryan, 2020). In journalism, readers leave more negative comments on race-related op-eds written by Black (versus White) journalists (Sumner et al., 2017). In our own work, we find that this backlash may stem from the notion that scholars' of color (but not White scholars') racial identity fundamentally shapes their perspective of all issues in terms of race. Underrepresented racial minorities are perceived as less objective and more biased than White journalists (Torrez et al., 2021).

Put simply, nonwork identities are expected to be neatly set aside when scholars conduct research (Acker, 2006; Ramarajan & Reid, 2013). When people enter the workplace, everything outside the scope of their work identity is expected to be left behind in an effort to create the ideal worker. This expectation stigmatizes a variety of self-relevant research, not solely race scholarship conducted by scholars of color (cf. Greenberg et al., 2019 for a perspective on working mothers studying pregnancy and motherhood; Amabile & Hall, 2018 for a perspective on retirees studying retirement; Jané et al., 2018 for a perspective on women conducting gender scholarship in management). In addition, such norms ignore and minimize how nonwork identities fundamentally shape the way people view and engage with their occupational contexts (Leigh & Melwani, 2019; Pitesa & Pillutla, 2019). For example, a Black woman cannot enter an organization and suddenly become a deracialized employee—this is an impossible and impractical expectation. Moreover, this assumption ignores and minimizes how some high-status nonwork identities (e.g., White, male, middle-class) are the ones that organizations center in their design of culture and norms (Ray, 2019; Rivera & Tilcsik, 2016) and thus are less likely to arouse concern over objectivity. Racial minorities—and their racial identities—by contrast are penalized for not fitting in with the standardized, dominant culture, both within the workplace and academia.

OBJECTIVITY INTERROGATION

Having reviewed the dynamics that shape perceptions of objectivity in race scholarship, we now turn to how interrogations of objectivity occur. We theorize that the primary sources shaping perceptions of objectivity (i.e., methodological rigor, interpretation that disrupts the status quo, or implication of ones' racial identity) are the exact sources that will be questioned, discredited, and discouraged in race scholarship. This can occur in a variety of spaces: presentation feedback, peer-reviews, and tenure and promotion committees. Most evaluative spheres in academia aim to provide a space in which a scholar can share their work and their peers can respond with constructive criticism to move the work forward in helpful ways. However, in an effort to uphold objectivity norms in race scholarship, this feedback can be obstructive, stifling efforts to improve and promote one's research.

Throughout this section, we provide examples of these interrogations from an early analysis of qualitative data. Over the course of 7 months, we interviewed 51 psychological scholars studying race-related topics in management and psychology departments. These scholars were racially diverse and came from a wide range of tenure in the field: graduate students, post-doctoral fellows, early-career faculty, and tenured faculty. The interviews explored topics related to research interests, scholarly motivations, and experiences sharing their research with the field broadly. Lastly, interviewees were asked if and how their racial identity influenced their experiences sharing their work.

Methodology Interrogations

One of the means through which a scholar's objectivity is questioned is through the interrogation of one's methodology. This focus on methodological rigor stems from the same foundational assumptions that devalue race-related research. Due to the historical focus on quantitative scholarship in management, methodology is perceived as a tool through which objectivity can be achieved (Zuberi & Bonilla-Silva, 2008). Thus, when a scholar's objectivity is called into question, such interrogation primarily occurs by discrediting or devaluing one's methods. These methods might include research design, data collection, and/or analysis techniques. Narratives from our own and others' research exemplify how these interrogations of methodology occur. For example, in his book Eduardo Bonilla-Silva, an Afro Puerto Rican sociologist, described an experience of sharing his work on colorblind racism to a mostly White sociology department. As he presented his work on subtle denial of racism, his colleagues questioned him, asking, "Who coded these data? Did you have White or Black coders? And what was the intercoder reliability index?" (Zuberi & Bonilla-Silva, 2008, p. 13).

Our own qualitative research revealed the same methodological interrogation (Torrez et al., in press). For example, one URM graduate student described a presentation in their department:

> The first question I got was about ... the race of the RAs [research assistants] and how did the race of the RAs impact [the study]. I felt like I was just getting lower-tier questions that were really basic. Obviously we accounted for that. (URM_9)

Black researchers are presumed less objective than White researchers, in part because of how their racial identities are conceptualized. White researchers, by contrast, are characterized as having less of a stake in attenuating racial issues in the United States, making them detached observers of racial justice scholarship. Hearkening back to the stigmatization of (traditionally race-related) qualitative methodology, a URM graduate student described their own experience:

So one of my other lab mates, she would present qualitative work and they would come at her very critical, in a very non-constructive manner, which didn't make sense because none of them did qualitative work. And then they were coming at it with a quantitative layman's approach. I'm like, "No, that's not how qualitative methodology works." It's just a very intimidating interaction. (URM_6)

Like many reviewers and editors in management, her peers lacked the familiarity and expertise with qualitative methods to appropriately evaluate it. Nonetheless, they were skeptical and critical, attempting to inject a quantitative perspective into qualitative methodology.

Another primary way in which objectivity is interrogated through methodology is by questioning the racial identity of the research *subjects*. As reviewed in the previous section, the majority of psychological research on race focuses on the experiences of White subjects. Indeed, most behavioral science research, including management, prioritizes the perspectives and psychology of conventionally Western, Educated, Industrialized, Rich, and Democratic (WEIRD) subjects (Bamberger & Pratt, 2010; Henrich et al., 2010). This normalizes White perspectives on race and diversity in the workplace and society, leaving the experiences of racial minorities largely understudied (Cox & Nkomo, 1990; Holvino, 2010). Racial minority subjects are therefore defined in opposition to White subjects, with insights being gleaned from research on racial minorities to the extent and degree it diverges from White samples. Thus, in order to achieve objectivity, researchers are often urged to incorporate White subjects' perspectives into their research on race. The following excerpt concerns a tenured URM faculty describing the enforcement of this standard in the review process:

If you have a sample that is the minority in a different country or whatever, people bring up all the time, "How can we generalize this?" When we have majority White samples, no one asks that question. It is just seen as a standard. And we expect that we should be able to generalize this research, this majority White sample, to everybody else. (URM_19)

Although this work was about how minorities relate to each other, this faculty was encouraged to include the perspectives of White people. The centering of White samples aligns research with the status quo, making it more palatable and closer to objectivity standards. Such incidents occur despite numerous attempts to push for an understanding of context, social structure, and race in management research (Colella et al., 2017; Cox & Nkomo, 1990; Gordon et al., 1990; Holvino, 2010; Katyal, 2009). Research that innovates by centering the experiences of racial minorities is, therefore, less likely to be seen as objective.

Ideological and Interpretation Interrogations

When it comes to racial scholarship, a researcher's methodological choice is not the only consideration subject to attack; their interpretation of data is often subject to objectivity interrogations. Bonilla-Silva provides another example in which his objectivity was questioned as he shared his interpretation of his work on colorblind racism. When presenting his work, one audience member questioned, "Since you do not have longitudinal data and are dismissive of survey results on racial attitudes, why should anyone believe your interpretation of these interviews?" (Zuberi & Bonilla-Silva, 2008, p. 13). Scholars' interpretation of data that promotes racial justice—or describes inequalities implicating White people as privileged by unearned advantages—directly challenges the status quo. The minimization of such research is merely part of the reliable tendency for high-status people to protect the status quo (e.g., Kraus et al., 2017). Unfortunately, such minimization in the process of peer review and scientific evaluation will deprive critical race scholarship and the people who produce it of the engagement they need to more fully develop the research and ideas. The following is an excerpt from a racial minority faculty member describing their experiences during their tenure and promotion process in management:

> So at the time, it was represented that at least one person, suggesting more than one person, questioned whether my research could ever be viewed as truly world class science because of the "ideologies behind them." And I asked [colleague] if he had anything of the sort in his review. He did not.... My review committee refused to take it out, and so it's ended up in my third-year review. It's still there. And if I ever open that file I boil over with rage at it. (RM_4)

Consistent with prior theorizing, research that challenges the status quo is susceptible to being perceived as more ideological than empirical. Such objectivity interrogations can look like attempts to frame the work as subjective rather than scientific:

> Whenever I give presentations, I don't ever get questions that [are] as critical of the work as what other people's questions are. It just seems like either they're taking it at face value or they're just not taking it at all. They feel I have like a lens that's coming to the work and so it's just like, okay, well that's your opinion more than that's scientific. (URM_8)

The above narrative from a Black graduate student represents how salient this notion of one's work as subjective becomes for URM scholars. This interrogation may not always be outwardly contentious. Indeed, White liberals engage in likely well-intentioned but nonetheless patronizing behavior toward Black Americans, using fewer words related to competence (e.g., "assertive," "powerful") in work assignments or introductory conversations with a Black (versus White) person (Dupree & Fiske, 2019). Across our work, we found a variety of patronizing monikers marking this ideological pushback (e.g., me-search, applied versus theoretical work, scholar-activism) that marginalizes racialized people and scholarship in management and psychology:

> So there's that expectation, and that expectation, sometimes it fits what people think but also, I feel like I've gotten some almost like annoyance from other scholars where they're like, "Oh yeah, okay, you're going to talk about race because you're a person of color and that's all you know about." So it definitely discredits critical thought that people of color put into their work, especially when they're studying race, and ignores the fact that bringing your own life experiences into that space adds an extra piece of labor that has to happen that white people don't have to do when they're talking about race within disparities and the harms that it creates to people. Like the idea is that all people of color studying race are the same and just doing the same "me-search." (URM_11)

Objectivity interrogation deindividuates people of color even as their lived experiences contribute unique insights to the field.

Overall, racial scholarship threatens the status quo and objectivity norms. This threat is reified in the objectivity interrogations launched at scholars of color, particularly those conducting research aimed at dismantling racial inequalities. These interviews highlight how racial scholarship elicits objectivity interrogation, a minimization process that increases barriers to publication and promotion. If these dynamics continue unchecked, it will prove difficult for racial scholarship—and marginalized scholars—to move from the periphery to the mainstream. In the following section, we document the interpersonal and structural impact of such dynamics on scholars of color and the scholarship of race relations in management.

IMPACT OF OBJECTIVITY INTERROGATION ON SCHOLARS OF COLOR AND RACIAL SCHOLARSHIP

As racial scholarship seeks legitimation in the field of management, it is up against the predominant norm of objectivity and thus faces intense scrutiny and interrogation. These norms devalue novel, innovative, and/ or qualitative approaches taken by scholars researching race, further marginalizing them, and undervaluing their work as low-quality and lacking in rigor. Crucially, this delegitimization process may disproportionately affect underrepresented scholars of color (Hofstra et al., 2020; Minefee et al., 2018) whose existence in academia is scarce, even in racial scholarship (Roberts et al., 2020).

The Battle for Belonging

Objectivity norms signal a lower sense of belonging to URM scholars, particularly those conducting racial scholarship. Racial minorities are often made to feel they do not belong in academic spaces due to a variety of factors (e.g., race-status associations; Dupree et al., 2021). Practices of objectivity may also effectively undermine a scholar's academic ability, integrity, and rigor (e.g., the assertion that studies of race conducted by URMs is "me-search"; Ray, 2016), further causing scholars of color to question their place in a field that has traditionally excluded people like them. Moreover, the dismissal of racial studies as specialized—and therefore unworthy of academic value—contributes to environments wherein scholars of color are made to feel that they, their work, and their perspectives are devalued. This, despite the fact that their perspectives mark a unique contribution to White management scholarship (Cox & Nkomo, 1990; Margolis & Romero, 1998). Unfortunately, such microaggressions likely recur in daily interactions (see the Competence Downshift; Dupree & Fiske, 2019) and in crucial evaluative spaces, such as tenure and promotion decisions.

Moreover, a historically White discipline often makes the development of racial scholarship particularly challenging for racial minorities (Brunsma et al., 2017; Minefee et al., 2018). Aside from the already significant challenges of tokenization (e.g., isolation, increased visibility, performance effects) and stereotype threat (Steele, 1997; Watkins et al., 2019; Wingfield & Wingfield, 2014), URM trainees of racial scholarship will have a scarcity of mentors who understand the challenges of objectivity interrogation in methods and practices in management scholarship. This means racial minorities likely lack safe venues to discuss issues of race and racism, let alone interrogations to their objectivity. Instead, URMs must constantly navigate and contend with majority White spaces to succeed in mainstream academia.

Navigating the White Space

Although much management work suggests that diversity is beneficial for organizations (Harrison & Klein, 2007; Herring, 2009; Mannix & Neale, 2005), the gains conferred by diversity can occur only when people are able to share their unique—and perhaps even controversial—perspectives. This happens when people can bring their full and authentic selves to the workplace (Dye & Golnaraghi, 2015; Ely & Thomas, 2001). Objectivity norms may dim racial minorities' authentic expression of their racial identity—as such expression will likely implicate one's objectivity. Racial minorities may thus employ compensation techniques, engaging in self-regulatory or self-presentational strategies (e.g., attending to appearance or shifting language; Dupree, 2021; Richeson & Shelton, 2007). While these self-regulatory strategies may be partially effective in mitigating interpersonal prejudice, they are cognitively and emotionally depleting (Shelton et al., 2005). Having to determine whether an audience members' questioning of your methodologies or interpretation is due to objectivity norms, pure racist motivations or, in the best case, a well-meaning attempt to improve your work is depleting. This acts as an additional barrier for URMs conducting racial scholarship in the already challenging context of graduate school (Ong et al., 2013; Wong, 2018).

Racial minority scholars may contend with prejudice or objectivity interrogations by engaging in self-regulatory or self-presentational strategies. However, these strategies may shape racial discourse and racial scholarship in the academy (Anderson, 2015; Goffman, 1963). Much like racial minorities downplay their stigmatized racial identities in the labor market (Kang et al., 2016), underrepresented racial minorities may disassociate themselves from characterizations of their racial group as less objective by attempting to objectify their work (Cha & Roberts, 2019; Shih & Young, 2016). This can lead URM researchers studying racialized topics to change research topics, reframe conclusions, or switch methodologies to adhere to objectivity norms. Deterred by frequent and unconstructive interrogations of their work, underrepresented racial minorities may start to present their work in ways that align with the status quo—ultimately stalling efforts to encourage radical and novel racial scholarship.

The Proliferation of Whiteness

A recent scoping review of research on race in psychology demonstrated that most publications tend to be authored by White authors, reviewed by White editors, and employ White samples (Roberts et al., 2020). The authors provide an intriguing thought experiment to understand the downstream implications of this bias for scholars of color:

> A researcher of color is invested in dismantling racial inequality and therefore conducts research on race with samples of color. The researcher submits a manuscript for publication to a White editor at a top-tier journal.

The manuscript is rejected by the editor, who feels unable or ill-equipped to handle it, perceives the researcher of color as less objective and credible than a White researcher, devalues or misunderstands the research, or criticizes the research for not including a White comparison sample. Subsequently, the researcher of color submits the work to an editor of color at a specialty journal who may be more invested in issues of race and more likely to publish the research. Ultimately, the research is published in a specialty journal that might be devalued by the author of color's institution, peers, students, and tenure committees, leaving mainstream psychology with theories, methods, and findings that do not reflect a diversity of perspectives (for similar arguments, see Hall & Maramba, 2001; Nzinga et al., 2018; Rowley & Camacho, 2015). (Roberts et al., 2020, pp. 9–10)

This process ultimately devalues research on race and racism by scholars of color by reducing its likelihood of receiving funding from research granting institutions (Hoppe et al., 2019), being cited (Hofstra et al., 2020), and being adopted by policymakers (Delgado, 1984) or organizational stakeholders (Hideg et al., 2020).

These dynamics elevate scholarship conducted by those best able to position themselves as objective outsiders—in the case of racial scholarship, this means members of the majority group (Jané et al., 2018; King et al., 2018). Race scholarship thus becomes filtered through Whitened narratives (Andersen, 2003; Bell & Hartmann, 2007; Gordon et al., 1990; Hikido & Murray, 2016). Such narratives, at best, ignore the complexity and nuances of racial issues, and, at worst, develop programs of research and new management practices that actively perpetuate racism (Clark, 1973). For example, the recent adoption of algorithms has led to an awareness that, even in a technological advancement presumed to lack human bias, the perspectives of the primarily White programmers creating these algorithms actually reinforce racism (Benjamin, 2019). In addition, colorblind or instrumental approaches to diversity (Apfelbaum et al., 2008; Apfelbaum et al., 2012) remain a significant part of our field's past and present connection with diversity management strategies in organizations. And yet, our field provides very little evidence of such approaches' hierarchy-attenuating utility (Georgeac & Rattan, 2021; Starck et al., 2021). Given current and historical attention to firm performance (Katyal, 2009), research that prioritizes how diversity relates to an organization's bottom line is more likely to be noticed by organizational stakeholders, further marginalizing those this research purportedly aims to help.

POTENTIAL SOLUTIONS AND CALLS TO ACTION

Having reviewed the ways in which racial minority scholars' objectivity is questioned through the interrogation of their methods and interpretation of their work on racial topics, this concluding section will discuss potential solutions. How can our field respond to these objectivity interrogations? Broadly, evaluators in our field such as editors, reviewers, and members of hiring and promotion committees must reconceptualize terms like rigor, objectivity, and bias—and reevaluate the meaning they possess in knowledge production. This means recognizing how detached and scientific observers have become synonymous with White and male perspectives, and deracialized scholarship. Contrary to staunch defenders of objectivity, this does not mean a complete abandonment of the scientific method, less attention to our own personal biases, or an opportunity for one's subjectivity to run rampant throughout the research process. Rather, it is a suggestion to internally investigate—with race at the forefront—what these standards mean and how they inadvertently exclude and silence the most vulnerable scholars in our field. We hope that upon recognizing the burdens on underrepresented racial minorities (particularly those conducting racial scholarship) and the impact on our understanding of race, diversity, and inclusion in management, this section encourages scholars to actively challenge traditional notions of objectivity through the solutions we suggest.

Reflexivity as a Solution to Systemic Subjectivity

Subjectivity is inevitable in scholarship. Reducing objectivity interrogations requires the deliberate and widespread proliferation of this fact. Objectivity is an impossible task. Rather than attempting to quantify and standardize management's path into scientific legitimacy through objectivity and scientific rigor, we must embrace bias and subjectivity, deepening our understanding of how our identities shape our science— including the research topics we choose, the people we study, and the outcomes we care about. Unlike the hierarchy-enhancing assumptions of management research that currently dominate our field, this stance considers the subjectivity of multiple parties, including White scholars conducting racial scholarship, scholars whose research is not explicitly racialized (but that undoubtedly has racial consequences), and scholars conducting quantitative research. From ideation and research design to analysis and interpretation of findings, all quantitative researchers, regardless of their racial identity, are inundated with subjective choices influenced by their backgrounds and identities.

One solution aimed at raising awareness of subjectivity in scholarship is the implementation of reflexivity statements. Here, we draw on lessons from other disciplines and methodologies to assert that researchers can, and should, reflect on their subjectivity in the research process. Typical academic norms would prescribe that scholars keep emotions and personal investments as separate from the research process as possible (Anteby,

2013; Nzinga et al., 2018). However, White scholars, as well as scholars of color, who study racial issues can and should make readers aware of their perspective, position, and privilege. Additionally, researchers who study topics they perceive to be race-neutral might reflect on how their positionality may nonetheless manifest in their work (Dupree & Kraus, 2021; Greenberg et al., 2019). Reflexivity statements would require all scholars to reflect on their true experiences as well as the "biases, past experiences, and beliefs" (Collins, 1986; Moorman, 2020, p. 436) that they intentionally or unintentionally infuse into the research process, from ideation to interpretation. Journals could require a statement of reflexivity prior to submission in all social scientific papers—a practice typically more common in qualitative research. Editors could reflect on their own positionality and require reviewers to do so as well before reviewing racial topics. In this way, scholars could personally reflect on their positionality in a way that invites structural changes by raising awareness of all scholars' subjectivity rather than interrogating the objectivity of the few scholars of color in our field.

Several examples of such reflexivity statements exist. Roberts and colleagues (2020) provide a note in the Acknowledgement section of their recent manuscript: "When the manuscript for this article was drafted, one author self-identified as U.S. Black-White American, and four authors self-identified as U.S. White American" (p. 12). Golash-Boza (2016) provides an example of a statement from a White scholar's perspective that could be integrated into the main manuscript:

> In the spirit of reflexivity, it is also crucial to consider one's positionality when doing race scholarship. I write this piece as a tenured professor and a white woman. My position as a tenured professor provides me with the academic freedom to write what I think without the fear of losing my job. As a white woman, I can be critical of racism without being labeled 'angry' in the same way that people of color may be. (p. 130)

An even more in-depth statement comes from Moorman (2020) which we perceive to be an exemplar (see Appendix for full text). Although we highlight these three examples, there may be more ways for scholars to reflect on their positionality: through the lens of other social identities, through a commitment to environmental justice and conservation, through the lens of life experiences or upbringings, or through reflection on their relative versus absolute social location.

Proactive Elevation of Critical Racial Scholarship as a Solution to Systemic Subjectivity

Another structural solution involves the prioritization and proliferation of racialized scholarship that challenges the status quo. In particular, we would like to see our field prioritize scholarship that not only investigates racial topics but does so from a critical lens. This could include, but is not limited to, a series of articles in every issue of the top journals in management focused on critical race psychology and management or qualitative methodologies that are authored by scholars of color. As reviewed previously, the status quo currently serves to marginalize these perspectives and approaches (Hoppe et al., 2019), and the relegation of this work to lower-tier specialty journals or special issues exacerbates racial inequality by contributing to racial disparities in publishing and citations (Hofstra et al., 2020; Roberts et al., 2020) A proactive approach that prioritizes this work across issues in top-tier journals would bring those perspectives from the periphery (e.g., special issues and specialty journals) into high-status, mainstream spaces and help alleviate these current disparities.

However, in order for such an approach to be successful, editors and reviewers in these mainstream journals must be required themselves to become more acquainted with these alternative perspectives and approaches in order to better evaluate and promote this work. Short-term changes might involve adding more expertise in qualitative methods and critical scholarship to editorial boards, whereas long-term changes would involve more training in these methodologies in management doctoral programs and adoption of the knowledge systems of underrepresented racial minorities in racial scholarship (Wright et al., 2019). These strategies would ensure that gatekeepers in our field appreciate the value of interdisciplinarity in management and the methodologies that privilege the perspectives and lived experiences of underrepresented racial minorities. As universities and academic societies grapple with a fuller understanding of the racialized nature of management, embracing these changes in training could position management scholarship to merge management and critical race scholarship, leading the way for sustainable, structural changes.

CONCLUSION

Objectivity is a foundational tenet of the scientific process. However, in a world where racism continues to pervade every sphere of society, the assumption that scholarship that is not explicitly racialized is more objective (or more race-neutral) is dangerous (Seamster & Ray, 2018). In this chapter, we have reviewed how objectivity norms disproportionately threaten racial scholarship and racially minoritized scholars, ultimately shaping how hierarchy-enhancing ideas about race relations are proliferated—with consequences for the application of this work in organizations. Currently, these norms dismiss the subjectivity of White scholars' racial experiences and interrogate racial minority scholars' authentic perspectives on issues of organizational racial equity. Racially minoritized scholars bring innovative perspectives of their lived experiences to bear on issues of racial scholarship which are discredited and minimized, further marginalizing their work, and reinforcing the dominance of White scholars in racial scholarship. Ultimately, without careful attention to the downstream consequences of traditional notions of objectivity, our adherence to its practices can reproduce the exact kinds of racial inequality scholars seek to remedy.

REFERENCES

Acker, J. (2006). Inequality regimes: Gender, class, and race in organizations. *Gender & Society, 20*(4), 441–464.

Adams, G., Dobles, I., Gómez, L. H., Kurtiş, T., & Molina, L. E. (2015). Decolonizing psychological science: Introduction to the special thematic section. *Journal of Social and Political. Psychology, 3*, 213–238.

Adams, G., Salter, P. S., Kurtiş, T., Naemi, P., & Estrada-Villalta, S. (2018). Subordinated knowledge as a tool for creative maladjustment and resistance to racial oppression. *Journal of Social Issues, 74*(2), 337–354.

Amabile, T. M., & Hall, D. T. (2018). The undervalued power of self-relevant research: The case of researching retirement while retiring. *Academy of Management Perspectives, 35*(3).

Andersen, M. (2003). Whitewashing race: A critical review essay on 'Whiteness. In A. Doane & E. Bonilla-Silva (Eds.), *Whiteout: The continuing significance of racism* (pp. 21–34). Routledge.

Anderson, E. (2015). The white space. *Sociology of Race and Ethnicity, 1*(1), 10–21.

Anteby, M. (2013). Relaxing the taboo on telling our own stories: Upholding professional distance and personal involvement. *Organization Science, 24*(4), 1277–1290.

Apfelbaum, E. P., Norton, M. I., & Sommers, S. R. (2012). Racial color blindness: Emergence, practice, and implications. *Current Directions in Psychological Science, 21*(3), 205–209.

Apfelbaum, E. P., Sommers, S. R., & Norton, M. I. (2008). Seeing race and seeming racist? Evaluating strategic colorblindness in social interaction. *Journal of Personality and Social Psychology, 95*(4), 918.

Armstrong, J. S. (1979). Advocacy and objectivity in science. *Management Science, 25*(5), 423–428.

Ashburn-Nardo, L., Morris, K. A., & Goodwin, S. A. (2008). The confronting prejudiced responses (CPR) model: Applying CPR in organizations. *Academy of Management Learning & Education, 7*(3), 332–342.

Bamberger, P. A., & Pratt, M. G. (2010). Moving forward by looking back: Reclaiming unconventional research contexts and samples in organizational scholarship. *Academy of Management Journal, 53*, 665–671.

Bell, E., Meriläinen, S., Taylor, S., & Tienari, J. (2020). Dangerous knowledge: The political, personal, and epistemological promise of feminist research in management and organization studies. *International Journal of Management Reviews*, 22(2), 177–192.

Bell, J. M., & Hartmann, D. (2007). Diversity in everyday discourse: The cultural ambiguities and consequences of "happy talk". *American Sociological Review*, 72(6), 895–914.

Benjamin, R. (2019). *Race after technology: Abolitionist tools for the new Jim code*. Polity.

Blackwell, J. E. (1988). Faculty issues: The impact on minorities. *The Review of Higher Education*, 11(4), 417–434.

Bluhm, D. J., Harman, W., Lee, T. W., & Mitchell, T. R. (2011). Qualitative research in management: A decade of progress. *Journal of Management Studies*, 48(8), 1866–1891.

Brunsma, D. L., Embrick, D. G., & Shin, J. H. (2017). Graduate students of color: Race, racism, and mentoring in the white waters of academia. *Sociology of Race and Ethnicity*, 3(1), 1–13.

Carbado, D. W., & Roithmayr, D. (2014). Critical race theory meets social science. *Annual Review of Law and Social Science*, 10, 149–167.

Cascio, W. F., & Aguinis, H. (2008). Research in industrial and organizational psychology from 1963 to 2007: Changes, choices, and trends. *Journal of Applied Psychology*, 93(5), 1062.

Cha, S. E., & Roberts, L. M. (2019). Leveraging minority identities at work: An individual-level framework of the identity mobilization process. *Organization Science*, 30(4), 735–760.

Chugh, D., & Brief, A. (2008). 1964 was not that long ago: A story of gateways and pathways. In A. P. Brief (Ed.), *Diversity at work* (pp. 318–340). Cambridge University Press.

Clark, C. X. (1973). The role of the white researcher in black society: A futuristic look. *Journal of Social Issues*, 29(1), 109–118.

Colella, A., Hebl, M., & King, E. (2017). One hundred years of discrimination research in the *Journal of Applied Psychology*: A sobering synopsis. *Journal of Applied Psychology*, 102(3), 500.

Collins, P. H. (1986). Learning from the outsider within: The sociological significance of Black feminist thought. *Social Problems*, 33(6), s14–s32.

Cox, T., Jr., & Nkomo, S. M. (1990). Invisible men and women: A status report on race as a variable in organization behavior research. *Journal of Organizational Behavior*, 11(6), 419–431.

Czopp, A. M., & Monteith, M. J. (2003). Confronting prejudice (literally): Reactions to confrontations of racial and gender bias. *Personality and Social Psychology Bulletin*, 29(4), 532–544.

Delgado, R. (1984). The imperial scholar: Reflections on a review of civil rights literature. *University of Pennsylvania Law Review*, 132(3), 561–578.

Delgado, R., & Stefancic, J. (Eds.) (2017). *Critical race theory: An introduction*. New York University Press.

Drury, B. J., & Kaiser, C. R. (2014). Allies against sexism: The role of men in confronting sexism. *Journal of Social Issues*, 70(4), 637–652.

Dupree, C. H. (2021). Black and Latinx conservatives upshift competence relative to liberals in mostly white settings. *Nature Human Behaviour, 5*(12), 1652–1662.

Dupree, C. H., & Fiske, S. T. (2019). Self-presentation in interracial settings: The competence downshift by White liberals. *Journal of Personality and Social Psychology, 117*(3), 579.

Dupree, C. H., & Kraus, M. (2021). Psychological science is not race neutral. *Perspectives on Psychological Science.* Advance online publication.

Dupree, C. H., Torrez, B., Obioha, O., & Fiske, S. T. (2021). Race–status associations: Distinct effects of three novel measures among White and Black perceivers. *Journal of Personality and Social Psychology, 120*(3), 601–625.

Dye, K., & Golnaraghi, G. (2015). Organizational benefits through diversity management. In R. Bendl, I. Bleijenbergh, E. Henttonen, & A. J. Mills (Eds.), *The Oxford handbook of diversity in organizations* (p. 255). Oxford University Press

Ely, R. J., & Thomas, D. A. (2001). Cultural diversity at work: The effects of diversity perspectives on work group processes and outcomes. *Administrative Science Quarterly, 46*(2), 229–273.

Gardner, D. M., & Ryan, A. M. (2020). What's in it for you? Demographics and self-interest perceptions in diversity promotion. *Journal of Applied Psychology.* Advance online publication.

Georgeac, O., & Rattan, A. (2021). *The business case for diversity backfires: Detrimental effects of organizations' instrumental diversity rhetoric for underrepresented group members' sense of belonging and performance.* Manuscript in preparation.

Goffman, E. (1963). Stigma and social identity. In E. Goffman (Ed.), *Stigma: Notes on the management of spoiled identity* (pp. 1–41). Simon & Schuster.

Golash-Boza, T. (2016). A critical and comprehensive sociological theory of race and racism. *Sociology of Race and Ethnicity, 2*(2), 129–141.

Gordon, E. W., Miller, F., & Rollock, D. (1990). Coping with communicentric bias in knowledge production in the social sciences. *Educational Researcher, 19*(3), 14–19.

Greenberg, D., Clair, J., & Ladge, J. J. (2019). A feminist perspective on conducting personally relevant research: Working mothers studying pregnancy and motherhood at work. *Academy of Management Perspectives, 35*(3). https://doi.org/10.5465/amp.2018.0087

Harrison, D. A., & Klein, K. J. (2007). What's the difference? Diversity constructs as separation, variety, or disparity in organizations. *Academy of Management Review, 32*(4), 1199–1228.

Hassard, J. (1995). *Sociology and organization theory: Positivism, paradigms and postmodernity* (No. 20). Cambridge University Press.

Hempel, C. G., & Oppenheim, P. (1948). Studies in the logic of explanation. *Philosophy of Science, 15*(2), 135–175.

Henrich, J., Heine, S. J., & Norenzayan, A. (2010). Most people are not WEIRD. *Nature, 466*(7302), 29–29.

Herring, C. (2009). Does diversity pay?: Race, gender, and the business case for diversity. *American Sociological Review, 74*(2), 208–224.

Hideg, I., DeCelles, K. A., & Tihanyi, L. (2020). From the editors: Publishing practical and responsible research in AMJ. *Academy of Management Journal, 63*(6), 1681–1686.

Hikido, A., & Murray, S. B. (2016). Whitened rainbows: How white college students protect whiteness through diversity discourses. *Race Ethnicity and Education*, *19*(2), 389–411.

Hofstra, B., Kulkarni, V. V., Galvez, S. M. N., He, B., Jurafsky, D., & McFarland, D. A. (2020). The diversity-innovation paradox in Science. *Proceedings of the National Academy of Sciences*, *117*(17), 9284–9291.

Holvino, E. (2010). Intersections: The simultaneity of race, gender and class in organization studies. *Gender, Work & Organization*, *17*(3), 248–277.

Hoppe, T. A., Litovitz, A., Willis, K. A., Meseroll, R. A., Perkins, M. J., Hutchins, B. I., Davis, A. F., Lauer, M. S., Valantine, H. A., Anderson, J. M., & Santangelo, G. M. (2019). Topic choice contributes to the lower rate of NIH awards to African-American/black scientists. *Science Advances*, *5*(10). https://doi.org/10.1126/sciadv.aaw7238.

Jané, S., Van Esch, C., & Bilimoria, D. (2018). "Why'd You Wanna Study That?" A process model of the under-legitimation of a research topic. *Academy of Management Learning & Education*, *17*(4), 401–424.

Kaiser, C. R., & Miller, C. T. (2001). Stop complaining! The social costs of making attributions to discrimination. *Personality and Social Psychology Bulletin*, *27*(2), 254–263.

Kang, S. K., DeCelles, K. A., Tilcsik, A., & Jun, S. (2016). Whitened résumés: Race and self-presentation in the labor market. *Administrative Science Quarterly*, *61*(3), 469–502.

Katyal, S. (2009). *Crirtical management studies: Perspectives on Information Systems*. Global India Publications.

King, E. B., Avery, D. R., Hebl, M. R., & Cortina, J. M. (2018). Systematic subjectivity: How subtle biases infect the scholarship review process. *Journal of Management*, *44*(3), 843–853.

Konrad, A. M. (2003). Special issue introduction: Defining the domain of workplace diversity scholarship. *Group & Organization Management*, *28*(1), 4–17.

Kraus, M. W., Rucker, J. M., & Richeson, J. A. (2017). Americans misperceive racial economic equality. *Proceedings of the National Academy of Sciences*, *114*(39), 10324–10331.

Kraus, M. W., & Torrez, B. (2020). A psychology of power that is embedded in societal structures. *Current Opinion in Psychology*, *33*, 86–90.

Leigh, A., & Melwani, S. (2019). #BlackEmployeesMatter: Mega-threats, identity fusion, and enacting positive deviance in organizations. *Academy of Management Review*, *44*(3), 564–591.

Lieberson, S., & Lynn, F. B. (2002). Barking up the wrong branch: Scientific alternatives to the current model of sociological science. *Annual Review of Sociology*, *28*(1), 1–19.

Mannix, E., & Neale, M. A. (2005). What differences make a difference? The promise and reality of diverse teams in organizations. *Psychological Science in the Public Interest*, *6*(2), 31–55.

Margolis, E., & Romero, M. (1998). "The department is very male, very white, very old, and very conservative": The functioning of the hidden curriculum in graduate sociology departments. *Harvard Educational Review*, *68*(1), 1–33.

Minefee, I., Rabelo, V. C., Stewart IV, O. J. C., & Young, N. C. J. (2018). Repairing leaks in the pipeline: A social closure perspective on underrepresented racial/ethnic minority recruitment and retention in business schools. *Academy of Management Learning & Education, 17*(1), 79–95.

Moorman, J. D. (2020). Socializing singlehood: Personal, interpersonal, and sociocultural factors shaping Black women's single lives. *Psychology of Women Quarterly, 44*(4). https://doi.org/10.1177/0361684320939070

Morris, A., & Ghaziani, A. (2005). DuBoisian sociology: A watershed of professional and public sociology. *Souls, 7*(3–4), 47–54.

Nzinga, K., Rapp, D. N., Leatherwood, C., Easterday, M., Rogers, L. O., Gallagher, N., & Medin, D. L. (2018). Should social scientists be distanced from or engaged with the people they study? *Proceedings of the National Academy of Sciences, 115*(45), 11435–11441.

O'Brien, L. T., & Crandall, C. S. (2005). Perceiving self-interest: Power, ideology, and maintenance of the status quo. *Social Justice Research, 18*(1), 1–24.

Ong, A. D., Burrow, A. L., Fuller-Rowell, T. E., Ja, N. M., & Sue, D. W. (2013). Racial microaggressions and daily well-being among Asian Americans. *Journal of Counseling Psychology, 60*(2), 188.

Parker, L., & Lynn, M. (2002). What's race got to do with it? Critical race theory's conflicts with and connections to qualitative research methodology and epistemology. *Qualitative Inquiry, 8*(1), 7–22.

Pfeffer, J., & Fong, C. T. (2002). The end of business schools? Less success than meets the eye. *Academy of Management Learning & Education, 1*(1), 78–95.

Pitesa, M., & Pillutla, M. M. (2019). Socioeconomic mobility and talent utilization of workers from poorer backgrounds: the overlooked importance of within-organization dynamics. *Academy of Management Annals, 13*(2), 737–769.

Porter, T. M. (1996). *Trust in numbers: The pursuit of objectivity in science and public life*. Princeton University Press.

Ramarajan, L., & Reid, E. (2013). Shattering the myth of separate worlds: Negotiating nonwork identities at work. *Academy of Management Review, 38*(4), 621–644.

Rasinski, H. M., & Czopp, A. M. (2010). The effect of target status on witnesses' reactions to confrontations of bias. *Basic and Applied Social Psychology, 32*(1), 8–16.

Ray, V. (2016, October 21). "The Unbearable Whiteness of Mesearch." *Inside Higher Ed.* https://www.insidehighered.com/advice/2016/10/21/me-studies-are-not-justconducted-people-color-essay

Ray, V. (2019). A theory of racialized organizations. *American Sociological Review, 84*(1), 26–53.

Ray, V. E., Randolph, A., Underhill, M., & Luke, D. (2017). Critical race theory, Afro-pessimism, and racial progress narratives. *Sociology of Race and Ethnicity, 3*(2), 147–158.

Richeson, J. A., & Shelton, J. N. (2007). Negotiating interracial interactions: Costs, consequences, and possibilities. *Current Directions in Psychological Science, 16*(6), 316–320.

Richter, J., Faragó, F., Swadener, B. B., Roca-Servat, D., & Eversman, K. A. (2020). Tempered radicalism and intersectionality: Scholar-activism in the neoliberal university. *Journal of Social Issues*.

Rivera, L. A., & Tilcsik, A. (2016). Class advantage, commitment penalty: The gendered effect of social class signals in an elite labor market. *American Sociological Review*, *81*(6), 1097–1131.

Roberts, S. O., Bareket-Shavit, C., Dollins, F. A., Goldie, P. D., & Mortenson, E. (2020). Racial inequality in psychological research: Trends of the past and recommendations for the future. *Perspectives on Psychological Science*, *15*(6). https://doi.org/10.1177/1745691620927709

Sablan, J. R. (2019). Can you really measure that? Combining critical race theory and quantitative methods. *American Educational Research Journal*, *56*(1), 178–203.

Salter, P., & Adams, G. (2013). Toward a critical race psychology. *Social and Personality Psychology Compass*, *7*(11), 781–793.

Schultz, J. R., & Maddox, K. B. (2013). Shooting the messenger to spite the message? Exploring reactions to claims of racial bias. *Personality and Social Psychology Bulletin*, *39*(3), 346–58.

Seamster, L., & Ray, V. (2018). Against teleology in the study of race: Toward the abolition of the progress paradigm. *Sociological Theory*, *36*(4), 315–342.

Shelton, J. N., Richeson, J. A., Salvatore, J., & Trawalter, S. (2005). Ironic effects of racial bias during interracial interactions. *Psychological Science*, *16*(5), 397–402.

Shih, M., & Young, M. J. (2016). *Identity management strategies in workplaces with color-blind diversity policies*. In H. A. Neville, M. E. Gallardo, & D. W. Sue (Eds.), *The myth of racial color blindness: Manifestations, dynamics, and impact* (pp. 261–274). American Psychological Association.

Starck, J. G., Sinclair, S., & Shelton, J. N. (2021). How university diversity rationales inform student preferences and outcomes. *Proceedings of the National Academy of Sciences*, *118*(16).

Steele, C. M. (1997). A threat in the air: How stereotypes shape intellectual identity and performance. *American Psychologist*, *52*(6), 613.

Sumner, R., Stanley, M. J., & Burrow, A. L. (2017). Room for debate (and derogation): Negativity of readers' comments on Black authors' online content. *Psychology of Popular Media Culture*, *6*(2), 113–122.

Syed, M. (2017). Why traditional metrics may not adequately represent ethnic minority psychology. *Perspectives on Psychological Science*, *12*(6), 1162–1165.

Torrez, B., Dupree, C. H., & Kraus, M. W. (2021). *Who tells your story: How racial expertise influences perceptions of objectivity and hiring in journalism* [Manuscript under review]. School of Management, Yale University.

Watkins, M. B., Simmons, A., & Umphress, E. (2019). It's not black and white: Toward a contingency perspective on the consequences of being a token. *Academy of Management Perspectives*, *33*(3). https://doi.org/10.5465/amp.2015.0154

Wingfield, A. H., & Wingfield, J. H. (2014). When visibility hurts and helps: How intersections of race and gender shape Black professional men's experiences with tokenization. *Cultural Diversity and Ethnic Minority Psychology*, *20*(4), 483.

Wong, A. (2018, November 27). Graduate school can have terrible effects on people's mental health. *The Atlantic*. Retrieved June 21, 2019, from https://www.theatlantic.com/education/archive/2018/11/anxiety-depression-mental-health-graduate-school/576769/

Wright, A. L., Gabel, C., Ballantyne, M., Jack, S. M., & Wahoush, O. (2019). Using two-eyed seeing in research with indigenous people: An integrative review. *International Journal of Qualitative Methods*, *18*. https://doi.org/10.1177/1609406919869695

Zuberi, T., & Bonilla-Silva, E. (2008). *White logic, White methods*. Rowman & Littlefield.

APPENDIX

Moorman, 2020: Research Reflexivity and Positionality

Reflexivity is the ongoing reflective practice of the researcher, wherein they describe how their own biases, past experiences, and beliefs influenced the execution and analysis of qualitative research (Berger, 2013; Wilkinson, 1988). At the time I designed this project, I was in my early 30s, never married, childless, and working on my PhD while living in Detroit. My friends and I were buzzing with the anxieties of Black women who had degrees, good jobs, and traveled the world but still had yet to meet that tall, handsome Black man with his own degrees, great career, baby fever, and a desire for marriage. Was it something we were doing? Had men changed? Were our expectations too high? I was not alone in my anxieties. Dating advice books that purported to help me learn the unspoken rules of love came to me as gifts by way of concerned godmothers and aunts. I received condescending advice from married women and sexist advice from my father about being single. While seemingly everyone had an opinion about what single Black women needed to heal, hide, or disavow in order to find a husband, seemingly no one was talking with us about our experiences, desires, and expectations of partnership. This project emerged from my own frustrations with being simultaneously subjected to and objectified by a broader social discourse that dissected unmarried Black women's lives, but did not engage us in that discussion.

My background, experiences, and training as a Black feminist social science researcher shaped why and how I executed this project. My positionality and experiences facilitated my ability to recruit and establish rapport with participants. As a fourth generation Detroiter and single Black woman researcher living in Detroit at the time of this study, I simultaneously occupied emic, group member status (e.g., single Black woman from Detroit), and etic, outsider (e.g., researcher) positionalities (Fetterman, 2019). My insider status fostered trust between participants and me, as many participants were excited to have the chance to speak about their experiences to a Black woman who understood what single life was like in Detroit. But for all of the benefits my background and identity conferred, these perspectives also created blind spots for me in this project, which in turn created limitations for my work.

As a Black feminist who was raised by a hardworking, high achieving single Black mother, I fundamentally view single life through the lenses of agency and resilience. In interviews, I found myself more critical of women who had difficulty embracing their single lives, which inhibited my ability to establish rapport with some participants. One way I accounted for issues in rapport building was through the Being Single Is... exercise. Although the power and privilege I had as a researcher was not eliminated, the Being Single Is... exercise created a space where interviewees set the terms for how they wanted their single lives to be interpreted.

CHAPTER 2

BROADENING THE CONTEXT

Addressing Systemic Oppression in Organizational Research

Catherine Warren
Ngoc S. Duong
Florida Institute of Technology

Nicholas P. Salter
Anmol Sachdeva
Hofstra University

ABSTRACT

Systemic oppression continues to be prevalent in organizations, despite efforts by researchers to ensure an equitable and inclusive workplace for all minority groups. In this chapter, we provide an understanding of systemic oppression in organizational and diversity, equity, and inclusion [DEI] research by describing what it means and its implications on organizational practices. Subsequently, we propose a shift in epistemology and research methods is needed to fully capture systemic oppression in organizations. Specifically, we suggest a shift from a functionalist perspective to a conflict perspective would better account for humanistic values that are largely overlooked in the

The Future of Scholarship on Race in Organizations, pp. 29–51
Copyright © 2022 by Information Age Publishing

functionalist perspective. We believe this focus on the conflict perspective needs to be a more purposeful and conscious effort in the field of industrial and organizational (I/O) psychology. Finally, we provided several research methods recommendations for researching the impact of systemic oppression in organizations. We hope that by producing more research investigating systemic oppression in the workplace that the field of DEI will further pave a path to help dismantle the historical barriers placed upon minorities.

BROADENING THE CONTEXT: ADDRESSING SYSTEMIC OPPRESSION IN ORGANIZATIONAL RESEARCH

The recent injustices against the African American community, such as the murders of George Floyd, Breonna Taylor, Elijah McClain, and many others, have sparked outcries across the country, highlighting the long-standing history of systemic oppression in the U.S. in the police and justice institutions. However, the insidious nature of systemic oppression reaches further, impacting nearly every other facet of life (i.e., economic, educational, and social institutions; Amis et al., 2018). For instance, systemic oppression is prevalent in the U.S. healthcare system, creating barriers for people of color to obtain equal access to health care (Feagin & Bennefield, 2014). In education, schools with a higher enrollment of White students receive better educational resources than schools with a higher enrollment of racial minority students (Feagin & Barnett, 2004). Similarly, individuals in the LGBTQ community often experience homelessness due to structural and systemic inequalities (Ecker et al., 2019).

The prevalence of systemic oppression throughout the U.S. also extends to the workplace context. That is, systemic oppression is inherent in organizational operations and has severe consequences for employees belonging to minority groups. However, organizational research on systemic oppression has yet to be fully explored, despite previous calls to do so (e.g., Gaucher et al., 2011). For instance, organizational research has largely focused on discrimination and bias that directly impact minority groups (e.g., Flage, 2019; Heilman & Caleo, 2018; Nadler et al., 2014; Walter et al., 2017), without fully addressing the impact of structural related issues has on organizations and minorities. This is likely because much of the existing organizational literature on systemic oppression or related topics have primarily focused on promoting equality through the lens of economic values. To put it simply, by demonstrating how diversity, equity, and inclusion (DEI) practices have clear linkages with enhancing organizational effectiveness and well-being, researchers assume that these practices can alleviate the disparate structural impact on various minority groups. In contrast, the lens of humanistic values emphasizes understanding the experiences of the oppressed. Humanistic values reflect the consideration of determining what is good, right, and fair for all individuals who would be impacted by an organization's decision, which can differ from the economic goals of the organization (Lefkowitz, 2013). Therefore, by focusing on humanistic values, researchers would better understand and combat the ingrained organizational barriers minorities encounter.

Directly aligning with these two values (i.e., economic and humanistic) are the functionalist and conflict perspectives, fundamental in sociology and anthropology (see Table 2.1). The functionalist perspective, aligned with economic values, suggests institutions are designed to fulfill and maintain necessary societal functions and order (Mahoney, 2004). In contrast, the conflict perspective, aligned with humanistic values, suggests institutions reinforce privilege and unfairly hinder minorities (Simon, 2016). Subsequently, these perspectives can be leveraged to inform the understanding of systemic oppression in organizations. Therefore, we suggest researchers can better account for systemic oppression in organizations by taking a multidisciplinary approach. Additionally, previous DEI research in industrial organizational (I/O) psychology has enhanced equality and inclusivity in organizations. However, we believe that the major focus of I/O psychology has been more aligned with the functionalist perspective of improving organizational effectiveness, resulting in overlooking the systemic barriers placed upon minority groups as suggested by the conflict perspective (Berrey, 2014). In other words, we argue that to fully embrace the notion of DEI and advance the future understanding of the field, we need to take on a conflict perspective and acknowledge the role of systemic oppression in organizations in harming the minority groups we are committed to help.

In addition, as systemic oppression is extended from other disciplines, research on this concept needs to also incorporate different epistemology and methodology. In other words, in the past, I/O Psychologists have largely relied on post-positivist and quantitative methodology, which assumes that there is a universal "truth," largely neglecting the lived experiences of minorities (Willis, 2007). Therefore, incorporating social constructivism paradigm and qualitative methodologies is needed to understand systemic oppression in organizations.

To support the points that we have highlighted above, we structure our chapter in the following structure. First, we introduce the concept of systemic oppression by extending on previous systemic racism theory (Feagin, 2006) and racial White frame (Feagin, 2013). Second, we discuss the importance of the conflict perspective in guiding the understanding of how systemic oppression impacts organizations. Third, we provide examples to demonstrate the prevalence of systemic oppression in organizations. Finally, we discuss specific methodologies that could be used to study systemic oppression in organizations.

Table 2.1

Summary of the Functionalist and Conflict Perspectives

Perspective	Belief	Focus	Example Research Question
Functionalist	Institutions are designed to fulfill the necessary functions and order within a society.	Organizational Effectiveness	How does performance appraisal systems motivate employees to perform better? Does incorporating artificial intelligence into selection systems improve financial cost? How does information sharing in teams improve team performance and organizational effectiveness?
Conflict	Institutions reinforce privilege and unfairly hinder minorities through systems embedded in social and historical context.	Context that influences barriers encountered by minorities.	How is the current performance appraisal system embedded in social and historical context to unfairly hinder women? What potential biases could be encountered by using artificial intelligence build with the current dominant narrative in organizations? How does racial white frame impact the distribution and allocation of social and organizational resources?

FROM SYSTEMIC RACISM TO SYSTEMIC OPPRESSION

Sociologist Joe Feagin (2006) first introduced systemic racism theory (also known as structural racism; Bailey et al., 2017), suggesting that within the U.S. there exists the phenomenon in which individuals who are of the racial minority groups, particularly those of African American descent, are discriminated against in various institutions. However, this discrimination is systemic in nature such that individuals do not only receive overt forms of negative treatment (e.g., name-calling), but deep-rooted issues exist, creating intangible barriers preventing individuals from being able to achieve their maximal and fullest selves.

According to Feagin (2006), the creation of this systemic form of oppression started as early as during the colonization of the North American continent. During this time frame, the existence of the slavery system, an exploitive economic labor system, served as the foundation for the creation of this form of discrimination. Individuals of African American descent were the primary target of this system, which gave rise to the cultural norms of mistreatment and negative attitudes toward this group of people. In other words, they were viewed as the bottom of the social hierarchy and given their inferior status within the social system.

Over time, this pattern of societal structure of hierarchy and oppression continued to persist today. As highlighted in the historical analysis by Feagin (2006), even with the abolishment of the slavery system, African Americans continued to be treated unfairly and oppressed within the U.S. system through the legal segregation era. During this time, many discriminatory practices (e.g., laws and policies) were developed to further prevent or limit these individuals from having access to many social institutions (e.g., education, healthcare, and services). Even though much of these practices are no longer legal today, the long-lasting negative effects of these policies have yet to be resolved. As a result, this issue becomes further deeply rooted within society. This cycle makes it difficult for people of this minority group to understand and recognize the barriers hindering them from accomplishing their lifelong goals.

In a follow-up development, Feagin (2013) suggested that the process in which these systemic issues continue to persist in the current time is because of the *racial White frame*. Feagin (2013) defined this concept as the "overarching white worldview that encompasses a broad and persisting set of racial stereotypes, prejudices, ideologies, images, interpretations and narratives, emotions, and reactions to language accents, as well as racialized inclinations to discriminate" (p. 3). The racial White frame can be understood as the dominant narrative consisting of a broad cultural phenomenon that reinforces the underlying cognitions, attitudes, beliefs, and values maintaining the societal domination for heterosexual Caucasian males. A central concept to the racial White frame is to paint the general "big picture" narratives and stories of White conquests, morals, superiority, hard work, and so forth, through the use of stereotypes, falsified images, and representation of minorities. These big picture stories and narratives then become cultural artifacts that further perpetuates the discrimination of minorities.

Both systemic racism theory and racial White frame (Feagin, 2006, 2013) predominantly focus on race. However, this form of oppression does not solely exist for racial minority groups but extends to other minorities categories. For example, women face various structural barriers such as unequal access to male-dominated networks (Blair-Loy, 2001) and stricter performance standards in comparison to men (Foschi, 1996). Similarly, those with disabilities face structural barriers that result in occupational segregation, limiting their earnings potential (Maroto & Pettinicchio, 2014). Furthermore, research indicates that LGBTQ individuals experience discrimination during the selection process (Flage, 2019). When they enter an organization, they continue to face discrimination at work, such as microaggression and ostracism (Casey et al., 2019; DeSouza et al., 2017). These pieces of evidence suggest structural and systemic forms of discrimination apply to other minority groups. Therefore, there is a need for an integrative concept describing how systemic forms of discrimination affect various minority groups.

Therefore, in this chapter, we adopt the concept of systemic racism (Feagin, 2006) and White racial frame (Feagin, 2013) and extend these concepts to encompass its effect on other minority groups such as gender, sexual orientation, nationality, disability status, etc. As a result, we will refer to this phenomenon as systemic oppression. Here, we define systemic oppression as a contextual factor developed through a series of historical events that systematically suppresses minority groups. Given this issue is systemic in nature, it would be important to point out that this is an external contextual factor, meaning that this factor exists and persists outside of the organization with implications for the organizations and institutions that reside within it.

THE FUNCTIONALIST AND CONFLICT PERSPECTIVES

Sociology and anthropology have a long history of incorporating systemic oppression in the societal context, which have utilized various frameworks to understand how institutions function in society. Both sociology and anthropology have approached systemic oppression in similar ways; however, anthropology literature focuses predominantly through the lens of culture. The major frameworks for examining institutions include functionalist and conflict. First, the functionalist perspective is a macro approach that suggests institutions are designed to fulfill the necessary functions and order within a society (Mahoney, 2004). In other words, organizations play an important role in providing and maintaining the structure to which society is functioning and peaceful. An example of the functionalist perspective regarding the workplace would be that organizations fulfill the necessary role of providing salaries to their employees to maintain order in society. Second, the conflict perspective acknowledges that although institutions fulfill necessary roles to maintain order, this "order" comes at a cost to minorities. More specifically, the conflict perspective is another macro approach that suggests that institutions reinforce privilege and unfairly hinder minorities (Simon, 2016). An example of the conflict perspective regarding the workplace is that although organizations provide salaries to maintain order in society, it also reinforces the privilege of majority groups by unfairly hindering minorities by enforcing the pay gap between the majority group and minority groups. In other words, the conflict perspective goes beyond the organization to incorporate the influence of social and historical context on organizational practices and policies. For example, a researcher may ask "Is the current organizational policy improving organizational effectiveness?", where a researcher asking a research question from the conflict perspective may ask "Does the current organizational policy differentially and unnecessarily harm minorities?"

Although the conflict and functionalist perspectives are both relevant in the organizational context, we posit that a majority of organizational research has relied on the functionalist perspective while largely unaware of the conflict perspective. One reason for the emphasis on the functionalist perspective in organizational literature is based on the focus on organizational effectiveness, which has overshadowed the need to focus on how these systems designed for organizational effectiveness hurt minority groups that we aim to protect through the conflict perspective (Lefkowitz, 2013). In other words, the goal for organizational effectiveness may not always align with the goals of promoting equality in the workplace, and by focusing through a functionalist perspective, organizational researchers may unintentionally maintain the barriers that minorities face in organizations. We believe that in order to combat systemic oppression in DEI research, we must shift our focus to a conflict perspective.

The Conflict Perspective in Management

The conflict perspective has been used in critical management studies (CMS), a stream of research in management related to I/O psychology. More specifically, the stream of research in CMS discusses concepts and issues due to the system which aligns with the conflict perspective discussed above. Adler and colleagues (2007) pointed out that CMS aims to bring attention to the perspectives that criticize structural related issues (e.g., capitalism or patriarchy), how they play a role in influencing the current HR and management practices within organizations, and how these practices serve to sustain these issues. In other words, CMS takes a humanistic approach to business and management in organizations, which was previously criticized to lack morality (see Anthony, 1986; Ghoshal, 2005). Additionally, CMS challenges the current status quo of current management practices in organizations, that are unethical and exploitative in nature, and tackle the issues that arise from them in ways that the mainstream perspectives in management are unable to fulfill (Klikauer, 2013).

Given the goal of CMS, this area of work had been discussed as a tenant of the Frankfurt School of Critical Theory (Adler et al., 2007; Klikauer, 2015), which focuses on understanding reality through the interplay between power and identity to address societal issues such as gender, sexual orientation, class, and so forth (Tyson, 2014). However, it is important to note that while CMS have been largely influenced by critical theory (Adler et al., 2007), the work under CMS is not limited to any single school of thought and has also incorporated other perspectives such as power and knowledge by Foucault (1980), labor process theory (Marx, 1977), and so forth. In summary, with these perspectives and the work done within CMS, one can understand the primary focus of CMS to be critically analyzing the domination structure within work organizations by using theories and perspectives that are not as well-known in the management and OB literature. Consequently, by taking this approach to management and organizations, CMS provides a better understanding of the feature of inequality within organizations, how to effectively tackle them, and provide a balance of power to different groups within an organization.

These perspectives from CMS are particularly relevant to understanding the impact of systemic oppression in organizations. We believe the inclusion of these perspectives could shed light on the mechanisms that reinforce and retain power for majorities that exacerbate the power differential between majority and minority members, reinforcing systemic oppression. For example, when I/O psychologists evaluate organizational dynamics, we should consider power dynamics between parties as an important contextual factor that influences subsequent outcomes. As power is an inherent and influential aspect in organizations (Ragins & Sundstrom, 1989), it is essential that researchers specifically examine this dynamic with minorities in organizations. By examining the mechanisms reinforcing individual and organizational power, researchers will be able to understand the impact of power on minorities and the differential development of power between minority and majority groups that reinforce the power of the majority group.

IMPLICATIONS FOR DIVERSITY, EQUITY, AND INCLUSION

There has been some research evidence from various organizational human resources (HR) and management practices (e.g., selection, performance management, etc.) that indicates the presence of systemic oppression affecting individuals in organizational settings. The research that we discuss here does not explain these issues in structural terms, as the structural lens is generally uncommon in the psychological perspective. However, it is important to leverage the findings from the HR and management literature to illustrate the presence of systemic barriers encountered by minorities. In this section, we discuss previous findings in the areas of staffing and performance management and leverage the conflict perspectives to describe how these issues are impacted by systemic oppression. Ultimately, incorporating the conflict perspective in organizational research will reframe objectives beyond organizational effectiveness to include broader involvement in society by contributing meaningful science (Lefkowitz, 2013).

Selection and Recruitment

Many organizations have developed a selection and recruitment system that aims to attract a diverse and competent pool of applicants for their job postings. However, existing research has consistently shown that selection and recruitment continue to create disparities against minorities on a systemic level. For instance, when job descriptions contain more masculine than feminine wording, applicants can perceive the job to be more suited for men and seem unattractive to their female counterparts (Gaucher et al., 2011). Similarly, subtle gender cues, such as using gender-exclusive language during the selection process, can result in female applicants withdrawing themselves from the recruitment and selection process (Stout & Dasgupta, 2011). This is particularly problematic as it continues to perpetuate gender disparity in organizations by attracting more male applicants than female applicants.

In addition to women experiencing negative systemic barriers from subtle gender cues, LGBTQ individuals also face similar barriers at work. More specifically, when organizations use binary gender language (i.e., he/she), it can signal to LGBTQ applicants that the organization does not have a pro-diversity and inclusion culture, potentially resulting in them feeling a sense of psychological discomfort and perceiving the organization to devalue stigmatized groups (McLemore, 2015). This is because some LGBTQ individuals identify their gender differently than traditional social norms (Carrera et al., 2012). Therefore, using binary gender language can result in LGBTQ individuals experiencing stigma due to misgendering (McLemore, 2015).

In addition to human biases making selection decisions, several organizations also use selection systems that include artificial intelligence (AI) systems. These organizations use AI systems with the intention of improving the quality of hiring decisions by attempting to eliminate the influence of applicant demographic characteristic cues and enhance efficiency (Purkiss et al., 2006). For example, negative stereotyping of a minority group (Kawakami et al., 1998) and activation of implicit bias pertaining to a particular group (e.g., an applicant's accent initiating perceptions of intelligence, kindness, national origin, ethnicity, etc.; Lippi-Green, 1994; Nesdale & Rooney, 1990) are cues that have been found to impair human decision-making and can lead to discriminatory decisions (Purkiss et al., 2006). As a result, implementing AI systems can potentially help with eliminating some of these biases and help select better applicants for a job.

Although AI has been included in selection systems for these benefits, the use of these AI systems can be problematic for minorities. For example, these AI systems were found to exacerbate the systemic racial disparity amongst the candidates, especially between Whites and African Americans (Koenecke et al., 2020). Previously, this happened when systems incorrectly transcribed the recordings from African American candidates during online interviews due to their accents, deeming these candidates less competent for the jobs (Andrews, 2020). Failure to detect the accents of African American candidates is due to the lack of audio data from this demographic group when designing the AI system (Andrews, 2020). Similarly, human biases that arise due to the social conceptions of stereotypes can also be built into and amplified in machine learning (Bolukbasi et al., 2016). For example, a study conducted by Caliskan and colleagues (2017) studied AI systems that adopted human-like semantic biases such as associating European American sounding names with pleasant words while negatively associating African American names with unpleasant words. The study further explained that this type of systemic bias would result in prejudicial outcomes for minority groups if used for organizational practices such as resume screening. In another instance, Angwin and colleagues (2016) found bias within the AI algorithms that incorrectly labeled Black defendants as higher risk criminals than White defendants while also incorrectly flagging White defendants as lower risk than Black defendants. These examples show that such human biases run the risk of amplifying their biases into AI systems, thereby causing gender and racial disparities among the minority groups.

Assessment and Performance Management

Organizations have long been considered to be a conduit to facilitate a meritocratic system (Young, 1958), where people are assessed and rewarded based on their own merits, which can serve as a function to dissolving the social inequalities that exist within the broader society largely mirroring the functionalist perspective (Pitesa & Pillutla, 2019). Research evidence on demographic subgroup membership in the organizational context, however, has not provided much support for this idea (van Dijk et al.,

2020) and instead suggest that there exist systemic hurdles that minority groups face. For instance, the research done by Yearby (2018) explains that to determine salary, employers often use past wages as an anchor, which can be a disadvantage for minority women. As a result, this approach to determining salary can further explain the reason why women, in general, are paid less in comparison to their male counterparts, even if they have similar or higher qualifications than them. Similarly, this wage disparity has also been found to be prominent amongst other minority groups (i.e., African American men) in comparison to their majority counterparts (i.e., White men; Huffman & Cohen, 2004).

When making decisions for managerial roles, women are often selected for such roles in times of crisis, thereby resulting in the "think crisis-think female" association (Ryan & Haslam, 2007). Additional research conducted by Ryan and colleagues (2010) further explained that females were chosen for such leadership positions as their feminine traits were seen as more desirable for crisis management. In other words, the historical and stereo-typical characteristics of women, such as tactful, sympathetic, and intuitive (Ryan et al., 2011), are seen as desirable for crisis management, creating a systemic barrier in that traditional feminine characteristics are more desirable when the organization is already failing. Selecting women for glass cliff positions during a crisis is setting them up for failure (Ryan & Haslam, 2007) and creating a systemic gender disparity among leadership positions.

Similarly, employees belonging to unconventional families, such as same-sex couples or families conceiving through surrogacy/foster/adoption methods, face structural barriers that prevent them from gaining access to family benefits. For example, in a qualitative interview study of LGBTQ families, Hanssen (2012) found that these individuals had to repeatedly explain and share their family situations if they had openly disclosed their sexual identity, causing psychological discomfort and strain at work. Fur-thermore, this repeated questioning of LGBTQ employees and their family situations makes it difficult for them to gain access to these benefits as their situations are entirely different from traditional conventional fami-lies. In other words, the inability of organizations to form policies that are inclusive of unconventional families could make such benefits and policies inaccessible for employees belonging to LGBTQ, thereby systemically dis-criminating against this minority group.

Given these findings, van Dijk and colleagues (2020) took a conflict per-spective and proposed a conceptual model, the cumulative social inequality in workplaces (CSI-W) model. The model describes how organizations play a role in sustaining or further perpetuating the social inequality that exists in the broader social system. More specifically, the CSI-W model suggests that when an employee enters an organization, they already have an initial set of opportunities and rewards that are given to them based on the social group that they belong in (e.g., White, Black, Asian, etc.). This initial set of opportunities and rewards then affect one's subsequent accumulation of knowledge, skill, ability (KSAs), social capital, and influence, such that the more opportunities and rewards that they have early on, the more of these resources that they can accumulate over time. Furthermore, the accumulation of these resources becomes more nuanced as the perceptions of others (i.e., stereotypes and status beliefs) and the organizational reward structures (i.e., segmentation, winner-take-all, and meritocratic ideology) are factored into the equation. In other words, employees that belong to a disadvantaged or a minority group would enter an organization with a lower set of opportunities and rewards in comparison to their majority counterparts. This inequality would then lead them to accumulate less personal and social resources over time, further perpetuating the social inequalities that exist in the broader social system. The development of the CSI-W makes it possible to understand the underlying mechanisms that further perpetuate these social and structural inequalities that exist in society and provides important implications for addressing systemic oppression in organizations.

RESEARCH METHODS FOR INCORPORATING SYSTEMIC OPPRESSION IN ORGANIZATIONAL RESEARCH

Based on the direct implications of systemic oppression within organizations and diversity and inclusion research, we have compiled a variety of methods that can be utilized to examine systemic oppression in organizational research. However, as systemic oppression is a complex phenomenon that is novel to the organizational context, it is important that researchers understand the relevance and practical contribution that utilizing multiple methods can provide. Specifically, we believe that triangulating the findings using multiple methods will provide a more holistic understanding of systemic phenomena. In other words, using multiple methods would better capture both the lived experiences of minorities and the macro mechanisms, which each add unique insight into the reinforcement of systemic oppression in organizations.

Qualitative Methods

There are a variety of qualitative methods utilized in sociological, psychological, and anthropological research that diversity and inclusion researchers should incorporate on systemic oppression (see Table 2.2). A reason that qualitative methods are utilized by many fields to investigate systemic oppression is the difference in epistemological and paradigmatic perspectives (Ladson-Billings, 2000). Such perspectives include critical theory, structural constructivism, social constructivism, which are founded on the conflict perspective and are useful in studying systemic oppression in the workplace since the focus of the research is the truth of the minority members and their lived experiences of how they are impacted by the larger societal system (Bourdieu, 1989; Ladson-Billings, 2000). Furthermore, qualitative methodology recognizes that in many situations, there is not only one "truth," allowing for minorities to express their own truth regarding the oppression they experience on a daily basis throughout different institutions and contexts (Kidder & Fine, 1997). For example, Pierre Bourdieu (1989) emphasizes the importance of investigating past objective states to examine the social world by incorporating one's perspectives and position as social reality is an object of perception. More specifically, he proposes that the social world is a product of double structuring, which includes both objective (e.g., the physical state of the space) and subjective components (e.g., perceptions of the individuals). This perspective is contrasted to the post-positivist approach that most quantitative research utilizes that states that there is only one truth or reality that exists.

Thematic Analysis. Thematic analysis is a foundational method for qualitative analysis (see Braun & Clarke, 2006, 2012 for guidelines on conducting thematic analysis). The general premise of thematic analysis is to identify, analyze, and report patterns within a qualitative dataset. By utilizing the rich descriptions provided in interview transcripts, researchers are able to tap into patterns that are not identifiable in quantitative measures. For example, previous research has used thematic analysis to understand the social dynamics of individuals with disabilities such as autism in adults by conducting semistructured interviews regarding their social dynamics (Crompton et al., 2020). Future research incorporating thematic analysis to investigate systemic oppression in the workplace can be done by conducting semistructured interviews with minorities and nonminorities to understand potential barriers during the selection process and identify themes for both groups and highlight any potential differences between them. For instance, participants could be asked questions such as "Please describe your experiences during interviews?", "Can you recall and describe what kind of small talk you engaged in during the interview?", and "Can you describe the salary negotiation process?"

Content Analysis. Another qualitative method that organizational researchers can utilize for studying systemic oppression is content analysis. Similar to thematic analysis, content analysis involves finding themes in the dataset; however, instead of finding the themes in interviews, a content analysis aims to find themes in qualitative data that was not originally purposed for research (e.g., social artifacts, Lune & Berg, 2017). Previous

Table 2.2

Summary of Research Methodologies and Best Practices That Incorporate Systemic Oppression in Organizational Research

Method	Example	Best Practices
Qualitative Methods		
Thematic Analysis	Crompton et al., 2020	Braun & Clarke, 2006, 2012
Content Analysis	Hatzithomas et al., 2016	Lune & Berg, 2017
Ethnography	Stuart & Benezra, 2018	Emerson et al., 2011
Participatory Action Research	Torre, 2009	Fine et al., 2003; Kemmis, 2006; Kemmis & Wilkinson, 1998
Quantitative Methods		
Big data	N/A	Tonidandel et al., 2018
Multilevel analysis	N/A	Aguinis et al., 2013
Social network analysis	Fang et al., 2020	Zwijze-Koning & de Jong, 2005

qualitative researchers have utilized content analysis to evaluate systemic oppression. For example, a previous content analysis aimed to longitudinally identify gender stereotype trends in Superbowl commercials by examining 20 years of commercials aired during the Superbowl (Hatzithomas et al., 2016). In this study, the author examined all of the advertisements the company produces for themes such as gender roles. Content analyses provide researchers with unique perspectives on the basis that the subjects being researched were not intended for the purpose of research, which may shed some light on implicit beliefs or attitudes of organizational members. An example of a future research direction that could utilize content analysis to investigate systemic oppression in the workplace could be examining workplace content (e.g., brochures, posters, etc.) for inclusivity (e.g., gendered words, picturing diverse sets of individuals in diverse positions, etc.).

Ethnography. A third qualitative method that could be used for researching systemic oppression in the workplace is an ethnographic method, which involves researchers immersing themselves in the setting that they are researching and recording all observations (Emerson et al., 2011). A benefit of ethnographic research is the researcher is able to make observations of the real experiences of organizational members in the context of interest.

Qualitative researchers have utilized ethnographic research to examine systemic oppression, such as observing the impact of increased policing and criminalization in predominantly African American communities (Stuart & Benezra, 2018). An example of a future research direction utilizing ethnography for investigating systemic oppression in the workplace would be a researcher immersing themselves in a workplace of interest and observing all interactions between managers and subordinates to identify potential patterns of barriers for minority groups.

Participatory Action Research. A final qualitative method we believe would be useful in studying systemic oppression in the workplace is participatory action research (PAR). Participatory action research involves democratic, collaborative relationships between participants and researchers to construct an understanding of individuals' lived experiences, allowing us to better understand the ways systemic oppression influences individuals' work lives (Fine et al., 2003). Previous research has utilized PAR as a method to study systemic oppression by examining educational injustices in low-income communities (Torre, 2009). A unique benefit of PAR is the collaborative process in which the research is cocreated and the action-focused objective to make a difference in the community (Fine et al., 2003). An example of a future direction that would utilize PAR to investigate systemic oppression within an organization is to develop a democratic and collaborative relationship with minority employees in which the researcher directly works with the employees to discuss their lived experiences regarding onboarding to identify any systemic barriers. Minority employees could help to identify and explain systemic issues that may be invisible to researchers who are not part of that group.

In essence, qualitative research has not been utilized in organizational research as often as quantitative research despite the numerous unique benefits of qualitative methods. These qualitative methods were designed to capture the conflict perspective by ensuring that the lived experiences of participants are reflected in the research. The rich data that qualitative methods produce allow researchers to understand the context in which minorities exist and navigate the workplace. By utilizing qualitative methods to investigate systemic oppression in the workplace, researchers will be better able to develop action plans to combat systemic barriers.

Quantitative Methods

Big Data. For instance, big data has been discussed to be an impactful approach to better understand research questions that are related to diversity, equity, and inclusion (Tonidandel et al., 2018). Big data refers to datasets that have a large number of data points, with different sources and types of data, and a high speed of data collection. With these features of big data, detection of subtle forms of discrimination (Botsford Morgan et al., 2015) and development of algorithms to make the workplace environment be more inclusive (Tonidandel et al., 2018) are possible. In the context of systemic oppression, big data can help researchers identify which organizational policies and practices are contributing to the oppression of minority groups. This can be done by applying text mining, natural language processing techniques, or machine learning to organizational policies and practices to quantify them so that researchers can directly assess the degree to which their organization is vulnerable to the effect of systemic oppression.

Multilevel Modeling. Furthermore, the obtained value using a big data approach from analyzing these policies and practices can also be used with multilevel modeling (Hox, 1998) to help uncover the effect systemic oppression directly has on lower levels factors, such as employee's motivation and turnover intentions (Kozlowski & Klein, 2000). For instance, if a researcher seeks to examine the effect of systemic oppression on the rate of minorities being promoted in organizations, they first need to quantify the value of systemic oppression from various organizations using big data techniques on historical systemic oppressive events. For example, the events that occurred on September 11, 2001, triggers a huge rate of discrimination toward the Muslims and Arabs communities in the United States (Anderson, 2002; American-Arab Anti-Discrimination Committee, 2003). This event can then be viewed as a systemic oppressive event as it changes the attitudes of the majority of Americans toward Muslims and Arabs people. As a result, organizations may adopt policies and practices, while not evident in nature, that are oppressive toward these groups of minorities. Assessing the historical artifacts (e.g., policies) from this event could provide a quantitative value of systemic oppression in organizations. Additionally, researchers would also need to obtain the rate of minorities being promoted from these organizations as well. Once these values have been obtained, researchers can then aggregate the systemic oppression values at the organizational level to the societal level, then examine their effect on the rate of minorities being promoted at the organizational level.

Social Network Analysis. A third quantitative method that can be utilized to investigate systemic oppression in the workplace is social network analysis (SNA). SNA is a quantitative method that examines relationships among social entities at varying levels of analysis (e.g., individuals, organizations, systems, etc.; Wasserman & Faust, 1994). Researchers can utilize SNA to investigate systemic oppression by examining the networks within and between organizations. For example, by examining the networks of minority groups compared to majority groups within an organization through a subgroup analysis, researchers may be able to uncover unique systemic barriers that minorities encounter. Researchers could examine the centrality of minority members compared to majority members, the access that subgroups have to influential members, resources, or differences in shared norms. Additionally, researchers could incorporate exponential random graph modeling (Robins et al., 2007) to understand how local social processes (i.e., within the organization) could impact the network structure (i.e., organization structure). A meta-analysis on studies using SNA techniques examined gender differences of brokerage positions (i.e., the person who connects two different networks together) within a network (Fang et al., 2020) and found women are less likely to occupy the brokerage position. However, proactive networking mediated this gender's effect on network brokerage in new employees, implying women may need to work harder for the same amount of privilege.

CONCLUSION

In this chapter, we introduced the concept of systemic oppression in organizations by drawing from systemic racism theory (Feagin, 2006). In addition, to highlight how systemic oppression impacts organizational entities, we take on the conflict perspective to illustrate how work organizations are vulnerable to structural inequities. We then discussed various methods that can be utilized to incorporate systemic oppression in future organizational research. While our discussion of these research methodologies is separated, we suggest that researchers use mixed-methods to enable effective triangulation of methods to fully understand its impact.

Overall, by incorporating systemic oppression in organizational research, we can advance our understanding of how organizations can contribute to developing a more equitable society for all minority groups. Although, it is important to mention that I/O psychologists have begun to use the conflict perspective primarily at the interface of social psychology (e.g., Morgenroth et al., 2020). We believe this focus on the conflict perspective needs to be a more purposeful and conscious effort in the field of I/O psychology. We hope that by producing more research investigating systemic oppression in the workplace that the field of DEI will further pave a path to help dismantle the historical barriers placed upon minorities.

REFERENCES

Adler, P. S., Forbes, L. C., & Willmott, H. (2007). Critical management studies. *Academy of Management Annals*, *1*(1), 119–179. https://doi.org/10.5465/078559808

Aguinis, H., Gottfredson, R. K., & Culpepper, S. A. (2013). Best-practice recommendations for estimating cross-level interaction effects using multilevel modeling. *Journal of Management*, *39*(6), 1490–1528. https://doi.org/10.1177/0149206313478188

Anderson, C. (2002, November 25). FBI: Hate crimes vs. Muslims rise. *Associated Press*. https://apnews.com/article/5e249fb6e4dc184720e3428c9d0bd046

Andrews, E. L. (2020, March 23). Stanford researchers find that automated speech recognition is more likely to misinterpret black speakers. *Stanford News*. https://news.stanford.edu/2020/03/23/automated-speech-recognition-less-accurate-blacks/

Angwin, J., Larson, J., Mattu, S., & Kirchner, L. (2016, May 23). Machine bias—There's software used across the country to predict future criminals. And it's biased against blacks. *ProPublica*. https://www.propublica.org/article/machine-bias-risk-assessments-in-criminal-sentencing

Anthony, P. (1986). *The foundation of management* (Vol. 324). Routledge Kegan & Paul.

American-Arab Anti-Discrimination Committee. (2003). *Report on hate crimes and discrimination against Arab Americans: The post-September 11 backlash, September 11, 2001–October 11, 2002*. American-Arab Anti-Discrimination Committee Research Institute.

Amis, J. M., Munir, K. A., Lawrence, T. B., Hirsch, P., & McGahan, A. (2018). Inequality, institutions and organizations. *Organization Studies*, *39*(9), 1131–1152. https://doi.org/10.1177/0170840618792596

Bailey, Z. D., Krieger, N., Agénor, M., Graves, J., Linos, N., & Bassett, M. T. (2017). Structural racism and health inequities in the USA: Evidence and interventions. *The Lancet*, *389*(10077), 1453–1463. https://doi.org/10.1016/S0140-6736(17)30569-X

Berrey, E. (2014). Breaking glass ceilings, ignoring dirty floors: The culture and class bias of diversity management. *American Behavioral Scientist*, *58*(2), 347–370. https://doi.org/10.1177/0002764213503333

Blair-Loy, M. (2001). It's not just what you know it's who you know: Technical knowledge, rainmaking, and gender among finance executives. *Research in the Sociology of Work*, *10*, 51–83. https://doi.org/10.1016/S0277-2833(01)80021-2

Bolukbasi, T., Chang, K. W., Zou, J. Y., Saligrama, V., & Kalai, A. T. (2016). Man is to computer programmer as woman is to homemaker? debiasing word embeddings. *Advances in neural information processing systems*, *29*, 4349–4357.

Botsford Morgan, W., Dunleavy, E., & DeVries, P. D. (2015). Using big data to create diversity and inclusion in organizations. In S. Tonidandel, E. King, & J. Cortina (Eds.), *Big data at work: The data science revolution and organizational psychology* (pp. 310–335). Routledge.

Bourdieu, P. (1989). Social space and symbolic power. *Sociological theory*, *7*(1), 14–25.

Braun, V., & Clarke, V. (2006). Using thematic analysis in psychology. *Qualitative Research in Psychology*, *3*(2), 77–101. https://doi.org/10.1191/1478088706qp063oa

Braun, V., & Clarke, V. (2012). Thematic analysis. In H. Cooper, P. M. Camic, D. L. Long, A. T. Panter, D. Rindskopf, & K. J. Sher (Eds.), *APA handbooks in psychology®. APA handbook of research methods in psychology, Vol. 2. Research designs: Quantitative, qualitative, neuropsychological, and biological* (pp. 57–71). American Psychological Association. https://doi.org/10.1037/13620-004

Caliskan, A., Bryson, J. J., & Narayanan, A. (2017). Semantics derived automatically from language corpora contain human-like biases. *Science*, *356*(6334), 183–186. https://doi.org/10.1126/science.aal4230

Carrera, M. V., DePalma, R., & Lameiras, M. (2012). Sex/gender identity: Moving beyond fixed and 'natural' categories. *Sexualities, 15*(8), 995–1016. https://doi.org/10.1177/1363460712459158

Casey, L. S., Reisner, S. L., Findling, M. G., Blendon, R. J., Benson, J. M., Sayde, J. M., & Miller, C. (2019). Discrimination in the United States: Experiences of lesbian, gay, bisexual, transgender, and queer Americans. *Health Services Research, 54*, 1454–1466. https://doi.org/10.1111/1475-6773.13229

Crompton, C. J., Hallett, S., Ropar, D., Flynn, E., & Fletcher-Watson, S. (2020). 'I never realised everybody felt as happy as I do when I am around autistic people': A thematic analysis of autistic adults' relationships with autistic and neurotypical friends and family. *Autism, 24*(6), 1438–1448. https://doi.org/10.1177/1362361320908976

DeSouza, E. R., Wesselmann, E. D., & Ispas, D. (2017). Workplace discrimination against sexual minorities: Subtle and not-so-subtle. *Canadian Journal of Administrative Sciences/Revue Canadienne des Sciences de l'Administration, 34*(2), 121–132. https://doi.org/10.1002/cjas.1438

Ecker, J., Aubry, T., & Sylvestre, J. (2019). A review of the literature on LBGTQ adults who experience homelessness. *Journal of Homosexuality, 66*(3), 297–323. https://doi.org/10.1080/00918369.2017.1413277

Emerson, R. M., Fretz, R. I., & Shaw, L. L. (2011). *Writing ethnographic fieldnotes.* University of Chicago Press.

Fang, R., Zhang, Z., & Shaw, J. D. (2020). Gender and social network brokerage: A meta-analysis and field investigation. *Journal of Applied Psychology.* https://doi.org/10.1037/apl0000841

Feagin, J. R. (2006). *Systemic racism: A theory of oppression.* Routledge/Taylor & Francis Group.

Feagin, J. R. (2013). *The White racial frame: Centuries of racial framing and counter-framing.* Routledge.

Feagin, J. R., & Barnett, B. (2004). Success and failure: How systemic racism trumped the *Brown v. Board* of education decision. *University of Illinois Law Review, 2004*(5), 1099–1130.

Feagin, J., & Bennefield, Z. (2014). Systemic racism and US health care. *Social Science & Medicine, 103*, 7–14. https://doi.org/10.1016/j.socscimed.2013.09.006

Fine, M., Torre, M. E., Boudin, K., Bowen, I., Clark, J., Hylton, D., Martinez, M., Missy, Roberts, R. A., Smart, P., & Upegui, D. (2003). Participatory action research: From within and beyond prison bars. In P. M. Camic, J. E. Rhodes, & L. Yardley (Eds.), *Qualitative research in psychology: Expanding perspectives in methodology and design* (pp. 173–198). American Psychological Association. https://doi.org/10.1037/10595-010

Flage, A. (2019). Discrimination against gays and lesbians in hiring decisions: A meta-analysis. *International Journal of Manpower, 41*(6), 671–691. https://doi.org/10.1108/IJM-08-2018-0239

Foschi, M. (1996). Double standards in the evaluation of men and women. *Social Psychology Quarterly, 59*(3), 237–254. https://doi.org/10.2307/2787021

Foucault, M. (1980). *Power/knowledge: Selected interviews and other writings, 1972–1977.* Vintage.

Gaucher, D., Friesen, J., & Kay, A. C. (2011). Evidence that gendered wording in job advertisements exists and sustains gender inequality. *Journal of Personality and Social Psychology*, *101*(1), 109–128. https://doi.org/10.1037/a0022530

Ghoshal, S. (2005). Bad management theories are destroying good management practices. *Academy of Management Learning & Education*, *4*(1), 75–91. https://doi.org/10.5465/amle.2005.16132558

Hanssen, J. K. (2012). 'My Rainbow Family'—Discomfort and the heteronormative logics. *Young*, *20*(3), 237–256. https://doi.org/10.1177/110330881202000302

Hatzithomas, L., Boutsouki, C., & Ziamou, P. (2016). A longitudinal analysis of the changing roles of gender in advertising: A content analysis of Super Bowl commercials. *International Journal of Advertising*, *35*(5), 888–906. https://doi.org/10.1080/02650487.2016.1162344

Heilman, M. E., & Caleo, S. (2018). Combatting gender discrimination: A lack of fit framework. *Group Processes & Intergroup Relations*, *21*(5), 725–744. https://doi.org/10.1177/1368430218761587

Hox, J. J. (1998). Multilevel modeling: When and why. In I. Balderjahn , R. Mathar, & M. Schader (Eds.), *Classification, data analysis, and data highways* (pp. 147–154). Springer-Verlag.

Huffman, M. L., & Cohen, P. N. (2004). Racial wage inequality: Job segregation and devaluation across US labor markets. *American Journal of Sociology*, *109*(4), 902–936. https://doi.org/10.1086/378928

Kawakami, K., Dion, K. L., & Dovidio, J. F. (1998). Racial prejudice and stereotype activation. *Personality and Social Psychology Bulletin*, *24*(4), 407–416. https://doi.org/10.1177/0146167298244007

Kemmis, S. (2006). Participatory action research and the public sphere. *Educational Action Research*, *14*(4), 459–476. https://doi.org/10.1080/09650790600975593

Kemmis, S., & Wilkinson, M. (1998). Participatory action research and the study of practice. In B. Atweh, S. Kemmis, & P. Weeks (Eds.), *Action research in practice: Partnerships for social justice in education* (pp. 21–36). Routledge. https://doi.org/10.4324/9780203024478

Kidder, L. H., & Fine, M. (1997). Qualitative inquiry in psychology: A radical tradition. In D. Fox & I. Prilleltensky (Eds.), *Critical psychology: An introduction* (pp. 34–50). SAGE.

Klikauer, T. (2013). *Managerialism: A critique of an ideology.* Springer.

Klikauer, T. (2015). Critical management studies and critical theory: A review. *Capital & Class*, *39*(2), 197–220. https://doi.org/10.1177/0309816815581773

Koenecke, A., Nam, A., Lake, E., Nudell, J., Quartey, M., Mengesha, Z., Toups, C., Rickford, J. R., Jurafsky, D., & Goel, S. (2020). Racial disparities in automated speech recognition. *Proceedings of the National Academy of Sciences*, *117*(14), 7684–7689. https://doi.org/10.1073/pnas.1915768117

Kozlowski, S. W. J., & Klein, K. J. (2000). A multilevel approach to theory and research in organizations: Contextual, temporal, and emergent processes. In K. J. Klein & S. W. J. Kozlowski (Eds.), *Multilevel theory, research, and methods in organizations: Foundations, extensions, and new directions* (pp. 3–90). Jossey-Bass.

Ladson-Billings, G. (2000). Racialized discourses and ethnic epistemologies. In N. Denzin & Y. Lincoln (Eds.), *Handbook of qualitative research* (2nd ed.). SAGE.

Lefkowitz, J. (2013). Values and ethics of a changing i-o psychology: A call to (further) action. In J. B. Olson-Buchanan, L. L. K. Bryan, & L. F. Thompson (Eds.), *Using industrial-organizational psychology for the greater good: Helping those who help others* (pp. 13–42). Routledge.

Lippi-Green, R. (1994). Accent, standard language ideology, and discriminatory pretext in the courts. *Language in Society, 23*(2), 163–198. https://doi.org/10.1017/s0047404500017826

Lune, H., & Berg, B. L. (2017). *Qualitative research methods for the social sciences* (9th ed.). Pearson.

McLemore, K. A. (2015). Experiences with misgendering: Identity misclassification of transgender spectrum individuals. *Self and Identity, 14*(1), 51–74. https://doi.org/10.1080/15298868.2014.950691

Mahoney, J. (2004). Revisiting general theory in historical sociology. *Social Forces, 83*(2), 459–489. https://doi.org/10.1353/sof.2005.0018

Maroto, M., & Pettinicchio, D. (2014). Disability, structural inequality, and work: The influence of occupational segregation on earnings for people with different disabilities. *Research in Social Stratification and Mobility, 38*, 76–92. https://doi.org/10.1016/j.rssm.2014.08.002

Marx, K. (1977). *Capital: Vol. 1.* Vintage.

Morgenroth, T., Kirby, T. A., Ryan, M. K., & Sudkämper, A. (2020). The who, when, and why of the glass cliff phenomenon: A meta-analysis of appointments to precarious leadership positions. *Psychological Bulletin, 146*(9), 797–789. https://doi.org/10.1037/bul0000234

Nadler, J. T., Lowery, M. R., Grebinoski, J., & Jones, R. G. (2014). Aversive discrimination in employment interviews: Reducing effects of sexual orientation bias with accountability. *Psychology of Sexual Orientation and Gender Diversity, 1*(4), 480-488. https://doi.org/10.1037/sgd0000079

Nesdale, A. R., & Rooney, R. (1990). Effect of children's ethnic accents on adults' evaluations and stereotyping. *Australian Journal of Psychology, 42*(3), 309–319. https://doi.org/10.1080/00049539008260128

Pitesa, M., & Pillutla, M. M. (2019). Socioeconomic mobility and talent utilization of workers from poorer backgrounds: the overlooked importance of within-organization dynamics. *Academy of Management Annals, 13*(2), 737–769. https://doi.org/10.5465/annals.2017.0115

Purkiss, S. L. S., Perrewé, P. L., Gillespie, T. L., Mayes, B. T., & Ferris, G. R. (2006). Implicit sources of bias in employment interview judgments and decisions. *Organizational Behavior and Human Decision Processes, 101*(2), 152–167. https://doi.org/10.1016/j.obhdp.2006.06.005

Ragins, B. R., & Sundstrom, E. (1989). Gender and power in organizations: A longitudinal perspective. *Psychological bulletin, 105*(1), 51–88. https://doi.org/10.1037/0033-2909.105.1.51

Robins, G., Pattison, P., Kalish, Y., & Lusher, D. (2007). An introduction to exponential random graph (p*) models for social networks. *Social Networks, 29*(2), 173–191. https://doi.org/10.1016/j.socnet.2006.08.002

Ryan, M. K., & Haslam, S. A. (2007). The glass cliff: Exploring the dynamics surrounding the appointment of women to precarious leadership positions. *Academy of Management Review*, *32*(2), 549–572. https://doi.org/10.5465/amr.2007.24351856

Ryan, M. K., Haslam, S. A., & Kulich, C. (2010). Politics and the glass cliff: Evidence that women are preferentially selected to contest hard-to-win seats. *Psychology of Women Quarterly*, *34*(1), 56–64. https://doi.org/10.1111/j.1471-6402.2009.01541.x

Ryan, M. K., Haslam, S. A., Hersby, M. D., & Bongiorno, R. (2011). Think crisis—think female: The glass cliff and contextual variation in the think manager—think male stereotype. *Journal of Applied Psychology*, *96*(3), 470–484. https://doi.org/10.1037/a0022133

Simon, R. M. (2016). The conflict paradigm in sociology and the study of social inequality: Paradox and possibility. *Theory in Action*, *9*(1), 1–31. https://doi.org/10.3798/tia.1937-0237.16001

Stout, J. G., & Dasgupta, N. (2011). When he doesn't mean you: Gender-exclusive language as ostracism. *Personality and Social Psychology Bulletin*, *37*(6), 757–769. https://doi.org/10.1177/0146167211406434

Stuart, F., & Benezra, A. (2018). Criminalized masculinities: How policing shapes the construction of gender and sexuality in poor black communities. *Social Problems*, *65*(2), 174–190. https://doi.org/10.1093/socpro/spx017

Tonidandel, S., King, E. B., & Cortina, J. M. (2018). Big data methods: Leveraging modern data analytic techniques to build organizational science. *Organizational Research Methods*, *21*(3), 525–547. https://doi.org/10.1177/1094428116677299

Torre, M. E. (2009). Participatory action research and critical race theory: Fueling spaces for nos-otras to research. *The Urban Review*, *41*(1), 106–120. https://doi.org/10.1007/s11256-008-0097-7

Tyson, L. (2014). *Critical theory today: A user-friendly guide*. Routledge.

van Dijk, H., Kooij, D., Karanika-Murray, M., De Vos, A., & Meyer, B. (2020). Meritocracy a myth? A multilevel perspective of how social inequality accumulates through work. *Organizational Psychology Review*, *10*(3-4), 240–269. https://doi.org/10.1177/2041386620930063

Walter, A. W., Ruiz, Y., Tourse, R. W. C., Kress, H., Morningstar, B., MacArthur, B., & Daniels, A. (2017). Leadership matters: How hidden biases perpetuate institutional racism in organizations. *Human Service Organizations: Management, Leadership & Governance*, *41*(3), 213–221. https://doi.org/10.1080/23303131.2016.1249584

Wasserman, S., & Faust, K. (1994). *Social network analysis: Methods and applications* (Vol. 8). Cambridge University Press.

Willis, J. W. (2007). *Foundations of qualitative research*. SAGE.

Yearby, R. (2018). Racial disparities in health status and access to healthcare: The continuation of inequality in the United States due to structural racism. *The American Journal of Economics and Sociology*, *77*(3–4), 1113–1152. https://doi.org/10.111/ajes.12230

Young, M. (1958). *The rise of the meritocracy*. Transaction.

Zwijze-Koning, K. H., & de Jong, M. D. T. (2005). Auditing information structures in organizations: A review of data collection techniques for network analysis. *Organizational Research Methods*, *8*(4), 429–453. https://doi.org/10.1177/1094428105280120

CHAPTER 3

WHAT DOESN'T KILL YOU, MAKES YOU STRONGER

Applying a Strength-Based Approach to Black Employees' Workplace Experience

Richard V. Burgess
University of North Carolina

Kalan R. Norris
University at Buffalo

ABSTRACT

Diversity research examining African American (hereafter, Black people or Black employees) employees overwhelmingly utilizes a deficit-based approach and, as a result, does not adequately capture their unique experiences at work. Also, this popular approach ignores the many strengths that Black employees may bring to work to succeed. We utilize a strength-based approach and offer a conceptual model to better understand Black employees' diversity-related workplace experiences. In addition, we offer guidance on what organizations can do to ensure that the burden of "fitting-in" at work does not rest solely on the shoulders of Black employees.

The Future of Scholarship on Race in Organizations, pp. 53–74
Copyright © 2022 by Information Age Publishing

WHAT DOESN'T KILL YOU, MAKES YOU STRONGER: APPLYING A STRENGTH-BASED APPROACH TO BLACK EMPLOYEES' WORKPLACE EXPERIENCE

In discussions of demographic diversity, one controversial issue has been the characterization of Black employees through the lens of a deficit-based approach (cf. Nkomo et al., 2019). African Americans are typically ascribed low-status group membership, and often treated with low regard, which makes them targets of stereotypes, prejudice, and discrimination (Colella et al., 2017; Roberson, 2019; Roberson et al., 2017). Further, researchers typically employ the use of status characteristics theory or social categorization lenses such that Black employees are universally deemed to occupy the same low status position, which disregards the multitude of ways an individual can experience race.

The deficit-based approach that is pervasive within literature falls short in capturing the normative development of Black employees in spite of experiences of racial discrimination. First, disparities in achievement, wealth, and quality of life between White and Black individuals are not necessarily the result of individual or cultural differences, but instead often structural racism (Kendi, 2019). In addition, while the Black employees often lack the material resource and career opportunities of employees of other races, they may possess higher levels of some nonmaterial resources (Yosso, 2005). Finally, in spite of widespread racial discrimination, many Black employees are often able to succeed and, in some cases, thrive at work. In fact, in 1970, only 6% of the Black population obtained a college degree. Now that number has quadrupled to 26% of the Black community (Lazonick et al., 2020). Further, a recent review on the evolution and future of diversity research (cf. Roberson et al., 2017) challenges researchers to account for the multidimensionality of intrapersonal identities, which may be useful for accurately capturing within-in group differences that exists among Black employees in the workplace. In light of this evidence, we propose a different approach to capture the richness of the Black experience within the workplace.

Within both the organizational sciences and the broader social sciences, scholars increasingly employ a strength-based approach to better understand the individual-level effects of various phenomena on Black people. In her classic community cultural wealth model, Yosso (2005) contends that communities of color have rich cultural assets that are often unrecognized and overlooked. In the same tradition, scholarship in psychology outlines the unique strengths of Black people and Black culture (Caldwell-Colbert et al., 2009; Mattis et al., 2016) that aid in normative development. The field of positive psychology examines the dynamic relationship between adversity and resilience such that an individual may experience positive psychological adjustment as a result (Mattis et al., 2016; Seligman & Csik-szentmihalyi, 2000). In management, positive organizational scholarship brings a similar lens to the field, focusing on capacity-enhancing dynamics that promote human thriving and excellence in individuals, groups, and organizations (Dutton et al., 2006). More recently, McCluney et al. (2017) use a strength-based approach to introduce their conceptual model in a recent paper on "calling-in-Black." In sum, numerous scholars across disciplines are highlighting the strengths (e.g., racial identity) that Black people possess.

Building off this work, we propose a strength-based approach for understanding Black employee experiences in the workplace. Strength-based models focus on how an individuals' resources and assets influence normative development. We argue that a strength-based approach is ideal for unpacking a Black employees' experience with managing intrapersonal identities in the workplace and its subsequent effects on both proximal and distal outcomes. We contend that Black cultural interdependence, the history of Black resistance to discrimination, and racial socialization may lead Black people to bring a collective sense of resilience to the workplace. Black employees utilize assets such as racial identity to serve as buffers to the negative experiences associated with being Black. We also argue that Black employees can best utilize their race-based strengths when they are fully included within their organization, thus enabling Black employees to bring their full selves to work. Finally, we argue that when fully included in organizations, Black employees engage in constructive deviance (Vadera et al., 2013), positive norm-defying behavior, that advance themselves, their organizations, and society as a whole.

In this chapter, we have three goals. First, we seek to extend positive organizational scholarship to our understanding of Black people in the workplace. A Strength-based approach can contribute to the positive psychology literature as we focus on the resources that aid in developing one's internal assets that may influence how one chooses to navigate the workplace. By focusing on the strengths Black employees have and the organizational practice that facilitates Black people to build on these strengths, we move beyond the deficit-based approach common to studies of Black people within the diversity literature and instead highlight potential sources of empowerment as experienced through social group membership. Second, we seek to establish a deeper understanding of Black strengths in the workplace. Although strength-based approaches are not novel, we situate the strength-based approach in the workplace context, using racial identity as the source of assets, to better understand the Black experience in an organizational context can aid in understanding the multidimensionality of intrapersonal identities (Roberson et al., 2017). By clearly articulating Black resilience in the face of discrimination and exploring its antecedents and resulting strengths, we focus on the unique assets and contributions Black employees can bring to the workplace. Finally, we offer up tangible actions organizations and managers can take to better support their Black employees. By developing a climate for inclusion, managers can not only increase Black employee well-being, but advance their organizations as a whole.

Figure 3.1

Conceptual Model of a Strength-based Approach

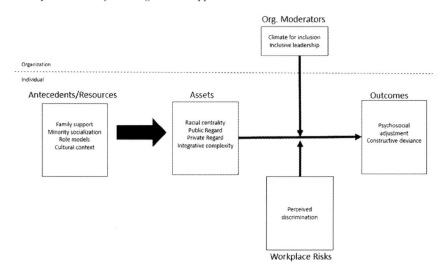

What Is a Strength-Based Approach?

To better understand the developmental trajectories of Black people, it is essential to consider how one's resources and cultural assets impact their potential to succeed in navigating the world. Before we proceed, we need to define a few important concepts for understanding the strength-based approach. Resources refer to positive factors external to the individual that promote positive development—for instance, positive child-rearing, support for a mentor, or membership in a social club. Assets refer to internal factors that aid in normative development and help one make sense of their external environment. Researchers use strength-based approaches in the fields of education and positive psychology to examine how personal (e.g., self-regulation, self-control) and cultural assets (e.g., racial identity) of Black people serve as protective factors, buffering the negative effects of various stimuli (Butler-Barnes et al., 2013; Fergus & Zimmerman, 2005). While a full review of strength-based approaches is outside the scope of this chapter, next, we will review relevant findings that serve to support why a strength-based approach is ideal for an organizational setting.

In a study of 220 Black adolescents, those students reporting higher levels of racial pride, self-acceptance, and self-efficacy reported higher levels of academic persistence despite experiencing school-based discrimination (Butler-Barnes et al., 2013). In a longitudinal study of Black students, racial identity was positively related to academic achievement, and private regard was positively related to school attachment, importance, and efficacy (Chavous et al., 2003). Strong racial identity beliefs buffered the negative impact of perceived racial barriers in the school context (Chavous et al., 2008). Researchers found significant relationships between racial pride and academic motivational outcomes (Altschul et al., 2006; Thompson & Gregory, 2012). Parental cultural socialization buffered the negative impact of teacher discrimination of Black adolescents' grade point average (Wang & Hughley, 2012). In other words, Black people that are taught positive messages concerning being Black performed better academically. Altogether, these findings provide support that Black individuals possess assets (e.g., knowledge, talent, capacities, and skill) and external resources (e.g., mentors, social networks, socialization processes) that can be used as building blocks as one pursues their aspirations despite facing adversity (Fergus & Zimmerman, 2005).

Could these same findings occur in the workplace setting? Prior empirical findings suggest yes. For instance, in a study of 211 college students, the researchers found an interaction between ethnicity and group identity as predictors of psychological empowerment and well-being (Molix & Bettencourt, 2010). To develop our conceptual model, we used two frameworks to understand how a strength-based approach, as a statistical tool, can allow researchers to begin unpacking the multidimensional complexities of one's intrapersonal identities. García-Coll et al.'s (1996) *Integrative Model of the Study of Developmental Competencies in Minority Children*, suggests that a minority individual's definition of the self is largely based on being a person of color (POC), and coping with experiences that are unique to being a POC at the intersection of social position (e.g., social class, race, ethnicity) and experiences (e.g., racism, discrimination, and segregation). This suggests that for Black people, race matters.

The second framework we draw on is Fergus and Zimmerman's (2005) resilience framework, emphasizing the protective model. The protective model is a means to understand how two individuals equally exposed to the same risk may experience different outcomes. Risk factors (e.g., perceived discrimination) refer to those stimuli that increase the probability of a negative outcome in one's life. When faced with risk while possessing assets, the Fergus and Zimmerman's protective model implies that in the face of a risk, such as discrimination, one's assets may buffer the negative effects of discrimination, which is the crux of the resilience framework. Resilience refers to the "dynamic process encompassing positive adaptation within the context of significant adversity" (Luthar & Cicchetti., 2000, p. 543). Resilience captures the interplay of assets and protective resources occurring over time, and it involves individual, family, and sociocultural influences (Masten et al., 1990; Rutter, 1987; Werner & Smith, 1992). Resilience is the process that explains how Black people hone and develop self-regulatory (i.e., assets) mechanisms that buffer their encounters with workplace mistreatment. Next, we introduce our conceptual model that displays some exemplar variables supporting a strength-based approach in the organizational context. Given the subjective nature of perceived discrimination, not all Black employees will experience the same level of threat. Discrimination research confirms problems of discrimination but fails to provide clear direction for its resolution (Hebl et al., 2020). We contend that for some Black employees, there individual assets will influence how they respond to negative situations in the workplace.

Resources as Antecedents

Black culture is a primary source of the assets that Black people bring to the workplace. Psychologist Nobles (1990) defines culture as a

> human process representing the vast structure of behaviors, ideas, attitudes, values, habits, beliefs, customs, language, rituals, ceremonies, and practices "peculiar" to a particular group of people, and that provides them with a general design for living and patterns for interpreting reality. (p. 12)

Within this context, Black culture represents the organizing structure Black people live within, interact with, and use to make meaning of life. While many outputs of Black culture are embraced by Americans more broadly (e.g., hip-hop music), Black culture is distinct from American culture. Black culture connects African-centered cultural values, a legacy of resistance to oppression, and strong support networks.

One core aspect of Black culture is the rich African-centered cultural values Black people draw upon. To start, Black cultural interdependence can be traced to West African traditions that capture Africans brought along into their new land (Jones, 1986; Nobles, 1991). Black culture puts a premium on relatedness to others within one's racial group, and views its members as deeply connected to each other and their common history

(Brannon et al, 2015). Additionally, African-center values are at the core of an "Afrocultural ethos" that permeates Black culture generally to guide the behavior and development of Black people (Mattis et al. 2016). Specifically, African-centered values such as communalism (a social interdependent orientation and prioritize on the social not the material gain) and harmony (reduction of competition) deeply permeate Black culture, resulting in the Black culture being particularly nurturing to Black people who engage with it (Boykin et al., 1997; Jagers et al., 1997). In total, Black culture offers substantial support that is accessible throughout the Black community.

In addition to African-centered principles, Black resistance to chattel slavery, Jim Crow, and systemic racism has also been fundamental to forming an interdependent Black culture in America. The horrors of oppression faced by Black people over the past 400 years led to a collective cultural response to protect Black bodies and affirm Black dignity. In antebellum America, Black culture (with the assistance of allies) actively resisted slavery through the creation of the Underground Railroad, where countless Black people worked together to better the Black community (Blassingame, 1979; Lawrence-McIntyre, 1987). After slavery, Black people were subject to the terror of the Jim Crow, a state administer apartheid system bolster by mob violence; in response, millions of Black people to fled to the North (Wilkerson, 2014) while others organized to launch the Civil Rights Movement which would ultimately lead to the system's demise. More recently, Black people have to face structural oppression in the form of educational disparities (Orfield, 2001), concentrated poverty (Sharkey, 2013), the wealth gap (Kraus et al., 2017), mass incarceration (Alexander, 2010), and the state-sanction murder of Black people by law enforcement. Still, Black people resist; as an example, Colin Kaepnernick risked his NFL career to make a statement protesting structural racism, and through his courage, launched a movement (Leigh & Melwani, 2019). As reflected in this and numerous other examples, an ethos of resistance is a core to the Black culture in America (Mattis et al., 2016).

Steeped in the African-centered cultural values and a tradition of resistance to oppression, Black American culture has built deep social support networks that are broadly accessible. One central place of support is the Black family. The Black family consists not only of the nuclear family, but also extended family members, adopted "fictive kin" (such as play uncles and play aunts), and the community at large (Taylor et al., 2013). These extended family networks provide emotional, practical, and financial support (Taylor et al., 2013). Beyond the family, other institutions such as churches and community groups connect Black people with important sources of support (Bagley & Carroll, 1998). In total, these institutions offer an affirming safe space for Black people in the face of the harsh, destructive forces of structural racism and racial discrimination.

The family context is recognized as the most influential socialization setting for forming a sense of self, values, and beliefs (Gecas, 1981). According to Peters (1985), building self-respect and pride via socialization messages/tactics is a significant component of Black child-rearing strategies. Socialization refers to the processes by which Black employees develop the perspective of their racial group (Neblett et al. 2009). Socialization is the process by which Black employees develop their assets (e.g., racial identity) through the developmental stages of life. Adolescents experience socialized to learn norms and practices in order to become well-functioning adults in society. Typically, Black families prepare adolescents and emerging adults via preparation for bias and promotion of messages (Hughes et al., 2006). Socialization tactics/messages linked in outcomes such as mature identity development (Barr & Neville, 2008), higher self-esteem (Neblett et al., 2008), reduced problematic behaviors (Bennett, 2007), academic adjustment (Anglin & Wade, 2007), and increased resilience (Brown, 2008). Further, parents' experiences with discrimination have been linked to communicating more racial socialization messages to prepare their offspring about dealing with Whites and how to cope with racial discrimination (Hughes, 2003; Hughes & Chen, 1997).

Interpersonal relationships may serve as resources for racial identity development via role modeling because individuals are motivated to act in accordance with their social and personal identities (Oyserman, 2009). Interpersonal relationships with friends and family, religious involvement, socioeconomic status, interracial interaction, and age are important determinants of racial identity (Demo & Hughes, 1990). Older parents are more likely to report using racial socialization than younger parents (Thornton et al., 1990). As one transitions into emerging adulthood, racial identity is reimagined with integrative complexity as part of the adult self, related to other identities, communities, and belief systems.

In addition to their connection to Black culture, Black people also deeply engage with the dominant American culture. American culture, based on Western values, prizes individualism, personal responsibility, and control (Bellah et al., 1985; Kitayama et al., 2007; Plaut et al., 2012). American culture views each individual as free from the more significant constraints of society, history, and the needs of other people. Contemporarily, the economic and political structure combine to emphasize the dominant American cultural ethos to filter broadly throughout society (Sanchez-Burke 2002). As a result, Black Americans are simultaneously immersed in the independent dominant American culture and the interdependent Black culture.

Black Employee Assets

Building of the resources of Black culture, Black people are able to develop a sense of racial identity. Racial identity support resilience and normative development (Spencer, 2006). We introduce the multidimensional model of identity development (cf. Sellers et al., 1998) to measure the assets one possesses. Racial identity refers to the significance of and meanings individuals attach to their racial group (Sellers et al., 1998). Racial identity is comprised of racial centrality, or how core one's race is to their self-concept, racial salience, or one's realization of social categorization in a specific context, and racial ideology, consisting of public and private regard. Public regard refers to how one feels dissimilar other's feels towards their racial group. Private regard refers to the extent to which one harbors positive feelings and attributions of their race. For Black people, resiliency, and normative development manifest through sociocultural factors (e.g., racial identity, racial socialization) that may develop personal strengths through adversity (McAdams et al., 2001). These scholars identify distinct dimensions of racial identity that are important for positive development. Racial identity has received empirical support as a buffer to some of the negative effects of racial discrimination (Caldwell et al., 2002). For instance, Jones et al. (2013) found Black college students higher in public regard felt tense, disgusted, angry, but unafraid after experiencing discrimination. High racial centrality is related to higher experiences of discrimination (Chae et al., 2017).

Black people also draw on their deep connection to both Black culture and the dominant American culture to gain a sense of integrative complexity. Integrative complexity is the ability and desire to accept competing perspectives on the same issue and forge conceptual links between them (Suedfeld et al., 1992; Tadmor et al., 2012). Due to the inherent "double consciousness" (cf. Dubois, 1903) of engaging with Black culture and the dominant American culture, many Black people utilize Black cultural beliefs and values to succeed in dominant cultural spaces. For instance, Brannon et al. (2015) show Black students utilized interdependent self-schemas and performed better on academic tasks in traditionally White spaces when engaged in Black culture. This ability to integrate the values of Black culture within the norms of the dominant culture is core is foundational to the strengths Black people bring to the workplace.

Why Are These Resources and Assets Important?

From an evolutionary psychology perspective, humans adapt and evolve to ecosystems to maximize their chances of survival—Black people are the epitome of "adaptability." For instance, there was a widely accepted belief that Blacks were inferior to the White race until in 1924, Allport suggested "the discrepancy in mental ability is not great enough to account for the problem which centers on the American Negro or to explain fully the ostracism to which he is subjected" (Allport, 1924, p. 21). Black people had to adapt to when schools were integrated for the first time in America. For instance, after *Brown vs. The Board of Education* (1954), Black Americans rallied together during the Civil Rights Movement to demand equal rights and justice for Black people. As such, we contend that throughout history there are numerous historical times to draw from which allude to Black people developing both assets and resources. Researchers have begun accumulating support for benefits of assets and resources. For example, researchers found assets such as self-esteem, internal locus of control, positive affect, and religiosity protected participants from the substance use consequences. Resources that buffer the negative effects of emotional distress are family connectedness, parental involvement with school, plans to attend college. Caldwell et al. (2002) show public regard and racial centrality buffer the effects of racial discrimination on violent behavior. Wong et al. (2011) found among Black participants who perceived higher discrimination, having a connection to one's racial group is associated with a higher self-competence beliefs and grade point average.

Supporting the Strengths of Black Employees

While Black employees bring unique assets to the workplace, they also face major barriers to leveraging those strengths. As previously discussed, Black people are broadly discriminated against in the workplace and society and large (cf. Avery et al., 2015), in some cases leading to Black employees being withdrawn (Volpone & Avery, 2013) and dissatisfied with their jobs (Greenhaus et al., 1990). Even when Black employees are not explicitly discriminated against at work, their life experiences can impact their experience in the workplace. Black employees often believe their racial identity does not align to their professional environment, causing Black employees to fear incorporating their racial identity at work (Bell & Nkomo, 2001). Additionally, Black employees face "Megathreats"— large scale, media covered, identity invoking episodes such as the police shooting of Black people—that Leigh and Melwani (2019) propose are uniquely challenging to the psyche of Black people and often overlooked by coworkers with a different racial background. Within many organizations, this confluence of factors dramatically hampers Black employees performance and impedes Black employees from bringing their full selves to work.

In order to utilize the strengths of their Black employees, organizations must be intentional about providing them with support. To truly feel included, employees must simultaneously have feelings of belonging and uniqueness (Shore et al., 2011). To help ensure Black employees feel included, firms should strive to build a climate for inclusion, defined by fairly implemented employment practices, integration of difference, and inclusion in decision making (Nishii, 2013). By engaging in each of the components to create an inclusive organizational climate, organizations can leverage the unique strengths the Black employees bring to the workplace, which may in turn improve firm performance (Gonzalez & DeNisi, 2009). We propose the following specific actions organizations can take to implement a climate of inclusion: recruiting Black employees, cultivating Black leadership, recognizing Black achievement, and supporting Black employees.

First, organizations must clearly and intentionally recruit Black talent. In alignment with the similarity-attraction paradigm (Byrne, 1971, Berscheid & Walster 1978), we propose Black employees feel more comfortable in firms that have other Black employees. In light of this, firms should ensure racial ethnic minorities, particularly Black people, are represented within their recruitment teams. Black job seekers are more attracted to organizations with recruiters that are Black or of another ethnic minority background (Avery et al, 2004; Knouse, 2009). Additionally, organizations should prominently feature diversity throughout their recruitment materials, as both diverse and nondiverse employees are attracted to organizations that clearly articulate their commitment to diversity (Avery & McKay, 2006; Ng & Burke, 2005; Williamson et al., 2008). Finally, organizations should engage in targeted, formal recruitment of diverse candidates, particularly at the collegiate level.

Not only must organizations recruit diverse talent, but they must work to include Black individuals within decision making in the organization. Within organizations, Black leaders often struggle to advance and are more viewed less favorably than White leaders (Avery et al., 2015; Rosette et al., 2008). To confront this, organizations must be intentional about elevating and valuing the voices of their Black employees. Additionally, organizations can use formal, structured mentorship programs to empower Black leaders and enhance their profile within the organization (Creary & Roberts 2017). Organizations must intentionally work to eliminate unfair structural barriers and support the work of Black employees.

Relatedly, organizations should also develop programs to support Black talent within the organization. While Black employees often take responsibility for work in the diversity, equity, and inclusion space, these efforts are often underappreciated, unrecognized, and uncompensated. Organizations should strive to fairly value diversity, equity and inclusion work and compensate employees who bring this expertise to firms. Firms cannot simply rely on diverse employees to support each other, as minority leaders often pay a penalty for enacting diversity valuing behaviors (Hekman et al., 2017). Instead, organizations must recognize the burdens Black employees face to engage in diversity work and properly compensate them the value this work brings. While diversity training has mixed results within organizations (Roberson, 2019), organizations should utilize needs assessments, use research-supported training models, and evaluate the training's impact to improve its effectiveness (Roberson et al., 2013). Similarly, firms should consider utilizing employee resource groups to advance the inclusion of their Black employees, though little research has emerged assessing their impact.

Succeeding in Strength

When Black employees feel included within the workplace, they often do not simply perform adequately within their jobs, but engage in constructive deviance that can benefit themselves, their organizations, and the society. Defined as "behaviors that deviate from the norms of the reference group depart from the norm of a reference group in honorable way" (Vadera et al., 2013), Leigh and Melwani (2019) theorize Black employees may engage in constructive deviance as a result of "identity fusion," or the "blurring of the boundaries between organizational and social identities" bringing their full selves to work (p. 581). Following this logic, by bringing their racial identity to the workplace, Black employees can utilize their strengths to enact norm defying behaviors with broad, cross-level benefits. We focus specifically on three aspects of constructive deviance: identity mobilization, creative performance, and progroup voice.

By utilizing their racial identity, Black employees can use identity mobilization, or leverage unique knowledge, perspective, and skills that other employees may not have. Recent studies have shown the individuals who engage across multiple cultures have greater levels of psychological adjustment (Nguyen & Benet-Martinez, 2013), so we might expect Black individuals, who live within both Black and the dominant American culture, to follow suit. Within the workplace, Cha and Roberts (2019) found Black journalists are able to utilize identity related insights to produce stories all readers can appreciate. Identity mobilization, which aligns to "taking charge" construct within constructive deviance (Vadera et al., 2013), has also been used by Black employees to provide increased access to minority customers (McKay et al., 2011). While the literature on identity mobilization is still emerging, there are a number of other ways in which Black culture awareness could plausibly result in tangible benefits for organizations.

Additionally, utilizing Black employees also helps organizations with creative performance. Black culture offers numerous opportunities for deep and sustained creativity; in fact, creativity is a core principle of optimal Black psychological functioning (Caldwell-Colbert et al., 2009). Additionally, scholars have seen resilience in the face of failure to be a major predictor of creative performance (Sweetman et al., 2011), as creative performance requires individuals to take risks that often do not pan out. Black individuals often bring a sense of integrative complexity to the workplace, which has been liked to creativity (Tadmor et al., 2009) Furthermore, Black people are underrepresented in many organizations, particularly knowledge work, meaning Black employees often bring a unique perspective, thus enhancing creativity (Williams & O'Reilly, 1998). Within teams, diversity produces outsized creative performance when all individuals feel included, mitigating the potential negative effects of social categorization (van Knippenberg & Mell, 2016). Within an inclusive environment, it follows Black employees will benefit their team's creative performance.

Finally, Black employees can lean on their strengths to engage in progroup voice behaviors to the benefit Black people and by extension, their organizations. Voice is generally viewed a speaking up regarding an organizationally relevant issue (for a review see Morrison, 2014) while progroup voice is speaking up to improve the organizational context (Leigh & Melwani, 2019). Due to their cultural connection, Black employees who bring their racial identity to work will be motivated to speak up on the behalf of Black people, even though progroup voice can be risky. The advocacy of Black workers has broad impacts beyond their employers; in the wake of #BlackLivesMatter protestor over the summer in 2020, Black employees are challenging their companies not only to engage in inclusive practices within the organization, but also to support Black communities and businesses more broadly. Through their advocacy for the needs of Black people, Black employees push their firms to engage in efforts that not just their group or their firm, but to benefit society as a whole.

CONCLUSION

Although the organizational behavior literature typically assumes a deficit-based approach with Black employees, Black people bring a number of strengths into the workplace. Immersed in an interdependent culture formed in part by African-centered values and strong familial support networks, Black people have developed a resilience and a number of assets that allow them to endure persistent discrimination within organizations. However, in order to best leverage their strengths, organizations should seek to create a climate of inclusion (Nishii, 2013) that affirms the personhood of Black employees. When fully included in organizations, Black employees will not only perform well in the workplace, but also engage in constructive deviance, leveraging their identity, engaging creative performance, and practicing pro-group voice to the benefit of themselves, the organizations that employ them, and society as a whole.

Utilizing a strength-based approach offers significant contribution to the diversity literature. Often, diversity scholars have focused on the challenges black employees face in the workplace, and proposed models to level the playing field for Black people. By contrast, we contend that Black people in the workforce bring unique benefits to organizations to be celebrated and appreciated. We also reframe the inclusion of Black employees within organizations; instead of focusing simply on achieving parity with White employees, Black workers can utilize their strengths to achieve performance that in some cases outpaces that of White workers. This approach builds on many of the benefits found in diversity literature. When making the case for diversity, scholars have often pointed to team level and organizational benefits based in the value diversity brings to the organizations (van Knippenberg & Mell, 2016). In this paper, we suggest individual Black employees can produce with excellence in the workplace, offering benefits to organizations who hire, include, and support these employees. Furthermore, this strength-based approach not only benefits the organization, but also individual Black employees within the organization.

Moreover, while this chapter focuses primarily on Black employees, the strength-based approach may also be applicable to other groups of employees that face discrimination within the workplace. Individuals bringing diverse identities into the workplace, often engage in supportive, tight knit cultures and have a legacy of overcoming discrimination, offering potentially similar strengths that have emerged among Black people. So, while Black employees are the focus of this text, employees of other backgrounds may have overlap in both their experiences, barriers to success and need for support.

Additionally, a strength-based approach has significant corporate and managerial implications. We contend that hiring Black employees is not only a moral imperative but offers a competitive advantage for companies. Black employees have the talent and ability to be stars in the workplace. The unique skills that Black employees bring to the workplace can offer firms a competitive advantage in the modern marketplace, if they are properly utilized and supported. When organizations create a climate of inclusion that allows Black employees to use their racial identity in the workplace, their effort can transform not only their companies, but also the world.

While the strength-based approach offers many potential benefits, there are some risks associated with fully implementing this approach. Black employees are not a monolith, and while there are common strengths Black employees can bring to the workplace, individuals will differ in their propensity to both have and utilize these strengths. Additionally, there are a number of other assets Black employees can bring to the workplace that. Scholars and practitioners alike must be careful not to reduce Black employees to their race, and instead take a holistic view of Black employees at work, treating them as individuals.

REFERENCES

Alexander, M. (2010). *The new Jim Crow: Mass incarceration in the age of colorblindness.* New Press, Distributed by Perseus Distribution,

Floyd Henry Allport. (1924). *Social psychology as a science of individual behavior and consciousness.* Houghton Mifflin Company.

Altschul, I., Oyserman, D., & Bybee, D. (2006). Racial-ethnic identity in mid-adolescence: Content and change as predictors of academic achievement. *Child Development,* 77(5), 1155–1169. https://doi.org/10.1111/j.1467-8624.2006.00926.x

Anglin, D. M., & Wade, J. C. (2007). Racial socialization, racial identity, and Black students' adjustment to college. *Cultural Diversity and Ethnic Minority Psychology,* 13(3), 207–215. https://doi.org/10.1037/1099-9809.13.3.207

Avery, D. R., Hernandez, M., & Hebl, M. R. (2004). Who's watching the race? Racial salience in recruitment advertising. *Journal of Applied Social Psychology,* 34(1), 146–161. https://doi.org/10.1111/j.1559-1816.2004.tb02541.x

Avery, D. R., & McKay, P. F. (2006). Target practice: An organizational impression management approach to attracting minority and female job applicants. *Personnel Psychology,* 59(1), 157–187. https://doi.org/10.1111/j.1744-6570.2006.00807.x

Avery, D. R., Volpone, S. D., & Holmes, O. (2015). *Racial discrimination in organizations.* A. J. Colella & E. B. King (Eds.), *The Oxford handbook of workplace discrimination* (Vol. 1). Oxford University Press.

Barr, S. C., & Neville, H. A. (2008). Examination of the link between parental racial socialization messages and racial ideology among Black college students. *Journal of Black Psychology,* 34(2), 131–155. https://doi.org/10.1177/0095798408314138

Bagley, C. A., & Carroll, J. (1998). Healing forces in African-American families. In H. I. McCubbin, E. A. Thompson, A. I. Thompson, & J. E. Fromer (Ed.), *Resiliency in African-American families.* (pp. 117–142). SAGE.

Blassingame, J. W. (1979). *The slave community: Plantation life in the antebellum South.* Oxford University Press.

Bell, E. L. J., & Nkomo, S. M. (2001). *Our separate ways: Black and White women and the struggle for professional identity.* Harvard University Press.

Bellah, R. N., Madsen, R., Sullivan, W. M., Swidler, A., & Tipton, S. M. (1985). *Habits of the heart: Individualism and commitment in American life.* Harper & Row.

Bennett, T. (2007). The work of culture. *Cultural Sociology, 1*(1), 31–47. https://doi. org/10.1177/1749975507073918

Berscheid, E., & Walster, E. (1978). *Interpersonal attraction* (2nd ed.). Addison-Wesley

Boykin, A. W., Jagers, R. J., Ellison, C. M., & Albury, A. (1997). Communalism: Conceptualization and measurement of an Afrocultural social orientation. *Journal of Black Studies, 27*(3), 409–418. https://doi.org/10.1177/002193479702700308

Brannon, T. N., Markus, H. R., & Taylor, V. J. (2015). "Two souls, two thoughts," two self-schemas: Double consciousness can have positive academic consequences for African Americans. *Journal of Personality and Social Psychology, 108*(4), 586–609. https://doi.org/10.1037/a0038992

Brown, D. L. (2008). African American resiliency: Examining racial socialization and social support as protective factors. *Journal of Black Psychology, 34*(1), 32–48. https://doi.org/10.1177/0095798407310538

Butler-Barnes, S. T., Chavous, T. M., Hurd, N., & Varner, F. (2013). African American Adolescents' academic persistence: A strengths-based approach. *Journal of Youth and Adolescence, 42*(9), 1443–1458. https://doi.org/10.1007/s10964-013-9962-0

Byrne, D. E. (1971). *The attraction paradigm.* Academic Press.

Caldwell, C. H., Zimmerman, M. A., Bernat, D. H., Sellers, R. M., & Notaro, P. C. (2002). Racial identity, maternal support, and psychological distress among African American adolescents. *Child Development, 73*(4), 1322–1336. https://doi.org/10.1111/1467-8624.00474

Caldwell-Colbert, A. T., Parks, F. M., & Eshun, S. (2009). Positive psychology: African American strengths, resilience, and protective factors. In H. A. Neville, B. M. Tynes, & S. O. Utsey (Eds.), *Handbook of African American psychology* (pp. 375–384). SAGE.

Cha, S. E., & Roberts, L. M. (2019). Leveraging minority identities at work: An individual-level framework of the identity mobilization process. *Organization Science, 30*(4), 735–760. https://doi.org/10.1287/orsc.2018.1272

Chae, D. H., Powell, W. A., Nuru-Jeter, A. M., Smith-Bynum, M. A., Seaton, E. K., Forman, T. A., Turpin, R., & Sellers, R. (2017). The role of racial identity and implicit racial bias in self-reported racial discrimination: Implications for depression among African American men. *Journal of Black Psychology, 43*(8), 789–812. https://doi.org/10.1177/0095798417690055

Chavous, T. M., Rivas-Drake, D., Smalls, C., Griffin, T., & Cogburn, C. (2008). Gender matters, too: The influences of school racial discrimination and racial identity on academic engagement outcomes among African American adolescents. *Developmental Psychology, 44*(3), 637–654. https://doi.org/10.1037/0012-1649.44.3.637

Chavous, T. M., Bernat, D. H., Schmeelk-Cone, K., Caldwell, C. H., Kohn-Wood, L., & Zimmerman, M. A. (2003). Racial identity and academic attainment among African American adolescents. *Child Development, 74*(4), 1076–1090. https://doi.org/10.1111/1467-8624.00593

Colella, A., Hebl, M., & King, E. (2017). One hundred years of discrimination research in the *Journal of Applied Psychology*: A sobering synopsis. *Journal of Applied Psychology, 102*(3), 500–513. https://doi.org/10.1037/apl0000084

Creary, S. J., & Roberts, L. M. (2017). G.I.V.E.-based mentoring in diverse organizations: Cultivating positive identities in diverse leaders. In A. J. Murrell & S. Blake-Beard *Mentoring diverse leaders: Creating change for people, processes, and paradigms* (pp. 3–24). Routledge/Taylor & Francis Group.

Demo, D. H., & Hughes, M. (1990). Socialization and racial identity among Black Americans. *Social Psychology Quarterly, 53*(4), 364–374. https://doi.org/10.2307/2786741

Dubois, W. E. B. (1903). *The souls of Black folk.* A. C. McClurg and Company.

Dutton, J. E., Worline, M. C., Frost, P. J., & Lilius, J. (2006). Explaining compassion organizing. *Administrative Science Quarterly, 51*(1), 59–96. https://doi.org/10.2189/asqu.51.1.59

Fergus, S., & Zimmerman, M. A. (2005). Adolescent resilience: A framework for understanding healthy development in the face of risk. *Annual Review of Public Health, 26,* 399–419. https://doi.org/10.1146/annurev.publhealth.26.021304.144357

García Coll, C., Lamberty, G., Jenkins, R., McAdoo, H. P., Crnic, K., Wasik, B. H., & Vázquez García, H. (1996). An integrative model for the study of developmental competencies in minority children. *Child Development, 67*(5), 1891–1914.

Gecas, V. (1982). The self-concept. *Annual Review of Sociology, 8,* 1–33.

Gonzalez, J. A., & Denisi, A. S. (2009). Cross-level effects of demography and diversity climate on organizational attachment and firm effectiveness. *Journal of Organizational Behavior, 30*(1), 21–40. https://doi.org/10.1002/job.498

Greenhaus, J. H., Parasuraman, S., & Wormley, W. M. (1990). Effects of race on organizational experiences, job performance evaluations, and career outcomes. *Academy of Management Journal, 33*(1), 64–86. https://doi.org/10.2307/256352

Hebl, M., Cheng, S. K., & Ng, L. C. (2020). Modern Discrimination in Organizations. *Annual Review of Organizational Psychology and Organizational Behavior, 7*(1), 257–282. https://doi.org/10.1146/annurev-orgpsych-012119-044948

Hekman, D. R., Johnson, S. K., Foo, M.-D., & Yang, W. (2017). Does diversity-valuing behavior result in diminished performance ratings for non-White and female leaders? *Academy of Management Journal, 60*(2), 771–797. https://doi.org/10.5465/amj.2014.0538

Hughes, D. (2003). Correlates of African American and Latino Parents' messages to children about ethnicity and race: A comparative study of racial socialization. *American Journal of Community Psychology, 31*(1), 15–33. https://doi.org/10.1023/A:1023066418688

Hughes, D., & Chen, L. (1997). When and what parents tell children about race: An examination of race-related socialization among African American families. *Applied Developmental Science, 1*(4), 200–214. https://doi.org/10.1207/s1532480xads0104_4

Hughes, D., Rodriguez, J., Smith, E. P., Johnson, D. J., Stevenson, H. C., & Spicer, P. (2006). Parents' ethnic-racial socialization practices: A review of research and directions for future study. *Developmental Psychology, 42*(5), 747–770. https://doi.org/10.1037/0012-1649.42.5.747

Jagers, R. J., Smith, P., Mock, L. O., & Dill, E. (1997). An Afrocultural social ethos: Component orientations and some social implications. *Journal of Black Psychology, 23*(4), 328–343. https://doi.org/10.1177/00957984970234002

Jones, J. M. (1986). Racism: A cultural analysis of the problem. In J. F. Dovidio & S. L. Gaertner (Eds.), *Prejudice, discrimination, and racism* (pp. 279–314). Academic Press.

Jones, S. C. T., Lee, D. B., Gaskin, A. L., & Neblett, E. W. (2013). Emotional response profiles to racial discrimination: Does racial identity predict affective patterns? *Journal of Black Psychology, 40*(4), 334–358. https://doi.org/10.1177/0095798413488628

Kendi, IX. (2019) *How to be an antiracist.* Random House.

Kitayama, S., Park, H., Sevincer, A. T., Karasawa, M., & Uskul, A. K. (2009). A cultural task analysis of implicit independence: Comparing North America, Western Europe, and East Asia. *Journal of Personality and Social Psychology, 97*(2), 236–255. https://doi.org/10.1037/a0015999

Knouse, S. B. (2009). Targeted recruiting for diversity: Strategy, impression management, realistic expectations, and diversity climate. *International Journal of Management, 26*(3), 347–353, 487.

Kraus, M. W., Rucker, J. M., & Richeson, J. A. (2017). Americans misperceive racial economic equality. *Proceedings of the National Academy of Sciences, 114*(39), 10324–10331. https://doi.org/10.1073/pnas.1707719114

Lawrence, M. C. C. (1987). The double meanings of the spirituals. *Journal of Black Studies, 17*(4), 379–401. https://doi.org/10.1177/002193478701700401

Lazonick, W., Moss, P., & Weitz, J. (2020). Employment and earnings of African Americans fifty years after: Progress? *Institute for New Economic Thinking Working Paper Series, 129.*

Leigh, A., & Melwani, S. (2019). #BlackEmployeesMatter: Mega-threats, identity fusion, and enacting positive deviance in organizations. *Academy of Management Review, 44*(3), 564–591. https://doi.org/10.5465/amr.2017.0127

Luthar, S. S., & Cicchetti, D. (2000). The construct of resilience: Implications for interventions and social policies. *Development and Psychopathology, 12*(4), 857–885. https://doi.org/10.1017/s0954579400004156

Masten, A. S., Best, K. M., & Garmezy, N. (1990). Resilience and development: Contributions from the study of children who overcome adversity. *Development and Psychopathology, 2*(4), 425–444. https://doi.org/10.1017/S0954579400005812

Mattis, J. S., Simpson, N. G., Powell, W., Anderson, R. E., Kimbro, L. R., & Mattis, J. H. (2016). Positive psychology in African Americans. In E. C. Chang, C. A. Downey, J. K. Hirsch, & N. J. Lin (Eds.), *Positive psychology in racial and ethnic groups: Theory, research, and practice.* (pp. 83–107). American Psychological Association.

McAdams, D. P. (2001). The psychology of life stories. *Review of General Psychology, 5*(2), 100–122. https://doi.org/10.1037/1089-2680.5.2.100

McCluney, C. L., Bryant, C. M., King, D. D., & Ali, A. A. (2017). Calling in Black: A dynamic model of racially traumatic events, resourcing, and safety. *Equality, Diversity and Inclusion: An International Journal, 36*(8), 767–786. https://doi.org/10.1108/EDI-01-2017-0012

McKay, P. F., Avery, D. R., Liao, H., & Morris, M. A. (2011). Does Diversity climate lead to customer satisfaction? It depends on the service climate and business unit demography. *Organization Science, 22*(3), 788–803. https://doi.org/10.1287/orsc.1100.0550

Molix, L., & Bettencourt, B. A. (2010). Predicting well-being among ethnic minorities: Psychological empowerment and group identity. *Journal of Applied Social Psychology, 40*(3), 513–533. https://doi.org/10.1111/j.1559-1816.2010.00585.x

Morrison, E. W. (2014). Employee voice and silence. *Annual Review of Organizational Psychology and Organizational Behavior, 1*(1), 173–197. https://doi.org/10.1146/annurev-orgpsych-031413-091328

Neblett, E. W., Smalls, C. P., Ford, K. R., Nguyên, H. X., & Sellers, R. M. (2009). Racial socialization and racial identity: African American parents' messages about race as precursors to identity. *Journal of Youth and Adolescence, 38*(2), 189–203. https://doi.org/10.1007/s10964-008-9359-7

Neblett Jr., E. W., White, R. L., Ford, K. R., Philip, C. L., Nguyên, H. X., & Sellers, R. M. (2008). Patterns of racial socialization and psychological adjustment: Can parental communications about race reduce the impact of racial discrimination? *Journal of Research on Adolescence, 18*(3), 477–515. https://doi.org/10.1111/j.1532-7795.2008.00568.x

Ng, E. S. W., & Burke, R. J. (2005). Person–organization fit and the war for talent: Does diversity management make a difference? *The International Journal of Human Resource Management, 16*(7), 1195–1210. https://doi.org/10.1080/09585190500144038

Nishii, L. H. (2013). The benefits of climate for inclusion for gender-diverse groups. *Academy of Management Journal, 56*(6), 1754–1774. https://doi.org/10.5465/amj.2009.0823

Nkomo, S. M., Bell, M. P., Roberts, L. M., Joshi, A., & Thatcher, S. M. B. (2019). Diversity at a critical juncture: New theories for a complex phenomenon. *Academy of Management Review, 44*(3), 498–517. https://doi.org/10.5465/amr.2019.0103

Nobles, W. W. (1990). *The infusion of African and African-American content: A Question of Content and Intent.* http://www.nuatc.org/articles/pdf/Nobles_article.pdf

Nobles, W. W. (1991). African philosophy: Foundations for black psychology. In R. L. Jones (Ed.), *Black psychology,* (3rd ed., pp. 47–63). Cobb & Henry.

Nguyen, A.-M. D., & Benet-Martínez, V. (2013). Biculturalism and adjustment: A Meta-analysis. *Journal of Cross-Cultural Psychology, 44*(1), 122–159. https://doi.org/10.1177/0022022111435097

Orfield, G. (2001) *Schools more separate: Consequences of a decade of resegregation.* Harvard University, Civil Rights Project.

Oyserman, D., Sorensen, N., Reber, R., & Chen, S. X. (2009). Connecting and separating mind-sets: Culture as situated cognition. *Journal of Personality and Social Psychology, 97*(2), 217–235. https://doi.org/10.1037/a0015850

Peters, M. F. (1985). Racial socialization of young Black children. In H. P. McAdoo & J. L. McAdoo (Eds.), *Black children: Social, educational, and parental environments* (pp. 159–173). SAGE.

Plaut, V. C., Markus, H. R., Treadway, J. R., & Fu, A. S. (2012). The cultural construction of self and well-being: a tale of two cities. *Personality and Social Psychology Bulletin, 38*(12), 1644–1658. https://doi.org/10.1177/0146167212458125

Roberson, L., Kulik, C. T., & Tan, R. Y. (2013). Effective diversity training. In Q. M. Roberson (Ed.), *Oxford library of psychology. The Oxford handbook of diversity and work* (pp. 341–365). Oxford University Press.

Roberson, Q., Holmes, O., & Perry, J. L. (2017). Transforming research on diversity and firm performance: A dynamic capabilities perspective. *Academy of Management Annals, 11*(1), 189–216. https://doi.org/10.5465/annals.2014.0019

Roberson, Q. M. (2019). Diversity in the workplace: A review, synthesis, and future research agenda. *Annual Review of Organizational Psychology and Organizational Behavior, 6*(1), 69–88. https://doi.org/10.1146/annurev-orgpsych-012218-015243

Roberson, Q., Ryan, A. M., & Ragins, B. R. (2017). The evolution and future of diversity at work. *Journal of Applied Psychology, 102*(3), 483–499. https://doi.org/10.1037/apl0000161

Rosette, A. S., Leonardelli, G. J., & Phillips, K. W. (2008). The White standard: Racial bias in leader categorization. *Journal of Applied Psychology, 93*(4), 758–777. https://doi.org/10.1037/0021-9010.93.4.758

Rutter, M. (1987). Psychosocial Resilience and Protective Mechanisms. *American Journal of Orthopsychiatry, 57*(3), 316–331. https://doi.org/10.1111/j.1939-0025.1987.tb03541.x

Sanchez-Burks, J. (2002). Protestant relational ideology and (in)attention to relational cues in work settings. *Journal of Personality and Social Psychology, 83*(4), 919–929. https://doi.org/10.1037/0022-3514.83.4.919

Seligman, M. E. P., & Csikszentmihalyi, M. (2000). Positive psychology: An introduction. *American Psychologist, 55*(1), 5–14. https://doi.org/10.1037/0003-066X.55.1.5

Sellers, R. M., Smith, M. A., Shelton, J. N., Rowley, S. A. J., & Chavous, T. M. (1998). Multidimensional model of racial identity: a reconceptualization of African American racial identity. *Personality and Social Psychology Review, 2*(1), 18–39. https://doi.org/10.1207/s15327957pspr0201_2

Sharkey, P. (2013). *Stuck in place: Urban neighborhoods and the end of progress toward racial equality.* University of Chicago Press.

Shore, L. M., Randel, A. E., Chung, B. G., Dean, M. A., Holcombe Ehrhart, K., & Singh, G. (2011). Inclusion and Diversity in Work Groups: A Review and Model for Future Research. *Journal of Management, 37*(4), 1262–1289. https://doi.org/10.1177/0149206310385943

Spencer, R. (2006). Understanding the mentoring process between adolescents and adults. *Youth & Society, 37*(3), 287–315. https://doi.org/10.1177/0743558405278263

Suedfeld, P., Tetlock, P. E., & Streufert, S. (1992). Conceptual/integrative complexity. In *Motivation and personality: Handbook of thematic content analysis* (pp. 393–400). Cambridge University Press.

Sweetman, D., Luthans, F., Avey, J. B., & Luthans, B. C. (2011). Relationship between positive psychological capital and creative performance. *Canadian Journal of Administrative Sciences/Revue Canadienne Des Sciences de l'Administration*, *28*(1), 4–13. https://doi.org/10.1002/cjas.175

Tadmor, C. T., Galinsky, A. D., & Maddux, W. W. (2012). Getting the most out of living abroad: Biculturalism and integrative complexity as key drivers of creative and professional success. *Journal of Personality and Social Psychology*, *103*(3), 520–542. https://doi.org/10.1037/a0029360

Tadmor, C. T., Tetlock, P. E., & Kaiping, P. (2009). Acculturation Strategies and integrative complexity: The cognitive implications of biculturalism. *Journal of Cross-Cultural Psychology*, *40*(1), 105–139. https://doi.org/10.1177/0022022108326279

Taylor, R. J., Chatters, L. M., Woodward, A. T., & Brown, E. (2013). Racial and ethnic differences in extended family, friendship, fictive kin, and congregational informal support networks: Racial and ethnic differences in informal support networks. *Family Relations*, *62*(4), 609–624. https://doi.org/10.1111/fare.12030

Thompson, C., & Gregory, J. B. (2012). Managing millennials: A framework for improving attraction, motivation, and retention. *The Psychologist-Manager Journal*, *15*(4), 237–246. https://doi.org/10.1080/10887156.2012.730444

Thornton, M. C., Chatters, L. M., Taylor, R. J., & Allen, W. R. (1990). Sociodemographic and environmental correlates of racial socialization by Black parents. *Child Development*, *61*(2), 401–409. https://doi.org/10.1111/j.1467-8624.1990.tb02786.x

Vadera, A. K., Pratt, M. G., & Mishra, P. (2013). Constructive deviance in organizations: Integrating and moving forward. *Journal of Management*, *39*(5), 1221–1276. https://doi.org/10.1177/0149206313475816

van Knippenberg, D., & Mell, J. N. (2016). Past, present, and potential future of team diversity research: From compositional diversity to emergent diversity. *Organizational Behavior and Human Decision Processes*, *136*, 135–145. https://doi.org/10.1016/j.obhdp.2016.05.007

Volpone, S. D., & Avery, D. R. (2013). It's self defense: How perceived discrimination promotes employee withdrawal. *Journal of Occupational Health Psychology*, *18*(4), 430–448. https://doi.org/10.1037/a0034016

Wang, M. T., & Huguley, J. P. (2012). Parental racial socialization as a moderator of the effects of racial discrimination on educational success among African American adolescents. *Child Development*, *83*(5), 1716–1731.

Werner, E. E., & Smith, R. S. (1992). *Overcoming the odds: High risk children from birth to adulthood*. Cornell University Press.

Wilkerson, I. (2014). *The warmth of other suns*. Vintage Books.

Williams, K. Y., & O'Reilly, C. A. III, (1998). Demography and diversity in organizations: A review of 40 years of research. *Research in Organizational Behavior*, *20*, 77–140.

Williamson, I. O., Slay, H. S., Shapiro, D. L., & Shivers-Blackwell, S. L. (2008). The effect of explanations on prospective applicants reactions to firm diversity practices. *Human Resource Management*, *47*(2), 311–330. https://doi.org/10.1002/hrm.20214

Wong, E. M., Ormiston, M. E., & Tetlock, P. E. (2011). The effects of top management team integrative complexity and decentralized decision making on corporate social performance. *Academy of Management Journal*, *54*(6), 1207–1228. https://doi.org/10.5465/amj.2008.0762

Yosso, T. J. (2005). Whose culture has capital? A critical race theory discussion of community cultural wealth. *Race Ethnicity and Education*, *8*(1), 69–91. https://doi.org/10.1080/1361332052000341006

CHAPTER 4

LET'S TALK ABOUT #BLM

The Role of Value Congruence on Supervisor-Subordinate Relationships

Lori Ramirez and Sarah Singletary Walker
Creighton University

ABSTRACT

Recent events have reignited discussions of race, equality, and justice in both work and nonwork contexts. Most recently, the videotaped images of George Floyd losing his life was watched by millions of individuals who in turn began to organize protests aimed at addressing racial inequality. Black Lives Matter (#BLM), regarded as one of the most visible protest movements today, has been credited with organizing a new generation of activists who are seeking restorative justice (Rickford, 2016). Drawing on event system theory, we argue that the #BLM movement, and events that trigger massive responses, disrupt the lives of individuals and organizations alike (Morgeson et al., 2015), influence business policies and processes (McCluney et al., 2017), and become a topic of discussion in the workplace (Liu, 2020). Although studies find a significant relation between external events and business decisions (Morgeson et al., 2015), there is a paucity of research examining the extent to which differing perceptions of events (e.g., protest movements) impact supervisor-subordinate relationships. The extant literature focuses primarily on

The Future of Scholarship on Race in Organizations, pp. 75–95
Copyright © 2022 by Information Age Publishing

exploring the need to modify organizational cultures and business practices in order to recognize and value Black workers (Opie & Roberts, 2017). The purpose of this chapter, however, is to examine how differing views of #BLM affect the supervisor-subordinate relationship and work-related outcomes.

The demographic composition of the workforce is becoming increasingly diverse. According to the U.S. Bureau of Labor Statistics (2020), people of color account for 23% of today's workforce. Recent research suggests that these changes are welcome. That is, a majority of Americans (80%) believe it is important to work in racially and ethnically diverse organizations (Pew Research Center, 2018). Though there is a large body of work examining the impact of diversity in organizations (Roberson et al., 2017), there is still a paucity of work-related research that examines race, in general, and the perspectives of Black employees in particular. The extant literature on the impact of *racial* diversity and organizations is mixed. Some studies reveal a link between racial diversity and a variety of positive organizational outcomes suggesting that greater racial diversity may lead to increased innovation, improved decision making, and higher financial returns (Cunningham, 2009; Richard, 2000; Richard et al., 2003; Rock & Grant, 2016). However, other research reveals negative impacts of diversity with employees reporting increased amounts of discomfort when working in diverse groups (Galinsky et al., 2015; Rock et al., 2016). In addition, and perhaps complicating the research on racial diversity, employees report a reluctance to discuss race at work resulting from a fear of provoking hostility and/or being perceived as an "agitator" (Hartmann, 2012; Hewlett et al., 2017; Roberts & Mayo, 2019). Given the increased salience of race, the potential for discussions about race may be more likely to emerge in the workplace. Therefore, work directed at understanding the impacts of such discussions is needed. Leigh and Melwani (2019) introduced a model of the influence of *mega-threats* defined as negative, large-scale, diversity-related episodes that receive significant media attention for Black employees. Their work predominantly explored the link between mega-threats and the social identity of Black employees at the individual-level. Little is known about how mega-threats may impact other organizationally relevant outcomes such as performance and satisfaction. In the current chapter, we focus on the extent to which discussions about race-related mega-threats affect the relationship between supervisors and subordinates, as well as the impacts of such discussions on other work outcomes. We first discuss previous work examining event system theory, mega-events, and focus on recent mega-threats in particular. Second, we discuss a model for understanding how discussions of mega-threats may have an impact on a variety of workplace outcomes. Specifically, we discuss how mega-threats may impact individuals' relationships at work and influence workplace outcomes (e.g., performance, satisfaction, commitment). Lastly, we suggest a number of recommendations for future research.

A growing body of literature examines the extent to which mega-events (i.e., sociocultural and political events) impact organizations (Tilcsik & Marquis, 2013). The extant literature examines how these events impact organizational initiatives related to marketing and philanthropy. For example, major sporting events, such as the Super Bowl and the Olympic Games, provide firms with access to consumers and opportunities to market their products during events (McGillivray & Frew, 2015). Similarly, unplanned events (e.g., natural disasters) affect the philanthropic spending and long-term initiatives of firms (Johnson et al., 2011; Tilcsik & Marquis, 2013). Of particular relevance to this chapter is a highly publicized video of George Floyd losing his life at the hands of Derek Chauvin, a White police officer. These images were watched by millions of individuals who in turn began to organize protests aimed at addressing racial inequality. The response to this mega-event was likely influenced by other recent killings of Black men and women (e.g., Ahmuad Arbery, Breonna Taylor). Leigh and Melwani (2019) extended previous work on mega-events and defined instances of police brutality and killings as mega-*threats* because such instances occurred as a result of one's membership in a specific group (in this case, being a Black person). Thus, the images of the murder of George Floyd may be conceptualized as a mega-threat for Black employees and may be considered a mega-event for White employees. In both cases, the recent events involving George Floyd can be considered a major event that impacted individuals across the globe. The George Floyd murder sparked global outrage as the salience of instances such as these (i.e., police violence against unarmed Black individuals) evoked negative, emotional reactions from the vast majority of people viewing the footage. In effect, the actions taken by Derek Chauvin awakened a racial (*in*)justice movement, the Black Lives Matter (#BLM) movement, which has become the largest social justice movement in United States history (Buchanan et al., 2020).

Black Lives Matter (BLM) was launched in 2013 (Black Lives Matter Foundation, n.d.) and has been credited with organizing a new generation of activists who are seeking social and economic restorative justice (Rickford, 2016). With a mission originally aimed at ending police brutality against Black Americans and "build local power" to promote Black liberation, BLM also advocates for social and economic justice, immigration reform, and LGBTQ+ rights to name a few. BLM primarily uses social media platforms and a large network of individuals and companies in support of the movement to "fight for Freedom, Liberation, and Justice" (Black Lives Matter Foundation, n.d.). The organization is largely seen as a mechanism for organizing protests around racial and economic inequity.

When organizations designed to address racial injustice mobilize (e.g., BLM), they often make headlines, raise awareness, drive change, and affect individuals in their work and personal lives (Hoffman et al., 2016; McCluney et al., 2017). It is important to note that the statement (i.e., #BLM), political movement, and decentralized BLM network of organizations are often confused. Moreover, the BLM organization and hashtags (i.e., #BLM; #Black Lives Matter) are at times used interchangeably. As a result, there are times when making this affirmation may be considered to be political in nature. In this chapter, we focus on #BLM as a movement that acknowledges the importance of addressing the racial inequity that has plagued Black people rather than the politicized attributions that might be made by supporters.

In spite of having a core value surrounding social justice, #BLM is, at times, viewed negatively. According to a Civiqs survey (2020), in the two weeks following the George Floyd killing, support for the #BLM movement increased significantly. For years the statement "Black Lives Matter" was met with significant resistance. The racial reckoning of Summer 2020 led to changes in the way the movement was viewed. With this unprecedented increase in public support, the #BLM movement served as the impetus for both individuals and major corporations to take action. For example, #BLM supporters united digitally for #BlackOutTuesday on June 2, 2020, by changing their social media profile photos to solid black images, signifying a day to reflect on racism and the need for societal change (Curtis, 2020). Moreover, some employers responded to a need to address racial inequity by providing workers paid time off for Juneteenth in celebration of the end of U.S. slavery on June 19 (Snider, 2020). In effect, the aftermath of the highly visible murders of Black Americans motivated both individuals and organizations to seek ways to address racial injustice.

There has been little discussion about how societal events whose mission is to fight for racial equality, such as the #BLM protests and rallies, spillover into workplace conversations and impact organizational relationships. To address this gap, we develop a conceptual framework to detail the process in which societal events affect supervisor-subordinate relationships and, ultimately, work outcomes. We draw from event system theory (Morgeson et al., 2015) and a mega-threats (Leigh & Melwani, 2019) framework to introduce how diversity-related societal events impact organizational decisions and individual responses. Using employee and organizational responses to the #BLM movement as a significant societal event, we then explore how such responses affect the supervisor-subordinate relationship. In particular, our framework explains how discussing dissimilar views of #BLM in the workplace impacts an employee's perception of their supervisor, which then affects the quality of the leader-member exchange relationship, and results in significant influence on work outcomes.

EVENT SYSTEM THEORY AND MEGA-THREATS

Event system theory (EST) suggests that significant events impact organizations when they are "novel, disruptive, and critical" (Morgeson et al., 2015). Recent events such as the #BLM protests and COVID-19 pandemic meet these criteria as both emerged unexpectedly, interrupted everyday lives, and quickly became a media spotlight. Scholars have long recognized that societal events affect people and organizations alike. Previous research focuses primarily on exploring the influence of mega-events (Tilcsik & Marquis, 2013). Mega-events can be: positive or negative, occur at regular intervals or happen spontaneously, and may vary in duration (i.e., lasting a few minutes or several months). Recent examples of mega-events include the annual Superbowl, the Olympics, the Pulse nightclub shooting, family separation at the U.S.-Mexico border, the #MeToo movement, and the COVID-19 Pandemic. Tilcsik and Marquis (2013) reveal that firms are more likely to respond to local events that take place within their communities suggesting that the relevance of the event is an important organizational consideration. Though the George Floyd murder occurred in Minneapolis, the publicization of the events was global and organizations headquartered in the United States and abroad responded to these events.

Early work on mega-events predominately explored the economic impacts of large-scale events on geographical areas. Scholars invested considerable efforts on developing models and methods to assess these economic impacts (Jones, 2005). Research suggests that planned mega-events (e.g., hosting international sporting events) are likely to generate positive outcomes for cities and firms, such as increased tourism (Fayos-Solá, 1998) and additional financial investments (Jones, 2005). For example, research has found that investments in capital infrastructure for the 1964 Olympic Games in Tokyo became a legacy for Japan, resulting in more efficient trains and improved highways (Jones, 2005; Müller, 2015). Furthermore, evidence indicates that unplanned major events (e.g., natural disasters) can produce similar positive economic effects to improve damaged infrastructure and generate needed revenue (Andersson et al., 2008). Thus, past literature demonstrates how large-scale events play a significant role in major strategic decisions for cities and organizations alike.

More recent work provides a conceptual framework for understanding how incumbents respond to a specific type of major event (i.e., mega-threats; Leigh & Melwani, 2019). Leigh and Melwani (2019) argue that, at the individual level, employees likely respond to societal events that are of particular relevance to their unique identities and values. Thus, they provide a framework for how mega-threats spill*over* into organizations. Specifically, they provide a structure for understanding how personal views on diversity-related major events (e.g., police brutality and killings) may impact organizational and individual-level outcomes. As with other instances of recent racism, the police violence inflicted upon George Floyd likely disrupted the lives of both individuals and organizations resulting in a number of employee and firm-level implications (McCluney et al., 2017). For organizations, it is likely that firms must consider ways to reduce any problematic behaviors that occur as a result of operational policies and practices that may lead to biases in the attraction, selection, and retention of underrepresented minorities. For individuals, it is likely that the events, protests, and responses have become a topic of discussion in the workplace (Liu, 2020). In the following section, we use the #BLM movement as an example of how societal events affect employee behaviors and organizational decisions. Then, we elaborate on how discussing #BLM while at work influences individual factors, specifically focusing on the relationship between supervisors and subordinates. Finally, we further discuss how these individual factors impact work outcomes which, in turn, affect the organization overall.

#BLM IN THE WORKPLACE/MEGA-THREATS

Though there is a growing body of research examining the extent to which major events impact organizations, there is a paucity of research examining the antecedents and consequences of very recent instances related to race and racism. As mentioned previously, the recent support for #BLM, as well as calls for change, is indicative of an increased awareness of the differential treatment experienced by individuals as a function of one's race. However, an important question remains. Specifically, to what extent do mega-threats spillover to both organizations and individuals working within them? This is an important question for organizations and individuals to understand given that recent mega-events and subsequent protests and reactions have influenced individuals across the globe. We provide a model to examine the relations between mega-threats (i.e., mega-events), perceptions of mega-threats, dyadic relationships, and organizational outcomes. Figure 4.1 provides an illustration of our conceptual model. We define each of the components of the model in the subsequent sections and conclude with a number of unanswered questions to direct future research.

Responding to Major Events. An increased attention on racial injustice reveals that organizational responses to mega-events are varied (Bonaparte, 2020). Specifically, some companies have strongly voiced their support for the #BLM movement. These actions have ranged from support on social media to actual policies designed to address inequity. Other firms have taken an approach that either ignores or downplays the significance of racial injustice. Subsequently, these firms are often perceived to be

Figure 4.1

Conceptual Model of the Effects of Discussing Dissimilar Views of Mega-Threats on Supervisor-Subordinate Relationships and Work Outcomes

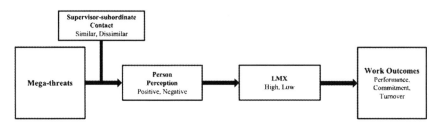

discriminatory as a result of "silencing Black Lives Matter" and face significant backlash from both customers and employees (Sacks, 2020). For example, during the recent COVID-19 pandemic, Costco employees were sent home or threatened with suspension for wearing masks with logos supporting #BLM. These experiences resulted in perceptions of harassment, discrimination, and frustration with their employer (Sacks, 2020). In response to negative reactions expressed by employees, Costco managers purported that such attire is political, which is a violation of their anti-harassment policy, however, some employees argued that the policy was inconsistently enforced, with managers taking action *only* when #BLM logos were worn (Sacks, 2020). Similar instances have occurred in other major corporations (e.g., Starbucks, Taco Bell). Though employees expressed discomfort with the way that these high-profile instances were handled, little is known about the extent to which these experiences led to other deleterious consequences.

Companies differ in whether the workplace is an appropriate place to express support for political movements like #BLM. Some firms allow their incumbents to openly demonstrate their support for organizations that address racial inequity. For example, Molly Moon Neitzel, owner of Molly Moon Neitzel ice cream stores, allowed her employees to wear #BLM logos on the job, stating "It makes me incredibly proud that so many of our employees are civically engaged" (Roberts, 2020). Other firms take a different approach and do not allow their employees to do so. The owner of K9 Korral kennel and doggy daycare (i.e., George Schlosser) stated "My employees can do what they want on their own time but not when I am pay-ing them" and has a policy that prevents employees from wearing political attire (Roberts, 2020).

The aforementioned examples highlight the dichotomy in how various companies differ significantly with respect to how employees can respond to mega-events while on the job. These two approaches likely have varied effects on individual outcomes (e.g., organizational culture, commitment, performance, cohesion). Given the recent mega-threats and the resulting outcry for organizational changes in light of social unrest, there is a pressing need to consider how support for diversity-related movements (e.g., #BLM) influence supervisor-subordinate relationships. This chapter explores these elements with particular focus on examining instances where individuals may have *opposing* views of #BLM. Although studies find a significant relation between external events and business decisions (Tilcsik & Marquis, 2013), there is a paucity of research examining the extent to which differing perceptions of mega-threats and #BLM impact supervisor-subordinate relationships. The purpose of this chapter, however, is to examine how differing views of #BLM affect the supervisor-subordinate relationship and other work-related outcomes (e.g., performance, commitment, turnover).

In addition to varied organizational responses, a recent survey by Pew Research Center (Perrin, 2020) provides evidence about the conflicting viewpoints that *individuals* have regarding the #BLM movement as a result of social media attention. Notable quotes include a #BLM supporter commenting that, "Reading articles on the BLM movement has opened my eyes to the degree of systemic racism in this country and the world." Meanwhile, another survey participant indicated that, "I used to support #BLM, but now I see them as violent domestic terrorists not interested in addressing the real problems within the Black community" (Perrin, 2020). In each of these comments, individuals describe how social media has informed their views on #BLM. Recent studies have found that using social media platforms can help movements expand and strengthen (Mundt et al., 2018) while shaping perceptions of race (Carney, 2016). The mega-threats that gave rise to the #BLM movement (i.e., acts of police brutality against Black individuals) were largely publicized through various social media platforms. The global spread of these social media posts, shares, and comments demonstrate how differences in feelings and thoughts about #BLM are prevalent. Thus, taken together with previous evidence from supervisors, we anticipate that everyday employees also likely have differing stances regarding the extent to which outward support for #BLM may be acceptable. Furthermore, we propose that when a supervisor and subordinate have dissimilar views about the mega-threats, discussions regarding #BLM are likely to influence their perceptions of one another.

Given the push for organizations to demonstrate internal and external support for racial equality, companies have taken action. Some of the most publicized outcries for organizational change include the 15 Percent Pledge for shelf space, a monetary pledge to donate towards #BLM-initiatives, and modifications to company policies and practices. Major retailers such as Sephora, Macy's, and Bloomingdales (Fifteen Percent Pledge, 2020) have agreed that because Black people represent nearly 15% of the U.S. population, they will give at least 15% of each store's shelf space to products manufactured by Black-owned businesses (Maheshwari, 2020). In addition to pledging to dedicate shelf space, some companies such as Uber, Zillow, and Ripple have joined The Board Challenge pledge to increase representation of Black leaders by pledging to appoint or keep at least one Black director on the board within the next year (The Board Challenge, n.d.). These practices are designed to address systemic issues related to racial inequity which were made more salient as a result of recent mega-events and subsequent responses.

Likewise, corporations have also made a public pledge to donate money to minority-owned nonprofits that carry out the #BLM mission and strategic company initiatives to help predominantly Black communities and minority consumers (Harper, 2020). CEOs have made similar pledge statements to show individual support for #BLM and for their organization's stance on #BLM. Companies realize that money alone will not ensure a lasting change for racial equality. Therefore, many organizations have pledged to make policy changes that will promote diversity and inclusion as well as changes to hiring and training practices to increase diversity, especially in leadership positions, and encourage racial dialogue.

Given the strategic decisions firms have made in response to the #BLM movement, the global awareness of mega-threats associated with #BLM, and the differing stances of #BLM, it is vital that organizations consider the likelihood that discussions about #BLM-related events will take place at work. We next focus on how mega-events and mega-threats have an impact on supervisor and subordinate dyads. The subsequent sections will explain how and why these mega-threats influence individual-level outcomes (e.g., performance, commitment) as well as the role that the supervisor-subordinate relationship plays in the link between mega-threats and employee outcomes.

SUPERVISOR-SUBORDINATE DYADIC RELATIONSHIPS

Perhaps one of the most important relationships within organizations is that of supervisor-subordinate dyads. Previous research reveals that as a result of positional power, supervisors may have a significant impact on subordinate behavior (Lewin, 1943). Moreover, the extent to which supervisors and subordinates have a positive relationship may also influence workplace behaviors (e.g., performance, motivation, turnover; van Breukelen et al., 2006) and organizational performance (Ostroff, 1992). Of more relevance to the current chapter, research reveals that mega-events highlighted in the media spill*over* into the workplace (Ballinger & Rockmann, 2010; Leigh & Melwani, 2019; Tilcsik & Marquis, 2013). While prior studies have examined the link between the supervisor-subordinate relationship and workplace outcomes, it has yet to consider the extent to which mega-events in general, and mega-threats in particular, have an impact on the dyadic relationship between supervisors and subordinates.

We anticipate that there are a variety of factors that may contribute to whether or not supervisors and subordinates discuss mega-threats while at work. Research has found that the quality of supervisor-subordinate relationships positively impacts employee voice (Van Dyne et al., 2008). Thus, employees with a high-quality supervisor-subordinate relationship are more likely to speak up than those with a low-quality relationship. We posit that in the context of the #BLM movement, a number of factors impact the extent to which individuals (i.e., supervisors and subordinates) discuss their opinions regarding the #BLM movement. Specifically, we anticipate that supervisor-subordinate dyads that have demographic similarities will be more likely to discuss mega-threats. In addition, we anticipate that the quality of the supervisor-subordinate dyad will impact whether or not such conversations are likely to occur. Lastly, we believe that the congruence of perceptions of mega-threats may impact work performance, organizational commitment, and turnover intentions.

Decisions about whether or not to discuss mega-threats at work is likely a complicated one. For instance, discussing differing views may fuel hostility and lead to polarization (Ely et al., 2006). The threat of negative outcomes for individuals who decide to discuss such events may have an impact on whether or not incumbents choose to discuss such events. Specifically, previous research indicates that hostility and polarization often result in decreased communication between individuals and reduced work performance (Ely et al., 2006). We next discuss two approaches to utilize for understanding how discussing opposing stances on significant events (e.g., #BLM) in the workplace influences employee perceptions, the quality of the supervisor-subordinate relationship, and, ultimately, work outcomes.

Similarity/Attraction Theory, Person Perception, and Work Outcomes. Similarity/attraction theory suggests that individuals are attracted to and develop closer relationships with similar others (Wetzel & Insko, 1982). The "similarity" has been examined with respect to a variety of surface-level demographic characteristics including race, gender, and age (Davidson et al., 2006; Gehrt et al., 2015; Young et al., 1997). Overall, research suggests that we are attracted to individuals with whom we share similarity. Moreover, evidence suggests that *perceived* similarity has a stronger relation with employee outcomes (e.g., job satisfaction) than *actual* similarity (Turban & Jones, 1988). Likewise, prior findings indicate that both perceived surface-level dissimilarity (e.g., observable differences in race, age) and perceived deep-level dissimilarity (e.g., invisible differences in beliefs, political stances, values, etc.) negatively impact work-related outcomes (Liao et al., 2008; O'Reilly et al., 1989). Thus, the more dissimilar individuals perceive themselves to be in the workplace, the worse work outcomes they will have. Relational demography research suggests that the effects of an individual's demographics on work behaviors extend beyond the individual and, instead, argues that it is the similarities and dissimilarities of characteristics amongst employees that explain work outcomes (Tsui & O'Reilly III, 1989). Much of the existing literature on relational demography focuses on surface-level differences while less research considers perceived deep-level dissimilarity (Liao et al., 2008). This chapter contributes to prior literature on relational demography by exploring the effects of deep-level dissimilarity in employee values, specifically differing #BLM stances, on work outcomes. We posit that perceived beliefs about #BLM, will function in a manner similar to that of previous research on surface and deep-level similarity.

Studies on similarity/attraction paradigm reveal that perceived dissimilarity often leads to lower work group performance, less group communication, and greater expectancy of turnover within a group (Neale et al., 1999; Riordan & Shore, 1997; Williams & O'Reilly, 1998). Likewise, Williams and O'Reilly (1998) found that dissimilarity in the supervisor-subordinate dyad results in negative employee behaviors and work performance. Şahin et al. (2019), furthermore, found that individuals who perceived themselves as having deep-level dissimilarity to others at work reported more decreased feelings of inclusion than those who perceived themselves as having deep-level similarity while perceived surface-level similarity or dissimilarity had no effect on felt inclusion.

We classify opposing stances of the #BLM movement as deep-level dissimilarity and posit that perceived dissimilarities likely cause negative perceptions of the supervisor as a person in the eyes of the employee. Therefore, we anticipate that perceived dissimilarity in support of the #BLM movement at the dyadic level negatively affects the ways in which the subordinate views their supervisor (and vice versa), and further impacts work outcomes including, but not limited to, performance, commitment, and turnover. Specifically, we propose that when dissimilar views about mega-threats are realized through #BLM-related dialogue between a supervisor and their employee, this supervisor-subordinate contact will moderate the link between the mega-threat and their perceptions of one another.

Scholars have recognized that person perception is a broad construct that encompasses various domains of judgment such as recognizing and judging others' emotions, judging others' thoughts, and judging status and relationship quality (Blanch-Hartigan et al., 2012; Hall & Bernieri, 2001). Person perception is defined as judgment of others' internal states, traits, and status. Bernieri (2001) found that individuals form such judgments quickly and with little effort. Therefore, we anticipate that employees will form judgements about their supervisors immediately following discussions regarding the #BLM movement.

In accordance with person perception theorizing and in light of the significant impact that mega-threats have on one's thoughts and behaviors (Leigh & Melwani, 2019), we propose that person perception will mediate the influence of mega-threats on the quality of a supervisor-subordinate relationship. Specifically, dissimilar stances on the #BLM movement will lead to a more negative perception of the supervisor from the subordinate's vantage point, which will further decrease the quality of the relationship between the employee and their supervisor.

LMX Theory and Subordinate Performance. A common underpinning for research on work relationships is leader-member exchange theory (LMX; Graen & Uhl-Bien, 1995). The premise of LMX theory is that the relationship between the leader and the employee develops through exchanges of information, resources, efforts, and emotions, and that LMX relationships can be categorized by high or low levels of interaction and information sharing (Liden et al., 1997). These exchanges result in a positive or negative impact on the relationship between the supervisor and subordinate. LMX research reveals that in-group subordinates (a higher quality supervisor-subordinate relationship) are more committed to their supervisors which in turn leads to increased organizational commitment (Truckenbrodt, 2000). Previous research also suggests that higher organizational commitment leads to better work performance (Meyer et al., 1989; Ostroff, 1992). In fact, a study by Ostroff (1992) showed that committed employees have a variety of impacts at both the individual and organizational levels (e.g., increased organizational performance, decreased absenteeism and turnover). Thus, a higher quality relationship (trust, etc.) can be associated with more supervisor and organizational commitment and, ultimately, better workplace outcomes.

Van Dyne et al. (2008) found that high quality relationships between employees and their supervisors motivate employee voice, which may likely result in improved employee performance and more dialogue while in the workplace. Likewise, research by Park and Nawakitphaitoon (2018) indicates that high quality supervisor-subordinate relationships allow employees more opportunities to share information and ideas with their supervisors and to speak up using more communication channels than lower quality relationships. Given that increased communication, trust, and satisfaction exist in such relationships, more positive workplace outcomes are likely to occur including increased organizational commitment and job satisfaction (Graen & Uhl-Bien, 1995; Meyer et al., 1989; Park & Nawakitphaitoon, 2018; Truckenbrodt, 2000). On the contrary, a low-quality dyadic relationship will likely lead to less communication and decreased job satisfaction. These negative factors may, in turn, result in worse employee performance and the employee feeling less committed to the organization.

As previously discussed, research has shown that mega-events/threats impact the internal environment of organizations (Morgeson et al., 2015). We anticipate that the quality of relationship between supervisors and subordinates may impact the extent to which individuals discuss mega-events/threats. Given the saliency of the #BLM movement in light of recent mega-events/threats, we anticipate that individuals with high quality relationships may be more likely to discuss such happenings. Moreover, we propose that discussions in support or opposition of #BLM while at work can affect the LMX relationship, ultimately influencing employee behaviors and actions.

Similarity/Attraction and LMX. Research reveals a connection between perceived similarity and the quality of LMX in a supervisor-subordinate relationship (Suazo et al., 2008). Given that similarity between employees likely influences the quality of the LMX relationship (Suazo et al., 2008) and such quality impacts employee behavior and performance, we posit that similarity in the supervisor-subordinate dyad can influence subordinate performance. Specifically, we propose that the supervisor-subordinate dyad will be influenced by the extent to which views of mega-threats and/or support for the #BLM movement are congruent or incongruent. This (dis)similarity will moderate the person perception of one another which will then impact the quality of the supervisor-subordinate relationship (i.e., LMX) and work outcomes. Thus, we expect that LMX will mediate the relation between person perception and work outcomes. In particular, when attitudes are congruent, we posit that the quality of the relationship will be high and that firm-relevant outcomes (e.g., performance, commitment, turnover intentions) will remain unchanged. However, when attitudes are incongruent, we posit that the mega-threat will have a negative impact on relationship quality and will also negatively impact organizationally relevant outcomes.

Extant research on supervisor-subordinate relationships have focused on similarities, however, this paper aims to emphasize the differences in this dyadic relationship relative to dissimilarity of perspectives on the #BLM movement. In line with evidence that perceived deep-level dissimilarity in the workplace can negatively affect employee relationships (Liao et al., 2008), we propose that dissimilarity in #BLM stances have a similar impact. Rimé (2009) explored how people engage in emotional sharing by discussing their feelings when an emotionally intense event occurs. For example, when a supervisor and subordinate have differing views of #BLM, a highly emotional mega-event, it is likely that discussions on the topic of #BLM will take place at work. This dissimilarity is likely to fuel negative emotions and perceptions of one another, leading to a lower quality relationship. Furthermore, this low-quality relationship may, ultimately, impact work performance such as decreased organizational commitment, worse employee performance, and employee turnover.

DISCUSSION

Examining ways to foster inclusive workplaces remains an important consideration as organizations become increasingly diverse (Opie & Roberts, 2017). As instances of racism and racist behaviors (both inside and outside of the workplace) are becoming more publicized, it is important to examine how such events impact employees. There is a scarce yet growing body of research examining mega-threats and perceptions of #BLM in the workplace. However, more research is needed to understand how employees respond to support (or lack thereof) for #BLM and/or other major events and mega-threats. This chapter focused on the #BLM movement; it is important, however, to acknowledge that there are a variety of other mega-threats that employees may experience. For example, highly publicized employment terminations may also serve as mega-threats that potentially impair performance, organizational commitment, and turnover intentions. Likewise, highly publicized instances of sexual violence in the workplace may also serve as mega-threats. More work is needed to better understand whether the *type* of mega-threat has a differential impact on workplace interactions and organizational outcomes.

We argue that mega-events, in general, and mega-threats, in particular, likely have significant implications for a variety of workplace outcomes. First, in line with affective events theory (Weiss & Cropanzano, 1996), mega-threats likely impact employee moods, emotions, and cognitive resources. Given that Black employees may highly identify with their race, instances of highly publicized racism likely elicit a number of negative emotions and rumination. We anticipate that mega-threats likely impact performance, however, empirical research is needed to address this gap in the literature. Future research should examine both the nature of the effects of mega-threats on workplace constructs as well as the duration of the impacts.

Second, future research should examine whether or not individuals view perceptions of mega-threats and protest movements as a way to categorize in-groups and out-groups. In line with similarity/attraction theory (Wetzel & Insko, 1982), #BLM is potentially a way in which individuals can be categorized. When at work, an individual's support for, or against, #BLM may be used to make a number of inferences about employee, or manager's, behavior. Future research is needed to examine how dyads change as a result of mega-events, mega-threats, and subsequent reactions to highly visible societal events.

Third, future research should examine the extent to which dyadic relationships have an impact on the relationships between mega-threats and work-related outcomes. That is, does high LMX buffer the effects of mega-threats on performance, commitment, and turnover? We anticipate that having supervisors or coworkers who share one's perspectives, will attenuate the impact of mega-threats on work related outcomes.

This chapter expands on Leigh and Melwani (2019) by providing a model for understanding the individual-level impacts of societal events. Previous work provides a conceptual framework for understanding how mega-threats can lead to positive outcomes for organizations. The current chapter, however, provides a mechanism for understanding how mega-threats can be deleterious for organizations, particularly in a context where perceptions of the event are incongruent. Specifically, examining dyadic relationships between supervisors and subordinates might provide some insight into how mega-threats can elicit negative outcomes including decreased performance, commitment, and increased turnover. Future research may view both of these processes simultaneously to obtain a clearer picture of how individuals respond to mega-threats.

Moreover, we extend the current literature by examining the extent to which contextual variables (e.g., dyadic relationships, deep-level similarity) impact the relation between mega-events, responses to mega-threats (e.g., support for the #BLM movement) and work outcomes. We propose a nuanced approach to exploring how perceived dissimilarities in views of the #BLM movement between an employee and a supervisor can generate negative outcomes. In addition, we posit that such impacts occur at both the employee and organizational levels.

Organizations should consider how best to respond to major societal events. Stakeholders have a variety of methods for influencing organizational responses to mega-events (Luo et al., 2016). Gupta and Briscoe (2020) examined organizational responses to social activism. Their examination of Fortune 500 companies revealed that the political affiliation of the organization influenced organizational responses, with liberal leaning organizations being more responsive to social protests than their more conservative counterparts. More work is needed to understand the extent to which such responsiveness is effective, as well as a structure for developing effective organizational responses for all organizations, regardless of political affiliation. Specifically, as #BLM may be considered a form of social activism, it may be important to examine whether activism related to mega-threats is also applicable.

A number of important questions remain about how support for #BLM in particular may impact individuals and organizations (Swigart et al., 2020). First, to what extent does support for #BLM function like a surface-level or deep-level indicator? Specifically, to what extent are the impacts of support for (or opposition to) impacted by time? Second, to what extent are interpersonal relationships impacted by support for (or opposition to) the #BLM movement? In other words, what are the implications for (in)civility when individuals have congruent and incongruent stances on the #BLM movement? Third and lastly, do individuals conceal or disclose their support of the #BLM movement? To what extent do individuals acknowledge their stance on the #BLM movement? Thus, future research is needed to examine these questions.

CONCLUSION

We anticipate that given the highly polarized climate of the United States, mega-threats and major events involving status characteristics will continue to occur and that such instances will likely continue to elicit responses from both individuals and organizations. More work is needed to understand the implications of mega-threats for both incumbents and organizations. In addition, it will also be important for organizations to proactively develop efficacious responses that enable employees to perform at optimal levels.

REFERENCES

Andersson, T. D., Armbrecht, J., & Lundberg, E. (2008). Impact of mega-events on the economy. *Asian Business & Management*, 7(2), 163–179.

Ballinger, G. A., & Rockmann, K. W. (2010). Chutes versus ladders: Anchoring events and a punctuated-equilibrium perspective on social exchange relationships. *The Academy of Management Review*, 35(3), 373–391.

Bernieri, F. J. (2001). Toward a taxonomy of interpersonal sensitivity. In J. A. Hall & F. J. Bernieri (Eds.), *Interpersonal sensitivity: Theory and measurement* (pp. 3–20). Psychology Press.

Black Lives Matter Foundation. (n.d.). *About*. Black Lives Matter. https://www.blacklivesmatter.com/about/

Blanch-Hartigan, D., Andrzejewski, S. A., & Hill, K. M. (2012). The effectiveness of training to improve person perception accuracy: a meta-analysis. *Basic and Applied Social Psychology*, 34(6), 483–498.

Bonaparte, Y. L. (2020). Meeting the Moment: Black Lives Matter, racial inequality, corporate messaging, and rebranding. *Advertising & Society Quarterly*, 21(3).

Buchanan, L., Bui, Q., & Patel, J. K. (2020, July 3). Black Lives Matter may be the largest movement in U.S. history. *The New York Times*. http://www.nytimes.com

Bureau of Labor Statistics, U.S. Department of Labor. (2020, December 1). *Labor force characteristics by race and ethnicity, 2019: BLS Reports*. U.S. Bureau of Labor Statistics. Retrieved May 14, 2021, from https://www.bls.gov/opub/reports/race-and-ethnicity/2019/home.htm

Carney, N. (2016). All lives matter, but so does race: Black lives matter and the evolving role of social media. *Humanity & Society*, *40*(2), 180–199.

Civiqs. (2020). "Black Lives Matter: Do you support or oppose the Black Lives Matter movement?, April 25, 2017–November 8, 2020 [Survey Report] in *Civiqs*. https://civiqs.com/results/black_lives_matter?uncertainty=true&annotations=true&zoomIn=true

Cunningham, G. B. (2009). The moderating effect of diversity strategy on the relationship between racial diversity and organizational performance. *Journal of Applied Social Psychology*, *39*(6), 1445–1460.

Curtis, C. (2020, June 2). What is Blackout Tuesday? The social media trend and controversy around it, explained. *USA Today*. https//ftw.usatoday.com/

Davidson, W. N., Nemec, C., & Worrell, D. L. (2006). Determinants of CEO age at succession. *Journal of Management & Governance*, *10*(1), 35–57.

Ely, R. J., Meyerson, D. E., & Davidson, M. N. (2006). Rethinking political correctness. *Harvard Business Review*, *84*(9), 78–87.

Fayos-Solá, E. (1998). The impact of mega events. *Annals of tourism research*, *25*(1), 241–245.

Fifteen Percent Pledge. (2020). *Who has taken the pledge*. Fifteen Percent Pledge. https://www.15percentpledge.org/pledged/

Galinsky, A. D., Todd, A. R., Homan, A. C., Phillips, K. W., Apfelbaum, E. P., Sasaki, S. J., Richeson, J. A., Olayon, J. B., & Maddux, W. W. (2015). Maximizing the gains and minimizing the pains of diversity: A policy perspective. *Perspectives on Psychological Science*, *10*(6), 742–748.

Gehrt, K., Louie, T. A., & Osland, A. (2015). Student and professor similarity: Exploring the effects of gender and relative age. *Journal of Education for Business*, *90*(1), 1–9. https://doi-org.cuhsl.creighton.edu/10.1080/08832323.2014.968514

Graen, G. B., & Uhl-Bien, M. (1995). Relationship-based approach to leadership: Development of leader-member exchange (LMX) theory of leadership over 25 years: Applying a multi-level multi-domain perspective. *The Leadership Quarterly*, *6*(2), 219–247. https://doi.org/10.1016/1048-9843(95)90036-5

Gupta, A., & Briscoe, F. (2020). Organizational political ideology and corporate openness to social activism. *Administrative Science Quarterly*, *65*(2), 524–563.

Hall, J. A., & Bernieri, F. J. (Eds.). (2001). *Interpersonal sensitivity: Theory and measurement*. Psychology Press.

Harper, S. R. (2020, June 16). Corporations say they support Black Lives Matter. Their employees doubt them. *The Washington Post*. https://www.washingtonpost.com/

Hartmann, D. (2012, March 1). Happy talk about diversity avoids difficult racial issues. *Scholars Strategy Network*. Retrieved July 15, 2020, from https://scholars.org/brief/happy-talk-about-diversity-avoids-difficult-racial-issues

Hewlett, S. A., Marshall, M., & Bourgeois, T. (2017, July 10). People suffer at work when they can't discuss the racial bias they face outside of it. *Harvard Business Review*. Retrieved July 15, 2020, from https://hbr.org/2017/07/people-suffer-at-work-when-they-cant-discuss-the-racial-bias-they-face-outside-of-it

Hoffman, L., Granger, N., Vallejos, L., Moats, M., Lemberger, M., & Lemberger-Truelove, T. (2016). An existential–humanistic perspective on Black Lives Matter and contemporary protest movements. *Journal of Humanistic Psychology*, *56*(6), 595–611.

Johnson, B. R., Connolly, E., & Carter, T. S. (2011). Corporate social responsibility: The role of Fortune 100 companies in domestic and international natural disasters. *Corporate Social Responsibility and Environmental Management*, *18*(6), 352–369.

Jones, C. (2005). Major events, networks and regional development. *Regional Studies*, *39*(2), 185–195.

Leigh, A., & Melwani, S. (2019). # BlackEmployeesMatter: Mega-threats, identity fusion, and enacting positive deviance in organizations. *Academy of Management Review*, *44*(3), 564–591.

Lewin, K. (1943). Defining the 'field at a given time.' *Psychological Review*, *50*(3), 292–310.

Liao, H., Chuang, A., & Joshi, A. (2008). Perceived deep-level dissimilarity: Personality antecedents and impact on overall job attitude, helping, work withdrawal, and turnover. *Organizational Behavior and Human Decision Processes*, *106*(2), 106–124.

Liden, R. C., Sparrowe, R. T., & Wayne, S. J. (1997). Leader-member exchange theory: The past and potential for the future. *Research in Personnel and Human Resources Management*, *15*, 47–120.

Liu, J. (2020, June 5). Talking about racial inequality at work is difficult-here are tips to do it thoughtfully. *CNBC*. https://www.cnbc.com/2020/06/05/how-to-thoughtfully-talk-about-racial-inequality-with-your-coworkers.html

Luo, X. R., Zhang, J., & Marquis, C. (2016). Mobilization in the internet age: Internet activism and corporate response. *Academy of Management Journal*, *59*(6), 2045–2068.

Maheshwari, S. (2020, June 10). Sephora signs '15 Percent Pledge' to carry more Black-owned brands. *The New York Times*. http://www.nytimes.com

McCluney, C., Bryant, C., King, D., & Ali, A. (2017). Calling in Black: Dynamic model of racially traumatic events on organizational resourcing. *Academy of Management Proceedings*, *2017*(1), 10399.

McGillivray, D., & Frew, M. (2015). From fan parks to live sites: Mega events and the territorialisation of urban space. *Urban Studies*, *52*(14), 2649–2663.

Meyer, J. P., Paunonen, S. V., Gellatly, I. R., Goffin, R. D., & Jackson, D. N. (1989). Organizational commitment and job performance: It's the nature of the commitment that counts. *Journal of Applied Psychology*, *74*(1), 152–156. https://doi.org/10.1037/0021-9010.74.1.152

Morgeson, F. P., Mitchell, T. R., & Dong L. (2015). Event system theory: An event-oriented approach to the organizational sciences. *Academy of Management Review*, *40*(4), 515–537. https://doi-org.cuhsl.creighton.edu/10.5465/amr.2012.0099

Müller, M. (2015). What makes an event a mega-event? Definitions and sizes. *Leisure Studies*, *34*(6), 627–642.

Mundt, M., Ross, K., & Burnett, C. M. (2018). Scaling social movements through social media: The case of Black Lives Matter. *Social Media + Society*, *4*(4), 2056305118807911.

Neale, M. A., Northcraft, G. B., & Jehn, K. A. (1999). Exploring Pandora's Box: The impact of diversity and conflict on work group performance. *Performance Improvement Quarterly*, *12*(1), 113–126.

O'Reilly, C., Caldwell, D., & Barnett, W. (1989). Work group demography, social integration, and turnover. *Administrative Science Quarterly*, *34*(1), 21–37. https://doi.org/10.2307/2392984

Opie, T., & Roberts, L. M. (2017). Do Black lives really matter in the workplace? Restorative justice as a means to reclaim humanity. *Equality, Diversity and Inclusion: An International Journal*, *36*(8), 707–719. https://doi.org/10.1108/edi-07-2017-0149

Ostroff, C. (1992). The relationship between satisfaction, attitudes, and performance: An organizational-level analysis. *Journal of Applied Psychology*, *77*, 963–974.

Park, J.-Y., & Nawakitphaitoon, K. (2018). The cross-cultural study of LMX and individual employee voice: The moderating role of conflict avoidance. *Human Resource Management Journal*, *28*(1), 14–30.

Perrin, A. (2020, October 15). 23% of users in U.S. say social media led them to change views on an issue; some cite Black Lives Matter. *Pew Research Center*. https://www.pewresearch.org/fact-tank/2020/10/15/23-of-users-in-us-say-social-media-led-them-to-change-views-on-issue-some-cite-black-lives-matter/

Pew Research Center. (2018). "Women and Men in STEM Often at Odds Over Workplace Diversity: % of U.S. adults who say it is _ important to have racial and ethnic diversity in the workplace today, July 11, 2017–August 10, 2017, [Survey Report] in *Pew Research Center*. https://www.pewsocialtrends.org/2018/01/09/women-and-men-in-stem-often-at-odds-over-workplace-equity/ps_2018-01-09_stem_4-01/

Richard, O. C. (2000). Racial diversity, business strategy, and firm performance: A resource-based view. *Academy of Management Journal*, *43*(2), 164–177.

Richard, O., McMillan, A., Chadwick, K., & Dwyer, S. (2003). Employing an innovation strategy in racially diverse workforces: Effects on firm performance. *Group & Organization Management*, *28*(1), 107–126.

Rickford, R. (2016). Black Lives Matter: Toward a modern practice of mass struggle. *New Labor Forum*, *25*(1), 34–42. https://doi.org/10.1177/1095796015620171

Rimé, B. (2009). Emotion elicits the social sharing of emotion: Theory and empirical review. *Emotion Review*, *1*(1), 60–85.

Riordan, C. M., & McFarlane Shore, L. (1997). Demographic diversity and employee attitudes: An empirical examination of relational demography within work units. *Journal of Applied Psychology*, *82*(3), 342–358.

Roberson, Q., Ryan, A. M., & Ragins, B. R. (2017). The evolution and future of diversity at work. *Journal of Applied Psychology*, *102*(3), 483.

Roberts, L. M., & Mayo, A. J. (2019, November 14). Toward a racially just workplace. *Harvard Business Review*. Retrieved July 14, 2020, from https://hbr.org/cover-story/2019/11/toward-a-racially-just-workplace

Roberts, P. (2020, October 3). Black Lives Matter logos in the workplace divide employers, workers, and customers. *The Seattle Times*. http://www.seattletimes.com

Rock, D., & Grant, H. (2016). Why diverse teams are smarter. *Harvard Business Review, 4*(4), 2–5.

Rock, D., Grant, H., & Grey, J. (2016). Diverse teams feel less comfortable—and that's why they perform better. *Harvard Business Review, 95*(9), 22.

Sacks, B. (2020, July 12). Costco didn't enforce its dress code—Until employees started wearing Black Lives Matter masks. *BuzzFeed News*. https://www.buzzfeednews.com/article/briannasacks/costco-black-lives-matter-masks-dress-code.

Şahin, O., van der Toorn, J., Jansen, W. S., Boezeman, E. J., & Ellemers, N. (2019). Looking beyond our similarities: How perceived (in) visible dissimilarity relates to feelings of inclusion at work. *Frontiers in Psychology, 10*, 575.

Snider, M. (2020, June 21). Off for Juneteenth: Will NFL, Nike, Twitter and corporate celebrations across America make a difference?. *USA Today*. https//www.usatoday.com/

Suazo, M., Turnley, W., & Mai-Dalton, R. (2008). Characteristics of the supervisor-subordinate relationship as predictors of psychological contract breach. *Journal of Managerial Issues, 20*(3), 295–312. Retrieved November 4, 2020, from http://www.jstor.org/stable/40604612

Swigart, K. L., Anantharaman, A., Williamson, J. A., & Grandey, A. A. (2020). Working while liberal/conservative: A review of political ideology in organizations. *Journal of Management*. https://doi.org/10.1177/0149206320909419

The Board Challenge. (n.d.). *In good company*. https://theboardchallenge.org/

Tilcsik, A., & Marquis, C. (2013). Punctuated generosity: How mega-events and natural disasters affect corporate philanthropy in U.S. communities. *Administrative Science Quarterly, 58*(1), 111–148.

Truckenbrodt, Y. B. (2000). The relationship between leader-member exchange and commitment and organizational citizenship behavior. *Acquisition Review Quarterly, 7*(3), 233.

Tsui, A. S., & O'Reilly, C. A., III. (1989). Beyond simple demographic effects: The importance of relational demography in superior-subordinate dyads. *Academy of management journal, 32*(2), 402–423.

Turban, D B, & Jones, A P. (1988). Supervisor-subordinate similarity: Types, effects, and mechanisms. *Journal of Applied Psychology, 73*(2), 228–234.

van Breukelen, W., Schyns, B. & Le Blanc, P., 2006. Leader-member exchange theory and research: Accomplishments and future challenges. *Leadership, 2*(3), 295–316.

Van Dyne, L., Kamdar, D., & Joireman, J. (2008). In-role perceptions buffer the negative impact of low LMX on helping and enhance the positive impact of high LMX on voice. *Journal of Applied Psychology, 93*(6), 1195.

Weiss, H. M., & Cropanzano, R. (1996). Affective events theory: A theoretical discussion of the structure, causes and consequences of affective experiences at work. *Research in Organizational Behavior, 18*, 1–74.

Wetzel, C. G., & Insko, C. A. (1982). The similarity-attraction relationship: Is there an ideal one? *Journal of Experimental Social Psychology, 18*(3), 253–276.

Williams, K. Y., & O'Reilly, C. A. (1998). Demography and diversity in organizations: A review of 40 years of research. *Research in Organizational Behavior*, *20*, 77–140.

Young, I. P., Place, A. W., Rinehart, J. S., Jury, J. C., & Baits, D. F. (1997). Teacher recruitment: A test of the similarity-attraction hypothesis for race and sex. *Educational Administration Quarterly*, *33*(1), 86–106.

CHAPTER 5

TRANSFORMING RACIAL MICROAGGRESSIONS INTO LEADER IDENTITY DEVELOPMENT THROUGH SELF-NARRATIVES

Amber Kea-Edwards and Rebecca J. Reichard
Claremont Graduate University

ABSTRACT

Understanding the inhibitors and accelerators of the development of leader identity, or the extent to which an individual views oneself as a leader, for Black, Indigenous, and people of color (BIPOC) is necessary to narrow the racial leadership gap. Developing a strong and integrated leader identity is a harbinger for developing dynamic leadership skills and attaining formal leadership roles. As a socially constructed phenomenon, leader identity development may be threatened by racial microaggressions, or subtle subversive slights directed towards an individual based on their racial group. Building on the foundation of the transformational learning theory of adult learning, aspiring BIPOC leaders can cope with racial microaggressions in a positive, proactive, and long-term manner. Specifically, they can craft a self-narrative to cultivate a positive racial identity to buffer the harmful effects of

The Future of Scholarship on Race in Organizations, pp. 97–117
Copyright © 2022 by Information Age Publishing

97

racial microaggressions on leader identity development. Understanding the role of racial microaggressions in leader identity development opens conversations about a more inclusive and diverse leadership pipeline. We suggest three strategies to inclusify future leader development research, including diversification of samples, reconceptualizing extant theory using a racial lens, and originating new theory grounded in BIPOC leaders' developmental experiences.

TRANSFORMING RACIAL MICROAGGRESSIONS INTO LEADER IDENTITY DEVELOPMENT THROUGH SELF-NARRATIVES

"When I hear about negative and false attacks, I really don't invest any energy in them, because I know who I am." —Michelle Obama

To create a fair and equitable society and optimize organizational effectiveness, leaders should represent their employees and customers. In the United States, Black, Indigenous, and people of color (BIPOC) are not adequately represented in formal leadership roles. Despite the passage of Title VII of the Civil Rights Acts of 1964, which prohibited organizations from discriminating against individuals based on their race, an increase in racial diversity has been limited to lower-level positions and middle-management roles (Roberts et al., 2019). The representation of BIPOC in top leadership positions within private businesses remains dismal (Hecht, 2020). Specifically, Asians hold 5.9%, non-White Hispanics hold 4.3%, and Blacks hold only 3.2% of executive-level leadership positions (Swerzenski, 2020). Previous studies point to race-related systemic issues such as the lack of hiring qualified individuals and discrimination in promotion practices (Roberson, 2019), and we discuss a previously unexamined inhibitor to BIPOC leader development—the development of leader identity.

Leader identity, or the extent to which an individual defines their sense of self through a leadership role (Day et al., 2008), is a proximal indicator of leader development. Possessing a strong and integrated leader identity catalyzes the development of advanced and dynamic leadership skills and complex meaning-making schemas (Day & Dragoni, 2015). In other words, when an individual internalizes a leader identity and integrates that identity into their sense of self, their thoughts and behaviors become aligned with that identity (Kegan, 1983). So, the development of a leader identity creates motivation and engagement in leadership-related tasks and practices (Chan & Drasgow, 2001; Kempster, 2006). Despite the surge of theory and research on the concept of leader identity (e.g., 150 articles published from 2007 to 2017; Epitropaki et al., 2017), the most influential leader development publications are based on White leaders by White authors (Vogel et al., 2021). We seek to add to this growing body of research by reenvisioning leader identity development through a racial lens. By doing so, we identify new insights and hypotheses, providing a pathway for more inclusive leader development research and, ultimately, better evidence needed to narrow the racial leadership gap.

Beyond the cultivation of expertise (Lord & Hall, 2005), leader identity development is a socially constructed process (DeRue & Ashford, 2010). As such, it is subject to both the claiming (or not) of leadership from the aspiring BIPOC leader and also the granting (or denying) of leadership from members of their social circles (e.g., supervisors, peers, subordinates, family/community members). Thus, although a BIPOC group member can reach for leadership, if their group explicitly or subtly denies their leadership attempts, then their leader identity development will be stunted. Viewing this social constructivist process through a racial lens, we unpack the influence of racial microaggressions as denials of BIPOC leader identity. We offer an individual-level solution by suggesting that aspiring BIPOC leaders engage in a self-narrative process designed to build a positive racial identity. We argue the latter will buffer the harmful effects of racial microaggressions on BIPOC leader identity development. In summary, we seek to answer two primary questions: (1) How do racial microaggressions impact the leader identity development process for aspiring BIPOC leaders? And (2) How can aspiring BIPOC leaders successfully cope with microaggressions to promote proactive and positive leader identity growth?

With a few exceptions (e.g., Leigh, Roberts, Rosette), leadership and leader development scholars have mostly disregarded the importance of race in theory development and practice (Vogel et al., 2021). Thus, we seek to expand a dominant leader development theory by examining the role of race and race-related events in the leader identity development process. Such theory expansion is a step in laying the ground for empirical research on the leader development process for BIPOC leaders. Additionally, when researchers *do* consider race-related issues in the workplace, they tend to ignore the agentic and internal strength of BIPOC leaders in favor of a focus on White individual's perceptions and actions (Ospina & Foldy, 2009). As a result, we have little research on the internal processes and personal development of BIPOC leaders. In response, we apply the concept of transformational learning to point to the proactive and agentic qualities of BIPOC leaders, particularly regarding racial microaggressions and leader identity development. Overall, research on diversity and inclusion is necessary within the leadership field, and attention toward the individual psychological process of BIPOC leaders is an opportunity to learn more about the meaning of diversity and the role of inclusivity (Eagly & Chin, 2010).

To answer our two primary questions, we first discuss leader identity development broadly and outline the impact of racial bias on the experience of leader identity development for BIPOC leaders. Next, we highlight racial microaggressions as a specific detrimental factor on leader identity development for BIPOC leaders. We then argue for the role of transformational learning as a strategy for aspiring BIPOC leaders to proactively cope with racial microaggressions. Specifically, we suggest using a positive racial identity self-narrative practice to buffer the negative impact of racial microaggressions on leader identity development. Finally, we conclude with a discussion on the practical implications and future research related to BIPOC leaders and their development.

BIPOC LEADER IDENTITY DEVELOPMENT

In general, identity is dynamic and consists of various sub-identities tied to different social roles (Hammond et al., 2017). Sub-identities can develop, weaken, and strengthen over time depending on their centrality to one's sense of self and activation in a particular context. Leader identity is one component of an individual's overall sense of self associated with one's conception of self as a leader (Epitropaki et al., 2017). According to identity theory, one's identity provides motivational properties that direct an individual's thoughts, emotions, and behaviors (Burke & Stets, 2009). For example, an individual who identifies as a leader is more likely to seek leadership opportunities, pursue leadership development training, accept challenging assignments, and assume a leadership role in a group or team meeting (Day et al., 2008). Overall, leader identity affects decision-making processes (Baumeister, 2010), social competence (Taylor & Hood, 2011), leadership effectiveness (Day & Sin, 2011), leadership emergence (Hogg, 2001), and leader development (Day & Dragoni, 2015). Ultimately, developing a strong leader identity for BIPOC leaders can support greater racial diversity in leadership emergence and leader development participation.

Given its importance, it is fortunate that leader identity is malleable and open to shifts toward or away from leadership. Throughout a seven-week leader development program, Miscenko et al. (2017) found that leader identity developed in a J-shaped pattern with those changes positively associated with leadership skills over time. Other researchers following developing leaders over five months and 12-time points found a positive, linear increase in leader identity (Middleton et al., 2019). Thus, due to its malleability, BIPOC leaders have the opportunity to develop a more central and strong leader identity over time.

However, prior scholars have not viewed the existing theory of leader identity development through a racial lens. Extant theory on how leader identity develops considers three overlapping approaches: (1) leader identity as skill development, (2) leader identity as social identity development, and (3) leader identity as relationship development (Ibarra et al., 2014). We argue that each operates uniquely for BIPOC leaders.

First, as one gains experience and skill as a leader, their leader identity develops to higher levels of complexity (Lord & Hall, 2005). Specifically, leaders interdependently advance through stages of expertise (i.e., novice, intermediate, expert) and corresponding stages of leader identity (i.e., individual, relational, and collective). However, BIPOC leaders differentially experience this link between expertise and leader identity development. For example, Ospina and Foldy (2009) conducted a 50-year review analysis on leadership and race and found that even highly qualified BIPOC leaders were perceived as ineffective. Carton and Rosette (2011) found that when BIPOC leaders are high performers in leadership, observers attribute that high performance to external attributions rather than internal attributions such as personal skills or expertise. For BIPOC leaders, the more direct association between skill development and leader identity may not be an internalized process due to the lack of a real-world personal association.

Second, the social identity theory of leadership describes leadership in relation to the context of one's specific group composition (Hogg, 2001). The most prototypical group member (i.e., typically White males; Rosette et al., 2008) represent the in-group and gain more significant influence in social settings (Rosette & Tost, 2010). Group members perceived to be more prototypical are more likely to have positive evaluations from peers than non-prototypical leaders (Lord & Maher, 1990). Group members are more attracted to socially similar members, which increases compliance and followership (Hogg, 2001). However, BIPOC employees represent a small portion within organizations, are less prototypical, are members of the outgroup, and are less likely to experience social attraction or gain influence (Hogg, 2001). Thus, a BIPOC leader's misfit with the group prototype determines their lower leadership positioning and hinders the development of their leader identity within that group.

Finally, relationship development as leader identity development is grounded in a social interactionist perspective (Baumeister, 2010), referred to as claiming and granting (DeRue & Ashford, 2010). From this perspective, individuals form a leader identity through social interactions embedded within a given social context (Mead, 1934). Therefore, a leader identity is an ongoing evaluation of the self, given the nature of enduring relationships and social interactions (Ibarra et al., 2014). Social interactions either validate (i.e., grant) or invalidate (i.e., deny) the leader's influence or effectiveness resulting in either positive or negative spirals of leader identity development (DeRue & Ashford, 2010). In this case, when an individual engages in leader-like behaviors (i.e., claiming), affirming interactions from one's peer group can lead to a stronger leader identity. On the other hand, acts of invalidation from one's peer group can create negative leader identity spirals. Based on this social constructivist perspective of leader identity development, denials of leadership unique to BIPOC leaders are racial microaggressions.

Racial Microaggressions as a Threat to BIPOC Leader Identity Development

Racial microaggressions inhibit the leader identity development of BIPOC leaders because these frequent, ambiguous, and unconscious slights create an identity threat propelling and perpetuating negative leader identity spirals. Racial microaggressions are "subtle, innocuous, preconscious, or unconscious degradations, putdowns, often kinetic but capable of being verbal and/or kinetic" directed towards an individual based on their racial group membership (Pierce, 1995, p. 281). A racial microaggression could look like shaming an Asian American individual who is terrible at math or stating that a Hispanic individual speaks good English. Racial microaggressions are negative interpersonal experiences that indicate "potential harm to the value, meanings, or enactment of an identity," creating an identity threat (Petriglieri, 2011, p. 641).

An identity threat is a disruptive and internalized emotion or thought which challenges an individual's current sense of self (Brown & Coupland, 2015). An identity threat occurs when an individual appraises their given environment as significant and potentially harmful (Folkman & Lazarus, 1984; Major & O'Brien, 2005). For BIPOC leaders, social interactions that bring attention to negative aspects of one's racial group membership, in addition to the leader's identification with one's race (i.e., in the form of a racial microaggression), can be appraised as significant and harmful events. Racial microaggressions are negative interpersonal experiences that indicate "potential harm to the value, meanings, or enactment of an identity" (Petriglieri, 2011, p. 641). Negative race-related comments or subtle actions of invalidation can trigger BIPOC leaders to reconsider their leader identity and perpetuate negative identity spirals (e.g., "Am I the leader I think that I am?", "How do I lead?"; Brown, 2015). Therefore, racial microaggressions create identity threats and, thus, impact leader identity development. Specifically, this negative relationship is significant due to the (1) frequent, (2) ambiguous, and (3) unconscious processing involved in racial microaggressions.

First, due to their high frequency (i.e., occurring every day or even multiple times in a day for individual BIPOC leaders; Wong et al., 2014), racial microaggressions reflect powerful denials of the aspiring BIPOC's leadership inhibiting their leader identity development. Racial microaggressions are prevalent because they often manifest through short blurts of verbal and/or nonverbal interactions. Phrases such as "you are so articulate," "where are you really from?," "there is only one race, the human race," "you people always...," and "some of my best friends are Black" are slight race-related comments that may be made to leaders daily from multiple sources, including their peers, subordinates, and superiors (Sue et al., 2007). Racial microaggressions are a unique experience for BIPOC leaders compared to their White counterparts (Sue et al., 2009). As a result, racial microaggressions are more visible and threatening for BIPOC leaders. Identity threats are more serious when the event is frequent (Burke, 1991). Thus, the higher the frequency of racial microaggressions, the more potent the identity threat resulting in negative leader identity spirals over time.

Second, the ambiguous nature of racial microaggressions can further inhibit leader identity development. Unlike overt forms of racial discrimination, such as finding a noose around your desktop, racial microaggressions are more challenging to identify or universally confirm (Sue, 2010). BIPOC leaders may struggle to establish whether experiences like being singled out or left out as signs of racial discrimination. In this case, the appropriate response or call to action is also ambiguous and complex. The ambiguity of racial microaggressions can cause higher stress and lower proactivity (Omi & Winant, 1994), inhibiting skill development, and thus, leader identity development. Due to ambiguous racial microaggressions, BIPOC leaders may experience adverse psychological outcomes and negative leader identity spirals.

Lastly, the unconscious nature of racial microaggressions may further inhibit BIPOC leader identity development. Similar to implicit bias (Jost et al., 2009), racial microaggressions may operate such that the perpetrator lacks awareness that a particular offense was due to their racial prejudice or that it constitutes a denial of leadership (Sue, 2010). Along with the high level of ambiguity, the unconscious pathways to racial microaggressions make it a challenge for BIPOC leaders to respond effectively. Consider an aspiring Asian American leader who, year after year, remains at the same level of leadership. The Asian American hears his colleagues speak about how vital he is to the team. Still, any time he attempts to informally or formally lead a group, someone talks over him or redirects others' attention (i.e., denies his leadership). In this example, is there evidence of a racial microaggression? Are his colleagues intentionally excluding him from advancing due to his race? Racial microaggressions present an identity threat with a large amount of ambiguity and could, but not in all cases, originate from an unconscious source, making it a challenge to correct. With this, common feelings associated with racial microaggressions create hopelessness due to the lack of understanding of how to respond appropriately (Wong et al., 2014).

COMMON RESPONSES TO RACIAL MICROAGGRESSIONS
AS LEADER IDENTITY THREATS

Commonly, individuals respond to identity threats in one of two ways: (1) maintain the threat or (2) eliminate the threat (Petriglieri, 2011). Maintaining the threat is a typical reactive coping response to an identity threat. In this case, BIPOC leaders tend to respond in a way that maintains the threat, prompting emotional and behavioral reactions that further isolate and debilitate successful leader identity growth. For example, an aspiring BIPOC leader facing daily racial microaggressions threatening their leader identity may react by engaging behaviors aligned with their unleader-like-ness, such as not attempting to influence their colleagues or going along even when they disagree with the group's direction. As their colleagues deny their leadership through racial microaggressions, aspiring BIPOC leaders stop attempts at claiming leadership. Over time, a negative leader identity spiral ensues, and they are no longer aspiring to leadership.

On the other hand, eliminating the threat is a more proactive coping response to an identity threat (Petriglieri, 2011). Eliminating the threat is a response that facilitates growth and development. Thus, we argue for the need to center efforts on building aspiring BIPOC leaders' capacity to eliminate the threat.

Because eliminating the identity threat is a proactive response, it requires significant cognitive and emotional energy (Major et al., 2000). Eliminating the threat assumes that the individual is able and willing either to (a) change the perspective of the individuals who presented the threat or (b) change their personal understanding of the threatened identity (Petriglieri, 2011). Regarding the former, aspiring BIPOC leaders may not have the ability or resources to change the perspective of the individuals engaging in racial microaggressions. Further, due to the unconscious nature of racial microaggressions, the perpetrator may not fully understand or accept that a change is necessary. Thus, changing the perspective of organizational members perpetuating racial microaggressions is the responsibility of the organization, an idea we return to in our discussion of practical implications.

On the other hand, BIPOC leaders do have the capacity to change their conceptualization of race and leadership. Thus, aspiring BIPOC leaders can attempt to eliminate the threat of racial microaggressions by creating a personal understanding of the positive connection between their race and successful leadership enactment. In this way, they conceptualize a proto-type of an effective leader that integrates their racial group membership. This method of eliminating the identity threat creates a pathway towards leader identity development (Kreiner & Sheep, 2009). Importantly for racial minorities, eliminating the threat can allow for an improved balance between their social identity and leader identity. So, what does eliminating the threat of racial microaggression entail, and how can this process create pathways towards a positive identity development for BIPOC leaders?

Learning From Racial Microaggressions

The ability to eliminate the threat of a racial microaggression requires a belief that positive change can occur from less than ideal or even adverse events. Kreiner and Sheep (2009) suggest that the opposing force of an identity threat can be flipped and used to counteract negative outcomes (e.g., "identity threat Jiu-Jitsu"). In this case, racial microaggressions in the workplace represent moments of identity threats and can act as a "catalyst for increased self-awareness and positive change" (Kreiner & Sheep, 2009, p. 32). However, this positive change does not spontaneously occur; on the contrary, it requires a practiced skill in learning. For example, Yip and Wilson (2010) argue that negative moments are viable pathways towards leader identity growth, specifically through a constructive learning process.

In this case, BIPOC leaders can learn from racial microaggressions through informational or transformational learning. Individuals engage in both forms of learning throughout the life span, with a particular proclivity for informational learning, which mimics traditional education. Informational learning is the practice of adding new information to a preexisting understanding (Kegan, 1983). In this case, a leader within a BIPOC group may experience a racial microaggression and use that experience to add to a preexisting understanding of racism or cross-cultural interactions (i.e., maintaining the threat). However, transformational learning can support the process of eliminating the threat for BIPOC leaders. Thus, we emphasize and argue for the unique role of transformational learning in buffering the negative relationship between racial microaggressions and leader identity development for BIPOC leaders.

Compared to informational learning, *transformational learning* (TL) changes how individuals make sense of the world around them. Through TL, individuals critically analyze their meaning-making systems, which may shift and change due to that analysis (Clark, 1993). TL coincides with eliminating the threat as a response to a racial microaggression. TL is a form of learning that shifts an individual's view of the world (Mezirow, 2002). Overall, informational learning "changes ... *what* we know," whereas TL "changes ... *how* [emphasis added] we know" (Kegan, 1983, p. 49). BIPOC leaders can eliminate the threat of racial microaggressions using TL As mentioned earlier, the frequency, ambiguity, and unconscious processing of racial microaggressions can make the response to the identity threat a challenging process for a racial minority.

TL is a nonlinear cognitive, emotional, and behavioral exploration of critical reflection triggered by a disorienting dilemma (Mezirow, 1990). When BIPOC leaders view racial microaggressions as opportunities to expand current ways of thinking through questioning assumptions and challenging personally-held beliefs, they can make a proactive impact on their leader identity growth even in the face of denials of their leadership. In this case, TL weakens the negative relationship between racial microaggressions and leader identity development for BIPOC leaders. However, the TL literature remains mainly in the education field, and the *process* to which an individual engages in TL, especially adults, has received little attention (Meyer, 2009). Bringing TL into the workplace and leader identity development, we discuss it in the context of crafting self-narratives. Crafting a self-narrative provides a positive long-term strategy for aspiring BIPOC leaders to cope and buffer the negative impact of racial microaggressions on their leader identity development.

Self-Narrative Approach as a Long-Term Strategy for Leader Identity Development

Self-narratives "refer to the individual's account of the relationships among self-relevant events across time" (Gergen & Gergen, 1986, p. 255). Self-narratives support the proactive reaction to racial microaggressions, eliminating the threat instead of maintaining it. A self-narrative facilitates the development of leader identity through the exploratory process of answering "Am I a leader?" and "How do I lead?" (Avolio & Gardner, 2005) and is vital for the development of leaders (Shamir & Eilam, 2005). For BIPOC leaders, it is essential to underscore the role of race and racial identity during a self-narrative process. Specifically, after experiencing racial microaggressions in the workplace, BIPOC leaders can leverage positive identities in an attempt to alleviate and even grow from the threat (Kreiner & Sheep, 2009). A focus on highlighting positive aspects of one's racial group membership throughout the lifespan can support the ability to eliminate the threat and enter the process of TL. In this case, crafting a self-narrative allows BIPOC leaders to strengthen their positive racial identity.

Positive racial identity. A positive identity creates a positive thrust for what is good and life-giving (Cameron et al., 2003). Dutton and colleagues (2009) argue that a positive identity allows an individual to express a more authentic version of self and increase overall feelings of self-respect. A positive identity can represent the content of identity, the process of identity, or the outcome of identity (Dutton et al., 2009). Positive racial identity represents the content of an identity, one's race. Maitlis (2009) outlines a positive identity content as a psychological resource that provides an individual with personal strength and a sense of meaning and purpose. Thus, positive racial identity reflects affirmative "attitudes and beliefs that one has about belonging to his or her racial group" (Helms, 1992, p. 241). With this, positive racial identity is an identity that can provide aspiring BIPOC leaders with the strength necessary to buffer the negative impacts of racial microaggressions on leader identity development (Brondolo et al., 2009; Forsyth & Carter, 2012; Harper, 2007).

Practically, a BIPOC leader can engage in race-specific and leader-specific self-narratives before and after a racial microaggression to buffer their adverse impacts on leader identity development (Avolio & Hannah, 2008). Thus, a self-narrative approach, which involves exploring racial identity, can evoke personal growth and development, increase well-being, and allow for effective leadership performance and leader development (Karp & Helgo, 2009). Next, we outline and describe the specific and practical steps BIPOC leaders can engage within their self-narrative to eliminate the threat, spark TL, and weaken the negative relationship between racial microaggressions and leader identity development.

Self-narrative as an intervention. The self-narrative approach, an internally driven process, can occur through an internal dialogue or written or verbal expressions to self (Singer & Blagov, 2004). The practice of self-narratives mimics TL and includes three key steps: (1) reflecting, (2) sharing, and (3) acting (Sandberg & Tsoukas, 2015). Each step is iterative, allowing this process to operate as a long-term strategy for BIPOC leaders (see Table 5.1 for a guided self-narrative practice). Further, because we view leader identity development through both a structural and social interactionist lens, this three-step process considers both leader-related and race-related experiences.

Reflect. Reflection is the first step in the self-narrative process. Reflection involves the practice of analyzing and questioning events throughout the life span. BIPOC leaders should reflect on race-specific events throughout the life span and explore how they relate to their everyday functioning as a leader. Further, BIPOC leaders can reflect on events that present elements of cultural pride and relate those events to the idea of leadership.

Share. Second, sharing facilitates the transformational learning process by providing an element of feedback. Sharing should be done intentionally and include members within one's network that the BIPOC leader can trust. The objective in the sharing step is to discover any gaps or oversights by gaining feedback from an individual that knows the leader well. Following this, the leader will return to step one to reflect on learning through the sharing process.

Act. Now that the BIPOC leader has undergone the iterative process of reflecting and sharing, they can now put their new understanding of self and the world into action. With this step, the leader aims to integrate

Table 5.1

A Guided Self-Narrative Practice for BIPOC Leaders

Guided Self-Narrative

The purpose of this guided self-narrative practice is to help you bolster and integrate a positive racial identity with your leadership role and leadership identity. This guided self-narrative practice includes three major sections that you should complete in sequential order: reflection, sharing, and action. You may revisit this self-narrative practice as often as needed.

Reflection. *Set a time for 5–15 minutes to reflect on each question. Your answers to these questions will create a personalized leadership narrative.*

1. Describe 2–3 events and/or experiences in your past that have shaped the way you understand and express your racial identity.
2. What does your evaluation of race lead you to DO and NOT DO in your leadership role?
3. Describe 2–3 events and/or experiences in your past that have shaped the way you view what it means to be an effective leader.
4. At what point in time did you begin to see yourself as a leader?
5. Has your racial identity conflicted with your leader identity? How have you coped with identity conflicts of this nature?
6. List 5–10 positive attributes that you believe relate to your racial identity or culture. Include ways that you have embodied or embraced these attributes in the past.
7. How can you or how have you used our own culture as a strength in your leadership roles?

Sharing. *Share your personal narrative with three people in your social network and ask the following questions.*

1. What aspects of this narrative do/don't demonstrate who I am to you?
2. Are there any aspects of my narrative that are largely left out or understated in my leadership practice?
3. If you were writing my narrative, what would you include or exclude that I didn't?

Action. *Answer the following questions based on the information that you gathered from your reflection and sharing.*

1. Considering your reflection, what leadership actions should you pay close attention to or monitor?
2. What leadership behaviors do you wish to eliminate? And when are these behaviors most likely to occur?
3. What leadership behaviors do you wish to amplify? And how can you incorporate those behaviors more?

the positive aspects of race and their practice of leadership to reach a personalized understanding of who they are as a leader. The leader can pay attention to the actions they once performed, which they may want to eliminate now. Or they may wish to amplify prior behaviors more than before. Although action is the final step in the process, we suggest that the leader cycles back through reflecting and sharing. In this regard, the self-narrative process is long-lasting and buffers the racial microaggressions over time.

The self-narrative process of reflecting, sharing, and acting works together to support the BIPOC's leader identity development in two ways. First, a self-narrative practice can facilitate the TL process, allowing for a proactive method to addressing racial microaggressions in the workplace. Second, a self-narrative practice focused on an individual's race across the lifespan can bolster a positive racial identity for BIPOC leaders. Overall, BIPOC leaders can use a positive racial identity to buffer the negative impact of microaggressions on leader identity development.

DISCUSSION

There is a lack of representation of BIPOC leaders in top leadership positions across the U.S. White men make up only 35% of the U.S. population, yet they hold 90% of Fortune 500 CEO positions (Zweigenhaft, 2020). Although many organizations indicate they aspire to be inclusive (Stark, 2021), inclusivity will not be achieved without the development and placement of BIPOC leaders. System-wide organizational change is needed to bridge the racial leadership gap. In this chapter, we focus on one crucial piece of building this bridge—BIPOC leader development. Specifically, we re-envision and expand extant dominant theories on leader identity development through a racial lens.

Identifying as a leader is an essential first step along any aspiring leader's leader development journey. When one integrates a leader identity into their sense of self, they are more likely to exert more effort toward their development and engage in more leader-like behaviors. These are critical endeavors for long-term leader development. In addition to the cultivation of expertise, leader identity development is considered a socially defined and constructed process. Aspiring leaders make claims toward leadership by engaging in leader-like behaviors (e.g., persuasion, initiating structure, decision-making), and their work circle responds by either granting or denying those claims (DeRue & Ashford, 2010). When granted, the aspiring leader continues with more leadership claims, and as others continue with more grants, an upward spiral of leader identity occurs as a result. Their leader identity strengthens and becomes integrated into their sense of self. On the other hand, when claims are met with denials, fewer claims follow, more denials continue, a negative spiral occurs, and the aspiring leader has a weakened leader identity.

Viewing this social constructivist perspective of leader identity development through a racial lens, we argue that racial microaggressions—or frequent, ambiguous, and unconscious slights related to one's race (Sue et al., 2009)—constitute denials of leadership for aspiring BIPOC leaders and threaten their leader identity development. Racial microaggressions are common occurrences within the workplace and predict adverse outcomes for racial minorities (Wong et al., 2014). Racial microaggressions send the message to aspiring BIPOC leaders that they do not belong. They are not part of the in-group. They are not a leadership prototype. They will not be followed by group members. These subtle but powerful messages undermine aspiring BIPOC leaders' leadership claims and threaten their leader identity development.

Prior research proposes more reactive strategies for coping with identity threats and focuses on the negative impact of identity threats (Kreiner & Sheep, 2009). However, a few scholars have urged for the exploration of positive buffers against adverse events, specifically identity threats (Maitlis, 2009). We argue that the practice of transformational learning through self-narratives strengthening one's positive racial identity can buffer the negative impact of racial microaggressions on BIPOC leaders' leader identity development. In this case, the practice of race-specific self-narratives can support the leader identity development process for BIPOC leaders.

This chapter adds to the literature by (1) addressing the context of race in leadership and (2) adding to the research on positive identities and positive growth through transformational learning theory. First, race is an essential contextual feature in the process of leadership and leader development (Ospina & Foldy, 2009). However, few studies address the role of race in the leader development process. Further, much of the research on race and leadership focuses on how others view and respond to BIPOC leaders (Ospina & Foldy, 2009). This chapter considers the role of race in the process of leader development by looking at the shift of an individual's leader identity as it relates to race-related events. In this way, the precursor and process of leader development are expanded and more inclusive of racial diversity.

Second, this chapter also adds to the positive lens of identity research and positive growth. With the advent of positive psychology, scholars have called for the consideration of more positive aspects of the human experience (Seligman & Csikszentmihalyi, 2014). This chapter looked towards the possibility of positive change for leaders due to racial microaggressions in the workplace. Kreiner and Sheep (2009) characterized identity threats as an opportunity to counteract an opposing force for personal gain. This area of research is growing. For example, Maitlis (2009) viewed posttraumatic events and experiences as an opportunity for growth. Although racial microaggressions are significant forms of identity threat for BIPOC leaders, there remains considerable room for growth and development. Specifically, through TL and the practice of crafting a self-narrative, BIPOC leaders can engage positive and proactive strategies to buffer the negative impacts of racial microaggressions.

Practical Implications

As explained, there are agentic and powerful actions that BIPOC leaders can take to support the development of a positive and integrated leader identity. BIPOC leaders should engage in self-narratives as a self-directed exercise. Specifically, BIPOC leaders can complete the guided self-narrative reflection found in Table 5.1. The self-narrative aligns with leader self-development initiatives and supports not only leader identity but also a positive racial identity (Reichard & Johnson, 2011). Organizations can facilitate this self-narrative process for BIPOC leaders by guiding them through the three-step self-narrative practice (i.e., reflect, share, and act) and by creating space for racial exploration and expression. Further, training initiatives can support the self-narrative process by providing structured courses on the malleability of identities such as a leader identity and racial identity.

Despite our focus in this chapter on what BIPOC leaders can do to buffer the negative impacts of existing racial microaggressions in the workplace, organizations have the responsibility to intentionally change perpetrators' points of view and behaviors related to racial microaggressions in the workplace. Accordingly, organizations must take steps to monitor, record, and respond to racial microaggressions. To better respond and prevent racial microaggressions from spreading across the workplace, organizations must analyze the impact of their culture and the behaviors of their top leadership team (Travis & Nugent, 2019). Prioritizing inclusivity and psychological safety can help reduce racial microaggressions in the workplace (Diaz, 2021). Overall, organizations should be mindful of the hidden barriers and obstacles that BIPOC leaders face in the workplace, especially those that hinder the leader development process. Understanding the role of racial microaggressions in leader identity development opens conversations about a more inclusive and diverse leadership pipeline.

Future Research

As mentioned, the most influential publications in the field of leader development have been written by and based on samples of White men (Vogel et al., 2021). As a result, evidence-based leader development practices to guide aspiring BIPOC leaders and supportive managers and organizations are nearly absent from the literature. There is a desperate need for more research on racial diversity and race-related concerns and experiences in the field of leader development. There is virtually no research on the leader development experience for BIPOC leaders. To move the field forward, future research can take on one or more of the following approaches ranging from incremental to holistic shifts.

Beginning with the basics, leadership and leader development researchers can aim to include more racially diverse samples in their studies. Currently, leader development research and practice are based on White samples, creating a gap and challenge for understanding how BIPOC leaders may differ in their developmental process. Accordingly, a basic standard for leader development research can include actively seeking a racially diverse sample. This approach may help researchers move in the right direction but may not tap into the nuanced and unique experiences of BIPOC leaders.

The second approach for researchers is to expand upon and re-envision existing leader development theory by including a racial lens. This approach is similar to one taken in this chapter, where we examined the dominant leader identity development theories through the lens of aspiring BIPOC leaders. As a result, we have opened up new research opportunities to empirically test the role of a positive racial identity as a buffering moderator of the negative effects of racial microaggressions on leader identity development. Similarly, scholars should re-envision other leader development theories and processes such as feedback interventions, job rotations, and stretch assignments through a racial lens. With this approach, researchers can better understand how the existing theories of leader development operate for BIPOC leaders and create opportunities for new empirical research. Although this approach of theory expansion is an improvement over simply diversifying the samples studied, it is still limited to reconceptualizing extant leader development theories, which originated from a White perspective. It is possible that the existing theories artificially confine and compromise the integrity of BIPOC leaders' experiences.

Therefore, the third and most holistic approach for researchers is to conceptualize new theories of leader development originating in BIPOC leaders' experiences. A grounded theory approach to the study of BIPOC leader development could contribute to not only new theories and research but new and more inclusive practices of leader development. Researchers can start with comprehensive and open-ended questions such as what is the experience of BIPOC leaders who desire to develop leadership skills in the workplace. Another area of investigation is to study when BIPOC leaders' experience the most leader development growth. With this frame-breaking approach, the experiences of BIPOC leaders are not only acknowledged but are affirmed as potential sources for theory creation.

CONCLUSION

Positive leader identity development is crucial for aspiring BIPOC leaders. Racial microaggressions are a common form of racial discrimination and frequently occur within the workplace. Racial microaggressions harm BIPOC employees' leader development journey as a threat to their leader identity. We provide a proactive and positive coping mechanism that aspiring BIPOC leaders can engage in, to help buffer the negative impact of racial microaggressions and develop a positive leader identity. This chapter adds to the literature on leader identity development by outlining the role of race and race-related events that impact leader development.

REFERENCES

Avolio, B. J., & Gardner, W. L. (2005). Authentic leadership development: Getting to the root of positive forms of leadership. *The Leadership Quarterly*, *16*(3), 315–338.

Avolio, B. J., & Hannah, S. T. (2008). Developmental readiness: Accelerating leader development. *Consulting Psychology Journal: Practice and Research*, *60*(4), 331.

Baumeister, R. F. (2010). The self. In R. F. Baumeister & E. J. Finkel (Eds.), *Advanced social psychology: The state of the science* (p. 139–175). Oxford University Press.

Brondolo, E., Brady VerHalen, N. B., Pencille, M., Beatty, D., & Contrada, R. J. (2009). Coping with racism: a selective review of the literature and a theoretical and methodological critique. *Journal of Behavioral Medicine*, *32*(1), 64–84.

Brown, A. D. (2015). Identities and identity work in organizations. *International Journal of Management Reviews*, *17*(1), 20–40.

Brown, A. D., & Coupland, C. (2015). Identity threats, identity work and elite professionals. *Organization Studies*, *36*(10), 1315–1336.

Burke, P. J. (1991). Identity processes and social stress. *American Sociological Review*, *56*(6), 836-849.

Burke, P. J., & Stets, J. E. (2009). *Identity theory*. Oxford University Press.

Cameron, K. S., Dutton, J. E., & Quinn, R. E. (2003). An introduction to positive organizational scholarship. *Positive Organizational Scholarship*, pp. 3–13.

Carton, A. M., & Rosette, A. S. (2011). Explaining bias against black leaders: Integrating theory on information processing and goal-based stereotyping. *Academy of Management Journal*, *54*(6), 1141–1158.

Chan, K. Y., & Drasgow, F. (2001). Toward a theory of individual differences and leadership: understanding the motivation to lead. *Journal of Applied psychology*, *86*(3), 481.

Clark, M. C. (1993). Transformational learning. *New Directions for Adult and Continuing Education*, *1993*(57), 47–56.

Day, D. V., & Dragoni, L. (2015). Leadership development: An outcome-orientated review based on time and levels of analyses. *Annual Review Organizational Psychology Organizational Behavior*, *2*(1), 133–156.

Day, D. V., & Sin, H. P. (2011). Longitudinal tests of an integrative model of leader development: Charting and understanding developmental trajectories. *The Leadership Quarterly*, *22*(3), 545–560.

Day, D. V., Harrison, M. M., & Halpin, S. M. (2008). *An integrative approach to leader development: Connecting adult development, identity, and expertise.* Routledge.

DeRue, D. S., & Ashford, S. J. (2010). Who will lead and who will follow? A social process of leadership identity construction in organizations. *Academy of Management Review*, *35*(4), 627–647.

Diaz, J. B. B. (2021). *Risky business: Leveraging psychological safety in the pursuit of workplace equity* [Manuscript submitted for publication]. Department of Behavioral and Organizational Sciences, Claremont Graduate University.

Dutton, J. E., Roberts, L. M., & Bednar, J. (2009). Positive identities and organizations: An introduction and invitation. In L. M. Roberts & James E. Dutton (Eds.), *Exploring positive identities and organizations: Building a theoretical and research foundation* (pp. 4–19). Psychology Press.

Eagly, A. H., & Chin, J. L. (2010). Diversity and leadership in a changing world. *American Psychologist*, *65*(3), 216.

Epitropaki, O., Kark, R., Mainemelis, C., & Lord, R. G. (2017). Leadership and followership identity processes: A multilevel review. *The Leadership Quarterly*, *28*(1), 104–129.

Folkman, S., & Lazarus, R. S. (1984). *Stress, appraisal, and coping*. Springer.

Forsyth, J., & Carter, R. T. (2012). The relationship between racial identity status attitudes, racism-related coping, and mental health among Black Americans. *Cultural Diversity and Ethnic Minority Psychology*, *18*(2), 128.

Gergen, K. J., & Gergen, M. M. (1986). Narrative form and the construction of psychological science. In T. R. Sarbin (Ed.), *Narrative psychology: The storied nature of human conduct* (p. 22–44). Praeger Publishers/Greenwood Publishing Group.

Hammond, M., Clapp-Smith, R., & Palanski, M. (2017). Beyond (just) the workplace: A theory of leader development across multiple domains. *Academy of Management Review*, *43*(3), 481–498.

Harper, S. R. (2007). Peer support for African American male college achievement: Beyond internalized racism and the burden of "acting White". *The Journal of Men's Studies*, *14*(3), 337–358.

Hecht, B. (2020). *Moving beyond diversity toward racial equity.* https://hbr.org/2020/06/moving-beyond-diversity-toward-racial-equity

Helms, J. E. (1992). Why is there no study of cultural equivalence in standardized cognitive ability testing? A*merican Psychologist*, *47*(9), 1083–1101.

Hogg, M. A. (2001). A social identity theory of leadership. *Personality and Social Psychology Review*, *5*(3), 184–200.

Ibarra, H., Wittman, S., Petriglieri, G., & Day, D. V. (2014). Leadership and identity: An examination of three theories and new research directions. In D. V. Day (Ed.), *The Oxford handbook of leadership and organizations*, (pp. 285–301). Oxford University Press.

Jost, J. T., Rudman, L. A., Blair, I. V., Carney, D. R., Dasgupta, N., Glaser, J., & Hardin, C. D. (2009). The existence of implicit bias is beyond reasonable doubt: A refutation of ideological and methodological objections and executive summary of ten studies that no manager should ignore. *Research in Organizational Behavior*, *29*, 39–69.

Karp, T., & Helgø, T. I. (2009). Leadership as identity construction: The act of leading people in organisations. *Journal of Management Development, 28*(10), 880–896.

Kegan, R. (1983). *The evolving self: Problem and process in human development*. Harvard University Press.

Kempster, S. (2006). Leadership learning through lived experience: A process of apprenticeship? *Journal of Management & Organization, 12*(1), 4–22.

Kreiner, G. E., & Sheep, M. L. (2009). Growing pains and gains: Framing identity dynamics as opportunities for identity growth. In L. M. Roberts & J. E. Dutton (Eds.), Exploring positive identities and organizations: *Building a theoretical and research foundation* (pp. 47–70). Routledge.

Lord, R. G., & Hall, R. J. (2005). Identity, deep structure and the development of leadership skill. *The Leadership Quarterly, 16*(4), 591–615

Lord, R. G., & Maher, K. J. (1990). Perceptions of leadership and their implications in organizations. J. S. Carroll (Ed.), *Applied social psychology and organizational settings* (pp. 129–154). Psychology Press

Maitlis, S. (2009). Who am I now? Sensemaking and identity in posttraumatic growth. In L. M. Roberts & J. E. Dutton (Eds.), *Exploring positive identities and organizations* (pp. 71–100). Psychology Press.

Major, B., & O'Brien, L. T. (2005). The social psychology of stigma. *Annual Review of Psychology, 56*, 393–421.

Major, B., Quinton, W., McCoy, S., & Schmader, T. (2000). Reducing prejudice: The target's perspective. In S. Oskamp (Ed.), *Reducing prejudice and discrimination* (pp. 211–237). Lawrence Erlbaum Associates

Mead, G. H. (1934). Mind, self and society (Vol. 111). In C. W. Morris (Eds.), *Quarrel between invariance and flux: A guide for philosophers and other players* (pp. 223–234). University of Chicago Press.

Meyer, P. (2009). Chapter 3: Learning space/work space: Can we make room for transformative learning in organizations? *Counterpoints, 341*, 43–63.

Mezirow, J. (1990). *How critical reflection triggers transformative learning. Fostering critical reflection in adulthood* (pp. 1–20). Jossey-Bass

Mezirow, J. (2002). Transformative learning: Theory to practice. *New Directions for Adult and Continuing Education, 1997*(74), 5–12.

Middleton, E. D., Walker, D. O., & Reichard, R. J. (2019). Developmental trajectories of leader identity: Role of learning goal orientation. *Journal of Leadership & Organizational Studies, 26*(4), 495–509.

Miscenko, D., Guenter, H., & Day, D. V. (2017). Am I a leader? Examining leader identity development over time. *The Leadership Quarterly, 28*(5), 605–620.

Omi, M., & Winant, H. (1994). *Racial Formation in the U.S.: From the 1960s to the 1990s*. Routledge.

Ospina, S., & Foldy, E. (2009). A critical review of race and ethnicity in the leadership literature: Surfacing context, power and the collective dimensions of leadership. *The Leadership Quarterly, 20*(6), 876–896.

Petriglieri, J. L. (2011). Under threat: Responses to and the consequences of threats to individuals' identities. *Academy of Management Review, 36*(4), 641–662.

Pierce, C. (1995). Stress analogs of racism and sexism: Terrorism, torture, and disaster. *Mental Health, Racism, and Sexism, 33*, 277–293.

Reichard, R. J., & Johnson, S. K. (2011). Leader self-development as organizational strategy. *The Leadership Quarterly, 22*(1), 33–42.

Roberson, Q. M. (2019). Diversity in the workplace: A review, synthesis, and future research agenda. *Annual Review of Organizational Psychology and Organizational Behavior, 6*, 69–88.

Roberts, L. M., Mayo, A. J., & Thomas, D. A. (2019). *Race, work, and leadership: New perspectives on the Black experience.* Harvard Business Press.

Rosette, A. S., Leonardelli, G. J., & Phillips, K. W. (2008). The White standard: racial bias in leader categorization. *Journal of Applied Psychology, 93*(4), 758.

Rosette, A. S., & Tost, L. P. (2010). Agentic women and communal leadership: How role prescriptions confer advantage to top women leaders. *Journal of Applied Psychology, 95*(2), 221.

Sandberg, J., & Tsoukas, H. (2015). Making sense of the sensemaking perspective: Its constituents, limitations, and opportunities for further development. *Journal of Organizational Behavior, 36*(S1), S6–S32.

Seligman, M. E., & Csikszentmihalyi, M. (2014). Positive psychology: An introduction. In M. Csikszentmihalyi (Ed.), *Flow and the foundations of positive psychology* (pp. 279–298). Springer.

Shamir, B., & Eilam, G. (2005). "What's your story?" A life-stories approach to authentic leadership development. *The Leadership Quarterly, 16*(3), 395–417.

Singer, J. A., & Blagov, P. S. (2004). Self-defining memories, narrative identity, and psychotherapy. In L. E. Angus & J. McLeod (Eds.), *The handbook of narrative and psychotherapy: Practice, theory and research,* (pp. 229–239). SAGE.

Stark, A. (2021). *Top ten work trends for 2021.* https://www.siop.org/Research-Publications/Items-of-Interest/ArtMID/19366/ArticleID/4914/Top-10-Work-Trends-for-2021

Sue, D. W. (Ed.). (2010). *Microaggressions and marginality: Manifestation, dynamics, and impact.* John Wiley & Sons.

Sue, D. W., Capodilupo, C. M., Torino, G. C., Bucceri, J. M., Holder, A., Nadal, K. L., & Esquilin, M. (2007). Racial microaggressions in everyday life: implications for clinical practice. *American Psychologist, 62*(4), 271.

Sue, D. W., Lin, A. I., & Rivera, D. P. (2009). Racial microaggressions in the workplace: Manifestation and impact. In J. L. Chin (Ed.), *Diversity in mind and in action, Vol. 2. Disparities and competence* (pp. 157–172). Praeger/ABC-CLIO.

Swerzenski, J. D. (2020). *Where are the Hispanic executives?* https://www.latinousa.org/2020/01/27/hispanicexecs/

Taylor, S. N., & Hood, J. N. (2011). It may not be what you think: Gender differences in predicting emotional and social competence. *Human Relations, 64*(5), 627–652.

Travis, D. J., & Nugent, J. S. (2019). *Culture matters: Unpacking change and achieving inclusion*. https://www.catalyst.org/wp-content/uploads/2019/02/culture_matters_unpacking_change_and_achieving_inclusion_1.pdf

Vogel, B., Reichard, R. J., Batistič, S., & Černe, M. (2021). A bibliometric review of the leadership development field: How we got here, where we are, and where we are headed. *The Leadership Quarterly, 32*(5), 101381.

Wong, G., Derthick, A. O., David, E. J. R., Saw, A., & Okazaki, S. (2014). The what, the why, and the how: A review of racial microaggressions research in psychology. *Race and Social Problems, 6*(2), 181–200.

Yip, J., & Wilson, M. S. (2010). Learning from experience. In E. V. Velsor, C. D. McCauley, & M. N. Ruderman (Eds.), *The Center for Creative Leadership handbook of leadership development* (pp. 63–95). Jossey-Bass.

Zweigenhaft, R. (2020). *Fortune 500 CEOs, 2000–2020: Still male, Still White*. https://thesocietypages.org/specials/fortune-500-ceos-2000-2020-still-male-still-white/

CHAPTER 6

THE IMPACT OF MEGA-THREATS AND POLITICAL IDEOLOGY ON BLACK EMPLOYEES

**Sydney N. Green, Gino J. Howard,
Hannah Perkins Stark**
Louisiana State University

Horatio D. Traylor,
University of Houston

Rachel Williamson Smith
Georgia Southern University

ABSTRACT

The purpose of this chapter is to push the boundaries of diversity research within the field of management to consider the impact of outside sources (i.e., mega-threats and political ideology) on Black employees. The chapter uses critical race theory and realistic group conflict theory to conceptualize the links between employee well-being and contextual (diversity climate and mega-threats) and individual (political ideology) factors. We review recent calls for scholars to address unanswered questions such as: How do mega-threats impact minority stress and employee interactions? How does knowing

The Future of Scholarship on Race in Organizations, pp. 119–136
Copyright © 2022 by Information Age Publishing
All rights of reproduction in any form reserved.

a coworker's political ideology affect interactions in the workplace? Are conflicts related to political ideology mega-threats? We also aim to further the development of human recourse strategies to mitigate and, perhaps, even prevent negative employee interactions, increased racial stress, and impaired employee performance following a mega-event or political ideology conflict.

THE IMPACT OF MEGA-THREATS AND POLITICAL IDEOLOGY ON BLACK EMPLOYEES

With over 23,000 incidents reported to the Equal Employment Opportunity Commission (EEOC) in the year 2019, workplace racial discrimination continues to be a large problem for racial minority (e.g., Black) employees (U.S. Equal Employment Opportunity Commission, 2020). Organizational leaders should be concerned with the way in which overt and more modern, subtle forms of racism in the work environment (e.g., microaggressions, social exclusion) function to exacerbate racial minority employee stress. The past three decades of discrimination research within the fields of management and psychology have made significant strides in the theoretical conceptualization of racial discrimination with the goal of increasing racial minority employee protection and reducing racial discrimination. Although research indicates that providing an environment for inclusivity (i.e., diversity climate) can significantly enhance employee performance (Boehm et al., 2014) and the well-being of racial minority employees (Holmes et al., 2020), workplace discrimination remains a major source of stress for many Black employees. We begin this chapter by exploring the concept of racial discrimination and diversity climate in the context of critical race theory (CRT; Delgado & Stefancic, 2001) and realistic group conflict theory (RGCT; Campbell, 1965). We then discuss the newly introduced construct of mega-threats, which are highly publicized, negative events that relate to diversity (Leigh & Melwani, 2019). Lastly, we explore the potential impact of political ideology on marginalized (i.e., Black) employee's experiences in the workplace.

Critical Race Theory

CRT originated in the 1970s in response to the increasingly popular argument that the progression of obtaining equal rights for Black Americans and reducing racial discrimination had slowed because it no longer converged with the interests of White Americans (Delgado & Stefancic, 2001). Racial discrimination is conceptualized as the unjustified mistreatment of racial minority individuals that ultimately undermines racial equity

(Fiske, 1998). The seminal book written by Delgado and Stefancic (2001) thoroughly synthesizes CRT and its components. The first and most central component of CRT asserts that the current laws prohibiting Anti-Black discrimination protects Black Americans from overt forms of racism (e.g., race-based violence) but not from subtle forms of racism. There are numerous forms of subtle racial discrimination Black Americans experience daily, including denial of bank loans, apartments, and jobs, being imprisoned and impoverished, and receiving worse medical care compared to White Americans (Delgado & Stefancic, 2001). Furthermore, compared to White Americans, Black Americans live shorter lives, complete fewer years of schooling, and occupy more menial jobs (Delgado & Stefancic, 2001).

Media-sensationalized events (i.e., mega-threats) signaling the social inferiority of Black Americans compared to White Americans, such as the higher rates of lethal police force toward Black individuals (Brown, 2021) is one of the more modern forms of racism potentially exacerbating the minority stress experienced by Black employees. DeCuir-Gunby and Gunby (2016) utilize CRT to understand the impact that racism can have on Black employees in the workplace. CRT posits that White supremacy is fundamental to work and life in the U.S. and that racially inequitable organizational procedures (e.g., unfavorably biased performance evaluations, less opportunity for career advancement) and subtle forms of racial discrimination outside of the workplace (i.e., mega-threats) are to be expected.

According to CRT, certain manifestations of racism in the workplace are unavoidable because racism is systematically engrained within society, socially and economically. Mega-threats involving violence toward Black Americans can be thought of as another manifestation of the systemic racism engrained within society. There is extensive evidence in the organizational diversity literature to suggest that the prejudice experienced by Black employees, even by proxy (i.e., seeing the murder of George Floyd on TV or social media), can have direct effects on their well-being and work outcomes (Himle et al., 2009); however, many cases of race-related stress go unnoticed, unreported, and untreated (Williams et al., 2018).

The racial stress resulting from discriminatory treatment has received considerable attention over the past couple of decades. Indeed, many scholars have observed racial discrepancies in the amount of psychological trauma experienced by Black individuals compared to White individuals and theorize that racial discrimination is the cause (Williams et al., 2018). Psychological trauma is a general term utilized in several disciplines to assess the link between physically or psychologically threatening circumstances and long-lasting functional impairment (Williams et al., 2018). The concept of racial stress is more common in diversity research and refers to the adverse physical and psychological consequences that results from repeatedly experiencing racial discrimination and subsequent feelings of distress, frustration, and anxiety (Comas-Díaz et al., 2019). Mega-threats such as the January 6, 2021, attack on the U.S. Capitol building, the police shootings of Black individuals, the unprovoked harassment of Black U.S. Army personnel, and the trial of Derek Chauvin in the death of George Floyd, ultimately threaten the livelihood of Black Americans and, potentially, lead to more feelings of fear, distress, frustration, and anxiety (Brown, 2021). Himle et al. (2009) noted that the prevalence of PTSD was 9.1% for Black Americans compared to 6.8% for non-Hispanic White Americans. Himle et al. (2009) also noted that the association between psychological trauma and impaired functionality at work is stronger for Black employees compared to White employees.

Furthermore, when compared to White Americans, Black Americans can provide written accounts of incidents of racial stress much easier, which is attributed to the stress levels of Black Americans being inherently greater (Plummer & Slane, 1996). Black Americans also exhibit more fluctuation in the types of coping strategies that they adopt. Given the higher levels of stress (in comparison to White Americans), Black Americans may have more experience coping in general, but engage in less coping from racially stressful situations than generally stressful situations. Scholars have theorized that White Americans may lack the appropriate coping skills for handling racial stressors (compared to Black Americans) because White Americans do not experience racial stressors as often (Plummer & Slane, 1996).

As corporations in America work to increase diversity, a culmination of ethnicities and ideologies (e.g., values and beliefs) will become ever-present and employee conflict may increasingly occur. Racial stress frequently arises from negative interracial interactions (e.g., microaggressions), or individuals of different cultures and ideologies engaging in conflict and can cause considerable psychological discomfort. According to Plummer and Slane (1996), an increasingly diverse society escalates the likelihood of experiencing racial stress. Examining the effect of stress experienced by Black employees has become even more critical for reducing racial discrimination in the workplace given the recent increase in race-related contention in the United States. A significant portion of the racial diversity research utilizes another theory, RGCT, to predict antecedents and outcomes of racial discrimination, which we discuss in detail next.

Realistic Group Conflict Theory

According to RGCT, intergroup conflict is commonly preceded by opposing group goals (i.e., the goals of one group interfere with the goals of another group) (Campbell, 1965). This conflict between groups, and the associated social tension, may be reduced when the groups' goals are convergent and when members from each individual group choose to cooperate with each other (Campbell, 1965). In addition to mega-threats, conflicts related to political ideology (i.e., liberal versus conservative ideals) may negatively impact Black employees' well-being (e.g., level of stress and anxiety) and their work outcomes (e.g., work engagement and performance).

Intergroup relations are influenced by internal and external group factors such as group history and the social context of the intergroup exchange (Tajfel & Turner, 1986). Stereotyping and social ostracism (i.e., the deliberate rejection of certain individuals) are frequently associated with "us" and "them" mentalities, or in other words, eliciting ingroups and outgroups (e.g., liberal employees versus conservative employees) in the workplace. When a conflict arises from one group's gain resulting in another group's loss, the losing group is even more likely to stereotype the winning group (Campbell, 1965). Over time, this stereotype is solidified, leading to increased group conflict. This is evident in the growing divide between major political parties in the United States. Stereotyping outgroup members is associated with greater intragroup solidarity, as group members continue to give greater meaning to their group identity and internalize group norms (Sherif & Sherif, 1979). Some racial diversity scholars utilize RGCT to help explain why conflict frequently occurs in racially diverse work groups, while other forms of diversity, such as educational diversity, is associated with increased group innovation (Mannix & Neale, 2005).

In line with RGCT, Brief et al. (2005) found that as perceptions of organizational diversity increased, White employees' perceptions of quality of work relationships decreased. Moreover, this relationship was strengthened as White employees reported increasing proximity to Black individuals in their neighborhoods. Brief et al. also found that White applicants who attributed higher levels of conflict in their neighborhoods to other racial groups viewed organizations as more unattractive when the organization reported high levels of diversity. Researchers suggest perceived threat experienced by White Americans will lead to more prejudice, reinforcing the ingroup-outgroup dynamic of RGCT (Zárate et al., 2004). These results support RGCT, such that outgroups perceived as a threat by ingroups are assigned negative stereotypes. While studying racial discrimination in hiring processes through the lens of RGCT, Goldman and colleagues (2019) found that Black applicants receive lower desirability ratings from White hiring managers compared to White applicants with equivalent criminal records. Additionally, White hiring managers justified their choice to reject Black applicants by reporting an increased risk of harm and poorer character of the applicant compared to a White applicant that committed the same crime. These results reflect RGCT such that, from the perspective of the hiring manager, the outgroup member is threatening to take a scarce resource (i.e., the job opportunity) from an ingroup member. Thus, by discriminating against outgroup members, the hiring manager is showing preference for other ingroup members. By highlighting the negative attributes of the outgroup members, the hiring manager, whether intentionally or inadvertently, appreciates the positive attributes of the ingroup, while simultaneously perpetuating the negative stereotypes of the outgroup.

RGCT posits that groups may only overcome intergroup conflict when they share a common goal which they are unable to achieve without collaborating with the other group (Sherif & Sherif, 1979). The communication and contact required to achieve the shared goal leads to reduced friction between groups and extinguishes the negative labels assigned during the conflict. As the groups engage in more positive experiences with one another, they improve their levels of intergroup understanding and acceptance. Sherif and Sherif (1979) highlight the importance of repeated positive interactions over an extended period. Repeatedly experiencing positive interactions, however, is just one instance of intergroup harmony, and is not influential enough to eliminate all the potential negative feelings about the outgroup. While studying intergroup hostility between groups at a boy's summer camp, Sherif et al. (1961) introduced multiple goals that required intergroup cooperation such as requiring the boys to pool their money to purchase a movie. Their results supported one of the core principles of RCGT, which states that if competing groups share multiple goals that are only attainable through intergroup cooperation, forced contact over a period will lead to decreased friction between group members and increased intergroup appreciation (Sherif et al., 1961).

Unfortunately, a lack of agreement regarding the antecedents of racial conflict in the workplace (e.g., diversity climate), ultimately impedes advances in research that could provide insight into strategies aimed at increasing feelings of equality among racial minority employees (Holmes et al., 2020). One obstacle often faced by discrimination scholars is the inconsistent theoretical conceptualization of diversity climate, a contextual factor that should, theoretically, moderate the association between racial discrimination and important outcomes like employee performance. Diversity climate refers to how much the organization promotes fair human resource policies and facilitates social cohesion among underrepresented employees (McKay et al., 2008). Cox's (1994) interactional model of cultural diversity (IMCD) asserts that a low diversity climate may lead to decreases in employee satisfaction, commitment, and performance (Holmes et al., 2020). On the other hand, a high diversity climate may prevent high rates of employee disengagement and turnover. Some scholars assert that the diversity climate-outcome association should only be studied at the group-level (i.e., individual perceptions of diversity climate are assessed for within-group agreement and then aggregated). However, compared to studies exploring the diversity climate-outcome association at the group-level, studies exploring the association at the individual-level are more common (Holmes et al., 2020).

One of the assumptions of another diversity climate theory, Nishii's (2013) climate for inclusion theoretical framework, argues that diversity climate is an individual-level construct. According to Nishi, a high climate for inclusion should, theoretically, allow individual employees to express more than one of their social identities (e.g., Black sexual orientation minority American), and to form connections with diverse others from all levels within their organization. Nishii also points out that to truly target and mitigate instances of racial discrimination experienced by Black employees, traditional training interventions may not suffice because they typically only address tangible instances of racial discrimination (e.g., racially biased rates of promotion). On the other hand, diversity climate, or climate for inclusion, addresses the interpersonal aspect of the environment. Employers are encouraged to allow their employees with different demographic backgrounds to get to know each other personally rather than relying on stereotypes and to collaborate in achieving prespecified goals (Nishii, 2013).

When marginalized employees observe instances of violence toward other marginalized individuals (i.e., mega-threats) and, perhaps, experience sadness, fear, or anger as a result, their work performance may be negatively impacted. Subsequently, organizations aiming to foster an inclusive work climate can benefit from providing marginalized employees with a dedicated space (e.g., engaging in active listening and developing actionable goals to address employee concerns) after a mega-threat has occurred (Brown, 2021). Although scholars have proposed strategies (e.g., mentoring and coaching) to improve organizations' diversity climate and reduce racial discrimination, theory (CRT and RGCT) and research indicates that incidents occurring outside of the organization (i.e., mega-threats and political ideology conflict) are becoming increasingly salient sources of employee stress (Humberd et al., 2015). Next, we discuss the concept of mega-threats and political ideology, followed by a discussion of their impact in the workplace.

Mega-Threats

According to CRT and RGCT, the complex experiences of Black employees may be significantly influenced by events taking place outside of the organization, including but not limited to the murder of and media-sensationalized instances of police brutality toward Black Americans

(Leigh & Melwani, 2019). The creation and subsequent development of the Black Lives Matter organization in 2013 has drawn the nation's attention to instances of human right violations against Black people in a novel way (Ashburn-Nardo, Thomas, & Robinson, 2017). It began as a way for social media users to connect over their outrage surrounding violence against young Black people, and has turned into an international movement, raising awareness against any form of mistreatment toward all Black individuals (i.e., man, woman, gender neutral, cis, queer, trans, citizen, undocumented). The collective outrage garnered by the organizers, followers, and allies of the Black Lives Matter organization has led to rallies, boycotts, town hall meetings, conferences between elected officials, and calls for legislative reform that may not have occurred otherwise (Ashburn-Nardo et al., 2017). Bringing attention to unacceptable violence against Black individuals can be critical to changing the current status quo. However, many Black individuals may experience increased stress from the constant reminder of such blatant discrimination occurring in a country that claims to treat all residents equally. Thus, mega-threats, or highly publicized, negative events relating to (anti-Black) discrimination (Leigh & Melwani, 2019), may be a unique and pervasive form of stress for Black individuals and have consequences extending into the organization.

Mega-threats may cause more fear and anxiety for individuals who can relate more to the victims' identities; however, the impact of mega-threats on employee well-being may be widespread such that all socially marginalized employees (e.g., racial minority, sexual orientation minority, and women) may feel sadness, hopelessness, fear, and/or anger after any mega-threat occurs. Though mega-threats are typically focused on a specific identity (e.g., Black Americans, Asian Americans, sexual orientation minority, women), witnessing mega-threats relating to the overt oppression of another marginalized group may lead to sadness, hopelessness, fear, and anger among Black employees though, perhaps, to a lesser extent. In line with CRT, mega-threats serve to perpetuate the systemic advantages given to able-bodied White heterosexual Christian males (e.g., receiving higher salaries, having more access to healthcare, being perceived as non-violent and more intelligent compared to other demographic groups). For instance, an LGBTQ Miami nightclub shooting that left 49 dead and 53 injured perpetuates the social inferiority of sexual orientation minority individuals. Along the same lines, legislation under the Trump administration allowed employers to fire an individual for identifying as gay, lesbian, or bisexual (Kalish Blair, 2016), and anti-Asian hate crimes spiked during the peak of the COVID-19 pandemic (e.g., violent attacks on Asian American owned businesses, overt harassment of Asian Americans). Both examples represent large-scale events that, ultimately, threaten the livelihood of all marginalized individuals.

Akin to the Black Lives Matter movement, anti-LGBTQ violence, the passing of legislation reducing access to reproductive healthcare (e.g., abortions) for women, the highly publicized instances of sexual harassment, and the resulting social movement, #MeToo, raises awareness against any form of mistreatment toward marginalized individuals (Wilson, 2020). Though these mega-threats may not be as salient to Black employees, they essentially increase awareness of inequities and injustices faced by other minority employees. Through both traditional (i.e., televised news) and social media outlets, these events highlight individuals' stories of discrimination and mistreatment that, according to CRT, expose the larger systems that maintain social inequalities and marginalize non-White, non-heterosexual men (Delgado & Stefancic, 2001).

In addition to providing victims with a platform to tell their story and a supportive community, the Black Lives Matter and #MeToo movements have shed light on workplace ostracism resulting from the disclosure of a discriminating or marginalizing experience (Brown & Battle, 2019). Before the Black Lives Matter and #MeToo movements, employees disclosing workplace discrimination or reacting to mega-threats were likely subjected to ostracism by their coworkers such that they may have been purposefully alienated or excluded from social exchanges by coworkers (Brown & Battle, 2019). Furthermore, privileged employees may be uncomfortable with discussing mega-threats because they feel helpless or guilty. Brown and Battle (2019) suggest that by drawing public attention to the negative effects that social isolation has on victims, these movements have increased bystander awareness of multiple forms of discrimination and the potential benefits of having constructive discussions surrounding these issues.

Organizations may have the potential to reduce some of the negative consequences associated with mega-threats (e.g., sadness, fear, anger, and hopelessness among marginalized employees, helplessness among privileged employees, and conflict between the two groups) through compassionate leadership and an inclusive work environment (Leigh & Melwani, 2019). Minority employees experiencing compassionate leadership and a high diversity climate may be better able to cope with their feelings (Leigh & Melwani, 2019). Plummer and Slane (1996) referenced two distinct types of coping that are particularly pertinent to racially stressful situations: problem-focused coping and emotion-focused coping (Lazarus & Folkman, 1984). Problem-focused coping (e.g., accepting responsibility, confrontive coping, planful problem solving, and seeking social support) involves behaviors and thoughts that attempt to address the source of stress. Emotion-focused coping (e.g., distancing, self-controlling, escape avoidance, and positive reappraisal) involves attempting to reduce the emotional responses experienced from a given stressor. Through problem-focused coping, both marginalized and privileged employees may be able to address issues relating to social marginalization (e.g., systemic racism and mega-threats). Unfortunately, mega-threats may continue cultivating fear and anxiety among marginalized employees; therefore, emotion-focused coping may be the more beneficial short-term strategy particularly for Black employees.

Oftentimes, Black employees are required to navigate racially charged work climates (i.e., low diversity climates), hoping to make sense of how they fit within the organization, the organization's broader geographic context, and their own marginalized social identity. This suggests that striving to effectively address racial discrimination and stress prompts organizations to focus on internal racially stressful events as well as the overall context in which the organization exists (Humberd et al., 2014; McCluney et al., 2017). If the organization provides support for their employees through a dedicated space and resources for marginalized employees to process their reactions to a particular mega-threat, in addition to fostering an inclusive climate, there may be a reduction in the detriment to employee well-being and withdrawal. Conversely, when organizations do not respond to or acknowledge mega-threats, the lack of appropriate response may manifest as stress and/or strain impacting marginalized and privileged employee behavior, as well as the broader organizational culture and climate.

Work attitudes (e.g., feelings of connectedness or alienation), in addition to the stress levels of Black employees, may be significantly impacted by mega-threats (Leigh & Melwani, 2019). Minority employees that feel their work environment is a safe place (i.e., high diversity climate) may choose to process mega-threats with their coworkers, such as through rumination, sharing the experiencing negative emotions, and engaging in group-level affective and/or cognitive processing. Mega-threats involving racial minority victims can frequently provoke revolutionary feelings in many employees, and especially racial minority employees. Employees in work environments with a high diversity climate may choose to decide whether they plan to actively respond (i.e., engage in positive deviance) with their workers. Positive deviance occurs when employees consciously defy rules or norms with the intent of benefitting their group and can occur internally or externally to the organization (Spreitzer & Sonenshein, 2004). Conversely, employees that do not feel that their work environment is a safe place for racial diversity (i.e., low diversity climate), or that they cannot share their attitudes about mega-threats with their coworkers, may be much less likely to engage in positive deviance (Leigh & Melwani, 2019). Their organizations may, eventually, miss the benefits that they would have gained had their employees engaged in risky behavior for the benefit of their group (e.g., making quality connections with diverse coworkers, defending their group) (Leigh & Melwani, 2019).

The #MeToo and Black Lives Matter movements have drawn substantial attention to the relationships between stigmatization, racism, and the undesirable individual, group, and organizational level outcomes previously stated in the chapter. Given that the future of the workforce (i.e., young adults) comprise the majority portion of Black Lives Matter movement followers, it is important that we understand the impact that social movements can have on members of the social identity group that is directly affected (Thomas & Ashburn-Nardo, 2020). For example, university faculty often witness the effects that the Black Lives Matter movement has on the experiences of their minority students (e.g., negative emotions, increased stress) (Thomas & Ashburn-Nardo, 2020). Because university faculty are disproportionately White, many of the social and educational inequalities, including instances of racial discrimination, experiences by racial minority students remain unidentified and unaddressed. Thomas and Ashburn-Nardo (2020) suggest that universities should increase faculty attention and support of racial minority students as they encounter stigmatization and racism in both the social and educational context. Moreover, universities and faculty members should provide minority students with the opportunity to form a collective group, to foster a sense of community and inclusion, and develop a voice to express group needs and to enact social change within their environment (Kanter, 2008; Thomas & Ashburn-Nardo, 2020). It is also recommended that, when hiring new faculty, universities should strive to increase racial diversity so that racial minority students have increased opportunities to form educational relationships with role models that have overlapping identities (Pietri et al., 2018; Thomas & Ashburn-Nardo, 2020).

Given the impact that mega-threats can have on employee outcomes and work group processes, methods typically utilized to improve the work experiences and outcomes of racial minority employees (e.g., diversity and inclusion training programs) may no longer be sufficient. To decrease workplace ostracism, Brown and Battle (2019) suggest that organizations explicitly address both intentional and unintentional ostracism as well as provide techniques that promote workplace cohesion. Such techniques may include interpersonal skill and conflict resolution trainings and guidelines for reporting instances of workplace ostracism. Organizations may implement these or similar programs to reduce the ostracism of other minority groups, as the intersectional identities of employees may result in compounding ostracism due to their membership in one or more minority groups (Cole, 2009; Crenshaw, 1991, as cited in Brown & Battle, 2019). Comparable to the faculty members studied by Thomas and Ashburn-Nardo (2020), organizational leaders should be cognizant of the inequalities faced by minority employees. For example, when hiring new employees, organizational leaders should also make efforts to increase racial diversity. A more racially diverse workforce may improve the well-being of racial minority employees and provide opportunities to reduce the underrepresentation of various groups. Organizational leaders must also understand the combined potential impact that social movements, the resulting publicity given to anti-Black discrimination, and opposing political ideologies can have on employee well-being.

Political Ideology

Political ideology is "a set of beliefs about the proper order of society and how it can be achieved" (Erikson & Tedin, 2003; Jost et al., 2009; Swigart et al., 2020, p. 1064). Research suggests that political ideology can be a major contributor to one's identity (Pew Research, 2014; Johnson & Roberto, 2018). In the past four years (i.e., since the 2016 presidential election), researchers have emphasized the importance of exploring the effects of political ideology on workplace outcomes (Larson, 2016), as the social categorization of liberals and conservatives has strengthened (Johnson & Roberto, 2018). Iyengar and Krupenkin (2018) found evidence suggesting that ingroups and outgroups based on political ideology may be associated with more hostility between coworkers compared to ingroups and outgroups based on race or sexual orientation. Given these findings, research exploring the workplace effects of political ideology in combination with mega-threats relating the oppression of a particular identity group (e.g., voting on legislation reducing access to reproductive healthcare for women or allowing employers to discriminate based on sexual orientation) may be particularly important.

Over the past four years, Americans have become less moderate and increasingly vocal about their political beliefs (Pew Research, 2014; Johnson & Roberto, 2018). Differences in political beliefs have always had the potential to create conflict; however, since the 2016 U.S. presidential election, conflict surrounding political ideology has increased exponentially. When surveyed, 91% of conservative Americans and 86% of liberal Americans reported that they viewed members on the other side of the other political spectrum as unfavorable (Pew Research, 2016). Given the increased popularity of social media platforms (e.g., twitter, parlor), Americans from all backgrounds can discuss politically related events in real-time and almost immediately signal their political ideology to their coworkers if they are connected on such platforms. A work team comprised of both Democrats and Republicans may create significant issues maintaining social harmony if political views enter the workplace. Additionally, because social media provides more anonymity compared to in-person interactions, employees may be more likely to engage in combative behaviors (e.g., name-calling, threatening or foul language). Given the current political climate, being labeled as a liberal or a conservative voter can carry potential consequences, even in the workplace. Scholars have called for research on the relationship between political ideology and specific outcomes, such as employment decisions, prosocial behaviors, and job performance (Carnahan & Greenwood, 2018).

A popular question among scholars has been the degree to which political ideology impacts specific work outcomes, such as employment decisions (Johnson & Roberto, 2018). Carnahan and Greenwood (2018) examined the impact of manager's political ideology on their managerial decisions of subordinates in a sample of large law offices. The authors found that law offices with a larger percentage of liberal partners hired more female associates, exhibited greater gender parity regarding rates of promotion, and were more likely to appoint female associates to client teams. Additionally, they observed that male manager's political ideologies were significantly more influential than female manager's political ideologies. This is in line with the work of Briscoe and Joshi (2017) who found that subordinates of liberal supervisors exhibited a reduced gender gap in performance-based pay compared to subordinates of conservative supervisors. In sum, a growing body of evidence suggests that manager's political ideology can impact their organizational decisions.

There have also been recent advancements on group-level political ideology. Specifically, Gupta and colleagues (2017) introduced the construct of organizational political ideology, which is defined as the beliefs of organizational members regarding how social worlds operate, such as which results are preferred and how to achieve such results. The authors predicted and found support for the relationship between organizational political ideology liberalism and advances in corporate social responsibility, which are "actions that appear to further some social good, beyond the interests of the firm and that which is required by law" (McWilliams & Siegel, 2001, p. 117). Additionally, these effects were stronger when human capital intensity is high, when organizational tenure of the CEO is large, and when corporate social responsibility is uncommon in the history of the firm.

Other research has examined the influence of political ideology on board level decisions. Park and colleagues (2020) found that when CEOs committed financial misconduct, politically conservative boards were more likely to terminate the CEO compared to politically liberal boards. The authors theorized that this was due to the ideo-attribution effect, which posits that conservatives tend to attribute causality of behaviors to dispositional traits (i.e., an individual's character), while liberals tend to attribute causality of behaviors to situational or external aspects (Bobbio et al., 2010). Park and colleagues (2020) findings were also in line with the threat management literature, in that conservative individuals tend to view the world as more dangerous and threatening (Duckitt, 2001), and seek to minimize these perceived events that could potentially impact their own reputation.

Mega-threats such as the passing of legislation to reduce reproductive healthcare (e.g., abortions) for women, allowing employers to discriminate based on sexual orientation, and, more recently, calls for legislation defunding the police, has close ties to political ideology. As the chasm grows between conservatives and liberals, perceptions of the other group's ideals and values becomes more general and less moderate. For example, conservative employees may perceive all liberal employees to endorse women's right to have an abortion, the legalization of recreational marijuana use, LGBTQ rights, and defunding the police. At the same time, liberal employees may believe all conservative employees endorse gun right's, are against immigration, tax programs (e.g., welfare), and women's reproductive rights.

Johnson and Roberto (2018) note the increasingly complex relationships between political ideology, demographic diversity (and mega-threats), and employee outcomes. The combination of controversial, media-sensationalized events (i.e., mega-threats) and everyone's ability to instantly broadcast their opinions may create the potential for conflict in the workplace. For example, since 2016, there have been multiple highly publicized events relating to political ideology: the deadly riot in Washington, D.C. three weeks before the 2020 presidential elect's inauguration, numerous violent attacks on abortion clinics, school shootings and subsequent calls for gun reform, and the passing of legislation banning transgender healthcare for minors in certain states. Unfortunately, as the social division between liberal and conservative employees continues to develop, organizational leaders may no longer be able to ignore the need to discuss the impact of political ideology and diversity on various work outcomes, especially for Black employees.

Multiple methods aimed at reducing racial discrimination in the workplace draw from CRT and RGCT to better understand interactions between racially dissimilar employees. In line with RGCT, competing political ideologies (and their associated sets of values and beliefs) related to mega-threats may lead to intense group conflict. Given the increase in media coverage of the recent violence and discrimination targeted towards Black Americans, personal values and beliefs that are frequently associated with political ideology may be more likely to influence employee interactions. Johnson and Roberto (2018) comment on the increasing divisiveness of liberal and conservative individuals and how the intense conflicts typically resulting from opposing religious values and beliefs are now frequently a result of differing political attitudes. Although widely cited in organizational diversity research, because of their time of publication, the methods of reducing discrimination drawn from CRT and RGCT did not consider the effects of mega-threats or political ideology, providing fertile opportunities for future research.

CONCLUSION

Although laws have been put into place from times of unprecedented social injustice such as women's suffrage and the civil rights movement, we have seen that discrimination has not been eradicated, but merely changed forms. Social movements such as Black Lives Matter and #MeToo have illuminated the need and moral obligation for organizations to address the injustices experienced by minority, marginalized, and underrepresented populations. The combination of repeated instances of unjustified violence against Black Americans (e.g., death by police-shooting) and the social divisiveness sparked by the 2016 and 2020 U.S. presidential elections could represent a new avenue for organizational diversity scholars.

The implications of mega-threats and political ideology have been echoed throughout the current social and political climate. As we have demonstrated in this chapter, CRT and RGCT illuminate the changes in how racism is functioning in society and the experiences of those who have been perpetrated. The reduction of workplace discrimination and the increase of inclusion must be at the core of organizational change as organizations strive to further understand the manifestations of mega-threats such as racial stress. From addressing group conflict antecedents of experienced stress, the potential for positive effects extends beyond that of understanding stress to the appropriate organizational and social responses for improving employee well-being.

REFERENCES

Ashburn-Nardo, L., Thomas, K., & Robinson, A. J. (2017). Broadening the conversation: Why Black lives matter. *Equality, Diversity and Inclusion: An International Journal, 36*(8), 698–706. https://doi.org/10.1108/EDI-09-2017-0198

Brief, A. P., Umphress, E. E., Dietz, J., Burrows, J. W., Butz, R. M., & Scholten, L. (2005). Community matters: Realistic group conflict theory and the impact of diversity. *The Academy of Management Journal, 48*(5), 830–844. https://doi.org/10.2307/20159700

Bobbio, A., Canova, L., & Manganelli, A. M. (2010). Conservative ideology, economic conservativism, and causal attributions for poverty and wealth. *Current Psychology, 29*, 222–234. https://doi.org/10.1007/s12144-010-9086-6

Boehm, S. A., Kunze, F., & Bruch, H. (2014). Spotlight on age-diversity climate: The impact of age-inclusive HR practices on firm-level outcomes. *Personal Psychology, 67*(3), 667–704. https://doi.org/10.1111/peps.12047

Briscoe, F., & Joshi, A. (2017). Bringing the boss's politics in: Supervisor political ideology and the gender gap in earnings. *Academy of Management Journal, 60*, 1415–1441. https://doi.org/10.5465/amj.2016.0179

Brown, K. (2021). The Fear Black Employees Carry. *Harvard Business Review*. https://hbr.org/2021/04/the-fear-black-employees-carry

Brown, S. E., & Battle, J. S. (2019). Ostracizing targets of workplace sexual harassment before and after the #MeToo movement. *Equality, Diversity and Inclusion: An International Journal, 39*(1), 53–67.

Campbell, C. A. (1965). *The embodied mind*. Wiley.

Carnahan, S., & Greenwood, B. N. (2018). Managers' political beliefs and gender inequality among subordinates: Does his ideology matter more than hers? *Administrative Science Quarterly, 63*, 287–322. https://doi.org/10.1177/0001839217708780

Cole, E. R. (2009). Intersectionality and research in psychology. *American Psychologist, 64*(3), 170–180.

Comas-Díaz, L., Hall, G. N., & Neville, H. A. (2019). Racial trauma: Theory, research, and healing: Introduction to the special issue. *American Psychologist, 74*(1), 1–5. https://doi.org/10.1037/amp0000442

Cox, T. (1994). *Cultural diversity in organizations: Theory, research and practice*. Berrett-Koehler.

Crenshaw, K. (1991). Race, gender, and sexual harassment. *Southern California Law Review, 65*(3), 1467–1476.

DeCuir-Gunby, J. T., & Gunby, N. W. (2016). Racial microaggressions in the workplace: A critical race analysis of the experiences of African American educators. *Urban Education, 51*(4), 390–414. https://doi.org/10.1177/0042085916628610

Delgado, R., & Stefancic, J. (2001). *Critical race theory: An introduction*. New York University Press.

Duckitt, J. (2001). A dual-process cognitive-motivational theory of ideology and prejudice. *Advances in Experimental Social Psychology, 33*, 41–113.

Erikson, R. S., & Tedin, K. L. 2003. *American public opinion: Its origins, content, and impact*. Routledge.

Fiske, S. T. (1998). Stereotyping, prejudice, and discrimination. In D. T. Gilbert & S. T. Fiske (Eds.), *Handbook of Social Psychology* (4th ed., pp. 357–411). McGraw-Hill.

Goldman, B., Cooper, D., & Kugler, T. (2019). Crime and punishment: A realistic group conflict approach to racial discrimination in hiring convicted felons. *International Journal of Conflict Management, 30*(1), 2–23.

Gupta, A., Briscoe, F., & Hambrick, D. C. (2017). Red, blue, and purple firms: Organizational political ideology and corporate social responsibility. *Strategic Management Journal, 38*(5), 1018–1040. https://doi.org/10.1002/smj.2550

Himle, J. A., Baser, R. E., Taylor, R. J., Campbell, R. D., & Jackson, J. S. (2009). Anxiety disorders among African Americans, Blacks of Caribbean descent, and non-Hispanic Whites in the United States. *Journal of Anxiety Disorders, 23*(5), 578–590. https://doi.org/10.1016/j.janxdis.2009.01.002

Holmes, O., Jiang, K., Avery, D. R., McKay, P. F., Oh, I.-S., & Tillman, C. J. (2020). A meta-analysis integrating 25 Years of diversity climate research. *Journal of Management, 47*(6). https://doi.org/10.1177/0149206320934547

Humberd, B. K., Clair, J. A., & Creary, S. J. (2015). In our own backyard: When a less inclusive community challenges organizational inclusion. *Equality, Diversity and Inclusion, 34*(5), 395–421. https://doi.org/10.1108/EDI-11-2013-0105

Iyengar, S., & Krupenkin, M. (2018). Partisanship as social identity: Implications for the study of party polarization. *Forum, 16*, 23–45.

Johnson, A. F., & Roberto, K. J. (2018). Right versus left: How does political ideology affect the workplace? *Journal of Organizational Behavior, 39*, 1040–1043.

Jost, J. T., Federico, C. M., & Napier, J. L. (2009). Political ideology: Its structure, functions, and elective affinities. *Annual Review of Psychology, 60*(1), 307–337. https://doi.org/10.1146/annurev.psych.60.110707.163600

Kalish Blair, Z. S. (2016). The pulse nightclub shooting: Connecting militarism, neoliberalism, and multiculturalism to understand violence. *North American Dialogue, 19*(2), 102–116. https://doi-org.libezp.lib.lsu.edu/10.1111/nad.12049

Kanter, R. M. (2008). *Men and women of the corporation: New edition.* Basic Books.

Larson, E. D. (2016). Black Lives Matter and bridge building: Labor education for a "new Jim Crow" era. *Labor Studies Journal, 41*, 36–66.

Lazarus, R. S., & Folkman, S. (1984). *Stress, appraisal, and coping.* Springer.

Leigh, A., & Melwani, S. (2019). #BlackEmployeesMatter: Mega-threats, identity fusion, and enacting positive deviance in organizations. *Academy of Management Review, 44*, 564–591.

Mannix, E., & Neale, M. A. (2005). What differences make a difference?: The promise and reality of diverse teams in organizations. *Psychological Science in the Public Interest, 2*, 31–55. https://doi.org/10.1111/j.1529-1006.2005.00022

McCluney, C. L., Bryant, C. M., King, D. D., & Ali, A. A. (2017). Calling in black: A dynamic model of racially traumatic events, resourcing, and safety. *Equality, Diversity and Inclusion, 36*(8), 767–786. https://doi.org/10.1108/EDI-01-2017-0012

McKay, P. F., Avery, D. R., & Morris, M. A. (2008). Mean racial-ethnic differences in employee sales performance: The moderating role of diversity climate. *Personnel Psychology, 61*(2), 349–374. https://doi.org/10.1111/j.1744-6570.2008.00116.x

McWilliams, A., & Siegel, D. (2001). Corporate social responsibility: A theory of the firm perspective. *Academy of Management Review, 26*, 117–127.

Nishii, L. H. (2013). The benefits of climate for inclusion for gender-diverse groups. *The Academy of Management Journal, 56*(6), 1754–1774.

Park, U. D., Boeker, W., & Gomulya, D. (2020). Political ideology of the board and CEO dismissal following financial misconduct. *Strategic Management Journal, 41*(1), 108–123. https://doi.org/10.1002/smj.3088

Pew Research Center. (2014). *14 striking findings from 2014.* https://www.pewresearch.org/fact-tank/2014/12/22/14-striking-findings-from-2014/

Pietri, E. S., Johnson, I. R., & Ozgumus, E. (2018). One size may not fit all: Exploring how the intersection of race and gender and stigma consciousness predict effective identity-safe cues for Black women. *Journal of Experimental Social Psychology, 74*, 291–306.

Plummer, D. L., & Slane, S. (1996). Patterns of coping in racially stressful situations. *Journal of Black Psychology, 22*(3), 302–315.

Sherif, M., Harvey, O. J., White, B. J., Hood, W. R., & Sherif, C. W. (1961). *Intergroup cooperation and competition: The robbers cave experiment*. University Book Exchange.

Sherif, M., & Sherif, C. W. (1979). Research on intergroup relations. In W. G. Austin & S. Worchel (Eds.), *The social psychology of intergroup relations*. Brooks/Cole.

Spreitzer, G. M., & Sonenshein, S. (2004). Toward the construct definition of positive deviance. *American Behavioral Scientist, 47*, 828–847.

Swigart, K. L., Anantharaman, A., Williamson, J. A., & Grandey, A. A. (2020). Working while liberal/conservative: A review of political ideology in organizations. *Journal of Management, 46*(6), 1063–1091. https://doi.org/10.1177/0149206320909419

Tajfel, H., & Turner, J.C. (1986) The social identity theory of intergroup behavior. In S. Worchel & W. G. Austin (Eds.), *Psychology of intergroup relation* (pp. 7–24). Hall Publishers.

Thomas, K., & Ashburn-Nardo, L. (2020). Black lives matter... still: Moving beyond acknowledging the problem toward effective solutions in graduate training and education. *Equality, Diversity and Inclusion: An International Journal, 39*(7), 741–747.

U.S. Equal Employment Opportunity Commission. (2020). *EEOC releases fiscal year 2019 enforcement and litigation data*. https://www.eeoc.gov/newsroom/eeoc-releases-fiscal-year-2019-enforcement-and-litigation-data

Williams, M. T., Metzger, I. W., Leins, C., & DeLapp, C. (2018). Assessing racial trauma within a DSM–5 framework: The UConn Racial/Ethnic Stress & Trauma Survey. *Practice Innovations, 3*, 242–277.

Wilson, J. C. (2020). Striving to rollback or protect Roe: State legislation and the Trump-Era politics of abortion. *Publius: The Journal of Federalism, 50*(3), 370–397. https://doi.org/10.1093/publius/pjaa015

Zárate, M. A., Garcia, B., Garza, A. A., & Hitlan, R. T. (2004). Cultural threat and perceived realistic group conflict as dual predictors of prejudice. *Journal of Experimental Social Psychology, 40*(1), 99–105. https://doi.org/10.1016/S0022-1031(03)00067-2

CHAPTER 7

BLACK LIVES MATTER

True Commitment or Tokenism?

Emily Moore and Anju Philip
University of Guelph

ABSTRACT

The goal of this investigation was to understand organizations' responses to Black Lives Matter, a social movement that gained momentum in response to the deaths of George Floyd and other Black American citizens in 2020. Using racialized decoupling from Victor Ray's racialized organizational theory, we resolved to investigate the congruency of companies' existing diversity and inclusion policies and statements before the mainstream BLM movement. To investigate review corporate statements, proposed actions, and corporate social media posts during the mainstream BLM movement of 2020. In doing so we assessed if organizations have engaged in tokenism or made true commitments to reduce internal racialized structures. In analyzing the three sets of publicly available information of the top 50 companies from the July 2020–Fortune 500 list we employ a content analysis methodology and contribute to the literature by identifying and developing a 4-category classification by which to distinguish organizations' varying commitments to reducing racial inequality. Our use of racialized organizational theory demonstrates an application of the theory to the BLM movement and provides argument for normative isomorphism's influence on diversity programming.

The Future of Scholarship on Race in Organizations, pp. 137–177
Copyright © 2022 by Information Age Publishing

Despite its creation in 2013, the #BlackLivesMatter hashtag, phrase and namesake non-profit organization did not receive mainstay media coverage and recognition as a social movement until the summer of 2020 (Burgess et al., 2019; Del Real et al., 2020; Maqbool, 2020). During this time the momentum for the Black Lives Matter (BLM) social movement became ubiquitous in North American media, appearing in the news, on social media platforms and referenced in statements of support from executives, celebrities and political leaders (Del Real et al., 2020). The underlying events which sparked the widespread advocacy for BLM were the horrific and publicized deaths of George Floyd, Breonna Taylor, and other Black American citizens (Buchanan et al., 2020; Maqbool, 2020). Throughout the summer of 2020, during the ongoing COVID-19 pandemic, millions of protesters demonstrated in the United States and across the world showing their support for BLM and demanding change for racial justice (Buchanan et al., 2020).

In response to the amplified awareness and social activism for the BLM movement, corporations too began pledging support and participation in efforts to combat systemic racism (Jan et al., 2020). Many companies participated in #blackouttuesday, sharing black boxes on their Instagram feeds to demonstrate solidarity with the BLM movement (Coscarelli, 2020). Support also took place through other social media platforms in statements and other shared media demonstrating corporations backing for BLM. Many of these outputs include statements from Corporate Executive Officer's (CEO) and other executives denouncing systemic racism within society and their organizations with commitments of support for the advancement of racial equality. Responses to the corporate pledges for BLM included mixed reviews, with critics questioning their intentions and longevity, asking if the demonstrations are true commitments for reform or acts of performative allyship or tokenism? (Batty, 2020; Jan et al., 2020).

To investigate this phenomenon, our study aims to explore the continuity between organizational support for the BLM movement and organizations' corporate diversity and inclusion policies (or lack of). By reviewing the corporate statements and social media posts made by organizations in support for the BLM movement throughout the summer of 2020 we ask the question, has corporate support for the BLM movement been an act of tokenism or do true corporate commitments for reducing organizational racism exist? Central to our inquiry are the actions taken to reduce the presence of racism within organizations.

Building on racialized decoupling, an aspect of Ray's (2019) racialized organizational theory, our study assesses three types of publicly available online information using the top 50 organizations from the 2020 Fortune 500 list (Fortune Media, 2020). Our sources include publicly available diversity and inclusion (D&I) policy statements or practices available on corporate websites, the corporate statements, or pledges of an action-oriented approach to advancing racial equality made on social media platforms in connection to the BLM movement and the social media posts made at the height of the BLM movement in 2020. Analysis of these policies and statements will determine answers to three primary questions regarding each of the top 50 Fortune 500 companies. Were any statements made commensurate with the BLM movement on social media during the summer of 2020? Do supporting D&I policies exist? Were changes made to these corporate policies based on responses to the BLM movement?

We approach this topic with a scholarly interest in workplace D&I practices and an intent to understand whether organizations' response to the BLM movement is congruent or not with their internal commitments and allyship for their Black employees. We do not seek to make any attempts to speak on behalf of the Black community or the Black employees who work at these organizations as we narrow our research scope to the organizational responses to this social movement.

Our analysis begins by setting the context for our study in reviewing BLM and racialized organizational theory. Following our methodology, the findings of our work produce a 4-category classification system for organizational responses to BLM and their level of commitment to reducing racism. This study advances the theory of racialized organizations (Ray, 2019) by demonstrating an application of how a social movement (BLM) may alter racialized organizational structures through normative isomorphic pressures. We further discover that the majority of organizations mobilize efforts for antiracism through alterations to diversity programming and that while advancements have been made, opportunities for further progress remain.

#BLACK LIVES MATTER

#Black Lives Matter (BLM), began as an online community targeting anti-Black racism in 2013 after 17-year-old Trayvon Martin's murderer was acquitted in Florida (Black Lives Matter, 2020; Ramaswamy, 2017). Martin was murdered after being targeted by George Zimmerman while walking home from a convenience store, and the subsequent acquittal of his killer created public outcry and led to the BLM social movement (Ramaswamy, 2017). The Black Lives Matter Global Foundation Inc. has since formalized as a global organization with a mission to "eradicate white supremacy and build local power to intervene in violence inflicted on Black communities by the state and vigilantes" (Black Lives Matter, 2020). BLM has grown to become a worldwide social movement through coordination and support on social media and public protests (Watson-Singleton et al., 2020). These public displays have brought awareness to the disproportionate way that African American's are killed by law enforcement and the presence of systemic racism across systems (Garza, 2014: Watson-Singleton et al., 2020).

During June of 2020 BLM protests were at their peak with some demonstrations spanning months in the United States with others taking place across the world, including the United Kingdom, Europe, and Canada (Buchanan et al., 2020; Maqbool, 2020). The 2020 protests were organized in response to the murder of George Floyd, and other Black Americans who lost their lives within weeks of each other (Maqbool, 2020). The protests and heightened awareness for the BLM movement received more recognition than ever before, which may be related to the events coinciding with the COVID-19 pandemic, a unique circumstance which may have allowed for more individuals to engage with protest activity (Gillion, 2020, as cited in Buchanan et al., 2020).

Understanding that BLM represents a broad social movement in bringing attention to systemic racism and the discriminatory treatment of African American's (Watson-Singleton et al., 2020) it has impact and influence on organizational life and rightly received organisational attention. As such, organizations and their leaders participated in support for BLM primarily during June of 2020 through corporate and social media updates, condemning racism within their organizations. To understand the connection between race and organizational life we turn to Ray's (2019) organizational theory to set the foundation for our current study.

RACIALIZED ORGANIZATIONAL THEORY

Organizations do not operate in isolation, and their positioning within society may influence their culture (van Oudenhoven, 2001) as was discovered in Hofstede's characterizing national cultures (Hofstede, 1991). As individuals our lifelong interaction with organizations demonstrates societies pervasive and intersecting relationship with organizations. As summarized by Etzioni (1964, p. 1), "Our society is an organizational society. We are born in organizations, educated in organizations and most of us spend our lives working in organizations." Further work has been done to demonstrate how the relationship between society and organizations may affect organizational culture in a way that contributes or perpetuates inequalities for employees. For example, Acker's research on the gendered substructures of organizations offers insight into why gender inequalities exist within organizations, constructed from the gendered assumptions held within organizations (Acker, 1990, 2012).

Aligned with the investigation of this paper, is Ray's (2019) theory of racialized organizations, which acknowledges that racialized processes take place within organizations and replaces the predominant view that organizations are race neutral. Defined as social structures which improve the agency of the dominant racial group at the expense of constraining the subordinate racial group's agency and efficacy, racialized organizations showcase how dynamics of race influence organizational life (Ray, 2019). The three proposed tenets of racialized organizations include, the imbalanced allocation of resources, credentialing of Whiteness and racialized decoupling (Ray, 2019).

We focus our attention within this analysis on the last characteristic, racialized decoupling. Racialized decoupling occurs when there is an internal deviation from the diversity policies adopted and publicly advertised by an organization (Ray, 2019). The practice of decoupling has been described in other employment equity literature as the "gap between policy and practice" (Agocs, 2002), or "window dressing" referring to the appearance of equality promotion without true reform (Baron, 1994). Racialized decoupling injects concepts of racial equality within existing decoupling theory, a concept found in corporate governance and institutional theory literature (Westphal & Zajac, 2001; Krenn, 2015). Importantly, racialized decoupling focuses on the lack of commitment by organizations to challenge internal racial hierarchies, alluding to the ceremonial function of diversity policies which fall short of mechanisms and measures needed to alter racial disparities within organizations (Ray 2019; Embrick, 2008, 2011).

Racialized decoupling has been described by the media as tokenism or performative allyship, referring to criticisms that organization's commitments for racial equality are not substantiated by actions to dismantle systemic racism (Jan et al., 2020; Batty, 2020). Such criticisms are built on previous instances of decoupled commitments for change and ongoing accounts that Black employees face discrimination in their workplace experiences (Jan et al., 2020). The continued stories of Black employees' experiences with workplace discrimination highlight the argued performative allyship nature of racialized decoupling particularly during a time of social pressure.

Therefore, our work brings attention to the commitments made by organizations to reduce internal racism. To remain consistent with the common terminology for racialized decoupling in the media we will refer to this phenomenon as tokenism throughout. We define tokenism as symbolic corporate effort(s) to represent a minority employee group (Black employees) by publicly displaying a commitment to diversity and inclusion without diligent action and ongoing commitments to support the employee group (Cloud, 1996: Torchia et al., 2011; Yoder, 1991).

A key factor in distinguishing tokenism from true commitments to reduce the racial structures of organizations is *intent*. Therefore, analysis of available corporate documents along with corporate statements assist in determining if the organization has meaningfully engaged in diversity efforts or strategic goals to reduce racialized structures within the organization. If the intent is the allusion to performative actions without actual action, then the organization is engaging in tokenism. However, if the organization truly intends to diversify their workforce, but is in the initial phases of the process, or hasn't been successful yet, then the presence of intent demonstrates a true commitment to reducing racial inequalities (Sherrer, 2018).

We feel it appropriate to apply the theory of racialized organizations to this temporal analysis as it is marked by a defining social movement through the increased societal awareness for BLM. Social movements, government policy and government relations are all considered external sources of influence on racialized organizations (Ray, 2019). In comparison, the internal sources which may influence organizational racialization include market share, diversity programming and distribution of resources through movement actors within the organization (Ray, 2019). We anticipate that our analysis will demonstrate the importance of diversity programming based on the nature of publicized anti-racism commitments by organizations.

METHODOLOGY

We employed a content analysis to investigate organizations' official corporate statements and social media responses to the BLM movement between May 25, 2020, and August 31, 2020, as well their commitments to diversity and inclusion preceding these dates. "Content analysis is a research method that uses a set of procedures to make valid inferences from text. These inferences are about the sender(s) of the message, the message itself, or the audience of the message" (Weber, 1990, p.11). According to Berelson (1952), content analysis has multiple uses depending on the substantive interests of the authors and accordingly we use this approach to identify and interpret the intentions of organizations through statements made via corporate websites and social media.

Fifty organizations were first selected based on their ranking on the Fortune 500 list (the top-ranked 50 companies within the list were selected). The Fortune 500 list represents the largest public companies in the United States based on revenue (Fortune Media, 2020). The rankings used for the present analysis were taken as of July 2020. Social media posts regarding BLM, racial justice, commitments to racial equality or related subject matter from each of the 50 companies' Twitter, Instagram, and LinkedIn accounts were catalogued. We only analyzed the social media accounts directly linked from corporate websites. Where Twitter, Instagram or LinkedIn accounts did not provide sufficient information we used other relevant social media accounts (i.e., Facebook). Information on the source of the post, its content, the date, and the associated URL were captured in a spreadsheet shared between both authors. As previously mentioned, the temporal range for the social media posts captured spanned from May 25, 2020, to August 31, 2020. As much of the momentum for the BLM movement began after the arrest and murder of George Floyd on May 25, 2020 (Hill et al., 2020) reviewing social media posts after this date would indicate an organizational response to the event. Furthermore, Blackout Tuesday, a social media campaign designed to disrupt "business as usual" was organized online and took place on June 2, 2020 (Gordon, 2020).

Information on workplace D&I was also captured from each of the 50 organizations' webpages. Data for each of the organizations were categorized into two different word document files. The first being D&I statements and practices taking place in the organization before the momentum of the BLM movement, hereafter referred to as pre-mainstream BLM commitments. Second, the announcements and actions taken by organizations throughout May 25, 2020–August 31, 2020, in response to BLM, hereafter referred to as responses or commitments during mainstream BLM. The authors importantly acknowledge that assessments of actual D&I programming prior to or after the mainstream BLM movement in June is not necessarily a rendering of complete information. Only the available information obtained through the above stated channels was used in the investigation. Some internal communications, for example, messages from CEO to employees were also published on social media (AmerisourceBergen, Verizon, etc.), however, we acknowledge that there might have been other internal communications which we have not included in our analysis as they are not publicly available.

We assessed the commitments of the 50 organizations to reduce the presence of racialized structures within their operations. To do so we first assessed and summarized information pertaining to specific activities the organization had in place for D&I, the actions they committed to as a response to BLM and the presence of their commitment to BLM on social media. Each author then documented all the available information on social media for 25 of the 50 organizations independently before both authors reviewed all information for the 50 of the organizations together. The authors then separately analyzed the contents of 10 organizations each, documenting emerging themes. The authors discussed the emerging themes and possible codes from first 40% of organizational social media information together before completing the analysis of the remaining data. The authors subsequently created a classification system using the refined codes and categories to apply to the companies based on the varying levels of organizational commitments addressing BLM.

FINDINGS

Using the text obtained from all three documents, that is, pre-mainstream BLM commitments, responses or commitments made during mainstream BLM movement and social media posts, a final table was created (see Appendix) to summarize each organization's statements and actions and to assess their commitment for reducing racial structures within their organizations. A final column was created to distinguish a company that demonstrated true commitment versus tokenism regarding racial equality. To be classified as making a commitment, a company would not only be making official statements but also establish a specific action-oriented approach to reducing racialized structures within the organization. Importantly, these actions had to be targeted towards improving the lives of their Black employees or increasing opportunities for new Black employees, such as creating opportunities for further education and training.

Our analysis revealed the creation of four categories that were used to classify the organizations using the terms commitment and tokenism as illustrated in Table 7.1. *No commitment* signified a company had made no commitments to reducing racialized structures pre-mainstream BLM, had no social media posts and no responses or commitments to reducing racialized structures during the mainstream BLM movement. *No new commitment* signified a company that made commitments to reducing racialized structures pre-mainstream BLM, made social media posts, but had no responses or commitments to reducing racialized structures during the mainstream BLM movement. *Tokenism* signified a company that had statements about reducing racialized structures pre-mainstream BLM, made social media posts, made statements about reducing racialized structures during the mainstream BLM movement but made no mention of specific actions or commitments. *True commitment* signified a company that made commitments to reducing racialized structures pre-mainstream BLM, made social media posts, and also made a commitment to reducing racialized structures during the mainstream BLM movement.

The results of our analysis demonstrated that only one company had no commitments to racial equality, Berkshire Hathaway (2021) had no D& I commitments on their webpage, made no comments on social media and had no references to actions to reduce racialized structures within the organization. While Berkshire Hathaway's subsidiaries have D&I and BLM commitments as a parent company they do not. Seventeen companies made commitments pre-mainstream BLM movement but had no new commitments; for example, Ford Motors has used its Ford Fund to support a wide range of educational programming & initiatives designed to help

Table 7.1

Four Category Classifications of Varying Levels of Commitment

Classification	Actions Pre-Mainstream BLM Movement	Actions/Response During Mainstream BLM Movement	Social Media Posts
No commitment	No	No	No
No new commitment	Yes	No	Yes
Tokenism	No (Only statements)	No	Yes
True Commitment	Yes	Yes	Yes

African American people improve their economic status and quality of life. Ford Fund also supports historically Black colleges and universities (HBCU), however, while Ford Motor made social media posts during the mainstream BLM movement, no additional commitments were made to reducing racialized structures in the organization.

Four companies displayed tokenism; for example, Costco Wholesale had existing D&I statements on their company website, made a statement expressing shock at the tragic death of George Floyd, condemning racism and injustice with a statement about a commitment to fairness and equality for employees but did not provide any commitments to reducing racial inequality within the organization. And lastly, 28 companies displayed true commitment; for example, Prudential Financial displayed pre-mainstream BLM commitment using specific D&I statements as well as the availability of an employee resource group (ERG) for Black employees, made social media posts condemning racial inequality and also displayed specific commitments during the mainstream BLM movement such as building participation and awareness in the workplace through advocacy for parental leave, retirements plans, planning innovative steps to banish racism in the workplace, mandating antiracism training, marking Juneteenth as a day of education and reflection, committing to reevaluate and improve hiring practices towards equal opportunities, and creating greater transparency in diversity data.

Table 7.2 provides examples and quotes of specific statements, action-oriented and otherwise, that were made by a few companies that fell into one of the four categories that were developed in our analysis. Detailed information for all 50 companies is available in the Appendix.

Table 7.2

Sample of Company Quotes, Statements, and Classification

No commitment	No New Commitment	Tokenism	True Commitment
Berkshire Hathaway	*Chevron*	*Costco*	*Apple*
Pre-mainstream BLM Actions – No information on D&I available on company webpage.	**Pre-mainstream BLM Actions** – "Our relationships and programs with historically Black colleges and universities are designed to encourage minority participation in science, technology, engineering and mathematics (STEM)…"	**Pre-mainstream BLM Actions** – "Inclusiveness and Equal Opportunity - We aim to have a diverse workforce that is representative of the communities where we do business, and to foster an inclusive environment…" – Corporate website (Costco, 2021)	**Pre-mainstream BLM Actions** – "53% of new hires in the U.S. are from historically underrepresented groups in tech. Underrepresented groups include women and people who identify as Black, Hispanic, Native American, or Native Hawaiian & Other Pacific Islander."
Response during mainstream BLM – No reference to BLM or D & I. **Social Media Posts** – No social media posts (Berkshire Hathaway, 2020) *Berkshire Hathaway as a parent company does not have distinct D&I commitments but their subsidiaries do*	To help ensure that our employees understand our policies and know how inclusion is practiced throughout our company, we provide opportunities such as diversity training, guidance on personal diversity action plans and lunchtime diversity learning sessions." – Corporate website (Chevron, 2021)	**Response during mainstream BLM** – "…Especially under the current circumstances, I want to remind Costco employees of our ongoing commitment to the values that are vital to our culture. We remain committed to taking care of our employees, building a diverse workforce, maintaining work environments that are free from discrimination and harassment, and treating each other in a fair, honest, respectful and inclusive way…" – Craig Jelinek, President and CEO (Costco, 2020a)	"We partner with community colleges, Historically Black Colleges and Universities (HBCUs), minority-serving institutions, and others through programs like AppleCare College and our Apple HBCU Scholars internship program. And we're developing partnerships to reach even more diverse talent across all ages and career stages." – Corporate website (Apple, 2021)

(Table continued on next page)

Table 7.2 (Continued)

Sample of Company Quotes, Statements, and Classification

No commitment	No New Commitment	Tokenism	True Commitment
Berkshire Hathaway	*Chevron*	*Costco*	*Apple*
	Response during mainstream BLM –	**Social Media Posts –**	**Response during mainstream BLM –**
	"As the human energy company, we are just that – humans, and we've felt the impact of what is happening in the United States around racial injustice. Our company is rooted in a diverse and inclusive culture, but we also understand it is our time to listen and learn."– Mike Wirth, CEO	"Dear Costco members, along with the rest of the country, we were shocked by the tragic and senseless death of George Floyd...." – Taken from Facebook post (Costco, 2020b)	"As part of its Community Education Initiative, Apple is partnering with an additional 10 Historically Black Colleges and Universities to bring coding and creativity opportunities to their campuses and broader communities." – Newsroom, Apple (Apple, 2020a)
	"We are fortunate to work for a company that lives its values. "Diversity and Inclusion" is the first value listed in The Chevron Way. That's not an accident. - Lee Jourdan, CDO (Chevron, 2020a)		**Social Media Posts** – "The senseless killing of George Floyd calls upon us all to speak and act against racism and injustice. Read the full message from Tim Cook (CEO) on apple.com" – (Instagram) (Apple, 2020b)
	Social Media Posts – "Black Lives Matter" – Photo (Twitter) (Chevron, 2020b)		

(Table continued on next page)

Table 7.2 (Continued)

Sample of Company Quotes, Statements, and Classification

No commitment	No New Commitment	Tokenism	True Commitment
	United Health Group	*FedEx*	*JPMorgan Chase*
	Pre-mainstream BLM Actions – "Sponsoring interns from INROADS, an international, nonprofit organization that places talented college students of color in internships with companies across the nation." – Corporate website (UnitedHealth Group, 2021) **Response during mainstream BLM** – "UnitedHealth Group and its team members will donate $10 million and 25,000 volunteer hours in response to Mr. Floyd's tragic death and the ensuing civil unrest." (UnitedHealth Group, 2020a).	**Pre-mainstream BLM Actions –** "Investing in our people and our diversity programs makes us stronger, and our workforce and leadership have been recognized consistently among top brands for diversity and inclusion…" – Corporate website (FedEx, 2021) **Social Media Posts –** "There is absolutely no place for racism or unequal treatment anywhere and we must unequivocally speak out and reject it when we see it "– CEO and COO (Twitter, LinkedIn) (FedEx, 2020b)	**Pre-mainstream BLM Actions –** "Today, over 35% of employees across 53 countries are a member of at least one of our BRGs, including: BOLD – Black Organization for leadership development. Advancing Black Pathways – Expanding Economic Opportunity for Black People" – Corporate website (JPMorgan Chase & Co, 2021) **Response during mainstream BLM –** "JPMorgan Chase is making a $30 billion commitment over the next five years to address some of the largest drivers of the racial wealth divide…… Part IV: Accelerate Investment in our Employees and Build a More Diverse and Inclusive Workforce" – Impact pledge, JP Morgan Chase (Corporate website) (JPMorgan Chase& Co, 2020)

(Table continued on next page)

Table 7.2 (Continued)

Sample of Company Quotes, Statements, and Classification

No commitment	No New Commitment	Tokenism	True Commitment
	United Health Group	*FedEx*	*JPMorgan Chase*
	"On Friday, June 19, UnitedHealth Group honors Juneteenth—the United States holiday also known as "Freedom Day" or "Emancipation Day" that recognizes a pivotal moment in the emancipation of enslaved people in Texas."– Newsroom, United Health Group \ (UnitedHealth Group, 2020b)	"Organizations dedicated to inclusion play a vital role in achieving an equal and justice society our role as a company is to help strengthen that work we are proud of the missions and initiatives we support that is promoting inclusion teaching acceptance and providing advancement for the African American community that's why we are devoting our social media platforms for the coming weeks to raising their voices and empowering communities to learn lead and take action" – FedEx (Twitter, LinkedIn) (FedEx, 2020c)	**Social Media Posts** – "We know there's work to do, and actions matter. Inequality for some of us demands change in all of us." – Link to website (LinkedIn) (JPMorgan Chase& Co, 2020)
	Social Media Posts – "The 325,000 people of UnitedHealth Group remain steadfast in our commitment to not only build a culture of inclusivity and diversity within our own organization, but to ensure our actions help create a more equitable society for the people we serve" – Dave Wichmann, CEO UnitedHealth Group (Image on Twitter) (UnitedHealth Group, 2020c)		

DISCUSSION AND CONCLUSION

The findings of our analysis demonstrate that the majority of responses to reducing organizational racialization were focused on alterations to diversity programming, one of the three internal processes included in organizational race theory (Ray, 2019). The precursor for these changes being the external BLM social movement. We argue that this is an appropriate assessment of the antecedent for these actions as all D&I programming alterations took place in conjunction with the increased momentum of BLM. Further, we offer that the pressure of this social movement can be explained through the mechanism of normative isomorphism, one of the three forces found in institutional theory (DiMaggio & Powell, 1983). Normative forces account for the influence that social beliefs, values, and norms have on organizations (Scott, 2008), such as is demonstrated through BLM. As normative isomorphic pressures have demonstrated influence on changes to human resources programming (Murphy & Garavan, 2009) which is the business unit where diversity programming is often mobilized, we suggest this link in theory. While Ray (2019), acknowledges the empirical nature of assessing which type of isomorphism promotes racial similarity in organizations, we posit that the social movement of BLM validates how societal values influence organizations through normative forces. In our study these social beliefs for racial equality demonstrated prominent alterations in diversity programming.

The alterations to diversity programming found in the organizations studied included: alterations to hiring practices, diversity targets for managers, anti-racism or discrimination training programs, D&I reporting initiatives, mentorship and cooperative education opportunities, educational partnership, discussion forums, new D&I commitments, and positions as well as general race-based education. These results indicate a contingency based approach by which organizations have individualized their response to BLM. The variety in these responses are solely focused on actions to reduce racial structures within organizations and do not include the other efforts made by the organizations to reduce systemic racism externally. We wish to highlight that while there were additional racial justice and equality commitments made by the organizations during this time such as efforts targeted to benefit local communities, educational institutions and policy reform, these actions did not seek to reduce internal organizational structures and therefore fell outside of the scope of our investigation.

All but one of the 50 reviewed organizations did not have a formal D&I statement. Organizations with these commitments often always listed them within a designated D&I segment of their webpage and were easy to navigate to. However, some of the reviewed D&I statement information was difficult to access and required the authors to perform a unique search on the organizational webpages. These voluntary D&I disclosures allow for organizations to express their congruence with social and legal diversity expectations (Singh & Point, 2009). The social expectation for organizations to manage their expressions of D&I was evident in our study as over 80% of organizations publicly acknowledged the importance of BLM and antiracism work. Importantly, the organizational displays for D&I commitments are marketing approaches to diversity which seek to connect with the target audience (Burgess et al., 2020). The perception of these displays as positive and facilitate belief congruence between the organization and their diversity marketing, whereas negative perceptions indicate a negative response and the perception of tokenism (Burgess et al., 2020). Therefore, individuals who perceive that diversity tokenism has occurred will have a negative response, believing that the organization has made deceptive claims (Lyon & Maxwell 2011; Torchia et al., 2011) which may create a negative narrative for the organization thereby influencing purchase intentions (Chen & Chang, 2013). It is important to note that similar perceptions might exist amongst employees of such organizations that have limited or no new commitments to diversity initiatives. This was apparent in our analysis as some employees commented on their employer's social media posts sharing frustrations based in their perceptions of an organization's weak response to internal racism.

In our investigation of actions taken to reducing racialized structures within organizations, an important finding was the presence of employee resource groups (ERGs) in many organizations, as 35 of the 50 companies in the analysis had ERGs. Such groups, initially referred to as a caucus in the 1960s, was established by Joseph Wilson, then CEO of Xerox to champion support and address discrimination issues for Black employees (Douglas, 2008). These groups are now more commonly known as employee networks, councils or forums, business resource groups, employee resource groups or affinity groups (Welbourne et al., 2017) and are defined by Catalyst as "groups of employees in an organization formed to act as a resource for both members and the organization" (Kaplan et al., 2009, p. 1). They are dedicated to fostering a diverse and inclusive work environment within the context of the organization's mission, values, goals, business practices and objectives" (Kaplan et al., 2009, p. 1). Therefore, if a company uses ERGs or similar groups, we assessed them as taking specific actions to reduce racialized structures, as ERG members may be regarded as "movement actors" who are deliberate in their attempt to redistribute resources within the organization (Bell, 2014; Ray, 2019). For example, some organizations mentioned executive support and participation in their ERGs, demonstrating their ability to redistribute resources through access to organizational power (e.g., Citigroup has executive-led affinity groups) and others create leadership development and other training programs through their existing ERGs (e.g., JPMorgan Chase has a business resource group BOLD—Black Organization for Leadership Development which is specifically aimed at providing an environment for empowerment and professional development).

We recognize that without direct access to policy and procedure documents or considering the experiences of Black employees in these companies, it is impossible to make causal statements about how companies are making efforts to reduce racialized structures. We also recognize that expressing that a company has made no new commitment does not necessarily mean that there is no commitment at all to racial equality. While this is a notable limitation within our study, we also do not believe that any company is free from racialized structures in the present day, therefore when a company does not make a statement recognizing the need for more to be done or take specific actions, it could be interpreted as a varying level of commitment to eradicating racial inequality in the workplace.

In recognizing that no organization is free from racialized structures we acknowledge that opportunities remain to initiate action-oriented commitments and measurable goals to reduce internal racism within all the organizations analyzed. The lack of additional actions to reduce organizational racism may be attributed to a variety of causes. Some causes highlighted by existing literature on decoupling include organizational financial constraints and a lack of knowledge or commitment to the subject area (Leck, 2002; Singh & Peng, 2010). However, the top 50 Fortune 500 organizations reviewed within this analysis have revenues ranging from $523, 296 to $67,684 million (Fortune Media, 2020). Therefore, we do not feel it appropriate to state that financial and knowledge deficits be plausible justifications for inaction. Corporations with resources of this magnitude can arguably hire qualified individuals to develop antiracism D&I programming and other actions targeted at benefiting Black employees.

Thus, we are left pondering why some organizations did not commit to doing more to dismantle organizational racism? And, if the social pressure of BLM was not enough to ignite action what would be? According to Ray (2019) other governmental or policy forces could lead to further anti-racism work, but we acknowledge that such actions take time, and the critical nature of this work warrants urgent action. In comparison, other organizations have demonstrated their agile ability to promptly pivot resources to diversity programming with defined commitments and actions towards their Black employees, and some targeted the full spectrum of the employee experience from recruitment through to promotion opportunities.

Furthering research on racialized decoupling within the current social context is imperative due to the implications it has for the study of justice, equity, diversity, and inclusion. In investigating organizations' responses to the BLM movement, we identified additional areas of inquiry. Most significant to continuing this analysis is for future research to determine if the studied organizations upheld their commitments to reduce racialized structures within their organizations or if decoupling took place. Researchers may also wish to conduct a textual analysis of social media posts and corporate statements. For example, while some companies' CEO statements condemned racialized violence and committed to actional outcomes, others were vague in reference to the events of police brutality. This might serve to produce further links to corporate statements of organizational action-oriented approaches. Another important line of inquiry would be to analyze the comments made on companies' social media posts. Our preliminary analysis identified negative comments and replies related to both organizational efforts to reduce racial inequality and additional hate speech. While most organizations did not engage with these users, some were quite active in condemning hate speech and even reporting inappropriate conduct. The level to which organizations uphold their D&I values by moderating the comments and engagement with their diversity content may provide indications on the strength of their programming or the governance used to create a culture of inclusion. Lastly, we suggest that the framework developed within this study to classify the commitments made by organizations in response to BLM may be applied to other social movements such as #MeToo or Climate Change.

To summarize, over 50% of the companies analyzed within our study showed signs of true commitment towards reducing racial inequality in their organizations. However, 22 of the 50 companies analyzed either had no commitment, no new commitments or showed signs of tokenism towards racial equality despite the escalated nature of the BLM movement. Our analysis demonstrates the application of Ray's (2019) racialized organizational theory to BLM and demonstrates empirical evidence of racialized decoupling by organizations.

Further, our research reveals how social movements like BLM may alter the racialized structures of organizations through altered diversity programming. We offer that this social movement showcases an application of normative pressures at work. Our creation and use of the four categories to organize company responses to BLM provides a means to classify organizational commitments to a social movement, a mechanism that we feel is of value for future tokenism research. Lastly, while we acknowledge that the majority of organizations studied were motivated to reduce the presence of racism internally, we are disheartened by the lack of commitment by others. We recognize the systemic and critical nature of racism in both our society and organizations and are optimistic that future research within this field may influence the greater adoption of anti-racism progress in organizations.

REFERENCES

Acker, J. (1990). Hierarchies, jobs, bodies: A theory of gendered organizations. *Gender & Society*, *4*(2), 139–158.

Acker, J. (2012). Gendered organizations and intersectionality: problems and possibilities. *Equality, Diversity and Inclusion an International Journal*, *31*(3), 214–224.

Agocs, C. (2002). Canada's employment equity legislation and policy, 1987–2000: The gap between policy and practice. *International Journal of Manpower*, *23*(3), 256–276.

Apple. (2020a, July 16). *Apple teams up with HBCUs to bring coding and creativity opportunities to communities across the US*. Press Release. https://www.apple.com/newsroom/2020/07/apple-teams-up-with-hbcus-to-bring-coding-and-creativity-opportunities-to-communities-across-the-us/

Apple. (2020b, June 4). *Follow the link in bio to read the full message from Tim Cook and learn about the actions we are* [Photograph]. Instagram https://www.instagram.com/p/CBB6DcGlhbj/

Apple. (2021). *Inclusion and diversity*. https://www.apple.com/diversity/

Baron, J. N. (1994). Organization evidence of ascription in labour markets. In P. Burnstein (Ed.), *Equal employment opportunity: Labour market discrimination and public policy* (pp. 71-84). Transaction.

Batty, D. (2020, July 6). Universities criticized for 'tokenistic' support for Black Lives Matter. *The Guardian*. https://www.theguardian.com/education/2020/jul/06/universities-criticised-for-tokenistic-support-for-black-lives-matter

Bell, J. (2014). *The Black Power Movement and American social work*. Columbia University Press.

Berelson, B. (1952). *Content analysis in communication research*. The University of Chicago Press.

Berkshire Hathaway. (2021). *Official home page*. https://www.berkshirehathaway.com

Black Lives Matter. (2020). *About*. https://blacklivesmatter.com/about/

Buchanan, L., Bui, Q., & Patel, J. (2020, July 3). Black Lives Matter may be the largest movement in U.S. history. *The New York Times*. https://www.nytimes.com/interactive/2020/07/03/us/george-floyd-protests-crowd-size.html

Burgess, A. J., Wilkie, D. C., & Dolan, R. (2020). Towards successful diversity initiatives: The importance of building audience connectedness. *Journal of Marketing Management*, 1–18.

Chen, Y. S., & Chang, C. H. (2013). Greenwash and green trust: The mediation effects of green consumer confusion and green perceived risk. *Journal of Business Ethics*, *114*(3), 489–500.

Chevron. (2020a, June). *Chevron leaders on racial injustice and discrimination*. News. https://www.chevron.com/stories/statements-from-chevron-leaders-on-racial-injusticeanddiscrimination?utm_source=twitter&utm_medium=social&utm_campaig=corporateresponsiblity

Chevron. (2020b, June 5). black lives matter. words from our leaders: https://chevron.co/blmtw [Thumbnail with link attached] [Tweet]. Twitter. https://twitter.com/Chevron/status/1268984687927705600

Chevron. (2021a). *Diversity and inclusion, enabling human progress*. Sustainability. https://www.chevron.com/sustainability/social/diversity-inclusion

Cloud, D. L. (1996). Hegemony or concordance? The rhetoric of tokenism in "Oprah" Oprah rags-to-riches biography. *Critical Studies in Media Communication, 13*(2), 115–137.

Coscarelli, J. (2020, June 2). #BlackoutTuesday: A music industry protest becomes a social media movement. *The New York Times*. https://www.nytimes.com/2020/06/02/arts/music/what-blackout-tuesday.html

Costco. (2020a). *CEO Message*. Home. https://www.costcobusinesscentre.ca/ceo-message.html

Costco. (2020b, June 6). *Dear Costco members, along with the rest of the country, we were shocked by the tragic and senseless death of* [Status update]. Facebook. https://www.facebook.com/Costco/posts/10158836181744947

Costco. (2021). *Inclusion at Costco. We support workplace equality*. Costco Jobs. https://www.costco.com/inclusion.html

Del Real, J., Samuels, R., & Craig, T. (2020, June 6). How the Black Lives Matter movement went mainstream. *The Washington Post*. https://www.washingtonpost.com/national/how-the-black-lives-matter-movement-went-mainstream/2020/06/09/201bd6e6-a9c6-11ea-9063-e69bd6520940_story.html

DiMaggio, P. J., & Powell, W. W. (1983). The Iron Cage revisited: Institutional isomorphism and collective rationality in organizational fields. *American Sociological Review, 48*(2), 147–160.

Douglas, P.H. (2008). "Affinity groups: catalyst for inclusive organizations." *Employment Relations Today, 34*(4), 11–18.

Embrick, D. G. (2008). The diversity ideology: Keeping major transnational corporations white and male in an era of globalization. *Globalization and America: race, human rights, and inequality*, 23–42.

Embrick, D. G. (2011). The diversity ideology in the business world: A new oppression for a new age. *Critical Sociology, 37*(5), 541–56.

Etzioni, A. (1964). *Modern Organizations*. Prentice-Hall.

FedEx. (2020a, June 1). *Letter from Frederick W. Smith and Raj Subramaniam to all FedEx team members and global leadership*. FedEx Newsroom. https://newsroom.fedex.com/newsroom/letter-from-frederick-w-smith-and-raj- subramaniam-to-u-s-employees-and-global-leadership/

FedEx. (2020b, June 1). *Read the full message to our team members from FedEx Corporation Chairman and CEO Frederick W. Smith and President and COO Raj Subramaniam*. [Thumbnail with link attached] [Tweet] Twitter. https://twitter.com/FedEx/status/1267505133216321542

FedEx. (2020c, June 12). *The conversation about treating people with respect, dignity, and acceptance is one that is necessary and one we must keep going*. [Thumbnail with link attached] [Tweet] Twitter. https://twitter.com/FedEx/status/1271522661441495040

FedEx. (2021). *Diversity & inclusion: our values in action*. https://www.fedex.com/en-us/about/diversity-inclusion.html

Fortune Media. (2020). *Fortune 500*. https://fortune.com/fortune500/

Garza, A. (2014, October 7). *A herstory of the #BlackLivesMatter movement by Alicia Garza*. http://www.thefeministwire.com/2014/10/blacklivesmatter-2/

Gordon, H. (2020, June 1). *Black Out Tuesday: music industry plans day of business disruption in solidarity with Black community*. CBC. https://www.cbc.ca/music/black-out-tuesday- music-industry-plans-day-of-business-disruption-in-solidarity-with-black-community-1.5592990

Hill, E., Tiefenthaeler, A., Triebert, C., Jordan, D., Willis, H., & Stein, R. (2020, May 31). How George Floyd was killed in police custody. *The New York Times*. https://www.nytimes.com/2020/05/31/us/george-floyd-investigation.html

Hofstede, G. (1991). *Cultures and organizations: Software of the mind*. McGraw-Hill Book Company.

Jan, T., McGregor, J., Merle, R., & Tiku, N. (2020, June 13). As big corporations say 'black lives matter,' their track records raise skepticism. *The Washington Post*. https://www.washingtonpost.com/business/2020/06/13/after-years-marginalizing-black-employees-customers-corporate-america-says-black-lives-matter/?arc404=true

JPMorgan Chase & Co. (2021). *Our* path forward. Impact. https://www.jpmorganchase.com/impact/path-forward

JPMorgan Chase & Co. (2021). *Employee programs*. Who we are. https://www.jpmorganchase.com/about/people-culture/employee-programs

Kaplan, M. M., Sabin, E., & Smaller-Swift, S. (2009), "Tool: The catalyst guide to employee resource groups, 1-Introduction to ERGs." www.catalyst.org/knowledge/catalyst-guide-employeeresource-groups-1-introduction-ergs

Krenn, M. (2015). Understanding decoupling in response to corporate governance reform pressures. *Journal of Financial Regulation and Compliance, 23*(4), 369–382.

Leck, J. D. (2002). Making employment equity programs work for women. *Canadian Public Policy, 28*, 85–100.

Lyon, T. P., & Maxwell, J. W. (2011). Greenwash: Corporate environmental disclosure under threat of audit. *Journal of Economics and Management Strategy, 20*(1), 3–41.

Maqbool, A. (2020, July 9). *Black Lives Matter: From social media post to global movement*. BBC News. https://www.bbc.com/news/world-us-canada-53273381

Murphy, A., & Garavan, T. N. (2009). The Adoption and Diffusion of an NHRD Standard: A Conceptual Framework. *Human Resource Development Review, 8*(1), 3–21.

Ramaswamy, C. (2017, February 13). *Trayvon martin's parents, five years on: 'Racism is alive and well in America'*. The Guardian. https://www.theguardian.com/us-news/2017/feb/13/trayvon-martin-parents-racism-alive-and-well-in-america

Ray, V. (2019). A theory of racialized organizations. *American Sociological Review, 84*(1), 26–53. https://doi.org/10.1177/0003122418822335

Scott, W. R. (2008). *Institutions and organizations: Ideas and interests*. SAGE.

Sherrer, K (2018). *What Is tokenism, and why does it matter in the workplace?* Vanderbilt University, News and Events. https://business.vanderbilt.edu/news/2018/02/26/tokenism-in-the-workplace/

Singh, P., & Peng, P. (2010). Canada's bold experiment with pay equity. *Gender in Management, 25*(7), 570–585.

Singh, P., & Point, S. (2009). Diversity statements for leveraging organizational legitimacy. *Management International, 13*(2), 23–34.

Torchia, M., Calabrò, A., & Huse, M. (2011). Women directors on corporate boards: From tokenism to critical mass. *Journal of Business Ethics, 102*(2), 299–317.

UnitedHealth Group. (2020a). *UnitedHealth Group announces support for Minneapolis-St. Paul in response to George Floyd tragedy and civil unrest.* Newsroom. https://www.unitedhealthgroup.com/newsroom/posts/2020-06-01-support-george- floyd.html

UnitedHealth Group. (2020b). *A closer look at Freedom Day.* Newsroom. https://www.unitedhealthgroup.com/newsroom/posts/2020-06-19-juneteenth-freedom-day.html

UnitedHealth Group. (2020c, June 2). *Our hearts are heavy with the tragic death of George Floyd. We're doing our part to help create a more equitable* [Thumbnail with link attached] [Tweet] Twitter. https://twitter.com/UnitedHealthGrp/status/1267794235601928193

UnitedHealth Group (2021). *Inclusion & diversity.* Culture. https://careers.unitedhealthgroup.com/culture/inclusion-and-diversity/

Walmart. (2020). Diversity equity and inclusion. https://corporate.walmart.com/global-responsibility/diversity-equity-and-inclusion

Watson-Singleton, N. N., Mekawi, Y., Wilkins, K. V., & Jatta, I. F. (2020). Racism's effect on depressive symptoms: Examining perseverative cognition and Black Lives Matter activism as moderators. *Journal of Counseling Psychology, 68*(1), 27–37. https://doi.org/10.1037/cou0000436

Weber, R. (1990). *Quantitative applications in the social sciences: Basic content analysis.* SAGE.

Welbourne, T. M., Rolf, S., & Schlachter, S. (2017). The case for employee resource groups: A review and social identity theory-based research agenda. *Personnel Review, 46*(8), 1816–1834.

Westphal, J., & Zajac, E. (2001). Decoupling policy from practice: The case of stock repurchase programs. *Administrative Science Quarterly, 46*(2), 202–228.

van Oudenhoven, J. (2001). Do organizations reflect national cultures? A 10-nation study. *International Journal of Intercultural Relations, 25*(1), 89–107.

Yoder, J. D. (1991). Rethinking tokenism: Looking beyond numbers. *Gender & Society, 5*(2), 178–192.

APPENDIX

Summary of Findings

Company	Pre-Mainstream	Response to Mainstream BLM Movement	Action(s) taken to reduce racialized organizational structures in response to BLM movement	ocial Media posts related to BLM (includes racism, racial justice etc.)	Classification
Walmart	• D&I Statement • Employee education program (achievement of college degree, high school diploma, skilled trade certificate and others) with 47% participation by employees of color	• CEO Statement • New racial equity commitment • Released Mid-Year Culture, Diversity, and Inclusion Report (2021) • Created a center for racial equity • Increased transparency in D & I reporting • Commitment to enhanced hiring practices, including diverse hiring teams, internal promotion, research to understand how to diversify talent			

(Appendix continued on next page)

APPENDIX (CONTINUED)

Summary of Findings

Walmart		• Offers a self-paced racial equity curriculum for all U.S. associates • Introduced Shared Value Network Team comprised of Black employees to guide racial equity advancements	Yes	Yes	True Commitment
Exxon Mobil	• D&I Statement • D&I Framework (Report) • ERG for Black Employees	No reference to BLM or D&I.	No	No	No New Commitment
Apple	• D&I Statement • Transparency in employee demographics • Partnerships with HBCUs • ERG for Black employees	• CEO Statement • Launched a Racial Equity and Justice Initiative focused on creating opportunity for communities of color • Increased HBCU partnerships to promote coding and workforce developing opportunities	Yes	Yes	True Commitment

(Appendix continued on next page)

APPENDIX (CONTINUED)

Summary of Findings

Berkshire Hathaway	No information on D&I available on company webpage. *Berkshire Hathaway's subsidiaries do make D&I and BLM commitments*	No reference to BLM or D&I .	No	No	No Commitment
Amazon.com	• D&I Statement • ERG for Black employees • Conversations on Race and Ethnicity (CORE) program, an internal conference led by scholars and activists	• Corporate Statement • Matched employee donations to initiatives focused on combating systemic racism (organizations were selected with the Black ERG) • Black ERG given a grant to fund local racial equality and education initiatives in various communities • Promoted Amazon products curated by the Black ERG	Yes	Yes	True Commitment

(Appendix continued on next page)

APPENDIX (CONTINUED)
Summary of Findings

United-Health Group	• D&I Statement • ERGs (unspecified) • Partnerships with Black organizations (i.e., Black MBA Association) • Internship, mentorship and scholarship programs targeted to diverse students	• Statement from CEO and other Executives	No	Yes	No New Commit-ment
McKesson	• D&I Statement • ERGs (unspecified) • Diversity champions and advisory board at an employee level	• CEO Statement	No	Yes	No New Commit-ment
CVS Health	• D&I Statement • Workforce diversity partnerships • Diversity recruiting initiatives and learning centers for prospective pharmacy apprentices	• CEO Statement • Five-year investment includes employee initiatives that address racial inequality including mentorship, sponsorship, and development of diverse employees, company-wide inclusion training	Yes	Yes	True Com-mitment

(Appendix continued on next page)

APPENDIX (CONTINUED)

Summary of Findings

CVS Health	• D&I Statement • Workforce diversity partnerships • Diversity recruiting initiatives and learning centers for prospective pharmacy apprentices	• Commitment to use position to advocate for public policy that addresses systemic inequalities	Yes	Yes	True Commitment
AT&T	• D&I Statement • D&I Annual Report • Transparency in employee demographics • Recruitment at HBCUs • Partnerships with Black organizations (over 20) i.e., Black Girls Code, National Black MBA Association • ERG for Black employees	• CEO Statement • Promote conversations on racial inequality in leadership town halls and team meetings • Commitment to purchase with Black-owned suppliers • Investment in economic opportunities for Black communities focusing on workforce readiness, technology, and entrepreneurship with HBCUs • Created diverse television content (Black News Channel)	Yes	Yes	True Commitment
Amerisource-Bergen	• D&I Statement • ERG for Black Employees	• CEO Statement	No	Yes	No New Commitment

(Appendix continued on next page)

APPENDIX (CONTINUED)

Summary of Findings

Chevron	• D&I Statement • Partnerships with diversity associations such as the National Society of Black Engineers (NSBE) — internships, FT opportunities for students • Programs with HBCUs are designed to encourage minority participation in STEM • Diversity Training • ERG for Black Employees	• Statements from CEO and other Executives (includes Black Employee Network President)	No	Yes	No New Commit-ment
Ford Motor	• Ford Fund supports educational programming & initiatives designed to help people improve their economic status and quality of life and supports HBCUs	•Corporate Statement	No	Yes	No New Commit-ment

(Appendix continued on next page)

APPENDIX (CONTINUED)

Summary of Findings

General Motors	• D&I State-ment • Co-op program (comprehensive, paid summer internship program for high school students in under-resourced communities)	• CEO Statement • Invested funding in antiracism work guided by ERGs	Yes	Yes	True Commitment
Costco Wholesale	• D&I Statement	• CEO Statement	No	Yes	Tokenism
Alphabet	• D&I report • Black Leadership Advisory Group • ERG for Black Employees • Commitment to increase Black+ and Latinx+ employees • Educational partnerships • State of Black Women EMEA Summit	• CEO announcement • Corporate statements • YouTube's—Trust and Safety team will work to strengthen product policies against hate and harassment. • Investment in Black business owners, startup founders, job seekers and developers, in addition to YouTube's fund to amplify Black creators and artists. • Google for Startups Accelerator for Black Founders, 3-month mentorship program	Yes	Yes	True Commitment

(Appendix continued on next page)

APPENDIX (CONTINUED)

Summary of Findings

Alphabet		• Funding targeted to closing the racial equity gaps in computer science education and increase Black+ representation in STEM fields and other education programming	Yes	Yes	True Commitment
Cardinal Health	• D&I Statement • Executive Group for Black Racial Equity	• Corporate Statement	No	Yes	No New Commitment
Walgreens Boots Alliance	• D&I Statement • D&I I Report • ERG for Black employees • Unconscious bias training	• Statement from CEO and other Executives • Unconscious bias training	No	Yes	No New Commitment
JPMorgan Chase	• D&I Statements • ERG for Black employees— BOLD—Black Organization for leadership development • Advancing Black Pathways— Expanding Economic Opportunity for Black People	• Statements from D&I executive • Financial commitment includes focus on employees (build a more equitable and representative workforce, upskill, and reskill	Yes	Yes	True Commitment

(Appendix continued on next page)

APPENDIX (CONTINUED)

Summary of Findings

Verizon Communications	• D&I Statement • ERG for Black Employees	• D&I Report • Statement from CEO and other Executives	No	Yes	No New Commitment
Kroger	• D&I Statement • ERG for Black employees	• ERG has developed an allyship resource guide • New Framework for Action: Diversity, Equity & Inclusion plan—Improve diverse talent recruiting by partnering with HBCU, Hispanic Association Colleges & Universities, and community college. • Creation of a D&I Advisory Council • Unconscious bias training	Yes	Yes	True Commitment
General Electric	• D&I Statement • ERG for Black employees	• CEO Statement • New Executive Position Related to D&I	Yes	Yes	True Commitment
Fannie Mae	• D&I Statement • ERG for Black employees	• CEO Statement • New executive position related to D&I	Yes	Yes	True Commitment

(Appendix continued on next page)

APPENDIX (CONTINUED)

Summary of Findings

Philips 66	• D&Statement • Executive D&I committee • ERG for Black employees	No reference to BLM or D&I	No	No	No New Commit-ment
Valero Energy	• D&I statement included in a PDF flyer on careers page • Educational engineering summit for minority students	No reference to BLM or D&I.	No	No	No New Commit-ment
Bank of America	• D&I Statement • ERG for Black employees • Partnerships with organizations focuses on promoting Black talent • Annual com-memoration and education events for Black History Month • Commit-ments to Black community partnerships	• Investment to address racial inequality includes focus on job training • Financial commitment to support women of colour in career advancement • Financial support to tutoring opportunities through Boys & Girls Club partnership • CEO Statement & Chief Diversity Officer Statement • Expanded connections with HBCUs • Encourage employees to review D&I priority, inclusion learning programs and other resources • Investment in internal D&I • Commitment to double Black managers and senior employees by 2025	Yes	Yes	True Com-mitment

(Appendix continued on next page)

APPENDIX (CONTINUED)

Summary of Findings

| Microsoft | • D&I Statement
• D&I report
• Transparency in employee demographic information
• Voluntary Allyship at Microsoft training
• Blacks at Microsoft program includes development of Black employees and scholarships for Black students to pursue careers technology | • Starting in 2021 all employees will be required to take training on allyship and privilege in the workplace with specific interest in the experience of Black employees
• Live training sessions for VPs
• Strengthened career planning for Black employees
• Expanded leadership development employees for Black employees at various levels
• Evaluate VP and GM's on diversity and inclusion
• Provide CVPs with D&I coaches to resolve systemic issues in their organizations
• Double Black owned suppliers over 3 years
• Double transaction volumes with Black owned financial institutions
• Additional funding to Black entrepreneurs
• Expand program to bring computer science education to Black schools
• Offer digital skill training to Black adults seeking jobs | Yes | Yes | True Commitment |

(Appendix continued on next page)

APPENDIX (CONTINUED)

Summary of Findings

Home Depot	• D&I Statement • Diversity based partnerships • ERG for Black employees	• CEO Statement	No	Yes	No New Commitment
Boeing	• D&I Statement • ERG for Black employees • Employee training and development	• CEO Statement • Board member Statement • Created a conversation guide for leaders with resources to discuss racial equity • Commitment to have transparency in employee demographics in 2021 • Commitment to increase representation of Black employees in the U.S. by 20%	Yes	Yes	True Commitment
Wells Fargo	• D&I Statement • Executive led EDI council • Quarterly diversity scorecard • ERG for Black employees	• CEO Statement • Commitment to double Black leadership representation in 5 years • Antiracism training for managers • Education sessions for employees • Leadership compensation based on diversity • New and expanded diversity role reporting to the CEO	Yes	Yes	True Commitment

(Appendix continued on next page)

APPENDIX (CONTINUED)

Summary of Findings

Citigroup	• D&I Statement • Executive led affinity groups, including one for Black employees, aimed to understand the needs of a demographic group • ERGs for Black employees • Diverse panel for director hiring • Offer unconscious bias training	• Statements from CEO and CFO • Initiate community partnerships serving racially diverse individuals • Funding for Black entrepreneurs • Commitment to spend with Black-owned suppliers • Commitment to produce inclusive software for banking clients • Increase representation in marketing and leadership • Create a senior leadership council to monitor racial equity commitments	Yes	Yes	True Commitment
Marathon Petroleum	• D&I Statement • Diversity and Inclusion Office leads a diversity strategy • ERGs for employees • D&I workshops and panels	No reference to BLM or D&I.	No	Yes	No New Commitment

(Appendix continued on next page)

APPENDIX (CONTINUED)

Summary of Findings

Comcast	• D&I Statement • Values Report (produced by external diversity advisory council • ERG for Black employees • ERG based mentorship program • Produces Black film and TV, includes media related to HBCU sporting events, tv, and playlists	• CEO Statement • Initiated program to support Black businesses impacted by COVID-19 with grants, marketing, and other supports • Initiated race-related conversations in Town Halls, speaker series • Mandatory antiracism and antibias training • Additional funding for ERGs	Yes	Yes	True Commitment
Anthem	• D&I Statement • ERG for Black employees • Offer unconscious-bias training • ERG's aid in promoting talent acquisition partnerships • Offers internship and scholarships for racially diverse students	• CEO Statement	Yes	Yes	No New Commitment

(Appendix continued on next page)

APPENDIX (CONTINUED)

Summary of Findings

Dell Technologies	• D&I Statement • D&I Report • ERG for Black employees • Black network alliance for recruitment and retention •Transparency in employee demographics •Commitments to Black and Hispanic representation in workforce and leadership by 2030 • Partnership to advance Black career opportunities in STEM	• Statement from Chief Diversity and Inclusion Officer	No	Yes	No New Commitment
DuPont de Nemours	• D&I Statement • Program to assist under-represented groups with career opportunities • ERG for Black employees	• CEO Statement • Commitment to advance racial equity through talent development, hiring, and overall reduction of racism • Team commitments will include members of the Black ERG	Yes	Yes	True Commitment

(Appendix continued on next page)

APPENDIX (CONTINUED)

Summary of Findings

State Farm Insurance	• D&I Statement • ERG for Black employees	• Pledge to advance education for Black community • CDO Statements (includes commitment for recruiting, hiring, employee learning paths, career development, and succession planning)	Yes	Yes	True Commitment
Johnson & Johnson	• D&I Statement	• CEO Statement • Series of listening tours and events for dialogue with leaders and fellow employees • Note to Black employees: take the time you need to process, stand up for your beliefs, and do whatever you need to do to take care of your families, communities, and yourselves.	Yes	Yes	True Commitment
IBM	• D&I Statement • ERG for Black employees	• IBM Will no longer offer or Develop Facial Recognition Software in Pursuit Of Racial Justice Reform (includes employees)	Yes	Yes	True Commitment
Target	• D&I Statement • ERG for Black employees	• CEO Statement • Juneteenth company holiday • Established REACH—our Racial Equity Action and Change committee—to create an action plan to guide our way.	Yes	Yes	True Commitment

(Appendix continued on next page)

APPENDIX (CONTINUED)

Summary of Findings

Freddie Mac	• D&I Statement • ERG for black employees • Polaris (training and teaching using a diverse group of VP-level mentoring and providing courses for Black ERG members)	• CEO Statement • Improved Polaris program (internal program for Black employees)	No	Yes	No New Commit-ment
United Parcel Service	• D&I Statement • ERG for black employees	• Commitment to support employment, education, small businesses, advocacy • Expansion to internal unconscious bias training, creating regular forums for additional discussion regarding topics surrounding racial equality and justice, and expanding its internship program with historically Black colleges, among other actions.	Yes	Yes	True Com-mitment
Lowe's	• D&I Statement • ERG Programs (unspecified)	• CEO Statement	No	Yes	No New Commit-ment

(Appendix continued on next page)

APPENDIX (CONTINUED)

Summary of Findings

Intel	• D&I Statements • D&I Report	• Statement from CEO and other Executives • Commitment to double investment in Black founders • Increasing investment to develop diverse employees— developing, mentoring, sponsoring, and promoting the diverse talent on our team	Yes	Yes	True Commitment
MetLife	• D&I Statement	• Corporate Statement (not employee specific)	No	Yes	Tokenism
Proctor and Gamble	• D&I Statement • ERG- for Black employees	• Statements from CEO and other Executives • Committed funding for racial equality • New films on bias, inequality, and racism	Yes	Yes	True Commitment
Raytheon Technologies	• D&I Statements	• CEO Statement • CEO article regarding listening to Black leaders within the organization	No	Yes	Tokenism
FedEx	• D&I Statement	• Statement from CEO and COO	No	Yes	Tokenism

(Appendix continued on next page)

APPENDIX (CONTINUED)

Summary of Findings

PepsiCo	• D&I Statement • D&I Report • Internal programs to promote Black history • ERG for Black employees	• CEO Statement • Initiative for Black representation at PepsiCo—(focusing on increasing representation; recruitment; and education, internships and apprenticeship expanding Black managerial population by 30% by 2025 through internal development and recruitment.)	Yes	Yes	True Commitment
Archer Daniels Midland	• D I Statement • Unconscious bias training	• Executive statements • Continue bias training • Will host forums for listening, discussion and learning.	Yes	Yes	True Commitment

(Appendix continued on next page)

APPENDIX (CONTINUED)

Summary of Findings

Prudential Financial	• D&I Statement • ERG for Black employees	• Statements from CEO and other Executives • Education funding commitment • Spotlighted in a series of case studies that outline innovative steps that the company is taking to banish racism in the workplace • Mandate antiracism and other inclusion training for all employees (U.S.) • Mark Juneteenth as a day of education and reflection to continue our learning. • Evaluate and improve talent practices—hiring, promotion, performance management, development and compensation— to ensure equal opportunity for all employees. • Commit to increase transparency in workforce demographics	Yes	Yes	True Commitment

CHAPTER 8

JUST GETTING STARTED

An Organizational and Management Scholar's Perspective on the Challenges Faced by Black Female Founders

Shana M. Yearwood
Teachers College, Columbia University

ABSTRACT

Black women are one of the fastest growing demographics of entrepreneurs in the United States. The number of Black women founders, a subset of entrepreneurs who create startups, which are high-growth or high-technology enterprises, is also increasing. Yet not much is known about the unique challenges Black women founders face, and how their challenges are similar to or different from the challenges of all Black women entrepreneurs. This chapter provides historical context and background on the motivations and current state of Black women entrepreneurs and founders and uses the metaphor of the "concrete wall" to explore what challenges Black women founders face as they try to launch, grow, and sustain their businesses. A single case study is used as an exemplar to elucidate these challenges—which include lack of access to startup capital, finding and attracting talent, and investor biases—and to compare them to challenges faced by other underrepresented groups

The Future of Scholarship on Race in Organizations, pp. 179–199
Copyright © 2022 by Information Age Publishing

of entrepreneurs. The chapter concludes with a proposed research agenda for management and organizational scholars to better understand Black women founders and the ecosystem within which they operate in order to inform potential solutions.

Over the course of 2020, two events compelled American organizations to not only rethink how and where they do business, but also to confront the inequities inherent in the United States economy. Beginning in March, the COVID-19 pandemic upended every realm of American organizational life, bringing much of the economy to a halt. At the same time, a series of high-profile police killings of Black men and women pressured the business community to contend with its role in perpetuating systemic racism. These two events directed public attention to the difficulties faced by business owners, and in particular, Black business owners (Presha & Yamada, 2020). Many Black entrepreneurs owned businesses in the industries most affected by the virus, such as accommodation and food services, retail, and health care and social assistance (Gould & Wilson, 2020) and were at greatest risk of being shut down. Three months after the shutdown, a preliminary report by the National Bureau of Economic Research found that both Black and women-owned businesses closed at disproportionate rates (Fairlie, 2020).

For Black women business owners in particular, 82% reported that their bottom lines fell sharply due to regulations that either severely limited their services, or shut them down altogether, for months on end (Digital Undivided, 2020; Umoh, 2020). Moreover, due to characteristics such as loan size and prior lending relationships, businesses owned by Black women were much less likely to receive much-needed financial support from the Payment Protection Plan (PPP), the federal assistance program for small businesses (Brooks, 2020; Hello Alice, 2020; Small Business Majority, 2020). For a particular subset of Black women entrepreneurs, founders, the economic shutdown highlighted a unique set of existing challenges. These challenges include access to funding and resources that would make their businesses sustainable, or that would allow them to pivot during an economic crisis. COVID-19 did not create these challenges; rather, it created a set of economic circumstances that brought the challenges to light.

Though research on underrepresented entrepreneurs has increased, much of prior research focused on either women entrepreneurs (Brush, 1992; Brush et al., 2019; Jennings & Brush, 2013; Moore & Buttner, 1997; Wheadon & Duval-Couetil, 2019) or minority or Black entrepreneurs (Fairlie, 2013; Fairlie & Robb, 2008; Morgan Stanley, 2018), which may subsume or obscure the experiences of Black women entrepreneurs. In addition, though research has begun to capture the experiences of Black women entrepreneurs running various types and sizes of ventures (Harvey, 2005;

Inman, 2000; Jackson & Sanyal, 2019; Jones, 2017; Smith, 2005), as well as women founders more broadly (Teare, 2020), less is known about Black women founders, and the nature and causes of their challenges. Project Diane, a biennial research project designed to focus specifically on this population, is one of the only research projects dedicated to understanding who Black women founders are and barriers to their success.

Black women founders are severely underrepresented; although Black women made up 15% of all women entrepreneurs in 2012, they were less than half of 1% of all women-led technology startups in 2015, leading researchers to refer to them as the "real unicorns of tech" (Finney & Rencher, 2016; U.S. Census Bureau, 2012). In addition, Black women founders face both gender and racial discrimination when trying to secure funding or access resources (Digital Undivided, 2020). Unfortunately, Black and Latina women founders received only 0.64% of all venture capitalist funding since 2018 and raised significantly less than their White male and female counterparts in 2020, despite showing a lower rate of failure than all startups tracked by Project Diane (Digital Undivided, 2020; Teare, 2019). These funding disparities can often mean failure to launch their ventures, as they do not secure enough funding to even construct prototypes of their ideas (Finney & Rencher, 2016).

Better understanding the experiences of Black women founders is critical for a few reasons. First, the number of Black women entrepreneurs and founders is a growing population. Businesses owned by Black women grew at double the rate of all women in the past five years (American Express, 2019). Project Diane (Digital Undivided, 2020) showed the number of Black women founders has increased by almost 200% since their inaugural survey in 2016, indicating that Black women remain motivated to participate in the American economy in new ways.

Second, the experiences of Black women founders differ in nature from those of other entrepreneurs. Black women founders are differentiated from other Black women entrepreneurs by the nature of their businesses; they create startups, fast-paced organizations designed to rapidly test and bring to market new ideas, often in the technology industry (Blank, 2013; Finney & Rencher, 2016; Riani, 2021). They are not only entering a space with fewer legal protections against discriminations than in traditional corporations but are also reliant on an industry—venture capitalism—that has been widely criticized for its discriminatory practices, as well as its reluctance and hesitance to change (Albergotti, 2020; Benner, 2017; Cutler, 2015; Fahs, 2019; Grant, 2020; Hinchliffe, 2019; Karake, 2020).

Lastly, this group represents sizable economic potential; if the gap between White women-owned businesses and businesses were to be closed, Black women-owned businesses would create an additional 2.4 million jobs, and more than $500 million in revenue would be introduced into the

American economy (American Express, 2019). Thus, Black women founders are critical not only to supporting the economic mobility of the Black community, but also to contributing to national economic prosperity.

The purpose of this chapter is twofold. First, to better understand the experiences of Black women founders. Due to limited research on this population, a case study of one Black woman founder is used as an exemplar to explore their challenges and compare them to the challenges faced by other Black women entrepreneurs. Second, to propose an agenda for future research on Black women founders by recommending how organizational and management scholars can build our understanding of this group.

A Brief History of Black Women's Entrepreneurship

Black women have long participated in the United States economy as business owners. However, their status as entrepreneurs has not always been recognized or acknowledged, given their skillsets, the jobs, and industries with which they were most associated, and the historical and market forces that lessened their agency (Boyd, 2000; Smith, 2005). The vast majority of research has focused on the challenges Black women faced in trying to access the primary labor market, and their denial of access (Abelda, 1986; Cunningham & Zalokar, 1992). This denial of access is impossible to ignore, as it means that Black women were largely segregated into agricultural or domestic work for decades, a trend that "exhibited striking continuity across space ... and time" (Jones, 1985, p. 161). This section traces the arc of Black women's entrepreneurship over time and shows how their entrepreneurial activity was both a result of and *in spite of* their broader context.

Smith (2005) contends that Black women, continuing in the tradition of their African ancestors, found ways to create successful businesses despite challenging circumstances. Similarly, Berry and Gross (2020) suggest that Black women exercised their agency, however limited, to participate in the American economy as entrepreneurs. During the period of slavery, though enslaved Black women's personal liberties were restricted, some women were able to sell crops or engage in agricultural brokering (Smith, 2005). In the 1800s, businesses owned by freed Black women included trading and bartering goods, food services, boarding homes, seamstress shops, and laundering (Schweninger, 1989, 1990; Smith, 2005). Following slavery, many Black women continued to leverage the skills they had built as enslaved women, hiring out their services as domestic workers, cooks, nurses, and seamstresses (Goldin, 1977; Jones, 1985). Though Black women were, by many accounts, were mainly relegated to domestic work during this time period, they still attempted to create boundaries around the type of work they did, as well as where they completed the work. For instance, Black women laundresses were able to bring washloads to their homes, and organized to protect their pay rates (White, 1999). They also engaged in harvesting activities above and beyond their sharecropping duties as a means of earning extra income (White, 1999).

By the early 20th century, Black women entrepreneurs began to become more established in the personal services and retail industries, and there were also cases of Black women owning financial institutions such as banks or insurance companies (Berry & Gross, 2020; Garrett-Scott, 2009; Smith, 2005). Black women also continued their tradition as cooks, selling food at public markets, and in some cases, owned restaurants, or catering services (Berry & Gross, 2020; Smith, 2005). Historians have also identified examples of former enslaved women who were able to invest in and create businesses that enabled them to become millionaires, such as investor and activist Mary Ellen Pleasant, midwife and daycare owner Bridget Mason, and Madam C. J. Walker's predecessor, Annie Tumbo Malone (Hayden, 1989; Wills, 2019).

Still, despite the successes of some Black women entrepreneurs, Black women's labor continued to be shaped by economic stability and exclusion. During the Industrial Revolution, Black women were excluded from some factory jobs in favor of poor European immigrants and were excluded from clerical and sales jobs created at the start of the 20th century, which more often went to White women or to Black men (Branch, 2011; Jones, 1985). Following the Great Depression, Black women, largely excluded from federal aid due to being segregated in agriculture and domestic work, were again pressured to create businesses for economic survival. Boyd (2000) found that Black women in Northern cities during this time period were likely to create boarding homes, serve as housekeepers, or provide hairdressing or personal services due to their familiarity with and history of participation in those industries.

In the decades following the Civil Rights Movement, minority-owned business received enough federal support and resources to experience a resurgence, particularly among smaller enterprises (Butler, 2005). Additionally, increased educational opportunities meant that Black women entrepreneurs were able to expand their skills and expertise, and by the 1980s, were able to enter the market for business services (Inman, 2000). By 1997, Black women owned more than 312,000 businesses, employing 189,000 employees, and generating nearly $14 billion in revenue (Smith, 2005).

It is evident that Black women took part in the economy as entrepreneurs from the time of their arrival in the United States up to the start of the 21st century. This history illustrates how Black women's entrepreneurial activity was a result of both "push" and "pull factors." Historical, sociopolitical, and economic factors such as enslavement, codified segregation, social safety nets, and legal protections were driving forces in Black women's ability to become entrepreneurs. Yet, Black women also have a longstanding tradition of displaying entrepreneurial aptitude and spirit and have taken pride in being able to use ingenuity to take care of themselves, their families, and their communities. Both trends continue today.

The Current State of Black Women Entrepreneurs and Founders

Black women entrepreneurs. Black women are now one of the most rapidly growing groups on entrepreneurs in the United States. Despite historical obstacles, businesses with a majority ownership of Black women grew 67% between 2007 and 2012 (Nielsen, 2017), and continued to grow at a rate of 50% between 2014 and 2019, such that Black women now own 21% of all women-owned businesses (American Express, 2019). More Black women are becoming entrepreneurs than ever before, with 17% starting or at the helm of new businesses, which is higher than that of White women or White men (Kelley et al., 2021). Today, Black women own nearly 2.6 million businesses, and operate across a wide array of industries (American Express, 2019). Nearly half of Black women-owned businesses with employees operate in healthcare and social assistance, followed by 13% in professional, scientific, and technical services (Baboolall et al., 2020).

The growth of the Black women entrepreneurial population is not without challenges. Black women entrepreneurs are segregated in industries that generate lower revenue (Baboolall et al., 2020). In 2012, Black women-owned businesses made up 9% of all businesses yet generated less than .5% of all sales and less than one third of the revenue generated by all Black-owned businesses (U.S. Census Bureau, 2012). Black women entrepreneurs are half as likely to be running mature businesses as White women, despite higher rates of starting businesses (Kelley et al., 2021). This is likely due to higher rates of business failure, with 49% of businesses created by Black women closing in the same year they were founded in 2007 (Mora & Davila, 2014).

Multiple reasons have been proposed as to why Black women continue to be drawn to entrepreneurship in large numbers, despite challenges. Some researchers continue to propose the "push" factors that historically drove Black women from the primary labor market. Black women continue to face significant wage gaps, with their wages having stagnated as of 1990 (Bureau of Labor Statistics, 2019; del Río & Alonso-Villar, 2015; Reeves & Guyot, 2017) and continue to face occupational segregation more broadly

(Alonso-Villar & del Rio, 2017; Catalyst, 2020; Matthews & Wilson, 2018. Indeed, Black women seem to be starting businesses as a means of supplementary income; they are more likely than any other group of women to be "sidepreneurs," and the majority spend fewer than 40 hours weekly on their enterprises (American Express, 2019; Balboolal et al., 2020)

Researchers also propose that for women professionals who work in traditional, large corporations, a glass or concrete ceiling may drive them to create their own enterprises (Heilman & Chen, 2003; Jackson & Sanyal, 2019). Bell and Nkomo (2001) call out the challenges faced by Black women in corporate America as being made of concrete, alluding to the fact that it is nearly impossible to break through; rather, one must "dig under, or find a way to climb over, or find a way to get around it" (Bernstein et al., 2018). Research has indicated that some Black women have become disillusioned with the lack of opportunities and barriers to advancement and have become discontented with the traditional labor market (Walker's Legacy, 2016).

In addition to those who want to evade or circumnavigate the corporate concrete ceiling, some Black women are also drawn to becoming entrepreneurs due to the attractiveness of what it means to "be your own boss." A growing body of research has identified more "pull" factors specific to Black women. They become entrepreneurs to have increased freedom and flexibility, especially around setting their own schedules, not having to be as concerned with childcare, and being able to spend more time with their families (Guidant Financial, 2020; Harvey, 2005; Heilman & Chen, 2003; Robinson et al., 2007). Black women are also interested in entrepreneurship as a potential means of economic mobility, with the strong desire to build or increase wealth for their families (Robinson et al., 2007; Walker's Legacy, 2016). Lastly, Black women are drawn to entrepreneurship in order to fulfill a specific need within or outside of their immediate community (Guidant Financial, 2020; Jones, 2017; Jackson & Sanyal, 2019).

Black women founders. Concurrent with the shift in growing number of Black women entrepreneurs, a shift has occurred within the economy that has, in some ways, lowered the barriers to becoming an entrepreneur. Technology and the rise of the digital age has caused the economy to evolve from more traditional products (Wheadon & Duval-Couetil, 2019). Technology and the rise of social media have created unique opportunities to market services directly to potential clientele. Much of what is known about Black women founders comes from the research project Diane, conducted by Digital Undivided. Black women have taken advantage of the changing economy in record numbers, launching startups in retail and consumer goods, business services, health, and education (Digital Undivided, 2020). Startups represent a unique opportunity for Black women entrepreneurs to rapidly ideate, design, create, and deploy new businesses that meet consumer needs.

Black women entrepreneurs are increasingly participating in this type of business ownership, with many ventures founded by Black women having been created in the last three years (Digital Undivided, 2020). Given the lack of specific designations given to entrepreneurial ventures in federal and other reporting, it is difficult to track the exact number of Black women-owned businesses that qualify as startup ventures. According to Project Diane's most recent report, which includes data on both Black and Latinx women founders, this group is highly educated, with 90% of their sample holding a bachelor's degree, and 50% holding more advanced degrees (Digital Undivided, 2020). These women founders are also more likely to be middle-aged, with more than 60% of the sample between 30 and 49 years of age, and 61% having grown up in a middle-class household (Digital Undivided, 2020).

These statistics describe Black women founders, but data on their experiences, and in particular the challenges they face and why they face them, continues to be limited. The metaphor of the concrete wall (Bell & Nkomo, 2001), as opposed to a ceiling, is an apt metaphor for Black women founders, as it implies that the journey of Black women founders is halted by an immovable hurdle, one that serves as a barrier to their progression forward, as opposed to the vertical ascent of a career ladder or hierarchy. In order to better understand the predicament of Black women founders, the case of one Black woman founder, who owns a successful company in consumer mobile technology, is explored. The next section traces her startup journey and some of the challenges she faced, and then uses existing data on Black women entrepreneurs and women founders more broadly to contextualize the case.

CASE STUDY

Our case study is one of a Black woman founder in the fast-paced software technology industry, named Michelle for the purpose of this chapter. Michelle is in her early 30s and is of African descent. The eldest in her family, Michelle grew up in the Northeastern United States, eventually majoring in engineering at an Ivy League university. Following her undergraduate studies, Michelle began working as a product engineer for an international consumer goods company. Early in Michelle's career, she began to excel in her role, which led her to form new insights about her work, as well as her ability to create value for the organization. As she developed new products for the organization, some of which became patented, she realized that though her intellectual capital was benefitting the organization, she ultimately did not own the output. In addition, she felt hampered by the organizational bureaucracy, which slowed the pace at which new products could be brought to market. Decisions about each product had to be reviewed by several stakeholders, and the entire review process would restart if significant enough changes were made to the product. Michelle began to view herself as more of a creator, and the idea of starting her own business became increasingly attractive to her. At that time, she was most interested in the freedom and flexibility entrepreneurship seemed to offer, as well as excited by the prospect of creating much-needed products at a more accelerated rate. She was excited by the consistent challenges of the entrepreneurial process, and the idea that anyone could start their own business if they were diligent and persistent enough.

Michelle was in her mid-20s when she launched her first business, a wellness subscription product, the experience of which compelled her to continue her formal education at a top 10 American business school. During business school, she followed trends related to the convenience industry, and took note of a new market need, by observing her own behavior and that of her classmates. Her second business was born, beginning as a consumer app, and has now been in business for just over four years. However, Michelle's journey to launch and grow her startup was difficult, and at times so challenging, she wondered whether to continue.

Michelle faced significant challenges in raising capital for her startup. In describing her experience pitching to investors in the early days of her business, Michelle described shortcuts she learned in order to predict what her experience might be with a particular investor, and to prepare accordingly. One indicator she used to discern this was whether or not their portfolios contained minorities, women, or other entrepreneurs from underrepresented backgrounds. If their portfolios did not contain anyone who looked like her, she knew they were likely not to invest. This strategy also helped her better insulate herself from disappointing results following what she believed to be otherwise successful pitches. Over the course of her time as a founder, she received more than 100 declines to fund her business. As a result, Michelle was forced to raise startup capital through other means. The first $250,000 she raised came from more than 800 donors, many of whom were either in her personal network, were college students with whom her business concept resonated, or both. Through equity crowdfunding, Michelle was able to raise enough money to build a prototype and launch at her graduate school. The prototype enabled her to do two things critical to securing additional funding—demonstrate consumer need and interest and collect data on how consumers were engaging with her product.

Another challenge Michelle faced was in attracting others to work with her, especially during the early stages of the company. She explained that Black founders are less likely to have cofounders because people are less likely to want to work for them for free. She felt that many in the pool of potential employees seemed to be "looking for the next Mark Zuckerberg." Early on, she could not afford to pay salaries, but though she was willing to offer equity, she found it difficult to find talent because, despite her credentials, she did not match up to others' image of a successful tech founder. As a result, she operated her business with the support of two other individuals until after the prototype had been developed. Interestingly, Michelle also shared experiences of attending large-scale events, and having attendees mistake her White male intern as the founder, which further indicated to her that others might not believe in her capabilities or competence based on her appearance.

A third challenge Michelle described was facing investor bias. When asked how that bias manifested, she explained that many venture capitalists are "pattern-matching" when they are listening to new pitches, but that at the time, examples of Black women founders who have generated outsized returns did not yet exist. She described being seated across the table from as many as eight White men at a time and being able to tell that they were "checked out" or had already decided whether or not they would be funding her venture before hearing her pitch. In addition, she felt investors asked many more questions of her than of her White or male colleagues, and in many cases, their questions were easy to identify as biased due to their content; they were asking her for information that no start-up would have in its early stages. From Michelle's perspective, it is common in industry for investors to "bet on the person," but in her case, they were focusing more heavily on the data. Michelle consistently felt as though investors were consistently attempting to "poke holes" in her concept. She described being told that her concept was too early in the process, that it "needed more traction," so that she could demonstrate more clearly her business was low-risk.

With the additional data from the prototype, Michelle was able to raise additional funding of more than $1.5 million. When the COVID-19 crisis hit, Michelle decided to pivot her business model. She realized being so heavily reliant on funding would no longer be sustainable given how her consumer markets had shifted during Covid-19, and rapidly evolved from a consumer mobile application to a business-to-business, or B2B, product, in order to be able to generate more revenue. Leveraging the existing application, her company rebranded and, as of the end of 2020, had generated more than $250,000 in revenue.

The Challenges Faced by Black, Women, Entrepreneurs, and Founders

While Michelle's case may seem like a success story, it is also illustrative of the "concrete wall" phenomenon, in that Michelle faced significant barriers to entry and growth throughout the different phases of her startup. In analyzing this case, the concrete wall is a more apt metaphor, as it constitutes a significant, and at times, seemingly unscalable barrier to forward progression. In the next section, her experience is contextualized via data on Black women founders, as well as the larger population of minority, women, and Black women entrepreneurs.

Access to startup capital. Michelle mentioned that startup capital was one of the most significant hurdles to launching her business, as without seed funding, she was unable to build the prototype that would demonstrate that her idea had both merit and more importantly, a market. The amount of capital raised is a key marker given that research suggests the amount of capital at the time of launch is connected to likelihood of business success (Fairlie, 2013). Without their first round of funding, founders may be unable to generate enough data to show the potential value of their ideas, preventing the business from gaining momentum (Finney & Rencher, 2016).

Research on Black women founders has emphasized access to startup capital as a significant barrier to entry. Almost 80% of Digital Undivided (2020) survey respondents, the majority of whom identified as Black, stated that limited access to funds and investment was their top challenge. Black and Latinx women founders received less than 1% of all venture capital funding between 2018 and 2020 and raise only 20% of the seed round median funding for all startup businesses (Digital Undivided, 2020). For Black women who have not yet been able to raise $1 million or more, their median seed totals are 5% of the median funding for all startups (Digital Undivided, 2020). As a result, a vast majority of these founders rely on their personal savings or salaries from more traditional employment in order to make their ideas a reality (Digital Undivided, 2020).

This experience is reflective of the fact that Black women entrepreneurs more broadly face difficulty in securing enough funding to launch their business (Walker's Legacy, 2016). Black women entrepreneurs have expressed that applying for loans is a wasted effort because they do not expect to receive the loan (Inman, 2000). As many as 61% of Black women entrepreneurs use their own funds to serve as startup capital (Kelley et al., 2021). While their experiences are similar, for Black women founders, the importance of capital is even more critical, as the ability to grow and attract additional investors is predicated on securing a baseline level of funding.

Access to talent. Michelle also mentioned the difficulties she faced in trying to identify and attract talent to help her build her business. She is not alone in this experience, as more than half of the Project Diane Black women founders are "solo" founders, which was twice the rate of Latinx women founders who were running their startups alone (Digital Undivided, 2020). The experience of running the business alone is reflective of Black women entrepreneurs more broadly; they are more likely to rely on their own labor to make the business a success (Smith, 2005). They are more likely to create sole proprietorships and have the lowest average rates of employment among all women-owned businesses, at an average of 0.2 employees (American Express, 2019).

Investor biases. Michelle also mentioned potential biases on the part of investors more than once. She seemed to attribute this bias to two factors— lack of representation within the industry, and potential beliefs about her own competence. Yet, she felt that if she showed enough data, investors would better understand and appreciate not only the near-term, but also the long-term viability of her product. She knew that overcoming this bias would be critical to sustained access to funding and investments.

Black women founders remain very underrepresented in the startup industry, which contributes to less investor exposure and lower prioritization of women and minority-owned ventures (Digital Undivided, 2020; Morgan Stanley, 2018). Black women present a racial and gender contrast to the majority of founders. Entrepreneurs are more likely to be perceived as male and less likely to be perceived as female (De Pillis & Meilich, 2006; Gupta et al., 2009; Gupta et al., 2020; Laguia et al., 2019). Moreover, entrepreneurs at the helm of high-growth or commercial ventures are viewed as similar to men (Gupta et al., 2020). White males in particular are overrepresented in the startup ecosystem, with 77% of founders being White and 90% being male, and the vast majority having graduated from Ivy League institutions (Rate My Investor, 2019).

Though Black women founders in the Project Diane (2020) database are highly educated, their race and gender may preclude them from matching investors' ideas of an entrepreneur. In addition to not matching the prototype of a founder, Black women founders may be evaluated using negative stereotypes about their race and gender. Indeed, entrepreneurs leading low-growth ventures are seen as having greater overlap with women, and investors are nearly twice as likely to believe minority-owned businesses perform below market average (Gupta et al., 2020; Morgan Stanley, 2018). Project Diane founders also report negative race and gender-related impacts on their entrepreneurial ventures (Digital Undivided, 2020).

One of the most cited datapoints as evidence of investor bias is funding, which for founders, is not only critical at the startup phase, but also as they advance through each round. In addition to industry type, revenue potential and size of the potential market, angel investors and venture capitalists may use prior amounts raised as a proxy for future success (Morgan Stanley, 2018). Unfortunately for Black women founders, though 60% are interested in external funding, only 24% have received external investments (Digital Undivided, 2020). Between 2018 and 2019, Black women founders secured only 0.27% of venture capital funds (Digital Undivided, 2020). This stands in stark contrast to the 14% of venture capital funding secured by women founders and mixed gender founding teams (AllRaise, 2020). Thus, it is critical to better understand the link between investor bias and decisions to invest in Black women founders.

Research on how the broader categories of Black, women, and Black women entrepreneurs experience discrimination also supports Michelle's perceptions of bias on the part of investors. Though research on Black women entrepreneurs is limited, a qualitative study revealed that they feel that they are seen by others as an atypical owner, and that consumers or investors expect them to have a bad attitude, be angry, intimidating, or unprofessional (Jackson & Sanyal, 2019). Furthermore, similar to ongoing investment funding for Black women founders, Black women entrepreneurs face significant challenges accessing capital and maintaining profitability. Black business owners are twice as likely as White business owners to report access to capital as a barrier to generating a profit and more than 50% more likely to state inadequate sales as a reason for business closure (Tareque et al., 2021).

This additional data suggests that Michelle's current success makes her an outlier among Black women founders and entrepreneurs. Her journey to success included several encounters with the concrete wall, which took various forms over the course of her business; these challenges are characteristic of many Black women founders' experiences. These encounters forced her to think of ways to innovate, generate revenue, and attract investment.

Areas for Future Research

Michelle's experiences, coupled with the experiences of other Black women founders and entrepreneurs, provide evidence of a concrete wall. However, research on Black women founders, remains in a nascent stage. Future research can help to deepen our understanding of the barriers and challenges faced by Black women founders and learn more about the environments within which they operate, in order to inform potential social, policy, and economic interventions. Management scholars and organizational psychologists can play a key role in leveraging what we know about the dynamics of traditional organizations and entrepreneurial ventures to clarify how the concrete wall manifests for Black women founders.

Scholars can continue to build our knowledge base on the experiences of Black women founders by first providing further clarification on who Black women founders are and bringing additional rigor to how they are defined. Entrepreneurship literature denotes high-growth, emerging growth, and high-tech ventures, but the U.S. Census Bureau data is not always align to these definitions (Kenney & Patton, 2015; Roberts, 1991). It is critical to better define Black women founders because the existing data demonstrates a continuation of labor market history trends that all Black women face; namely, that they are unable to access opportunities that would create true economic mobility (Robinson et al., 2007). Building upon data by Digital Undivided (2020) to understand these Black women founders' backgrounds, motivations, and areas of expertise could also help to identify the extent of the disparity between their business performance and the response of the investor community. Research on women entrepreneurs indicates they are less likely to want to grow their businesses, while survey data on Black-owned businesses suggests they are more averse to debt than their White and Latino peers (Zampetakis et al., 2016; Tareque et al., 2021).

It is also important to understand who Black women founders are in order to better differentiate between the experiences of Black women founders and other racial and gender categories of entrepreneurs. This chapter has shown some of the ways in which their experiences are similar, such as in access to startup capital, access, and ability to afford hiring help, and potential biases of investors. However, less is known about Black women founders' challenges in generating revenue, and the role of consumer perceptions for Black women-owned startups is also unknown. Lastly, researchers can also better elucidate how Black women founders navigate the challenges outlined in this chapter and other barriers. Research on Black women entrepreneurs suggests covering, professionalism, and reliance on social relationships as ways Black women business owners respond to the pressures they face (Jackson & Sanyal, 2019; Smith, 2019).

Organizational and management scholars can also apply well-established theories in their field to deepen our understanding of the experiences of Black women founders, as well as form and test new theories altogether. The growing body of research on the intersectional stereotypes of Black women could be used to better understand how those in the startup ecosystem perceive Black women entrepreneurs. Current research suggests that they are seen as angry, strong, and dominant, masculine (Rosette et al., 2018; Goff et al., 2008; Ghavami & Peplau, 2012), as well as to be associated with unemployment, lower-skilled, or service roles (Koenig & Eagly, 2014). In addition, research on intersectional invisibility and (in)visibility could be applied to the experiences of Black women founders (Buchanan & Settles, 2018; Purdie-Vaughns & Eibach, 2008; Jones, 2017). While the lack of research on Black women founders provides some evidence of their invisibility, some of the Project Diane founders named their race and gender as helping their entrepreneurial endeavors, indicating that their visibility may change depending on context (Digital Undivided, 2020).

Theories related to race and gender stereotypes could also be applied to Black women founders. For instance, shifting standards theory may help to understand why they claim such small proportions of venture capital funding (Biernat, 2012; Biernat & Kobrynowicz, 1997). Michelle suggested that investors asked her more questions, or needed more data, suggesting that the burden of proof for her concept may be higher. Research on women entrepreneurs suggests they are more likely to be asked "prevention questions," or are required to demonstrate evidence that their venture is low-risk than are men entrepreneurs, and that these questions are directly related to the amount of funds raised (Kanze et al., 2018). In addition, researchers could explore the lack of fit model and social identity theory (Heilman, 1983; Tajfel & Turner, 1986). Research on women tech entrepreneurs shows that women are perceived as less competent than their male counterparts (Tinkler et al., 2015, that there are some differences between how men and women perceive entrepreneurs (Gupta et al., 2009; Gupta et al., 2009), and that these differences can result from a lack of industry and gender fit (Kanze et al., 2020). Venture capitalists, who are largely White and male (Rate My Investor, 2019; Walker's Legacy, 2016), play a large role in deciding whether or not to invest, and yet, are unaware of the funding inequities women and minority entrepreneurs face (Morgan Stanley, 2018). Better integrating judgment and decision-making theories with theories on discrimination and bias can help to elucidate which criteria are used to evaluate new ventures, and what becomes salient when evaluating a non-traditional founder.

Lastly, organizational psychologists can and should be invested in further research with the intent to inform potential interventions. Digital Undivided and others have proposed that the venture capital industry diversify as a means of leveling the playing field for Black women founders. (Finney & Rencher, 2016; Lang & Van Lee, 2020). However, despite rapid growth in the participation of Black and women investors in the industry, diversification is likely a longer-term solution. Similarly, initiatives that proliferated in 2020 as a result of the Black Lives Matter movement, such as #BuyBlack, are helpful in creating a short-term infusion of capital into Black-owned businesses (Porter et al., 2021), but may not address more systemic, entrenched challenges. These include lack of exposure, knowledge, and resources, as well as more limited social networks (Baboolall et al., 2020). In the fast-paced technology start-up ecosystem, government regulations may lag behind, leaving certain groups more vulnerable to discriminatory practices, with no avenues for reporting (Albergotti, 2020). Understanding the ecosystem would help to contextualize the many challenges Black women founders face and how to address them. It would also ensure that Black women are able to fully participate in, contribute to, and benefit from the American labor market.

REFERENCES

Albelda, R. P. (1986). Occupational segregation by race and gender, 1958–1981. *ILR Review, 39*(3), 404–411.

Albergotti, R. (2020, July 26). Black startup founders say venture capitalists are racist, but the law protects them. *Seattle Times.* https://www.seattletimes.com/business/black-startup-founders-say-venture-capitalists-are-racist-but-the-law-protects-them/

AllRaise (2020). Annual Report 2020. *AllRaise.* https://allraise.org/assets/all-raise-annual-report-2020.pdf

Alonso-Villar, O., & Del Río, C. (2017). The occupational segregation of African American women: Its evolution from 1940 to 2010. *Feminist Economics, 23*(1), 108–134.

American Express. (2019). *State of women-owned businesses: Summary of key trends.* https://s1.q4cdn.com/692158879/files/doc_library/file/2019-state-of-women-owned-businesses-report.pdf

Baboolall, D., Cook, K., Noel, N., Stewart, S. and Yancy, N. (2020, October 29). Building supportive ecosystems for Black-owned U.S. businesses. *McKinsey & Company.* https://www.mckinsey.com/industries/public-and-social-sector/our-insights/building-supportive-ecosystems-for-black-owned-us-businesses

Bell, E. L. J., & Nkomo, S. M. (2001). *Our separate ways: Black and White women and the struggle for professional identity.* Harvard Business School Press

Benner, K. (2017, June 3). Women in tech speak frankly on culture of harassment. *The New York Times.* https://www.nytimes.com/2017/06/30/technology/women-entrepreneurs-speak-out-sexual-harassment.html

Bernstein, A., & Gallo, A. (2018, November 5). *HBR women at work: Sisterhood is scarce* [Audio podcast]. https://hbr.org/podcast/2018/11/sisterhood-is-scarce

Berry, D. R., & Gross, K.N. (2020). *A Black women's history of the United States.* Beacon Press.

Biernat, M. (2012). Stereotypes and shifting standards: forming, communicating, and translating person impressions. *Advances in Experimental Social Psychology, 45,* 1–59. https://doi.org/10.1016/B978-0-12-394286-9.00001-9

Biernat, M., & Kobrynowicz, D. (1997). Gender- and race-based standards of competence: Lower minimum standards but higher ability standards for devalued groups. *Journal of Personality and Social Psychology, 72*(3), 544–557. https://doi.org/10.1037/0022-3514.72.3.544

Blank, S. (2013). Why the lean start-up changes everything. *Harvard Business Review, 91*(5).

Boyd, R. L. (2000). Race, labor market disadvantage, and survivalist entrepreneurship: Black women in the Urban North during the Great Depression. *Sociological Forum, 15*(4), 647–670.

Branch, E. H. (2011). *Opportunity denied: Limiting Black women to devalued work*. New Rutgers University Press.

Brooks, R.A. (2020, July 17). Black-owned businesses may not survive COVID-19. *National Geographic.* https://www.nationalgeographic.com/history/2020/07/black-owned-businesses-may-not-survive-covid-19/#close

Brush, C. G. (1992). Research on women business owners: Past trends, a new perspective and future directions. *Entrepreneurship theory and practice, 16*(4), 5–30.

Brush, C., Edelman, L. F., Manolova, T., & Welter, F. (2019). A gendered look at entrepreneurship ecosystems. *Small Business Economics, 53*(2), 393–408.

Bureau of Labor Statistics (2020). *Highlights of women's earnings in 2019*. BLS Reports. https://www.bls.gov/opub/reports/womens-earnings/2019/home.htm#:~:text=Earnings%20by%20race%20and%20ethnicity,(%24642)%20earned%2063%20percent

Buchanan, N. T., & Settles, I. H. (2019). Managing (in) visibility and hypervisibility in the workplace. *Journal of Vocational Behavior, 113,* 1–5. https://doi.org/10.1016/j.jvb.2018.11.001

Butler, J. S. (2005). *Entrepreneurship and self-help among black Americans: A reconsideration of race and economics*. SUNY Press.

Catalyst. (2021). *Women of color in the United States: Quick take.* https://www.catalyst.org/research/women-of-color-in-the-united-states/

Cunningham, J. S., & Zalokar, N. (1992). The economic progress of black women, 1940–1980: Occupational distribution and relative wages. *ILR Review, 45*(3), 540–555.

Cutler, K. (2015, October 6). *Here's a detailed breakdown of racial and gender diversity data across U.S. venture capital firms.* Tech Crunch. https://techcrunch.com/2015/10/06/s23p-racial-gender-diversity-venture/

Del Río, C., & Alonso-Villar, O. (2015). The evolution of occupational segregation in the United States, 1940–2010: Gains and losses of gender–race/ethnicity groups. *Demography, 52*(3), 967–988.

de Pillis, E., & Meilich, O. (2006). Think entrepreneur, think male? Business students' assumptions about a hypothetical entrepreneur. *International Review of Entrepreneurship, 4,* 3–18.

Digital Undivided (2020). *The state of Black women entrepreneurs during COVID-19.* https://www.digitalundivided.com/covid-19-report

Digital Undivided. (2020). *The state of Black and Latinx women founders.* https://www.projectdiane.com/

Fahs, G. (2020, September 5). Silicon Valley's toxic culture requires a legal fix. *The Atlantic.* https://www.theatlantic.com/ideas/archive/2019/09/change-harassment-silicon-valley-change-law/597373/

Fairlie, R. W. (2020). *The impact of COVID-19 on small business owners: Evidence of early-stage losses from the April 2020 current population survey.* National Bureau of Economic Research. https://www.nber.org/system/files/working_papers/w27309/w27309.pdf

Fairlie, R. W. (2013). Entrepreneurship, economic conditions, and the great recession. *Journal of Economics & Management Strategy, 22*(2), 207–231.

Fairlie, R. W., & Robb, A. M. (2008). *Race and entrepreneurial success*. The MIT Press.

Finney, K., & Rencher, M. (2016). *The real unicorns of tech: Black women founders*. Digital Undivided. https://www.digitalundivided.com/data-research

Garrett-Scott, S. (2009). A historiography of African American business. *Business & Economic History On-Line*, 7, 1–33.

Ghavami, N., & Peplau, L. A. (2012). An intersectional analysis of gender and ethnic stereotypes: Testing three hypotheses. *Psychology of Women Quarterly*, 37(1), 113–127.

Goff, P. A., Thomas, M. A., & Jackson, M. C. (2008). "Ain't I a woman?": Towards an intersectional approach to person perception and group-based harms. *Sex Roles*, 59(5), 392–403. https://doi.org/10.1007/s11199-008-9505-4

Goldin, C. (1977). Female labor force participation: The origin of Black and White differences, 1870 and 1880. *Journal of Economic History*, 37(1), 87–108.

Gould, E., & Wilson, W. (2020). *Black workers face two of the most lethal preexisting conditions for coronavirus—Racism and economic inequality*. Economic Policy Institute. https://www.epi.org/publication/black-workers-covid/

Grant, N. (2020, August 24). Black venture capitalists confront Silicon Valley's quiet racism. *Bloomberg*. https://www.bloomberg.com/news/features/2020-08-24/black-venture-capitalists-confront-silicon-valley-s-quiet-racism

Guidant Financial. (2020). *Black entrepreneurs—2020 trends: A look at African-American-owned businesses in 2020*. https://www.guidantfinancial.com/small-business-trends/african-americans-in-business/

Gupta, A., Batra, S., & Gupta, V. K. (2020). Gender, culture, and implicit theories about entrepreneurs: a cross-national investigation. *Small Business Economics*, 1–17. https://doi.org/10.1007/s11187-020-00434-9

Gupta, V. K., Turban, D. B., Wasti, S. A., & Sikdar, A. (2009). The role of gender stereotypes in perceptions of entrepreneurs and intentions to become an entrepreneur. *Entrepreneurship theory and practice*, 33(2), 397–417.

Harvey, A. M. (2005). Becoming entrepreneurs: Intersections of race, class, and gender at the Black beauty salon. *Gender and Society*, 19(6), 789–808. https://doi.org/10.1177/0891243205280104

Hayden, D. (1989). Biddy Mason's Los Angeles 1856–1891. *California History*, 68(3), 86–99.

Heilman, M. E. (1983). Sex bias in work settings: The lack of fit model. *Research in organizational behavior*, 5, 269–298.

Heilman, M. E., & Chen, J. J. (2003). Entrepreneurship as a solution: the allure of self-employment for women and minorities. *Human Resource Management Review*, 13, 347–364. https://doi.org/10.1016/S1053-4822(03)00021-4

Hello Alice. (2020). *Hello Alice impact report: What Black business owners need right now*. https://blog.helloalice.com/hello-alice-covid-black-business-impact-report/

Hinchliffe, E. (2019, January 28). Funding for female founders stalled at 2.2% of VC dollars in 2018. *Fortune*. https://fortune.com/2019/01/28/funding-female-founders-2018/

Inman, K. (2000). *Women's resources in business start-up: A study of Black and White women entrepreneurs*. Routledge Taylor & Francis Group.

Jackson, T. M., & Sanyal, P. (2019). Struggles and strategies of Black women business owners in the U.S. *Journal of Business Anthropology*, *8*(2), 228–249. https://doi.org/10.22439/jba.v8i2.5850

Jennings, J. E., & Brush, C. G. (2013). Research on women entrepreneurs: challenges to (and from) the broader entrepreneurship literature? *Academy of Management Annals*, *7*(1), 663–715.

Jones, J. (1985). *Labor of love, labor of sorrow: Black women, work, and the family, from slavery to the present*. Basic Books.

Jones, N. N. (2017). Rhetorical narratives of Black entrepreneurs: The business of race, agency, and cultural empowerment. *Journal of Business and Technical Communication*, *31*(3), 319–349. https://doi.org/10.1177/1050651917695540

Kanze, D., Conley, M. A., Okimoto, T. G., Phillips, D. J., & Merluzzi, J. (2020). Evidence that investors penalize female founders for lack of industry fit. *Science advances*, *6*(48), 1–10.

Kanze, D., Huang, L., Conley, M. A., & Higgins, E. T. (2018). We ask men to win and women not to lose: Closing the gender gap in startup funding. *Academy of Management Journal*, *61*(2), 586–614.

Karake, M. (2020, June 10). *"We existed in parallel universes"—What it's like to be Black in Silicon Valley*. World Economic Forum. https://www.weforum.org/agenda/2020/06/being-black-in-silicon-valley-systemic-racial-injustice/

Kelley, D., Majbouri, M., & Randolph, A. (2021, May 11). Black women are more likely to start a business than White men. *HBR*. https://hbr.org/2021/05/black-women-are-more-likely-to-start-a-business-than-white-men

Kenney, M., & Patton, D. (2015). Gender, ethnicity and entrepreneurship in initial public offerings: Illustrations from an open database. *Research Policy*, *44*(9), 1773–1784.

Koenig, A. M., & Eagly, A. H. (2014). Evidence for the social role theory of stereotype content: Observations of groups' roles shape stereotypes. *Journal of Personality and Social Psychology*, *107*(3), 371–392.

Laguía, A., García-Ael, C., Wach, D., & Moriano, J. A. (2019). "Think entrepreneur-think male": a task and relationship scale to measure gender stereotypes in entrepreneurship. *International Entrepreneurship and Management Journal*, *15*(3), 749–772. https://doi.org/10.1007/s11365-018-0553-0

Lang, I., & Van Lee, R. (2020, August 27). Institutional investors must help close the race and gender gaps in venture capital. *HBR*. https://hbr.org/2020/08/institutional-investors-must-help-close-the-race-and-gender-gaps-in-venture-capital

Matthews, M., & Wilson, V. (2018, August 6). Separate is still unequal: How patterns of occupational segregation impact pay for Black women. *Economic Policy Institute*. https://www.epi.org/blog/separate-is-still-unequal-how-patterns-of-occupational-segregation-impact-pay-for-black-women/

Moore, D. P., & Buttner, E. H. (1997). *Women entrepreneurs: Moving beyond the glass ceiling*. SAGE.

Mora, M. T., & Dávila, A. (2014). Gender and business outcomes of Black and Hispanic new entrepreneurs in the United States. In M. T. Mora & A. Davila (Eds.), *Proceedings of one hundred twenty-sixth annual meeting of the American Economic Association (104)*, 245–249.

Morgan Stanley. (2018). *The growing market investors are missing*. https://www.morganstanley.com/pub/content/dam/msdotcom/mcil/growing-market-investors-are-missing.pdf

Nielsen. (2017). *African American women: Our science, her magic*. https://www.nielsen.com/us/en/insights/reports/2017/african-american-women-our-science-her-magic.html

Porter, G., Holman, J., & Shanker, D. (2021, February 26). *Bloomberg*. https://www.bloomberg.com/news/articles/2021-02-26/buy-black-trend-sees-staying-power-with-corporate-america-buy-in

Presha, A., & Yamada, H. (2020, October 23). 'Buy Black' movement helps Black-owned businesses amid COVID-19: It's 'more than a trend'. *ABC News*. https://abcnews.go.com/US/buy-black-movement-helps-black-owned-businesses-amid/story?id=73797139

Purdie-Vaughns, V., & Eibach, R. P. (2008). Intersectional invisibility: The distinctive advantages and disadvantages of multiple subordinate-group identities. *Sex roles, 59*(5), 377–391. https://doi.org/10.1007/s11199-008-9424-4

Rate My Investor. (2019). *Diversity in U.S. startups*. Rate My Investor, Diversity VC. https://ratemyinvestor.com/diversity_report

Reeves, R.V., & Guyot, K. (2017, December 4). *Black women are earning more college degrees, but that alone won't close race gaps*. Brookings Institute. https://www.brookings.edu/blog/social-mobility-memos/2017/12/04/black-women-are-earning-more-college-degrees-but-that-alone-wont-close-race-gaps/

Riani, A. (2021, April 22). The difference between an entrepreneur and a startup founder. *Forbes*. https://www.forbes.com/sites/abdoriani/2021/04/22/the-difference-between-an-entrepreneur-and-a-startup-founder/?sh=6cbb760f3eed

Roberts, E. B. (1991). High stakes for high-tech entrepreneurs: Understanding venture capital decision making. *MIT Sloan Management Review, 32*(2), 9.

Robinson, J., Blockson, L., & Robinson, S. (2007). Exploring stratification and entrepreneurship: African American women entrepreneurs redefine success in growth ventures. *Annals of the American Academy of Political and Social Science, 612*(2), 131–154. https://doi.org/10.1177/0002716207303586

Rosette, A. S., Ponce de Leon, R., Koval, C. Z., & Harrison, D. A. (2018). Intersectionality: Connecting experiences of gender with race at work. *Research in Organizational Behavior, 38*, 1–22. https://doi.org/10.1016/j.riob.2018.12.002

Schweninger, L. (1990). Property owning free African-American women in the South, 1800-1870. *Journal of Women's History, 1*(3), 13–44.

Schweninger, L. (1989). Black-owned businesses in the South, 1790–1880. *The Business History Review, 63*(1) ,22–60.

Smith, C. A. (2005). *Market women: Black women entrepreneurs—Past, present, and future*. Praeger.

Small Business Majority. (2020). *The agenda for America's entrepreneurs of color*. https://smallbusinessmajority.org/policy-agenda/agenda-for-americas-entrepreneurs-of-color

Tajfel, H., & Turner, J. C. (1986). The social identity theory of intergroup behavior. In S. Worchel & W. Austin (Eds.), *Psychology of intergroup relations* (pp. 7–24). Nelson-Hall.

Tareque, I., Orozco, M., Oyer, P., & Porras, J. (2021). *US Black-owned businesses: Pre-pandemic trends & challenges.* Center for Entrepreneurial Studies. https://www.gsb.stanford.edu/faculty-research/publications/us-black-owned-businesses-pre-pandemic-trends-challenges

Teare, G. (2019, January 15). 2018 Sets all-time high for investment dollars into female-founded startups. *Crunchbase News.* https://news.crunchbase.com/news/2018-sets-all-time-high-for-investment-dollars-into-female-founded-startups/

Teare, G. (2020, December 21). Global VC funding to female founders dropped dramatically this year. *Crunchbase News.* https://news.crunchbase.com/news/global-vc-funding-to-female-founders/#:~:text=Crunchbase%20data%20shows%20more%20than,the%20same%20period%20last%20year

Tinkler, J. E., Whittington, K. B., Ku, M. C., & Davies, A. R. (2015). Gender and venture capital decision-making: The effects of technical background and social capital on entrepreneurial evaluations. *Social Science Research, 51,* 1–16. https://doi.org/10.1016/j.ssresearch.2014.12.008

Umoh, R. (2020, October 26). Black women were among the fastest-growing entrepreneurs—then COVID arrived. *Forbes.* https://www.forbes.com/sites/ruthumoh/2020/10/26/black-women-were-among-the-fastest-growing-entrepreneurs-then-covid-arrived/?sh=6e7416cd6e01

U.S. Census Bureau. (2012). Survey of business owners (SBO) 2012 survey results. https://www.census.gov/library/publications/2012/econ/2012-sbo.html

Walker's Legacy. (2016). *Black women entrepreneurs: Past & present conditions of Black women's business ownership.* https://drive.google.com/file/d/0B559IwAA2nWYV21LZWk4bkhKQzg/view

Wheadon, M., & Duval-Couetil, N. (2019). Token entrepreneurs: a review of gender, capital, and context in technology entrepreneurship. *Entrepreneurship and Regional Development, 31*(3–4), 308–336. https://doi.org/10.1080/08985626.2018.1551795

White, D. G. (1999). *Too heavy a load: Black women in defense of themselves, 1894–1994.* WW Norton & Company.

Wills, S. (2018). *Black fortunes: The story of the first six African Americans who escaped slavery and became millionaires.* HarperCollins.

Zampetakis, L. A., Bakatsaki, M., Kafetsios, K., & Moustakis, V. S. (2016). Sex differences in entrepreneurs' business growth intentions: An identity approach. *Journal of Innovation and Entrepreneurship, 5*(1), 1–20.

CHAPTER 9

THE AUTHENTICITY PARADOX

A Double Consciousness Perspective of Race, Gender, and Authenticity at Work for Black Women

Karoline M. Summerville
University of North Carolina at Charlotte

Enrica N. Ruggs
University of Memphis

ABSTRACT

Research on authenticity in the workplace has exploded in recent years yet scholars have ignored the implications of social identity on the subjective experience of authenticity for individual employees. As a result, little is known about how stigmatized identities such as race and gender affect one's ability to be authentic at work. In this chapter, the authors apply double consciousness theory to understand how organizational contextual factors including organizational culture, diversity climate, and discrimination affect Black women's double consciousness and psychological safety at work—two psychological mechanisms that can foster or hinder Black women's authentic expression in the workplace from a job-demands resources perspective. This conceptual framework provides an illustration of the experience of authenticity at work using an intersectional lens.

The Future of Scholarship on Race in Organizations, pp. 201–232
Copyright © 2022 by Information Age Publishing

Many organizations have recently embraced and encouraged employee authenticity at work; however, research suggests that the ability to be authentic at work may not be equally accessible or beneficial for all employees (Schmader & Sedikides, 2018). Authenticity is the degree to which one is able to enact their "true self." Often, authenticity is discussed in terms of behaving in ways that reflect one's self-concept (Lehman et al., 2019). There are benefits to employees behaving authentically at work such as increased well-being, work engagement, and empowerment (Gan et al., 2018; Ménard & Brunet, 2011; Sutton, 2020). However, developing or expressing authenticity may be difficult, particularly for individuals with marginalized identities (Zhang & Noels, 2013).

One group that often struggles with deciding whether they can behave authentically at work is Black women. Many Black women experience discrimination and bias in the workplace due to their multiple minority race and gender identities (Sanchez-Hucles & Davis, 2010), and as such, many feel the need to alter their behavior at work to resist negative stereotypes and consequences (Carrim & Nkomo, 2016). For example, many Black women reported carefully regulating their emotions, identities, and behavior at work to avoid stereotypes like "the angry Black woman" stereotype (Smith & Nkomo, 2003; Jones & Shorter-Gooden, 2009). If Black women feel like they have to adapt their appearance and change their behavior to manage impressions related to their race and gender identities at work, it is likely they may have difficulty expressing their true selves at work. As such, experiences of discrimination and pressures from society and organizations can inhibit authenticity in Black women and also inhibit the benefits organizations seek to gain from having authentic employees.

In this chapter, we explore factors that influence the expression of authentic behavior at work for Black women from an intersectional lens. The purpose of this chapter is to develop an inclusive theory of authenticity for employees with intersecting minority race and gender identities. It is likely that the factors examined here influence the decision to be authentic for individuals with varying intersecting marginalized race or gender identities, although the level of influence may be different depending on the intersection of race and gender identities (e.g., Black men vs. Asian women). In this chapter, we focus specifically on Black women. Overall, we suggest that multiple minority race and gender identities make achieving authenticity at work more complex for Black women compared to people with majority race and gender identities (i.e., White men). Our framework outlines how specific contextual variables enable or constrain authenticity. As seen in Figure 9.1, we develop a conceptual framework to explain how societal, organizational, and individual-level factors can influence Black women's decision to be authentic at work. We outline a model illustrating the ways that contextual factors influence psychological processes of how

Black women perceive their social identities and the psychological safety of their work environments, which in turn influences their behavioral organization-specific identity management strategies. These factors and processes ultimately affect their levels of authenticity as their appraisal of the environment helps to inform whether or not they believe it's safe to behave as their true selves at work. We draw on theories from psychology, management, and sociology to develop a model to help describe the ways in which cultural context, organizational factors, and individual experiences can influence psychological processes that affect one's authentic behavior expression.

Our conceptual framework is important for three key reasons. First, most of the research on authenticity explores outcomes of authenticity such as well-being and work engagement; yet it often fails to address factors that influence the extent to which authentic behavior is possible. We address this gap by examining individual and organizational antecedents to authenticity to combat the assumption that authenticity is a behavior that exists without restrictions. Second, our framework answers the call for scholars to consider authenticity in context and examine how contextual factors may foster or hinder authentic expression in the workplace (Chen, 2019). Third, this framework aims to provide a perspective of authenticity that challenges the underlying assumptions that perpetuate an overly optimistic view of authenticity in the workplace. One assumption underlying

Figure 9.1

Conceptual Framework for Understanding Black Women's Experienced Authenticity at Work

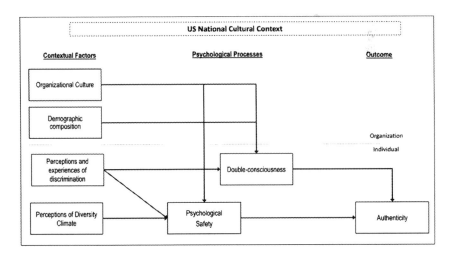

authenticity is that all individuals have an equal capacity to be authentic at work. We contend that authenticity is a more complex phenomenon for individuals who possess identities that are marginalized in the workplace. Thus, our framework involves an examination of both the positive and negative aspects of authenticity in terms of how possessing one or more minority identities encourages or restricts individuals from being their true selves at work. From a practical perspective, our framework provides a starting point for organizations who are seeking ways to support employees from diverse backgrounds in ways that can improve their ability to be themselves at work in an effort to improve their subjective experience at work and overall well-being.

In the sections that follow, we will begin by providing a brief overview of the construct of authenticity. Next, we discuss our conceptual model which outlines antecedents to authenticity. In this section, we describe contextual factors at the societal, organizational and individual-levels that inform the psychological processes that likely play a role in Black women's decisions to be authentic at work. Broadly, we build on double consciousness theory (DuBois, 1903) to discuss how contextual factors affect Black women's double consciousness as well as psychological safety at work. Lastly, we explain how double consciousness and psychological safety relate to authenticity using the job-demands resources (JDR) model (Bakker & Demerouti, 2007).

What Is Authenticity?

The construct of authenticity has been defined in many different ways, and it has been used to refer to a variety of entities including individuals, brands, and organizations (Lehman et al., 2019). Across the various definitions, a core theme is that authenticity commonly refers to being or behaving as "one's true self." Individuals experience authenticity when there is alignment between one's internal sense of self and the external expression of that self (Caza et al., 2018). Cha et al. (2019) conducted an integrative review of authenticity studies and found that many conceptualizations of authenticity can be characterized as either experienced authenticity (i.e., self-rated; alignment between one's own self-concept and behaviors) or externally perceived authenticity (i.e., other-rated; beliefs that someone is behaving in a way that aligns with their values). A second integrative review found that authenticity has been approached from three perspectives: (1) authenticity as consistency between one's values and external behaviors, (2) authenticity as conformity to a social category or group, and (3) authenticity as connection to other people or places (Lehman et al., 2019). In this chapter, we are particularly concerned with experienced authenticity, or the extent to which Black women *feel* authentic at work. This falls under the perspective of authenticity as consistency.

Authenticity has been conceptualized as both a trait and state construct, with the former referring to enduring characteristics of authenticity and the latter referring to authenticity as behavior that is variable across time and situations. In this chapter, we examine authenticity as a state-like construct that "results from the congruence between the person and the specific environment in which s/he operates" (van den Bosh et al., 2019, p. 248). State authenticity refers to the experience of being *currently* in sync with one's real or genuine self or the perception that one is being true to who one is (Sedikides et al., 2019; Sedikides et al., 2017).

We propose that Black women uniquely experience authenticity (or inauthenticity) due to contextual factors within a work environment. At the societal level, attitudes, values, and norms associated with Black female identity in the United States (U.S.) national culture affects how Black women understand, experience, and enact their identities at work. Organizations that are not race or gender neutral exacerbate the extent to which Black women see themselves through racialized and gendered lenses (Acker, 1990; Ray, 2019; Welang, 2018). We contend that norms within organizational cultures often reflect expectations of professionalism that are biased in ways that perpetuate a racialized and gendered ideal worker image and hinder authentic expression for Black women (Acker, 2006). For instance, Black women may receive a "hair penalty," meaning they may be deemed as less professional, when they wear their hair in natural or "Afro-centric" hairstyles (Koval & Rosette, 2020; Opie & Phillips, 2015). This, and other racialized gender norms, influence not only others' perceptions of acceptable appearance, but also Black women's perceptions that what is acceptable may not be aligned with what is authentic to their true selves.

Overview of Conceptual Model

We now turn our discussion to factors that may enhance or inhibit authenticity for Black women at work. We examine specific macro, meso and micro-level contextual factors that affect how Black women understand, experience, and express their identities. At the societal level, U.S. national culture conveys attitudes, values, and norms about Black female identities developed throughout history that we argue, affects Black women's experiences and understanding of their race and gender identities. When such values and norms trickle down to organizational contexts, organizational cultures reflect the shared, hegemonic cultural beliefs about race and gender identities at the societal level. Further, in many corporate organizations, organizational demography (the composition of an organization in terms of its members' attributes) contains lower representation of racial and gender minorities due to the social relegation of individuals to certain occupations and occupational levels (Acker, 2006). At the individual-level, we examine how perceptions of diversity climate, or the extent to which an organization is perceived to value diversity, and experiences of discrimination affect Black women's authenticity through the psychological processes of psychological safety and double consciousness.

We draw upon double consciousness theory to propose that racialized and gendered organizations enhance the likelihood that Black women will situate their self-concepts in terms of their race and gender (Welang, 2018). DuBois (1903) explains racialization as the process of socially constructing racial categories and attaching meanings to those categories that structure the experiences of groups and individuals. Gendered processes work much in the same ways (Acker, 1990). Racialized and gendered contexts do not explicitly acknowledge race or gender yet disregard the humanity of racially and gender oppressed individuals. As such, racialized work environments can be defined as work environments that constrain Black women's agency, legitimate the unequal distribution of resources, consider whiteness a credential, and separate the formalization of diversity, equity, and inclusion from policies and practices aimed at reinforcing racial inequality (Ray, 2019). In gendered work environments, gender is interwoven into processes such that exploitation, control, behavior, emotion, and advantage developed and granted based on gender and what (or who) is considered masculine and feminine (Acker, 1990). In gendered organizations, distinctions between men and women help to create meaning and identity within the organization. A single organization can be both racialized and gendered simultaneously.

Within such work environments, Black women become more aware of their inferior status and thus, feel less psychologically safe, or feel like they cannot take interpersonal risks in their organizations without risk of a negative consequence (Hewlin et al., 2014). Experiences with discrimination inside of work and society more broadly, along with the lack of racial diversity at work, can also inform the extent to which Black women experience double consciousness, or internal conflict with regard to their race identity, because such experiences make one's racial identity salient particularly through an external or outward lens. Double consciousness describes a sense of "twoness" that Black individuals feel in regard to their identity due to learning or developing racial identities in a context where they are made aware, at an early age, that their racial identity is considered a "minority" or "inferior" identity (Sellers et al., 1998; Whaley, 2016). We suggest that the extent to which Black women grapple with double consciousness will affect their perceptions of psychological safety in their work environments.

We draw upon the theory of double consciousness (DuBois, 1903) to help explain why Black women may vary in the extent to which they feel they are able to be authentic at work. We posit that double consciousness, characterized as a multidimensional experience of one's identities (i.e., seeing oneself from the perspectives of others) may enable Black women to navigate their external environment in ways that do not require them to sacrifice expressing themselves authentically at work. In contrast, those who feel conflicted by their contrasting racial (i.e., Black) and cultural (i.e., American) identities likely feel they need to assimilate or conform to their external environments, will feel less psychologically safe, and will be less likely to express their true selves at work. Lastly, we contend that double consciousness and psychological safety will be directly related to authentic expression at work. In the sections that follow, we discuss each element of the conceptual model in more detail. First, we provide a brief overview of double consciousness.

Double Consciousness

Double consciousness is a theory of the consciousness of oneself (Pittman, 2016). Early conceptualizations of double consciousness are seen in clinical psychology (Binet, 1905) to describe shifting between a primary and secondary consciousness. Sociologist W. E. B. Dubois' (1903) used the term in his writings to describe the subjective experience of social stratification, particularly from the perspective of the oppressed groups of people of African descendants (Levine, 1998). According to Meer (2019), double consciousness theory acknowledges four significant conditions involved when oppressed individuals form their self-concepts. First, DuBois explains the experience of developing one's sense of self in a context where one is subject to minority-majority power relations. Meer refers to this process as the conflicted construction of the self. Secondly, the creation of an additional perspective emerges from the experience of double consciousness. This is a condition that emerges when Black individuals internalize the majority group's external perceptions of their identities, and their true self-concept becomes distorted by racial prejudices. Dubois calls this new perspective "the gift of a second sight" that is given to minority individuals who are behind "the veil." The veil is like a one-way mirror that allows Black individuals to perceive things that "escapes the notice of the majority, specifically the distance between democratic ideals and the practice of racial exclusion" (p. 53).

The third condition of double consciousness addresses racial dualism or the hyphenated experience of Black Americans, in particular, who are expected to fulfill their citizenship duties while not receiving equal rights

208 K. M. SUMMERVILLE and E. N. RUGGS

and freedoms and simultaneously being excluded from the public culture (Meer, 2019; Pittman, 2016). This duality results in a sense of "twoness"—a sensation racial minorities may feel that stems from their dual attachment and commitment with their majority (e.g., American) and minority identities (e.g., Black, woman). This twoness reflects the dualism between the two cultures embedded in the lives of many Black Americans—a mainstream American culture and Black American culture. Gooding-Williams (2009) argues this sense of twoness is a *conflict* between two sets of ideals and strivings. For DuBois, the "merging" of the two selves can only take place if White prejudice and racism has been eliminated from the environment's culture (Pittman, 2016). The fourth condition of double consciousness states that oppressed individuals aim to affirm both of their dual identities such that Black individuals would seek to validate both their African descendant (Black) and American identities. In this condition, oppressed individuals attempt to merge one's double-self into a better, truer self (Dubois, 1903).

In summary, double consciousness explains how racialization processes inform self-formation and explains the link between racialized societies and the lived experiences of racialized people, including Black women (Itzigsohn & Brown, 2015). Welang (2018) expands on double consciousness theory and argues that due to their multiple minority race and gender identities, Black women suffer a triple consciousness such that they become aware of their identities through three identity lenses as opposed to two: national culture, race, and gender.

Empirical research on double consciousness supports the notion that Black Americans have dualistic identities. Brannon et al. (2015) found experimental evidence that Black individuals who were often exposed to both mainstream cultural contexts (or contexts dominated by cultural ideals associated with the majority) and subcultural contexts (or cultural contexts dominated by cultural ideals associated with the minority) identified with two different self-schemas: an independent self-schema and an interdependent self-schema. The independent self-schema aligns with American cultural ideals and perceives the self as relatively separate and autonomous from others whereas the interdependent self-schema aligns with African American/Black cultural ideals and construes the self as relatively connected to and related to others. Similarly, prior work has shown that career-oriented Black women have reported perceptions of living in two distinct cultural contexts—one Black and the other White (Bell, 1990). Cross cultural scholars refer to this phenomenon as biculturalism or identifying with two cultures (Nguyen & Benet-Martínez, 2013; Toomey & Ting-Toomey, 2013).

Double consciousness is a common psychological phenomenon among Black people; however, this psychological process may manifest in different ways for different people and in different contexts (Allen & Bagozzi, 2001; Walker, 2018). Namely, double consciousness may sometimes manifest as a positive psychological process, yet at other times or for other people it may be a negative process. On the positive side, double consciousness can be seen as a coping mechanism that may operate similar to biculturalism. According to a recent meta-analysis, biculturalism is strongly and positively related to psychological adjustment (Nguyen & Benet-Martínez, 2012). However, double consciousness can also function negatively as a source of identity conflict that may result in psychological and behavioral outcomes similar to those associated with assimilation, such as identity conflict and conformity (Mok & Morris, 2009). The effects of double consciousness are dependent on how the individual appraises the sensation of double consciousness.

Double consciousness theory provides a framework for understanding how national culture affects Black women's identity development in the United States and ultimately affects their experienced authenticity at work. Next, we provide a brief overview of the treatment of Black women in U.S. national culture to situate the contextual background of our model.

Black Women in U.S. National culture

National culture, or a society's attitudes, values, and norms, are reflected in larger contextual systems such as language, media, political rhetoric, and organizations (Hofstede, 1980). The treatment and representation of Black women in U.S. national culture influences the messages they receive about their race and gender identities from an early age (Shorter-Gooden, 1996).

Black women have unique historical experiences in the United States in that they belong to the only racial identity group the U.S. constitution once legally regarded as property rather than as human. The beginning of Black women's relationship with America is a story of enslavement and harassment and presently, Black women are the primary population of workers who experience some of the highest rates discrimination and mistreatment in the workplace (Jones & Shorter-Gooden, 2009). Research has shown that there is a link between slavery and the racialized gendered perceptions of Black women who have been historically depicted (e.g., in film) and stereotyped as "Mammies," "Sapphires," or "Jezebels." Mammies were originally slaves who served as nannies or housekeepers in the slave master's house and are often physically portrayed as obese and dark-skinned (Thomas et al., 2013). The stereotypical Mammy is considered a nurturing caretaker who is good at problem-solving and is selfless. Sapphires refer to Black women portrayed as controlling, harsh, and loud. These women represent "the angry Black woman" stereotype. Jezebels represent the stereotype of Black women as hyper-sexual and seductive. All of these stereotypical images inform others' perceptions and expectations of Black women and are still present today (Thomas et al., 2013).

Black women become hyper aware of these historical images and stereotypes through negative messages perpetuated in the media and through interpersonal interactions with others over their lifetime including teachers, guidance counselors, and peers. Indeed, as girls, Black women are more likely than women of other races to have experienced school discipline as Black girls are disciplined at a higher rate than girls of other races (Morris & Perry, 2017). Black girls are also more likely to be disciplined at school for defiance and disobedience than White girls, which relies on subjective evaluations of behavior that confirms and punishes Black girls' agentic behavior as "angry" and "noncompliant" (Annamma et al., 2019; Morris & Perry, 2017). Additionally, images in the media trigger cognitive comparisons between oneself and images portrayed on screen and thus, it is not surprising that media images have been found to negatively affect Black women's self-perceptions and self-esteem (Makkar & Strube, 1995). A more recent study found that awareness of negative stereotypes reduces well-being for Black women (Jerald et al., 2017). Taken together, these experiences grounded in negative stereotypes can complicate the identity and career development processes of Black women as they develop their sense of self (Reynolds-Dobbs et al., 2008; Thomas et al., 2013).

Black women have also reported receiving positive messages from family members and others intended to buffer the negative messages in U.S. culture about Black women. One such message often received is to "be strong." Such messages contain an emphasis on the importance of achievement no matter the adversity and are tied to stereotypes of the Black woman as a "superwoman" who can overcome any challenge because her ancestors have endured the adversaries of slavery (Thomas et al., 2013). Although well intended, such messages may not always lead to positive outcomes as Black women may become exhausted by trying to live up to the ideal of being strong in the face a constant oppression. Further, Black women may internalize competing positive and negative stereotypes and experience identity conflict, particularly in relation to external contexts. This identity conflict can lead to double consciousness for Black women when deciding how to interact with people at work so as to avoid confirming negative stereotypes and display the expected positive stereotypes even if this does not align with how they feel.

Thus, Black women develop their overall self-concept in relation to the historical context that informs both their race and gender identities. Research supports this notion and suggests that Black women do not separate race from their female identity and in some cases, may see their race identity as more central than their gender identities to their overall self-concept (Settles, 2006; Shorter-Gooden & Washington, 1996; Thomas et al., 2011). Therefore, we contend that Black women's double consciousness also affects Black women's gendered identity such that for many Black women, gender identity is grounded in or develops in the backdrop of her racial identity, especially with respect to the labor force (Jones & Day, 2018).

Although we do not provide an elaborate historical exploration of the collective experiences of various race and gender minorities in America, the logic behind our framework is inherently linked to the broader discourses around minority race and gender identities in Western culture. It is imperative that we do not ignore the delicate intricacies of more macro social discourses that may inform Black women's social identity processes within organizations. More presently, social movements intended to celebrate the beauty, power, and resilience of Black women, such as the natural hair movement and #BlackGirlMagic, likely also affect Black women's attitudes toward and enactment of authenticity in the workplace. For instance, although natural hair may be a direct expression of authenticity in the Black community, many Black women choose to suppress the behavior in workplace settings for years. Recently, more Black women are choosing to wear their hair naturally in organizational contexts, even though they may be more likely to face social repercussions (Koval & Rosette, 2020). Therefore, authenticity becomes a complex phenomenon that is itself embedded with sociocultural meanings associated with race and gender identity that impacts how individuals understand their identities, especially in relation to their social contexts.

As such, double consciousness may derive as a positive or negative psychological state depending on how Black women view themselves in relation to mainstream culture. Some Black women may perceive double consciousness as a resource, such that double consciousness helps them integrate their multiple identities and promote health and well-being. These women are likely able to shift between the two identities in ways that are fluent, and thus, may be better able to adjust and cope in racialized organizational cultures. As a result, Black women who appraise their double consciousness as a resource may be able to feel more comfortable in these environments and thus, may also achieve a stronger sense of authenticity at work because they can navigate between their professional and personal contexts more seamlessly. On the other hand, Black women who perceive their double consciousness as an internally conflicting experience tend to experience psychological distress as a result (Whaley, 2016). Such individuals are likely to feel a reduced sense of belonging and may be at greater risk for experiencing self-alienation, perceiving misfit between their identities and environments where either their race or American identity is the dominant group (Walker, 2018). Although Black women who identify more with their race identity may reap the social benefits of a greater internal sense of belonging to this group (Szymanski & Lewis, 2016), the reality of their daily experience in racialized and gendered work contexts likely makes them feel socially distanced or alienated from their race identity group (Allen & Bagozzi, 2001).

Organizational Contextual Factors

Societal culture informs the development of many organizational cultures in the United States. Many organizations reflect the inequality and inequity seen at a larger societal level because organizations have adopted the ideologies associated with race and gender used in broader society (Acker, 1990: Ray, 2019). Next, we explore the role of organizational contextual factors on influencing Black women's authenticity through double consciousness and psychological safety.

Organizational culture. Management scholars have long understood organizations as "little societies" where socialization processes, norms, and structures that make up culture manifest (Allaire & Firsirotu, 1984). Organizational culture constitutes the shared values and basic assumptions that explain why organizations do what they do and focus on what they focus on; it exists at a fundamental, perhaps preconscious, level of awareness grounded in history and tradition and is a source of collective identity and commitment (Ehrhart et al., 2014; Martin, 1992; Pettigrew, 1979; Schein, 1990; Schneider et al., 2017).

Following DuBois' (1903) examination of Black individuals' experiences within a racialized world, we propose that double consciousness helps explain how Black women may internalize the experience of being the racialized and gendered other in the workplace and how they grapple with outsiders' beliefs and expectations about their self-concept in the context of the workplace in an effort to achieve authentic self-expression. Feminist and critical race theorists converge in having long examined how organizations perpetuate culturally shared meanings and values associated with gender and race (Acker, 2006; Ridgeway & Kricheli-Katz, 2013). Such theorists insist that organizations are not race and gender-neutral contexts rather, race and gender meanings are embedded within the "ideal worker norm" in organizations and trickles down from organizational ideology down to the very nature of work and the organizational structures (e.g., policy, hierarchies, facilities) designed to control how work gets done (Acker; 1990, 2006; Ely & Padavic, 2007; Ray, 2019). Differences in men's and women's contributions to family work and varying cultural expectations of men and women's roles within family units, especially for women make it difficult for women to mold their lives according to the ideal worker norm (Blair-Loy, 2003). Gender is further complicated by race; however, very little research exists that examines the intersection of work-life balance and diversity (Özbilgin et al., 2011).

According to our model, racialized and gendered organizational cultures increase Black women's double consciousness and do not promote Black women's core aspects of the self. Ironically, racialized work environments often do not acknowledge race and gendered work environments do not account for the role of gender stereotyping on organizational decision-making. Organizational cultures provide cues and expectations on how to behave (Cox, 1991), and often those cues are based on gender and race stereotyping. Racialized and gendered organizational cultures may be particularly harmful for Black women as they are ignored in both, and the intricacies of their intersecting identities are less likely to be taken into account. Black women are keenly aware of the negative stereotypes associated with their race and gender identities that may determine how their behavior is perceived in the workplace (Reynolds-Dobbs et al., 2008). As such, we argue that Black women likely feel hyperaware of their race and gender identities and feel less psychologically safe than their majority identity counterparts (e.g., White men and women) when the organizational culture perpetuates negative social meanings tied to their race and gender identities.

For many Black women, organizational cultures signal devaluation with regard to race and gender social identities and constitute norms, values, and beliefs that strongly influence how these minority-status groups are treated by their majority counterparts. A prevalent example of this is organizations that refuse to acknowledge "Black Lives Matter" and racism in response to recent police shootings involving Black people in the United States (Opie & Roberts, 2017). Additionally, Black women may be negatively evaluated when they wear their hair naturally (Koval & Rosette, 2020). Indeed, others may view this as a racial performance and associate doing so a form of masculinity and dominance reminiscent of largely male, militant leaders of the Black Panther party (Kelley, 1997).

Black women must often carefully choose to express or suppress their racial identity in organizational contexts based on the situation and as a result, they do not often have the luxury of processing their identities at work in a fluent manner. That is, their self-concept cannot be separated from race or gender, resulting in increased levels of double consciousness. In other words, instead of feeling relatively unaware of themselves at work, Black women may experience more cognitive friction with regard to their race and gender identities at work that is induced by subtle threats to their identity embedded in organizational cultures. A plethora of research evidence shows that Black women are not equally compensated for performing the same and sometimes more work than others (e.g., Fisher &

Houseworth, 2017), are not equally represented in the senior ranks (e.g., Byrd, 2009), and are among the most discriminated populations at work (e.g., Ortiz & Roscigno, 2009). In these ways, Black women are constantly reminded of their inferior position in racialized and gendered organizational cultures.

Organizations also signal value toward race and gender through images, artifacts, and policies. For example, work-life policies like maternity leave policies may indicate that the organization accounts for women who become pregnant during their time of employment; however, the ways in which taking advantage of the policy impacts women's career advancement may send a stronger message to employees about the organization's views on women's experiences in the workplace (Kirby & Krone, 2002). Additionally, linguists and cognitive scientists are finding evidence that the predominant language spoken within organizations may affect how gender norms are perceived and enacted in the workplace and beyond. For instance, gendered language (e.g., describing things using masculine and feminine phrases) has been found to be related to gendered division of labor (Gay et al., 2018), reduced female board presence, and lower entrepreneurial activity among women (Prewitt-Freilino et al., 2012). Further, work environments that are racialized and gendered may signal to Black women that in order to succeed, they must embrace masculinity and hide their femininity while also embracing Whiteness and disregarding or downplaying their Blackness. Possessing one or multiple minority identities in a dominant work environment within the broader context of a society that perpetuates complex, negative stereotypes associated with one's minority identities can result in ongoing complex cognitive and behavioral responses for Black women. They must choose to express or suppress parts of their identity, especially those aspects of their identity that may be considered performances of race or gender that may be misconstrued as stereotypical behavior (Gond et al., 2016; Tyler & Cohen, 2010).

We suggest external consequences such as unequal racial and gender patterns in promotion, pay, and other organizational decisions may contribute to the behavioral choices of Black women who may feel pressured to change their behaviors at work to achieve awards and avoid costs. As a result of working in gendered and racialized organizations, Black women may shift their identities to conform to the professional standards and dominant cultural values of the workplace when interacting with coworkers who do not identify as Black in an effort to relate to and help make others more comfortable around them. However, such shifting of behavior can also result in negative outcomes for Black women such as internal conflict, lack of authentic relationships with others, and psychological stress (Dickens & Chavez, 2018; Gamst et al., 2020). As such, organizational cultures that promote the dominant culture can send signals to Black women that diminishes their psychological safety, or the extent to which they feel they can speak up and take risks in their organizations without risk of negative consequence (Edmondson, 1999).

Proposition 1: Racialized and gendered organizational cultures will increase Black women's double consciousness at work.

Proposition 2: Racialized and gendered organizational cultures will decrease Black women's perceptions of psychological safety at work.

Organizational demography. Organizational demography, in this case, the race and gender composition of a work group, organization, or community, has been shown to affect organizational attitudes and behavior including organizational attachment, diversity climate, turnover intentions, and voluntary turnover in top management teams (McKay et al., 2011; Pugh et al., 2008). Organizational demography exacerbates the conditions of double consciousness.

In organizations where race and gender organizational demography are skewed such that Black women are underrepresented, Black women have to grapple with stark identity contrasts between themselves and their coworkers – who are mostly White and male. This means that Black women have less opportunities for their identities to be validated by others who can relate to them (Denton, 1990), and they are more likely to be more negatively evaluated by dissimilar others (Mattan et al., 2019). These challenges can lead to a stifling of authentic behavior as Black women work to try to conform to the others around them, thereby engaging in identity management strategies such as shifting to suppress their race and gender identities (Gamst et al., 2020). When organizational demography is more diverse and similar others are present, people with minority identities are likely to not only feel more validated but also feel more comfortable expressing their true selves. Thus, low representation of racially and gender similar others in the organization increase Black women's hyperawareness of their minority identities. Thus, many Black women develop a new professional identity that integrates their race and gender identities to one that is often more muted and more aligned with the dominant culture (Smith & Nkomo, 2003).

Beyond obstacles Black women may face in constructing their professional identities, organizations that lack diverse representation of race and gender minorities signal to Black women that they are a part of the organization and are expected to fulfill their employee duties, however, the benefits of doing so are not promised. Monolithic organizations signal to minority individuals that there is a lack of care and intention from the organization around hiring and/or retaining diverse employees. As such,

Black women often find themselves in the minority in many US organizations, and the numbers of similar race and gender others decrease as Black women move up in rank. In this way, underrepresentation signals to Black women that they are a part of the organization but likely will not receive the same organizational support as others. Black women are often excluded from predominantly White informal networks in the workplace (Ibarra, 1995) and even when they hold powerful positions in organizations, Black women receive less instrumental and social support from such networks (McGuire, 2002). When Black women are in environments that lack gender and racial diversity, they likely perceive themselves as outsiders and experience greater friction as a result. It is likely that psychological safety may be increased for Black women in environments where the proportion of similar others is higher because the presence of similar others helps reduce feelings of isolation, discomfort, interpersonal obstacles, and decreased identification with the organization (Davis & Afifi, 2019; Pelled et al.,1999; Stewart & Garcia-Prieto, 2008).

As Black women increasingly occupy predominantly White and male contexts, they run the risk of sensing a decline in closeness with their racial identity group (Allen & Bagozzi, 2001). From a double consciousness perspective, increased exposure to one's racial or gender group may help individuals engage their identities from an internal perspective rather than an external perspective and increase well-being for Black women (Driscoll et al., 2015; Lyubansky & Eidelson, 2005; Walker, 2018). For example, Lee (2018) found that gender diversity had a positive moderating effect on the relationship between status conflict and team psychological safety likely due to the high proportion of women. The authors suggest that gender diversity may reduce interpersonal challenges among team members because research has shown women to be more reluctant to engage in competition and to be more socially sensitive to others than men (Lee, 2018). Based on previous research, we posit that organizational demography is related to double consciousness and psychological safety for Black women such that low representation of women and Black people, specifically Black women, spurs greater double consciousness and lower levels of psychological safety.

Proposition 3: Low representation of racial and gender minorities in work environments increase Black women's double consciousness.

Proposition 4: Low representation of racial and gender minorities in work environments will decrease Black women's psychological safety.

Perceptions and experiences of discrimination. Black women experience high rates of workplace harassment and discrimination and are more likely to deal with high-risk situations that set them up for failure (Hall et al., 2012; Hewlett et al., 2005; Haslam & Ryan, 2008; Mays et al., 2007). Also, Black women are often overlooked and ignored (Purdie-Vaugns & Eibach, 2008) and when they do speak up, they are often not given credit for their ideas (Sesko & Biernat, 2010). Black women likely experience psychological tension as a result of discriminatory experiences that prevent them from reaching their full potential at work. Racial discrimination at work has been linked to higher levels of work-stress and reduced levels of well-being, especially among Black women (Ortiz & Roscigno, 2009; Wadsworth et al., 2007).

Discrimination informs Black women's psychological safety because it conveys to them that their identities are not socially validated in positive ways and that they are not perceived to be in equal standing with others. In general, Black women have to counteract stereotypes that penalize them for dominance and expressions of anger, and they experience penalties when their appearance highlights racial features, such as natural hair (Koval & Rosette, 2018; Rosette et al., 2018). Black women can face discrimination linked to stereotypes attributed to their race and gender identities that affect the rates at which they are hired, their occupational roles, how they are perceived when they are in leadership positions, and attainment of organizational support (Holder et al., 2015). As discrimination can negatively affect psychological safety, we also posit that it increases Black women's double consciousness because they are more likely to engage in identity management strategies that deemphasize their race and gender identities as a way to reduce discrimination.

Proposition 5: Perceptions and experiences with discrimination will increase Black women's double consciousness at work.

Proposition 6: Perceptions and experiences of discrimination will decrease Black women's psychological safety.

Individual perceptions of diversity climate. At the individual level, diversity climate refers to employee perceptions that an employer uses fair personnel practices and socially integrates underrepresented employees into the workplace culture (McKay & Avery, 2015). Some might suggest that diversity climate is a contextual variable given that it concerns employee perceptions of characteristics associated with organizations' structural environment (e.g., policies, leadership structure). Many studies have shown that diversity climate perceptions are related to a host of job attitudes including organizational commitment and job satisfaction (Holmes et al., 2020). Research suggests that diversity climate matters for all employees regardless of identification with diverse backgrounds; nonetheless, levels of diversity climate perceptions and behavioral outcomes are stratified according to race and gender identities (McKay et al., 2007; McKay et al., 2008). For example, compared to White men, racial minorities placed greater value on employer efforts to promote diversity, and held more favorable attitudes about the qualifications of women and ethnic minorities (McKay et al., 2008). Further, the relationship between diversity climate and turnover intentions has been shown to be strongest among Black employees compared to other racial groups (McKay et al., 2007) and greater racial and ethnic diversity can strengthen the relationship between diversity climate and positive outcomes (Holmes et al., 2020).

Diversity climate is likely to be a salient source of information for Black women to understand the extent to which their race and gender identities are valued in the organization. Diversity climate also may influence the extent to which Black women feel they can trust and approach interpersonal relationships with others in the workplace in an authentic manner. Research has shown that environments that fostered inclusion enhanced the relationship between diversity practices and trust in the organization (Downey et al., 2015). In a similar fashion, we believe organizations where Black women perceive high diversity and inclusion climates will engender greater trust in how these women approach interpersonal relationships with others.

We propose that positive diversity climates may help facilitate Black women's authentic expression at work because they will feel more psychologically safe and hence, feel less of a need to self-monitor in environments that value their identities. Psychological safety has also been found to mediate the effects of diversity climate on performance and for racial minorities, this relationship was stronger for racial minorities (Singh et al., 2013), suggesting that positive diversity climates may help minorities devote more cognitive resources to performing on the job.

Proposition 8: Positive perceptions of diversity climate will foster higher levels of psychological safety for Black women.

Double Consciousness, Psychological Safety, and Authenticity

From a job-demands resources perspective, lack of psychological safety at work likely manifests in inauthenticity at work for Black women because those who feel less psychologically safe at work are more likely to devote cognitive resources to monitoring their behavior, rather than behaving and being in the moment, resulting in job stress. The job-demands resources model (JDR) states that job demands (i.e., physical, social, or organizational aspects of the job that require sustained effort) and job resources (i.e., physical, social, organizational aspects of the job that help employees achieve work-related goals, reduce job demands, and stimulate personal growth) must be in equilibrium for employees to remain motivated and avoid stress and burnout (Bakker & Demerouti, 2007; Xanthopoulou et al., 2007). We contend that Black women face unique social demands and performance pressures at work while simultaneously receiving less instrumental and social support due to their non-prototypical race and gender identities. High job demands have been found to be related to negative individual outcomes such as exhaustion likely due to the physical and psychological effort needed to meet those demands (Crawford et al., 2010). Black women experience psychological tension as a result of discriminatory experiences that can create strain and can reduce trust in coworkers (Holder et al., 2015). Hence, work characteristics create conditions of invisibility and hypervisibility that can complicate Black women's ability to control their optimal levels of belongingness and distinctiveness that enhance individual well-being (McCluney & Rabelo, 2019).

Since Black women, like many others, have a personal stake in their career outcomes (e.g., financial stability), they may take a cost-benefit perspective and approach their behavior in the workplace in more strategic ways given that they may experience social and professional penalties for behavior that deviates from the biased professional standards present in homogenous organizational contexts. For instance, Black individuals often perform "racial tasks" such as self-presentation, emotion work, and other behaviors that ease the discomfort of White coworkers and ultimately uphold racial hierarchies in the workplace (Wingfield & Alston, 2014). Black women may perceive such behaviors to be necessary responses to obligatory, hindering job demands that require them to shift their behavior to strike a balance between their self-perceptions and the expectations of others (Burke & Stets, 2009), even if this means possibly sacrificing an internal sense of self. Doing so requires Black women to devote more personal resources (i.e., aspects of the self that are generally linked to resiliency) in their work environments for the sake of their careers (Xanthopoulou et al., 2007).

Double consciousness may operate as a job demand or as a job resource for Black women depending upon how they appraise this psychological process. For some Black women, double consciousness may create tension as the acknowledgment of their "twoness" leads to increased identity conflict. For other Black women, however, double consciousness may serve as a personal resource they rely upon, as it may enable them to navigate their work environments in ways that help them combat the negative outcomes associated with stereotypes and discrimination. In either case, double consciousness may ultimately lead to less authentic behavior as Black women consciously alter their behavior at work to avoid negative outcomes associated with poor contextual factors; however, the intrapersonal consequences of this behavior may differ (i.e., for those who view double consciousness positively, less authenticity may lead to positive psychological outcomes; whereas those who view it negatively may experience more negative outcomes).

> **Proposition 9:** Double consciousness will mediate the relationship between organizational contextual factors and authenticity at work. Specifically, when Black women are in racialized and gendered organizations and organizations with low representation of Black employees and women, or when they experience discrimination or perceive low diversity climates, they will have experience greater levels of double consciousness, which will result in them expressing less authentic behavior.

Psychological safety is considered an organizational resource, or a physical, social, and organizational aspect that helps individuals achieve one's work-related goals. Thus, we argue that Black women may perceive socially-related job demands that hinder them from feeling comfortable being their authentic selves at work, particularly with regard to their authentic racial and gender identities because they feel less psychological safe than their race and gender identity counterparts.

> **Proposition 10:** Psychological safety will mediate the relationship between individual level contextual factors and authenticity. Specifically, when Black women are in racialized and gendered organizations and organizations with low representation of Black employees and women, or when they experience discrimination or perceive low diversity climates, they will have less psychological safety, which will result in them expressing less authentic behavior.

DISCUSSION

There has been a great deal of discussion about authenticity at work; however, there has been little consideration of how social identities such as race and gender affect one's ability to achieve authenticity at work. To address this limitation in the literature, our framework interrogates authenticity for Black women at work. Double consciousness permits a lens through which to understand how external perceptions and expectations associated with Black women's identities can affect their authentic behavior at work. Our model builds on the current literature by explaining authenticity from a person-environment fit perspective and discusses how organizational contextual factors signal the extent to which organizations value race and gender identities in the workplace. With Black women as our main focus, our framework outlines how organizational demography, perceptions of diversity climate, and perceptions and experiences of discrimination act as antecedents to authenticity via psychological mechanisms.

Black women are not passive subjects who allow external perceptions to control their cognitions, emotions, or behavior. Rather, double consciousness may give Black women an advantage in terms of understanding which behaviors are deemed "appropriate" in a professional environment. In other words, it is possible that *in*authenticity may be a strategy that Black women use to manage their identities in the workplace in order to advance. For example, Black women may shift their identities to conform to the professional standards and dominant cultural values of the workplace when interacting with coworkers who do not identify as Black or female (Bell, 1990). Smith and colleagues (2019) found some evidence of this through interviews with executive Black women who reported sometimes engaging in behaviors that aligned with dominant culture and veiled their own identities in order to avoid negative treatment toward themselves resulting from the social identity as a Black woman. Although identity shifting permits Black women to relate to others and help make others more comfortable around them, it can also result in negative outcomes such as internal conflict, lack of authentic relationships with others, and psychological stress (Dickens & Chavez, 2018; Gamst et al., 2020).

Overall, societal and organizational culture, as well as individual perceptions of diversity climate and discrimination experiences, influence psychological processes that affect whether or not Black women choose to be authentic at work. Societal culture helps to contribute to low levels of race and gender diversity in some occupations and industries, which often leads to Black women being one of the few minority women in their organizations or work units. The lack of racial and gender diversity, and importantly the lack of intersectional racial and gender diversity all contributes to organizational cultures that may be experienced as less inviting and comfortable for Black women. As such, stereotypes about Black women in the broader society as well as organizational factors that contribute to an isolation effect for Black women are related to lower levels of psychological safety in the workplace. Experiences with discrimination are likely related to lower levels of psychological safety because these experiences reduce feelings of trust in colleagues. In organizational cultures that allow instances of discrimination to go unchecked, particularly subtler forms of discrimination, Black women may feel particularly vulnerable and less likely to want to trust colleagues. Negative stereotypes embedded in societal culture about Black women inform how these women experience their workplaces and approach interactions with colleagues.

We propose that Black women's double consciousness is inherently linked to the broader discourses around Black female identity in the Western culture. Macro social discourses inform Black women's social identity processes, which can affect how contextual factors influence their willingness to be authentic at work. When Black women enter organizations, societal factors and double consciousness developed through experiences can inform how safe they feel within organizations that: (a) do not acknowledge their unique identity experience within the culture or demographic representation of the organization, (b) allow discrimination to occur, or (c) do not foster positive diversity climates. Such organizations fail to foster inclusive work environments that enable a healthy balance of various cultural identities that exist within Black women's self-concept. As a result, Black women may have a more difficult time being authentic at work.

Theoretical Contributions

The theoretical contribution of this framework lies first in the focus on the subjective experiences of individuals with multiple minority identities. Our focus on Black women in this chapter helps frame the role of social identity in understanding the psychological or internal aspects of authenticity and how these operate for individuals with historically marginalized identities. Our work builds on intersectionality, role congruity, social role theories, as well as the literature on stereotypes. Our framework also helps build an understanding of how race and gender identities inform the ways in which employees are able to be and feel authentic at work.

Intersectionality is a theory of multiple identities and explains how social identities (e.g., race, gender, class, age, religion, etc.) combine to create interlocking systems of oppression and privilege that result from processes of differentiation. Intersectionality research has demonstrated that the intersection of race and gender complicates processes of power and privilege in different contexts. For instance, individuals who share one common demographic but differ on another (e.g., White men and Black men) may be evaluated differently based on positive and negative stereotypes associated with their identities that are both contradictory and mutually reinforcing (Hall et al., 2018). Hall et al. (2018) put forth the MOSAIC model (i.e., a model of stereotyping through associated and intersectional categories) to explain how stereotypes associated with multiple demographic categories and their ancillary categories (e.g., intersectional and associated categories) combine to influence outsiders evaluations based on the degree to which an individual and their behaviors (i.e., visibility) are noticed or attended to, proscriptive templates that declare that an individual "should not" enact a certain behavior, and prescriptive templates or directives that an individual "should" enact a certain behavior (Hall et al., 2018). Future research may integrate these ideas to inform research questions such as how do Black women express their authentic selves at work and when are they penalized or rewarded for doing so?

Our framework can also be used to build on prior work on social role theory (Eagly & Wood, 2016; Livingston et al., 2012) to explain how stereotypes associated with various intersecting identities inform the extent to which race and gender matter to achieving authenticity at work. For instance, women leaders may experience more difficulty being authentic and developing authentic relationships at work because followers may not perceive their authentic selves as legitimate or in line with their work roles (Eagly, 2005; Hopkins & O'Neal, 2015). Thus, there are a plethora of opportunities for future research to unpack ways race and gender complicate the subjective experience of authenticity at work as well as how external perceptions of race and gender identities affect how authenticity may result in positive or negative consequences at work.

Practical Implications

From a practical standpoint, our framework can help organizations better understand the subjective experiences of employees from diverse identity backgrounds in order to learn ways to improve them. The role of context in our framework can help make recommendations for organizations more concrete in terms of how they can foster inclusive work environments that foster or promote authentic behavior in all employees, rather than certain groups only. Lastly, our framework sheds light on the costs and benefits associated with authenticity for multiple minority individuals such that there may be risks associated with authenticity for individuals with stigmatized identities and thus the motivation to be one's true self at work may be low. Additionally, there may be negative health outcomes associated with the attempt to be authentic at work such as race-related stress associated with authenticity. We propose that considering a more objective view of authenticity may be beneficial in uncovering the realistic experience and expectations of authenticity at work for Black women and other individuals who identify with race and gender minority identities.

CONCLUSION

Overall, authenticity is a complex phenomenon that is embedded with sociocultural meanings associated with race and gender identity, and therefore may not be as easily attainable for all employees. Black women may take cost-benefit perspective and approach their behavior in the workplace in more strategic ways given that they may experience social and professional penalties for behavior that deviates from the biased standards of what is considered professional in homogenous organizational contexts. Some Black women may not feel comfortable being their authentic selves at work and perceive inauthenticity to be a social demand at work rather than a resource they have equal access to, particularly with regard to their authentic racial and gender identities because they feel less psychological safe than their race and gender identity counterparts.

REFERENCES

Acker, J. (1990). Hierarchies, jobs, bodies: A theory of gendered organizations. *Gender & Society, 4*(2), 139–158. https://doi.org/10.1177/089124390004002002

Acker, J. (2006). Inequality regimes gender, class, and race in organizations. *Gender & Society, 20*(4), 441–464. https://doi.org/10.1177/0891243206289499

Allaire, Y., & Firsirotu, M. E. (1984). Theories of organizational culture. *Organization Studies, 5*(3), 193–226. https://doi.org/10.1177/017084068400500301

Allen, R. L., & Bagozzi, R. P. (2001). Cohort differences in the structure and outcomes of an African American belief system. *The Journal of Black Psychology, 24*(4), 367–400. https://doi.org/10.1177/0095798401027004001

Annamma, S. A., Anyon, Y., Joseph, N. M., Farrar, J., Greer, E., Downing, B., & Simmons, J. (2019). Black girls and school discipline: The complexities of being overrepresented and understudied. *Urban Education, 54*(2), 211–242. https://doi.org/10.1177/0042085916646610

Bakker, A. B., & Demerouti, E. (2007). The job demands-resources model: State of the art. *Journal of Managerial Psychology, 22*(3), 309–328. https://doi.org/10.1108/02683940710733115

Bell, E. L. (1990). The bicultural life experience of career-oriented Black women. *Journal of Organizational Behavior, 11*(6), 459–477. https://doi.org/10.1002/job.4030110607

Binet, A. (1905). *On double consciousness: Experimental psychological studies*. Open Court.

Blair-Loy, M. (2009). *Competing devotions: Career and family among women executives*. Harvard University Press.

Brannon, T. N., Markus, H. R., & Taylor, V. J. (2015). "Two souls, two thoughts," two self-schemas: Double consciousness can have positive academic consequences for African Americans. *Journal of Personality & Social Psychology, 108*(4), 586–609. https://doi.org/10.1037/a0038992

Byrd, M. Y. (2009). Telling our stories of leadership: If we don't tell them they won't be told. *Advances in Developing Human Resources, 11*(5), 582–605. https://doi.org/10.1177/1523422309351514

Burke, P. J., & Stets, J. E. (2009). *Identity theory*. Oxford University Press.

Carrim, N. M. H., & Nkomo, S. M. (2016). Wedding intersectionality theory and identity work in organizations: South African Indian women negotiating managerial identity. *Gender, Work & Organization, 23*(3), 261–277. https://doi.org/10.1111/gwao.12121

Caza, B. B., Moss, S., & Vough, H. (2017). From synchronizing to harmonizing: The process of authenticating multiple work identities. *Administrative Science Quarterly*, 1–43. https://doi.org/10.1177/0001839217733972

Cha, S. E., Hewlin, P. F., Roberts, L. M., Buckman, B. R., Leroy, H., Steckler, E. L., Ostermeier, K., & Cooper, D. (2019). Being your true self at work: Integrating the fragmented research on authenticity in organizations. *Academy of Management Annals*, *13*(2), 633–671. https://doi.org/10.5465/annals.2016.0108

Chen, S. (2019). Authenticity in context: Being true to working selves. *Review of General Psychology*, *23*(1), 60–72. https://doi.org/10.1037/gpr0000160

Cox, T., Jr. (1991). The multicultural organization. *The Executive*, *5*(2), 34–47. https://doi.org/10.5465/ame.1991.4274675

Crawford, E., Lepine, J., & Rich, B. (2010). Linking job demands and resources to employee engagement and burnout: A theoretical extension and meta-analytic test. *The Journal of Applied Psychology*, *95*, 834–848. https://doi.org/10.1037/a0019364

Davis, S. M., & Afifi, T. D. (2019). The strong black woman collective theory: Determining the prosocial functions of strength regulation in groups of black women friends. *Journal of Communication*, *69*(1), 1–25. https://doi.org/10.1093/joc/jqy065

Denton, T. C. (1990). Bonding and supportive relationships among Black professional women: Rituals of restoration. *Journal of Organizational Behavior*, *11*(6), 447–457. https://doi.org/10.1002/job.4030110606

Dickens, D. D., & Chavez, E. L. (2018). Navigating the workplace: The costs and benefits of shifting identities at work among early career US Black women. *Sex Roles*, *78*(11-12), 760-774. https://doi.org/10.1007/s11199-017-0844-x

Downey, S. N., Werff, L. van der, Thomas, K. M., & Plaut, V. C. (2015). The role of diversity practices and inclusion in promoting trust and employee engagement. *Journal of Applied Social Psychology*, *45*(1), 35–44. https://doi.org/10.1111/jasp.12273

Driscoll, M. W., Reynolds, J. R., & Todman, L. C. (2015). Dimensions of race-related stress and African American Life Satisfaction: A test of the protective role of collective efficacy. *Journal of Black Psychology*, *41*(5), 462–486. https://doi.org/10.1177/0095798414543690

DuBois, W. E. B. (1903). *The souls of Black folk*. First Avenue Editions.

Eagly, A. H. (2005). Achieving relational authenticity in leadership: Does gender matter? *The Leadership Quarterly*, *16*(3), 459–474. https://doi.org/10.1016/j.leaqua.2005.03.007

Eagly, A. H., & Wood, W. (2016). Social role theory of sex differences. In *The Wiley Blackwell Encyclopedia of Gender and Sexuality Studies* (pp. 1–3). American Cancer Society. https://doi.org/10.1002/9781118663219.wbegss183

Edmondson, A. (1999). Psychological safety and learning behavior in work teams. *Administrative Science Quarterly*, *44*(2), 350–383. https://doi.org/10.2307/2666999

Ehrhart, M. G., & Raver, J. L. (2014). The effects of organizational climate and culture on productive and counterproductive behavior. In *The Oxford handbook of organizational climate and culture* (pp. 153–176). Oxford University Press.

Ely, R., & Padavic, I. (2007). A feminist analysis of organizational research on sex differences. *Academy of Management Review*, *32*(4), 1121–1143. https://doi.org/10.5465/amr.2007.26585842

Fisher, J. D., & Houseworth, C. A. (2017). The widening black-white wage gap among women. *LABOUR: Review of Labour Economics & Industrial Relations*, *31*(3), 288–308. https://doi.org/10.1111/labr.12099

Gamst, G., Arellano-Morales, L., Meyers, L., Serpas, D., Balla, J., Diaz, A., Dobson, K., Feller, C., Rought, S., Salazar, B., Garcia, S., & Aldape, R. (2020). Shifting can be stressful for African American women: A structural mediation model. *Journal of Black Psychology*, *46*(5), 364–387. https://doi.org/10.1177/0095798420939721

Gan, M., Heller, D., & Chen, S. (2018). The power in being yourself: Feeling authentic enhances the sense of power. *Personality and Social Psychology Bulletin*, *44*(10), 1460–1472. https://doi.org/10.1177/0146167218771000

Gay, V., Hicks, D. L., Santacreu-Vasut, E., & Shoham, A. (2018). Decomposing culture: An analysis of gender, language, and labor supply in the household. *Review of Economics of the Household*, *16*(4), 879–909. https://doi.org/10.1007/s11150-017-9369-x

Gond, J.-P., Cabantous, L., Harding, N., & Learmonth, M. (2016). What do we mean by performativity in organizational and management theory? The uses and abuses of performativity. *International Journal of Management Reviews*, *18*(4), 440–463. https://doi.org/10.1111/ijmr.12074

Hall, J. C., Everett, J. E., & Hamilton-Mason, J. (2012). Black women talk about workplace stress and how they cope. *Journal of Black Studies*, *43*(2), 207–226. https://doi.org/10.1177/0021934711413272

Hall, E., Hall, A., Galinsky, A., & Phillips, K. (2018). MOSAIC: A model of stereotyping through associated and intersectional categories. *Academy of Management Review*, *44*. https://doi.org/10.5465/amr.2017.0109

Haslam, S. A., & Ryan, M. K. (2008). The road to the glass cliff: Differences in the perceived suitability of men and women for leadership positions in succeeding and failing organizations. *The Leadership Quarterly*, *19*(5), 530–546. https://doi.org/10.1016/j.leaqua.2008.07.011

Hewlett, S. A., Luce, C. B., & West, C. (2005). *Leadership in your midst: Tapping the hidden strengths of minority executives*. Harvard Business Review. https://hbr.org/2005/11/leadership-in-your-midst-tapping-the-hidden-strengths-of-minority-executives

Hewlin, P. F., Dumas, T. L., & Burnett, M. F. (2014). Is it safe to be me?: The effects of psychological safety, race and leadership on creating facades. *Academy of Management Proceedings*, *2014*(1), 14515. https://doi.org/10.5465/ambpp.2014.14515abstract

Hofstede, G. (1980). Culture and organizations. *International Studies of Management & Organization*, *10*(4), 15–41. https://doi.org/10.1080/00208825.1980.1165 6300

Holder, A. M. B., Jackson, M. A., & Ponterotto, J. G. (2015). Racial microaggression experiences and coping strategies of Black women in corporate leadership. *Qualitative Psychology*, *2*(2), 164–180. https://doi.org/10.1037/qup0000024

Holmes IV, O., Jiang, K., Avery, D. R., McKay, P. F., Oh, I. S., & Tillman, C. J. (2020). A meta-analysis integrating 25 years of diversity climate research. *Journal of Management*, 1–26. https://doi.org/10.1177/0149206320934547

Hopkins, M. M., & O'Neil, D. A. (2015). Authentic leadership: Application to women leaders. *Frontiers in Psychology*, 6, 1–31. https://doi.org/10.3389/fpsyg.2015.00959

Ibarra, H. (1995). Race, opportunity, and diversity of social circles in managerial networks. *The Academy of Management Journal*, 38(3), 673–703. https://doi.org/10.5465/256742

Itzigsohn, J., & Brown, K. (2015). Sociology and the theory of double consciousness: W.E.B. Du Bois's phenomenology of racialized subjectivity. *Du Bois Review*, 12(2), 231–248. https://doi.org/10.1017/S1742058X15000107

Jerald, M. C., Cole, E. R., Ward, L. M., & Avery, L. R. (2017). Controlling images: How awareness of group stereotypes affects Black women's well-being. *Journal of Counseling Psychology*, 64(5), 487–499. https://doi.org/10.1037/cou0000233

Jones, M. K., & Day, S. X. (2018). An exploration of Black Women's gendered racial identity using a multidimensional and intersectional approach. *Sex Roles*, 79(1), 1–15. https://doi.org/10.1007/s11199-017-0854-8

Jones, M. C., & Shorter-Gooden, K. (2009). *Shifting: The double lives of Black Women in America*. HarperCollins.

Kelley, R. (1997). Nap time: Historicizing the afro. *Fashion Theory*, 1, 339–352. https://doi.org/10.2752/136270497779613666

Kirby, E., & Krone, K. (2002). "The policy exists but you can't really use it": Communication and the structuration of work-family policies. *Journal of Applied Communication Research*, 30(1), 50–77. https://doi.org/10.1080/00909880216577

Koval, C. Z., & Rosette, A. S. (2020). The natural hair bias in job recruitment. *Social Psychological and Personality Science*, 1–10. https://doi.org/10.1177/1948550620937937

Lee, C. (2018). Does gender diversity help teams constructively manage status conflict? An evolutionary perspective of status conflict, team psychological safety, and team creativity. *Organizational Behavior and Human Decision Processes*, 144, 187–199. https://doi.org/10.1016/j.obhdp.2017.09.005

Lehman, D. W., O'Connor, K., & Carroll, G. R. (2019). Acting on authenticity: Individual interpretations and behavioral responses. *Review of General Psychology*, 23(1), 19–31. https://doi.org/10.1177/1089268019829470

Levine, R. F. (1998). *Social class and stratification: Classic statements and theoretical debates*. Rowman & Littlefield.

Livingston, R. W., Rosette, A. S., & Washington, E. F. (2012). Can an agentic Black woman get ahead? The impact of race and interpersonal dominance on perceptions of female leaders. *Psychological Science*, 23(4), 354–358. https://doi.org/10.1177/0956797611428079

Lyubansky, M., & Eidelson, R. J. (2005). Revisiting Du Bois: The relationship between African American double consciousness and beliefs about racial and national group experiences. *Journal of Black Psychology*, 31(1), 3–26. https://doi.org/10.1177/0095798404268289

Makkar, J. K., & Strube, M. J. (1995). Black women's self-perceptions of attractiveness following exposure to white versus black beauty standards: The moderating role of racial identity and self-esteem. *Journal of Applied Social Psychology*, *25*(17), 1547–1566. https://doi.org/10.1111/j.1559-1816.1995.tb02632.x

Martin, J. (1992). *Cultures in organizations: Three perspectives*. Oxford University Press.

Mattan, B. D., Kubota, J. T., Li, T., Venezia, S. A., & Cloutier, J. (2019). Implicit evaluative biases toward targets varying in race and socioeconomic status. *Personality and Social Psychology Bulletin*, *45*(10), 1512–1527. https://doi.org/10.1177/0146167219835230

Mays, V. M., Cochran, S. D., & Barnes, N. W. (2007). Race, race-based discrimination, and health outcomes among African Americans. *Annual Review of Psychology*, *58*(1), 201–225. https://doi.org/10.1146/annurev.psych.57.102904.190212

McCluney, C. L., & Rabelo, V. C. (2019). Conditions of visibility: An intersectional examination of Black women's belongingness and distinctiveness at work. *Journal of Vocational Behavior*, *113*, 143–152. https://doi.org/10.1016/j.jvb.2018.09.008

McGuire, G. M. (2002). Gender, race, and the shadow structure: A study of informal networks and inequality in a work organization. *Gender & Society*, *16*(3), 303–322. https://doi.org/10.1177/0891243202016003003

McKay, P. F., & Avery, D. R. (2015). Diversity climate in organizations: Current wisdom and domains of uncertainty. *Research in Personnel and Human Resources Management*. Emerald Publishing Limited.

McKay, P. F., Avery, D. R., Liao, H., & Morris, M. A. (2011). Does diversity climate lead to customer satisfaction? It depends on the service climate and business unit demography. *Organization Science*, *22*(3), 788–803. https://doi.org/10.1287/orsc.1100.0550

McKay, P. F., Avery, D. R., & Morris, M. A. (2008). Mean racial-ethnic differences in employee sales performance: the moderating role of diversity climate. *Personnel Psychology*, *61*(2), 349–374. https://doi.org/10.1111/j.1744-6570.2008.00116.x

McKay, P. F., Avery, D. R., Tonidandel, S., Morris, M. A., Hernandez, M., & Hebl, M. R. (2007). Racial differences in employee retention: Are diversity climate perceptions the key? *Personnel Psychology*, *60*(1), 35–62. https://doi.org/10.1111/j.1744-6570.2007.00064.x

Meer, N. (2019). WEB Du Bois, double consciousness and the 'spirit'of recognition. *The Sociological Review*, *67*(1), 47–62.

Ménard, J., & Brunet, L. (2011). Authenticity and well-being in the workplace: A mediation model. *Journal of Managerial Psychology*, *26*(4), 331–346. https://doi.org/10.1108/02683941111124854

Mok, A., & Morris, M. W. (2009). Cultural chameleons and iconoclasts: Assimilation and reactance to cultural cues in biculturals' expressed personalities as a function of identity conflict. *Journal of Experimental Social Psychology*, *45*(4), 884–889. https://doi.org/10.1016/j.jesp.2009.04.004

Morris, E. W., & Perry, B. L. (2017). Girls behaving badly? Race, gender, and subjective evaluation in the discipline of African American girls. *Sociology of education, 90*(2), 127–148.

Nguyen, A.-M. D., & Benet-Martínez, V. (2013). Biculturalism and adjustment: A meta-analysis. *Journal of Cross-Cultural Psychology, 44*(1), 122–159. https://doi.org/10.1177/0022022111435097

Opie, T. R., & Phillips, K. W. (2015). Hair penalties: The negative influence of Afrocentric hair on ratings of Black women's dominance and professionalism. *Frontiers in Psychology, 31*, 1-14. https://doi.org/10.3389/fpsyg.2015.01311

Opie, T., & Roberts, L. M. (2017). Do Black lives really matter in the workplace? Restorative justice as a means to reclaim humanity. *Equality, Diversity and Inclusion: An International Journal, 36*(8), 707–719. https://doi.org/10.1108/EDI-07-2017-0149

Ortiz, S. Y., & Roscigno, V. J. (2009). Discrimination, women, and work: Processes and variations by race and class. *The Sociological Quarterly, 50*(2), 336–359. https://doi.org/10.1111/j.1533-8525.2009.01143.x

Özbilgin, M. F., Beauregard, T. A., Tatli, A., & Bell, M. P. (2011). Work-life, diversity and intersectionality: A critical review and research agenda. *International Journal of Management Reviews, 13*(2), 177–198. https://doi.org/10.1111/j.1468-2370.2010.00291.x

Pelled, L., Ledford, G. E., Jr., & Albers Mohrman, S. (1999). Demographic dissimilarity and workplace Inclusion. *Journal of Management Studies, 36*(7), 1013–1031. https://doi.org/10.1111/1467-6486.00168

Pettigrew, A. M. (1979). On studying organizational cultures. *Administrative Science Quarterly, 24*(4), 570–581. https://doi.org/10.2307/2392363

Pittman, J. P., (2016). "Double Consciousness." In E. N. Zalta (Ed.),*The Stanford encyclopedia of philosophy* (Summer 2016 Edition).

Prewitt-Freilino, J. L., Caswell, T. A., & Laakso, E. K. (2012). The gendering of language: A comparison of gender equality in countries with gendered, natural gender, and genderless languages. *Sex Roles, 66*(3), 268–281. https://doi.org/10.1007/s11199-011-0083-5

Pugh, S. D., Dietz, J., Brief, A. P., & Wiley, J. W. (2008). Looking inside and out: The impact of employee and community demographic composition on organizational diversity climate. *Journal of Applied Psychology, 93*(6), 1422–1428. https://doi.org/10.1037/a0012696

Purdie-Vaughns, V., & Eibach, R. P. (2008). Intersectional invisibility: The distinctive advantages and disadvantages of multiple subordinate-group identities. *Sex Roles, 59*(5), 377–391.

Ray, V. (2019). A theory of racialized organizations. *American Sociological Review, 84*(1), 26–53. https://doi.org/10.1177/0003122418822335

Reynolds-Dobbs, W., Thomas, K. M., & Harrison, M. S. (2008). From mammy to superwoman: Images that hinder Black Women's career development. *Journal of Career Development, 35*(2), 129–150. https://doi.org/10.1177/0894845308325645

Ridgeway, C. L., & Kricheli-Katz, T. (2013). Intersecting cultural beliefs in social relations: Gender, race, and class binds and freedoms. *Gender & Society, 27*(3), 294–318. https://doi.org/10.1177/0891243213479445

Rosette, A. S., Ponce de Leon, R., Koval, C. Z., & Harrison, D. A. (2018). Intersectionality: Connecting experiences of gender with race at work. *Research in Organizational Behavior, 38,* 1–22. https://doi.org/10.1016/j.riob.2018.12.002

Sanchez-Hucles, J. V., & Davis, D. D. (2010). Women and women of color in leadership: Complexity, identity, and intersectionality. *American Psychologist, 65*(3), 171–181. https://doi.org/10.1037/a0017459

Schein, E. H. (1990). Organizational culture. *American Psychologist, 45*(2), 109–119. https://doi.org/10.1037/0003-066X.45.2.109

Schmader, T., & Sedikides, C. (2018). State authenticity as fit to environment: The implications of social identity for fit, authenticity, and self-segregation. *Personality and Social Psychology Review, 22*(3), 228–259. https://doi.org/10.1177/1088868317734080

Schneider, B., González-Romá, V., Ostroff, C., & West, M. A. (2017). Organizational climate and culture: Reflections on the history of the constructs in the *Journal of Applied Psychology. Journal of Applied Psychology, 102*(3), 468–482. https://doi.org/10.1037/apl0000090

Sedikides, C., Slabu, L., Lenton, A., & Thomaes, S. (2017). State authenticity. *Current Directions in Psychological Science, 26*(6), 521–525. https://doi.org/10.1177/0963721417713296

Sedikides, C., Lenton, A. P., Slabu, L., & Thomaes, S. (2019). Sketching the contours of state authenticity. *Review of General Psychology, 23*(1), 73–88. https://doi.org/10.1037/gpr0000156

Sellers, R. M., Smith, M. A., Shelton, J. N., Rowley, S. A. J., & Chavous, T. M. (1998). Multidimensional model of racial identity: A reconceptualization of African American racial identity. *Personality and Social Psychology Review, 2*(1), 18–39. https://doi.org/10.1207/s15327957pspr0201_2

Sesko, A. K., & Biernat, M. (2010). Prototypes of race and gender: The invisibility of Black women. *Journal of Experimental Social Psychology, 46*(2), 356–360. https://doi.org/10.1016/j.jesp.2009.10.016

Settles, I. H. (2006). Use of an intersectional framework to understand Black women's racial and gender identities. *Sex Roles, 54*(9–10), 589–601. https://doi.org/10.1007/s11199-006-9029-8

Shorter-Gooden, K., & Washington, N. C. (1996). Young, Black, and female: The challenge of weaving an identity. *Journal of Adolescence, 19*(5), 465–475. https://doi.org/10.1006/jado.1996.0044

Singh, B., Winkel, D. E., & Selvarajan, T. T. (2013). Managing diversity at work: Does psychological safety hold the key to racial differences in employee performance? *Journal of Occupational and Organizational Psychology, 86*(2), 242–263. https://doi.org/10.1111/joop.12015

Smith, E. L. J. B., & Nkomo, S. M. (2003). *Our separate ways: Black and White women and the struggle for professional identity.* Harvard Business Press.

Smith, A. N., Watkins, M. B., Ladge, J. J., & Carlton, P. (2019). Making the invisible visible: Paradoxical effects of intersectional invisibility on the career experiences of executive Black women. *Academy of Management Journal, 62*(6), 1705-1734. https://doi.org/10.5465/amj.2017.1513

Stewart M. M., & Garcia-Prieto, P. (2008). A relational demography model of workgroup identification: Testing the effects of race, race dissimilarity, racial identification, and communication behavior. *Journal of Organizational Behavior, 29*(5), 657–680. https://doi.org/10.1002/job.523

Sutton, A. (2020). Living the good life: A meta-analysis of authenticity, well-being and engagement. *Personality and Individual Differences, 153*, 1–14. https://doi.org/10.1016/j.paid.2019.109645

Szymanski, D. M., & Lewis, J. A. (2016). Gendered racism, coping, identity centrality, and African American college women's psychological distress. *Psychology of Women Quarterly, 40*(2), 229–243. https://doi.org/10.1177/0361684315616113

Thomas, A. J., Hoxha, D., & Hacker, J. D. (2013). Contextual influences on gendered racial identity development of African American Young Women. *Journal of Black Psychology, 39*(1), 88–101. https://doi.org/10.1177/0095798412454679

Thomas, A. J., Hacker, J. D., & Hoxha, D. (2011). Gendered racial identity of Black young women. *Sex Roles, 64*(7), 530–542. https://doi.org/10.1007/s11199-011-9939-y

Toomey, A., Dorjee, T., & Ting-Toomey, S. (2013). Bicultural identity negotiation, conflicts, and intergroup communication strategies. *Journal of Intercultural Communication Research, 42*(2), 112–134. https://doi.org/10.1080/17475759.2013.785973

Tyler, M., & Cohen, L. (2010). Spaces that matter: Gender performativity and organizational space. *Organization Studies, 31*(2), 175–198. https://doi.org/10.1177/0170840609357381

Van den Bosch, R., Taris, T. W., Schaufeli, W. B., Peeters, M. C., & Reijseger, G. (2019). Authenticity at work: A matter of fit? *The Journal of Psychology, 153*(2), 247–266.

Wadsworth, E., Dhillon, K., Shaw, C., Bhui, K., Stansfeld, S., & Smith, A. (2007). Racial discrimination, ethnicity and work stress. *Occupational Medicine, 57*(1), 18–24. https://doi.org/10.1093/occmed/kql088

Walker, S. M. (2018). Empirical study of the application of double-consciousness among African-American men. *Journal of African American Studies, 22*(2–3), 205–217. https://doi.org/10.1007/s12111-018-9404-x

Welang, N. (2018). Triple Consciousness: The reimagination of Black female identities in contemporary American culture. *Open Cultural Studies, 2*(1), 296–306. https://doi.org/10.1515/culture-2018-0027

Whaley, A. L. (2016). Identity conflict in African Americans during Late adolescence and young adulthood: Double Consciousness, multicultural, and Africentric Perspectives. *21st Annual Conference of the National Association of African American Studies & Affiliates*, 106–113.

Wingfield, A. H., & Alston, R. S. (2014). Maintaining hierarchies in predominantly white organizations: A theory of racial tasks. *American Behavioral Scientist, 58*(2), 274–287. https://doi.org/10.1177/0002764213503329

Xanthopoulou, D., Demerouti, E., & Schaufeli, W. (2007). The role of personal resources in the Job Demands-Resources model. *International Journal of Stress Management, 14*(2), 121–141. https://doi.org/10.1037/1072-5245.14.2.121

Zeus, L. (2002) The souls of White folk: Critical pedagogy, Whiteness studies, and globalization discourse, *Race Ethnicity and Education, 5*(1), 29–50. https://doi.org/10.1080/13613320120117180

Zhang, R., & Noels, K. A. (2013). When ethnic identities vary: Cross-situation and within-situation variation, authenticity, and well-being. *Journal of Cross-Cultural Psychology, 44*(4), 552–573. https://doi.org/10.1177/0022022112463604

CHAPTER 10

DOUBLE JEOPARDY OR INTERSECTIONAL INVISIBILITY?

Reconciling (Seemingly) Opposing Perspectives

James T. Carter
Columbia University

Rebecca Ponce de Leon
Duke University

ABSTRACT

Scholars across numerous disciplines are increasingly examining the experiences of individuals with multiple subordinated identities. Two of the dominant theoretical perspectives that have investigated these experiences—the double jeopardy (Beal, 2008) and intersectional invisibility (Purdie-Vaughns & Eibach, 2008) hypotheses—draw from intersectional perspectives (Crenshaw, 1989) to make predictions about these individuals' outcomes. However, despite their shared underpinnings, these theories are often pitted against one another, as they ultimately posit competing predictions. The double jeopardy hypothesis highlights how multiply marginalized individuals face compounded prejudice corresponding to each of their identities, whereas the intersectional invisibility hypothesis suggests

The Future of Scholarship on Race in Organizations, pp. 233–258
Copyright © 2022 by Information Age Publishing

that these individuals are rendered "invisible" members of their identity groups, evading typical forms of prejudice corresponding to their identities. Instead of aiming to establish the superiority or increased explanatory value of one of these theories, in this chapter we seek to understand the conditions under which outcomes consistent with each approach are likely to emerge. In selectively reviewing the literature that draws on double jeopardy and intersectional invisibility, we (a) offer a timely review of a growing research area, (b) offer propositions to help elucidate the nuances between these two perspectives, and (c) suggest new directions ripe for continued research on these ideas. We hope to address a significant and critical gap in the literature that, at present, undermines our understanding of individuals with multiple subordinated identities.

The 2020 U.S. Presidential race was a groundbreaking election.[1] Not only were voter participation and campaign finance records shattered, but Vice President-elect Kamala Harris made national history as the first Black, first Indian, and first woman to be elected to the vice presidency. The road to this historic moment was not easy; indeed, as a woman of color, Harris contended with stereotyping and prejudice on the campaign trail (e.g., McGee, 2020). Despite the numerous attacks on Vice President-elect Harris's identity, however, it remains unclear how her treatment may have differed if she only possessed *one* of these subordinated identities. From one dominant theoretical perspective, Harris likely contended with "double jeopardy," experiencing compound discrimination as a woman *and* a person of color. In turn, she may have faced a combination of both racism and sexism. However, another perspective suggests that the intersection of these marginalized identities likely rendered her socially "invisible." In turn, although they may have buffered her from some forms of racism and sexism, her dual subordinated identities may also have resulted in unique, intersectional forms of oppression. As existing research supports both arguments, a looming question remains: When and why might we expect either outcome to occur?

Social scientists are increasingly exploring questions like these that attend to the experiences of individuals with *multiple, intersecting* marginalized identities. Specifically, this work attends to intersectionality, or "overlapping social categories, such as race and gender, that are relevant to a specified individual or group's identity and create a unique experience that is separate and apart from its originating categories" (Rosette et al., 2018, p. 3). Grounded in critical race theory and coined by legal scholar Kimberlé Crenshaw (1989, 1991), intersectionality was originally conceived to emphasize the unique experiences of Black women that are separate and apart from the experiences of White women or Black men. Intersectional frameworks have subsequently been applied to reveal how the experiences of those with multiple marginalized individuals often diverge from the experiences of those with a single marginalized identity (Cole, 2009) and have been integrated into studies of class (e.g., Cuadraz & Uttal, 1999; Freeman et al., 2010), sexuality (e.g., King et al., 2013), and disability (e.g., Artiles, 2013). Organizational scholars have also increasingly adopted intersectional perspectives in their research, with a particular focus on uncovering the differential workplace experiences of women of color and White women (for a review, see Rosette et al., 2018).

Research across diverse disciplines (e.g., sociology, Collins, 2015; psychology, Purdie-Vaughns & Eibach, 2008; gender and feminist studies, Nash, 2008; Thomsen & Finley, 2019) has considerably advanced our theoretical understanding of intersectionality. These explorations overwhelmingly support the notion that the possession of multiple marginalized identities creates unique experiences and outcomes (Browne & Misra, 2003; Collins & Bilge, 2020; Crenshaw, 1990). However, empirical results documenting the specific consequences of intersecting subordinated identities have been mixed at best. In particular, whereas one line of work has documented outcomes associated with *double jeopardy* (Beal, 2008; Berdahl & Moore, 2006; Rosette et al., 2018), another has focused on experiences of *intersectional invisibility* (Purdie-Vaughns & Eibach, 2008).

The double jeopardy and intersectional invisibility hypotheses represent two of the most influential theoretical perspectives used to understand the experience of multiple marginalization. The double jeopardy hypothesis[2] asserts that people with more than one subordinated identity (e.g., lesbians) are discriminated against based on each of these separate identities (e.g., gender and sexuality) and, consequently, experience cumulative discrimination. As a result, multiply subordinated individuals experience worse outcomes than people with just one of these identities (e.g., heterosexual women or gay men; Barnum et al., 1995, Cole, 2009; Meyer, 2010). Conversely, intersectional invisibility argues that those with multiple subordinated identities are non-prototypical of their constituent identity groups and, in turn, frequently overlooked or discounted as members of these groups (Purdie-Vaughns & Eibach, 2008). This relative invisibility can result in both disadvantages and advantages. From this perspective, rather than being subjected to compound discrimination, multiply subordinated individuals may be buffered from some of the single-axis prejudice that prototypical members typically face (e.g., Livingston et al., 2012). However, their non-prototypicality may also lead to unique forms of intersectional oppression, such as being ignored or neglected (e.g., Schug et al., 2015; Sesko & Biernat, 2010).

Thus, when directly compared, the double jeopardy and intersectional invisibility hypotheses ultimately propose competing predictions. Although these perspectives have contributed immensely to theorizing on intersectionality, the apparent contradictions in their theorizing have also led to a significant gap in the literature: The conditions under which double jeopardy or invisibility may occur remain unclear. To truly advance the position of the most disadvantaged people in our organizations and communities, it is critical to better understand the conditions under which multiply subordinated individuals may experience "cumulative" oppression, commensurate with prejudice based on each marginalized identity, versus "invisible" oppression, evading some of prejudice corresponding to each of their marginalized identities while suffering the unique marginalization of diminished prototypicality. In service of this goal, this chapter provides a review of extant research leveraging the double jeopardy and intersectional invisibility hypotheses. Through selectively reviewing these seemingly disparate findings, we offer considerations for a path forward with a particular focus on the complexities and influence of stereotypes and prototypes on the experiences of marginalized groups. Ultimately, when we critically consider stereotype integration, prototypicality, and the frames of reference used to measure discrimination, we can better understand when double jeopardy or intersectional invisibility may occur.

Through this analysis of double jeopardy and intersectional invisibility, we aim to contribute to the literature on diversity and inclusion in several key ways. First, we address a significant and critical gap in the literature that, at present, undermines our understanding of individuals with multiple subordinated identities. By offering a nuanced perspective on how to understand what appear to be competing findings in extant research on intersectional identities, we help to clarify current theorizing about intersectionality. Second, we respond to recent calls in diversity scholarship that ask us to evaluate intersectionality critically and thoroughly (e.g., Hebl et al., 2020; Roberson, 2019; Rosette et al., 2018). Overall, we hope that this chapter pushes scholars to increasingly consider the effect of contexts, stereotypes, and prototypes on how we observe and measure the experiences of people with intersectional identities in organizations and beyond.

DEFINING DOUBLE JEOPARDY
AND INTERSECTIONAL INVISIBILITY

The Double Jeopardy Hypothesis: Multiple
Disadvantages Lead to Cumulative Penalties

The double jeopardy hypothesis (e.g., Beal, 2008; Epstein, 1973) seeks to understand the *cumulative* disadvantages of people with multiple subordinated identities. For instance, according to the double jeopardy hypothesis, women of color face the effects of both race and sex prejudice in society (e.g., King, 1988). Though classically theorized about Black women, the argument and logic very aptly apply to any person with more than one subordinated identity (e.g., Barnum et al., 1995; Derous et al., 2015; Lincoln & Allen, 2004; Meyer, 2010).

The double jeopardy hypothesis is conceptualized in two distinct, yet related ways. The first is the additive perspective. From this perspective, women of color and White women, for instance, experience equal amounts of sex-based discrimination; women of color and men of color experience equal amounts of race-based discrimination. Adding the two sources of discrimination together (e.g., sex and race) results in immense, additive discrimination and adversity for women of color that exceeds the oppression experienced by either White women or men of color (e.g., Almquist, 1975; Brown & Misra, 2003). As noted elsewhere, this perspective suggests that each form of discrimination is equivalent and additive in the mathematical, quantitative sense. For instance, the additive perspective would suggest that a low-SES, Black lesbian woman would experience a sort of "quadruple jeopardy" stemming from racism + sexism + classism + heterosexism (King, 1988). Key to this argument is that each of these forms of discrimination poses a "single, direct, and independent" adverse effect on the person, such that their individual effects are equal and can be disentangled from one another (King, 1988, p. 47).

The second conceptualization of double jeopardy—the multiplicative perspective—suggests that social identity categories—like gender and race—do not independently influence outcomes as they do in the additive approach (Crenshaw, 1991; Settles, 2006). Theorists have long asserted that the additive approach is a reductive approach to understanding the experiences of those with multiple subordinate identities (e.g., Bowleg, 2008; Davis, 1981; King, 1988). Specifically, scholars have argued that over-looking the ways in which identities interact with one another ignores the interdependent nature of social hierarchies and systems of control (King, 1988; Crenshaw, 1990). That is, disadvantages corresponding from race and sex *compound* one another, making their effects significantly greater than the sum of their parts. In keeping with the additive example above, multiplicative double jeopardy would suggest that a low-SES Black lesbian woman would experience discrimination akin to multiplying racism, sexism, classism, and heterosexism. From this perspective, Black women would be expected to experience more discrimination than both Black men and White women along race and sex dimensions due to the interaction of their marginalized social identities (Berdahl & Moore, 2006).

Whether adopting an additive or multiplicative approach, empirical investigations of the double jeopardy hypothesis overwhelmingly demonstrate that multiple subordinated identities lead to unique adverse outcomes (see Klonoff et al., 1995). Most early organizational work on

double jeopardy sought to examine the effect of intersecting subordinated identities on salaries and wages. This research found that racially
minoritized women earn lower wages than both racially minoritized men
and White women (Browne, 1999), and, importantly, that the pay gap for
racially minoritized and female employees (compared to White and male
employees) widens significantly with age (Barnum et al., 1995). Not only
are wages explained, in part, by multiple subordinated social identities,
but so are job opportunities: research examining the careers of Hollywood
actors finds negative effects of being female *and* of being older on the
number of film roles received by actors (Lincoln & Allen, 2004).

A large body of this work has also documented the ways in which social
identities negatively affect mental and physical health (e.g., Szymanski &
Stewart, 2010), revealing that elderly women have worse objective health
than both elderly men and young women (Chappell & Havens, 1980).
Other work in this vein finds that Black and Hispanic Americans have
worse health outcomes than their White counterparts and that this health
gap is even larger among the elderly (Carreon & Noymer, 2011). Scholars
have also applied this hypothesis to other marginalized groups and shown
that sexual minorities of color exhibit more psychological distress than
sexual minorities (who are not people of color) or people of color (who are
not sexual minorities; Hayes et al., 2011).

Research has also documented the insidious interpersonal consequences
of double jeopardy. In organizations, racially minoritized women face more
workplace harassment than racially minoritized men and White women
(Berdahl & Moore, 2006). Further, studies of workplace incivility, or "low-
intensity deviant behavior with ambiguous intent to harm the target, in
violation of workplace norms for mutual respect" (Andersson & Pearson,
1999, p. 457), have revealed that gender and race affect respondents' vul-
nerability to uncivil treatment on the job, with women of color reporting the
worst treatment (Cortina et al., 2001; for a review, see McCord et al., 2018).

Additionally, the COVID-19 pandemic provides further evidence of double jeopardy for Latinx and Black women. Specifically, Latinx women—who
tend to be overrepresented in service-based labor (e.g., hospitality)—have
experienced greater rates of unemployment relative to Latinx men, White
women, and White men (Gould et al., 2020). Relatedly, Black women have
faced the largest increase in unemployment rates during the pandemic,
surpassing White men, White women, and Black men (Gould & Wilson,
2020). Although it would be inaccurate to attribute these unemployment
and work outcomes wholly to the pandemic (e.g., McCall, 2003), this global
phenomenon does provide clear examples of how multiply minoritized
populations are particularly affected during times of societal hardship.

Overall, research in the double jeopardy tradition reveals, on balance,[3]
that multiply subordinated individuals experience worse outcomes than

their singly subordinated counterparts. Next, we turn our attention to another pioneering framework that has posited different predictions about the effects of multiple subordination: intersectional invisibility.

The Intersectional Invisibility Hypothesis: Multiple Disadvantages Lead to Diminished Recognition

In contrast to the double jeopardy hypothesis, the intersectional invisibility hypothesis (Purdie-Vaughns & Eibach, 2008) was proposed to emphasize and delineate the unique forms of oppression experienced by individuals with multiple, intersecting subordinated identities. The basic premise of intersectional invisibility states that social identity prototypes tend to reflect normative societal ideologies, rendering those with multiple subordinate group identities socially "invisible." That is, because society centers certain groups as more normative than others (e.g., men as the normative standard for gender, Eagly & Kite, 1987; Whiteness as the normative standard for race, Bonilla-Silva, 2000; Devos & Banaji, 2005), those who deviate from these norms on more than one dimension will tend to be ignored or overlooked in certain situations.

The invisibility of multiply marginalized group members was central to the original conceptualization of intersectionality, which in large part served to criticize the inability of the law to attend to the unique discrimination Black women face. Specifically, Crenshaw (1989) pointed out several court cases (e.g., *DeGraffenreid v. General Motors; Moore v. Hughes Helicopter*) that had dismissed Black women's discrimination claims in the absence of evidence that White women or Black men had systematically experienced discrimination. That is, the courts argued that Black women could not substantiate their claims of gender discrimination unless White women had been affected and could not support their claims of racial discrimination unless Black men had been affected. Black women's experiences were thus rendered "invisible" in the court because they did not correspond to the workplace outcomes of singly subordinated individuals.

Although this theoretical perspective originated more recently than double jeopardy, a range of empirical research has provided evidence for the "invisibility" of those with multiple marginalized identities. For instance, cognitive research has demonstrated that Black women are viewed as non-prototypical of their constituent gender and racial groups and, in turn, are categorized as members of these groups less readily than White women or Black men (e.g., Goff et al., 2008; Johnson et al., 2012; Sesko & Biernat, 2010; Thomas et al., 2014). Stated otherwise, Black women are less accurately and quickly categorized as "Black," compared to Black men, and as "women," compared to White women. Research on person perception has also demonstrated that gay men of color are attributed fewer traits stereotypic of their race than their heterosexual counterparts (Petsko & Bodenhausen, 2019), again suggesting that multiply subordinated group members are contrasted away from their identity categories.

This relative invisibility may result in a constellation of positive and negative outcomes for multiply disadvantaged individuals. For instance, both older women and Black women have been shown to evade typical backlash for enacting dominance, compared to their more prototypical, singly subordinated counterparts (i.e., younger women and older men, Martin et al., 2019; White women and Black men, Livingston et al., 2012). Similarly, age appears to buffer Black men from some of the harmful stereotyping they may experience relative to White men. That is, although young Black men are perceived as more hostile and angry than young White men, this pattern reverses for the elderly (Kang & Chasteen, 2009). Scholars also argue that whereas White women may face penalties for masculine behavior, Black women may be buffered from the same reprisals (Biernat & Sesko, 2013). Despite these positive effects, however, intersectional invisibility can also lead to unique disadvantages: Multiply subordinated individuals are often neglected, misremembered, or discounted, relative to singly subordinated individuals (e.g., Schug et al., 2015; Sesko & Biernat, 2010, 2018). Indeed, multiple studies have revealed that statements made by Black women are more often forgotten than those of Black men or White women (Schug et al., 2015; Sesko & Biernat, 2010). Highlighting the benefits and challenges associated with intersectional invisibility, interviews with Black female executives revealed that these women felt that their dually subordinated identities freed them from typical racialized and gendered expectations, but also left them overlooked and misunderstood in many professional situations (Smith et al., 2019).

Thus, whereas double jeopardy proposes an additive or multiplicative model of compounding prejudice, findings supporting the intersectional invisibility model uncover "how the forms of oppression that people with intersecting disadvantaged identities experience differ from the forms of oppression that people with a single disadvantaged identity experience" (Purdie-Vaughns & Eibach, 2008, p. 380). In doing so, intersectional invisibility places a special focus on how outcomes for multiply marginalized individuals may fundamentally differ from those of singly subordinated individuals, due to their diminished prototypicality.

RECONCILING DOUBLE JEOPARDY AND INTERSECTIONAL INVISIBILITY

Are multiply subordinated individuals subjected to double jeopardy, or are they rendered "invisible?"[4] We suggest that although these theoretical perspectives may appear to be in direct opposition, considering the stereotypes and role congruity perceptions at play in distinct contexts, and attending to the reference groups and prototypes used in comparative analyses can help to elucidate situations in which double jeopardy or intersectional invisibility may be observed. In general, a consideration of these factors supports the idea that multiply-subordinated individuals can simultaneously experience outcomes associated with each perspective.

Intersectional Stereotyping, Prototypicality, and Contextual Fit

Based on the propositions of the MOSAIC model of stereotyping (Hall et al., 2019), attending to group stereotypes may help to disentangle contexts in which outcomes reflecting double jeopardy versus intersection invisibility may be observed. MOSAIC is an intersectional framework that emphasizes the role of social category integration in person-perception and comparative evaluation. The theory suggests that when comparing the experiences of two individuals, the influence of social categories that the targets have in common (i.e., the "foundational" category) must be integrated with salient categories that differ between the two individuals (i.e., "intersectional" categories). Importantly, the degree of overlap between expectations and stereotypes for these categories determines the prototypicality of group members within the group overall. When stereotypes of an individuals' foundational and intersectional categories align with one another, foundational category stereotypes are amplified, or applied strongly. Conversely, when foundational and intersectional categories do *not* align, foundational category stereotypes are diluted, or applied weakly.

To illustrate this framework, consider a comparison of White and Black women. Because "White," as the racial standard (e.g., Rosette et al., 2008), has no gendered associations or stereotypes (Galinsky et al., 2013; Hall et al., 2015), communal feminine stereotypes emphasizing sensitivity, warmth, and kindness (Ellemers, 2018; Kite et al., 2008; Rudman & Glick, 1999, 2001) are applied to White women unaltered (Ghavami & Peplau, 2013; Rosette et al., 2016). In contrast, Black women's masculine racial stereotypes that emphasize their dominance, strength, and anger (Ghavami & Peplau, 2013; Niemann et al., 1994; Rosette et al., 2016) conflict with traditional feminine stereotypes and result in the dilution of these stereotypes for Black women. As such, White women are more prototypical of women in general than are Black women (e.g., Schug et al., 2015; Sesko & Biernat, 2010).

The pattern of stereotype application that MOSAIC illustrates can help to shed light on the disparate findings in the intersectional invisibility and double jeopardy literatures. Specifically, foundational group prototypicality can have positive or negative effects, depending on the fit between foundational group stereotypes and expectations for the context (Wong & McCullough, 2021). Indeed, work on person-position fit suggests that when evaluating individuals in a given role, people assess the extent to which the person's traits align with those required for the role (Eagly & Karau, 2002; Heilman, 1983; Lord et al., 1984; Lord & Maher, 1993). For instance, a woman may be viewed as a good fit for a customer service position—as feminine gender stereotypes align with expectations for such a role—but a poor fit for a leadership position—as feminine gender stereotypes misalign with agentic expectations for leaders (Eagly & Karau, 2002). We suggest that a similar process can help to explain when being non-prototypical of their constituent identity groups may either advantage or disadvantage multiply subordinated individuals.

As one illustrative example, although Black female leaders who display dominant behavior evade the backlash experienced by both White female and Black male leaders (Livingston et al., 2012), they are also more strongly penalized than either of these groups when they make mistakes on the job (Rosette & Livingston, 2012). Stereotyping and perceptions of contextual fit may help account for these and other similar findings that are in apparent opposition. In the current example, intersectional stereotypes are advantageous for Black women when perceptions of dominance are the focus, but detrimental when perceptions of competence are the focus.[5] These findings make sense when the stereotypes applied to women and to Black people are considered. As a foundational group, women are proscribed from enacting dominance due to stereotypes casting them as inherently communal and warm (Eagly & Karau, 2002; Phelan & Rudman, 2010; Rudman, 1998; Rudman & Glick, 1999, 2001), and Black people are proscribed from displaying dominance due to stereotypes casting them as highly threatening and dangerous (Livingston & Pearce, 2009; Navarrete et al., 2010). As the respective prototypes of women and Black people, White women and Black men are also proscribed from displaying dominance. Black women, however, appear to benefit from the integration of the opposing stereotypes corresponding to their racial and gender identities. That is, integrating feminine stereotypes emphasizing communal traits with racial stereotypes comprising threatening traits dilutes each set of expectations. In turn, in a context that requires dominance, Black women benefit from relaxed proscriptions against such behavior, relative to White women and Black men (Hall et al., 2019; Rosette et al., 2016, 2018).

When evaluations of competence are of central importance, however, the integration of these categories simply emphasizes Black women's perceived incompetence and lack of fit for leadership positions. Because both women *and* Black people are descriptively stereotyped as lacking the technical competence for leadership (Eagly & Karau, 2002; Fiske et al., 2002;

Rosette et al., 2008), this expectation of incompetence is likely amplified for Black women in the context of organizational failure, enhancing their penalization relative to either Black men or White women. Thus, when the context shifts from one centered on dominant behavior to one focused on competence, Black women's intersectional stereotypes may lead to penalties consistent with the double jeopardy hypothesis.

In a similar vein, the amplification of negative competence-related stereotypes may account for the observation that Black and Latinx women suffer a wage and promotion gap, relative to White men, greater than that of White women or Black and Latinx men (Labor force characteristics by race and ethnicity, 2019); Women in the Workplace, 2020). Findings suggesting that lesbians—who are stereotyped as more masculine and, in particular, more competent than women in general (Fiske et al., 2002; Freeman et al., 2010; Glick & Fiske, 2001; Kite & Deaux, 1987)—experience hiring and salary benefits, relative to heterosexual women (Daneshvary et al., 2008; Klawitter, 2015), further suggest the role of stereotypes in driving outcomes reflecting either invisibility or double jeopardy. Similarly, Biernat and Sesko (2013) found that a pro-male gender bias was observed for White, but not Black, women paired with a man on a masculine task. Black women's avoidance of gender bias in this task again supports the idea that unique masculine stereotypes ascribed to Black women contributed to their invisibility in these contexts. Together, these findings emphasize the importance of considering intersectional effects on stereotyping and, consequently, the distinct perceptions of fit that may arise among those who share an identity.

Stereotype integration may also help to explain research suggesting that among Asian people, Asian *men* experience more cognitive invisibility than Asian women (Johnson et al., 2012; Schug et al., 2015; Schug et al., 2017). Although this finding appears to conflict with the propositions of intersectional invisibility, when considered alongside research on gendered races (Galinsky et al., 2013; Hall et al., 2015; Wilkins et al., 2011), these findings again suggest the importance of categorical integration in shaping outcomes. That is, because Asian people as a superordinate category are stereotyped as highly feminine, Asian women's gender category is more consistent with their race than Asian men's gender category. As a result, Asian *women* are more prototypical of Asian people than Asian men, despite their dual subordinated identities (Schug et al., 2015).

As the principles of MOSAIC, alongside the above examples, illustrate, attending to the role of categorical integration in shaping stereotyping and prototypicality can elucidate contexts in which specific group members may face heightened or diminished prejudice. Specifically, the content of stereotypes corresponding to identities, their interactive effect, and their contextual fit may be more important for shaping outcomes than the mere number of marginalized identities a person has.

Proposition 1a: When the integration of multiple subordinated identities results in stereotypes better suited for the context—compared to superordinate group stereotypes—advantages associated with intersectional invisibility will be observed

Proposition 1b: When the integration of multiple subordinated identities results in stereotypes worse suited for the context—compared to superordinate group stereotypes—disadvantages associated with double jeopardy will be observed

Measurement and Frames of Reference in Discrimination Research on Intersectional Identities

Another important step in reconciling these disparate theories is attending more closely to the reference points used in these bodies of work. Specifically, scholars must consider the groups and individuals to which multiply subordinated individuals are compared and the implicit standards used to quantify and measure prejudice. As previously articulated, prototypicality (the extent to which an individual is representative of the category or group they belong to; Mervis & Rosch, 1981; Strom et al., 2012; Rosch & Mervis, 1975) and stereotypes (fixed beliefs we hold about individuals based on the groups they belong to; Hilton & Von Hippel, 1996; Operario & Fiske, 2001; Stangor & Lange, 1994) dominate our frames of reference for discrimination, and thus, have serious implications for how we assess the very presence of discrimination. As such, it is critical that scholars consider the interaction between prototypicality and stereotypes as we examine how individuals with multiple subordinate identities are evaluated.

Again, drawing from MOSAIC, considering the dilution and amplification of stereotypes and their effects on prototypicality can shed light on how certain measures of discrimination center the experiences of singly subordinated individuals. As suggested above, MOSAIC argues that the extent to which foundational group stereotypes are applied to individuals "is contingent upon how prototypical the individual is of the category such that category stereotypes are more strongly applied to individuals who are perceived to be more representative of that category" (Hall et al., 2019, p. 645). As such, prototypicality determines how stereotypes are applied to group members through processes of *dilution* and *amplification*.

Consider the effects of amplification and dilution in light of research demonstrating that Black men experience more adverse outcomes compared to Black women in "shoot/don't shoot" paradigms (Plant et al., 2011). In these studies, participants assume the role of police officers who must quickly decide whether to shoot potentially dangerous suspects, depending on whether they visually process the suspect as wielding a gun or a benign object (e.g., a cell phone). Although Black people as a superordinate group are stereotyped as violent and threatening to some extent, these stereotypes are amplified for Black men (the prototype for Black people) but diluted for Black women. As such, using decisions to shoot as measures of racial prejudice likely center prototypical group members (i.e., Black men) and marginalize the distinct forms of racialized prejudice Black women may face, for example.

Consider also recent work on perceptions of gay men of color. Across several experiments, Petsko and Bodenhausen (2019) rigorously test and find evidence that gay racially minoritized men become "deracialized," concluding that gay men of color might, consequently, be less susceptible to racial discrimination than heterosexual men of color. However, given the complexity of identity and the inability to cleanly delineate whether experiences emanate from one social identity or another, it is incumbent upon us to consider how racial prejudice, in this case, might *fundamentally differ* for straight and gay men of color due to the interactive effects of race and sexual orientation on group prototypicality. That is, although "de-racialization" may indeed occur for gay men of color, we suggest that this process might simply change how they experience racial discrimination, rather than reduce or eliminate it. To use conceptualizations of prejudicial experiences that do not examine how racial discrimination might also be informed by sexuality obscures and further marginalizes these experiences. For instance, a Black gay man may face unique racial discrimination because he is a non-prototypical Black person and "de-racialized." For instance, he may be perceived by others as not "Black" enough and face specific interpersonal consequences as a result. It is thus imperative that we undertake a more nuanced approach to exploring prejudice and discrimination for individuals with multiple subordinated identities who may not be subjected to prototypical superordinate group stereotypes.

When they belong to groups with consistent stereotype content, multiply marginalized individuals may be attributed *amplified* group stereotypes. As suggested above, this process might be best exemplified in work that demonstrates Black women's outcomes in occupational contexts (e.g., more negative outcomes than White women and Black men; for a review, see Sayce et al., 2012) because stereotypes of incompetence are attributed more strongly to Black people than to White people and also more strongly to women than to men. As such, for Black women, these stereotypes of incompetence are consistent with one another and can combine to produce more negative competence evaluations for Black women (Bavishi et al., 2010).

Foundational work conducted by Almquist (1975) reports results consistent with these claims. Using labor force data, she finds that Black women are disadvantaged in three important ways in the labor market: they secure fewer jobs overall, even fewer high-level jobs, and experience wage discrimination. All three of these findings are consistent with the stereotype amplification hypothesis, as these evaluations tend to be based on evaluations of occupational competence.

Additionally, in a study of teaching evaluations, Bavishi and colleagues (2010) find that Black female professors were evaluated as the least competent, legitimate, and having the worst interpersonal skills compared to White and male professors. Suggesting the role of stereotyping in this process, the students who provided the evaluations had not met these fictitious professors, but instead drew upon their cognitive schemas to provide their expectations of these faculty members.

In general, as the above example illustrate, by studying discrimination in ways that reflect superordinate group stereotypes, our theorizing and hypothesizing likely centers the experiences of those who are most prototypical of these stereotypes. It is clear that if this is indeed the case, our empirical approach to mapping and mitigating discrimination *within* subordinated groups may not always capture the unique circumstances of multiply subordinated group members. Since these individuals view their identities as inseparable (e.g., Williams, 2014), it is logical to surmise that they also view the discrimination they face as tied to *all* of their identities. For instance, a Black man being harassed might easily deduce that this experience is because of his race. However, a Black woman facing harassment might encounter more ambiguity in the source of the mistreatment and surmise that her experienced harassment is due to both her race *and* gender (Smith & Nkomo, 2003). As such, is it critically important to reflect on how dissecting discrimination into neat, singular social identity categories[6] robs us of the ability to consider how discrimination might look distinct for those who share a single identity. In turn, when we ask about specific forms of prejudice, we may be obscuring unique forms of identity-based prejudice that less prototypical group members face.[7]

Supporting this possibility, quantitative research on workplace harassment finds that racially minoritized women are subject to "not-man-enough" forms of sexual harassment at a higher rate than White women (Berdahl & Moore, 2006, p. 433), while qualitative work concludes that Black executive women are subject to unique forms of discrimination and invisibility because of their race and gender (Smith et al., 2019). Indeed, feminist scholar Moya Bailey termed the distinct anti-Black sexism that Black women experience "misogynoir" (Bailey, 2013; Bailey & Trudy, 2018) to emphasize that racial and gender bias are experienced differently for Black women, compared to Black men and White women, respectively.

Taken together, these examples underscore two critical points: first, the necessity for scholars to consider what is (or is not) prototypical of subordinate groups, and second, that measuring discrimination without critically interrogating said prototypicality obfuscates our understanding of individuals with multiple subordinated identities.

Proposition 2a: When the integration of multiple subordinate identities amplifies superordinate group stereotypes, researchers will observe results consistent with double jeopardy.

Proposition 2b: When the integration of multiple subordinate identities dilute superordinate group stereotypes, researchers will observe results consistent with intersectional invisibility.

DISCUSSION

The double jeopardy and intersectional invisibility hypotheses are often pitted against one another. However, we suggest that a closer consideration of stereotype integration, prototypicality, and consequent contextual fit can help to explain how and when outcomes associated with each perspective may arise. By studying discrimination in ways that likely correspond to more prototypical group members, researchers may not capture the full extent to which multiple identities may interactively inform stereotypes.[8] In turn, scholars may overlook the specific forms of prejudice that subgroup members who are ascribed diluted superordinate identity stereotypes may face. Multiply marginalized targets may be systematically excluded from this research, given that these individuals are often non-prototypical of their constituent identity groups. Further, as articulated above, research has documented time and time again that the experiences of people with multiple subordinated identities are distinct and deserve to be studied in their own right. We thus propose that moving forward, we as researchers must do a better job of studying discrimination in a way that accounts for multiple sources of discrimination, rather than privileging more prototypical experiences.

Interestingly, this review and our suggestions for moving forward reveal the influence of intersectional invisibility on the way discrimination itself has been studied. Throughout this chapter, we have discussed and explicated how studies of intersectional discrimination may have rendered invisible those we have intended to study by privileging more prototypical forms of prejudice. As such, a necessary (but often missing) piece of the puzzle in better understanding how prejudice and discrimination might differ for multiply (vs. singly) subordinated individuals is the development and implementation of approaches that center these individuals.

Future Directions for Double Jeopardy and Intersectional Invisibility

Although research across the social sciences has increasingly incorporated intersectional frameworks, these studies have tended to focus on juxtaposing the experiences of Black women with those of White women and Black men. Resultantly, much of the empirical work demonstrating double jeopardy and intersectional invisibility is based on studies of Black women. Although this work is critically important, it limits the scope of what intersectionality research can and should do. Stated otherwise, to better understand the diverse outcomes of multiply subordinated individuals, intersectional research should broaden to consider the intersection of other social identities, beyond race and gender. Consider that organizational scholarship has largely neglected the importance of social class (Côté, 2011), and when it is considered, "SES indicators, such as occupational position, education, and income, have usually been treated as nuisance variables" (Christie & Barling, 2009, pp. 1474–1475). As interest in the role of social class in organizations has notably increased over the last decade (see Martin & Côté, 2019), exploring how social class might interact with other social identities to impact workplace outcomes may reveal important nuances in existing findings on organizational experiences. Further, disability is another aspect of identity that has largely been neglected by management scholars (Colella et al., 2017). Although interest in the effect of (dis)ability is steadily increasing, "it still lags behind that of other diversity dimensions, such as gender, race, and ethnicity" (Beatty et al., 2019, p.119). Future work should consider how often neglected aspects of identity, like class and disability, intersect with other, perhaps more observable, identities to influence organizational outcomes. And subsequently, core management journals should ensure space for this work.

Relatedly, another fruitful avenue for continued research on these topics is the effects of stigma concealability on invisibility and double jeopardy. Specifically, how might double jeopardy versus intersectional invisibility emerge for individuals who possess both a concealable (e.g., HIV positive status, a history of mental illness) and visible (e.g., race, gender) stigmatized identity? For example, a person with two visible subordinated identities may be more likely to experience outcomes consistent with double jeopardy because their identities are visible, accessible, and more easily used in judgments than those who bear some mix of visible and invisible stigmatized identities or only invisible stigmatized identities. In line with recent calls for research that considers concealable stigmas and identities (e.g., Hallett, 2015; Williams & Frederick, 2015), we encourage and call for management scholars to empirically address these questions.

As quantitative research leveraging the intersectional invisibility hypothesis has tended to measure invisibility as cognitive non-prototypicality (e.g., Johnson et al., 2012; Schug et al., 2015; Thomas et al., 2014), continued research on this topic should explore more outcomes explicitly tied to discrimination. For instance, this literature could benefit from continued studies that examine invisibility in terms of status conferral, salary allocation, or hireability (see Biernat & Sesko, 2013; Livingston et al., 2012; Martin et al., 2019). Given that double jeopardy research typically considers these types of outcomes—rather than more perceptual consequences of intersectionality—extending the invisibility literature to include additional studies that explicitly measure discrimination may facilitate more direct comparisons between these literatures. Further, as the possession of multiple subordinate identities does not always diminish prototypicality (e.g., Asian men), continued explorations of intersectional invisibility that transcend issues related to prototypicality may enrich our understanding of the outcomes multiply marginalized individuals in particular are likely to encounter.

CONCLUSION

Describing the challenges she has faced as a woman of color in politics, Vice President-elect Kamala Harris noted "when I first ran for office that was one of the things that I struggled with, which is that you are forced through that process to define yourself in a way that you fit neatly into the compartment that other people have created."[9] As this observation suggests, by forcing people with multiple (subordinated) identities into a singular box, we create a problematic dynamic for these individuals and for the study of marginalization. Stated otherwise, the treatment of identities as orthogonal to one another obscures the nuanced effects of intersectionality on experiences of prejudice and discrimination. With conversations around the increased representation of *all underrepresented* individuals at the forefront of diversity, equity, and inclusion, it is imperative that we have a tighter focus on the processes and challenges to studying the experiences of the changing workforce. We hope that this chapter pushes both applied and research-oriented conversations forward in service of this goal.

REFERENCES

Abele, A. E., Cuddy, A. J. C., Judd, C. M., & Yzerbyt, V. Y. (2008). Fundamental dimensions of social judgment. *European Journal of Social Psychology, 39,* 1063–1065.10.1002/ejsp.574

Almquist, E. M. (1975). Career counseling for women in 1884: The more total view. *Vocational Guidance Quarterly, 23*(4), 298–300. https://doi.org/10.1002/j.2164-585X.1975.tb02175.x

Andersson, L. M., & Pearson, C. M. (1999). Tit for tat? The spiraling effect of incivility in the workplace. *Academy of management review, 24*(3), 452–471. https://doi.org/10.5465/amr.1999.2202131

Artiles, A. (2013). Untangling the racialization of disabilities: An intersectionality critique across disability models. *Du Bois Review: Social Science Research on Race, 10*(2), 329–347. https://doi.org/10.1017/S1742058X13000271

Bailey, M. (2013). New terms of resistance: A response to Zenzele Isoke, *Souls, 15*(4), 341–343. https://doi.org/10.1080/10999949.2014.884451

Bailey, M., & Trudy. (2018) On misogynoir: Citation, erasure, and plagiarism. *Feminist Media Studies, 18*(4), 762–768. https://doi.org/10.1080/14680777.2018.1447395

Barnum, P., Liden, R. C., & Ditomaso, N. (1995). Double jeopardy for women and minorities: Pay differences with age. *Academy of Management Journal, 38*(3), 863–880. https://doi.org/10.2307/256749

Bavishi, A., Madera, J. M., & Hebl, M. R. (2010). The effect of professor ethnicity and gender on student evaluations: Judged before met. *Journal of Diversity in Higher Education, 3*(4), 245.

Beal, F. M. (2008). Double jeopardy: To be Black and female. *Meridians, 8*(2), 166–176. http://www.jstor.org/stable/40338758

Beatty, J. E., Baldridge, D. C., Boehm, S. A., Kulkarni, M., & Colella, A. J. (2019). On the treatment of persons with disabilities in organizations: A review and research agenda. *Human Resource Management, 58*(2), 119–137. https://doi.org/10.1002/hrm.21940

Berdahl, J. L., & Moore, C. (2006). Workplace harassment: Double jeopardy for minority women. *Journal of Applied Psychology, 91*(2), 426–436. https://doi.org/10.1037/0021-9010.91.2.426

Biernat, M., & Sesko, A. K. (2013). Evaluating the contributions of members of mixed-sex work teams: Race and gender matter. *Journal of Experimental Social Psychology, 49*(3), 471–476. https://doi.org/10.1016/j.jesp.2013.01.008

Bonilla-Silva, E. (2000). "This is a White Country": The racial ideology of the Western nations of the world-system. *Sociological Quarterly, 70*, 188–214. https://doi.org/10.1111/j.1475-682X.2000.tb00905.x

Bowleg, L. (2008). When Black + Lesbian + Woman ≠ Black Lesbian Woman: The methodological challenges of qualitative and quantitative intersectionality research. *Sex Roles, 59*(5), 312–325. https://doi.org/10.1007/s11199-008-9400-z

Browne, I. (Ed.). (1999). *Latinas and African American women at work: Race, gender, and economic inequality.* Russell Sage Foundation. Retrieved December 15, 2020, from http://www.jstor.org/stable/10.7758/9781610440943

Browne, I., & Misra, J. (2003). The intersection of gender and race in the labor market. *Annual Review of Sociology, 29*, 487–513. Retrieved December 15, 2020, from

Carreon, D., & Noymer, A. (2011). Health-related quality of life in older adults: Testing the double jeopardy hypothesis. *Journal of Aging Studies*, *25*(4), 371–379. https://doi.org/10.1016/j.jaging.2011.01.004

Carter-Sowell, A. R., & Zimmerman, C. A. (2015). Hidden in plain sight: Locating, validating, and advocating the stigma experiences of women of color. *Sex Roles*, *73*(9), 399–407.

Chappell, N. L., & Havens, B. (1980). Old and female: Testing the double jeopardy hypothesis. *Sociological Quarterly*, *21*(2), 157–171. https://doi.org/10.1111/j.1533-8525.1980.tb00601.x

Christie, A. M., & Barling, J. (2009). Disentangling the indirect links between socioeconomic status and health: The dynamic roles of work stressors and personal control. *Journal of Applied Psychology*, *94*(6), 1466–1478. https://doi.org/10.1037/a0016847

Cole, E. R. (2009). Intersectionality and research in psychology. *American Psychologist*, *64*(3), 170–180. https://doi.org/10.1037/a0014564

Colella, A., Hebl, M., & King, E. (2017). One hundred years of discrimination research in the *Journal of Applied Psychology*: A sobering synopsis. *Journal of Applied Psychology*, *102*(3), 500–513. https://doi.org/10.1037/apl0000084

Collins, P. H. (2015). Intersectionality's definitional dilemmas. *Annual Review of Sociology*, *41*, 1–20. https://doi.org/10.1146/annurev-soc-073014-112142

Collins, P. H., & Bilge, S. (2020). *Intersectionality*. John Wiley & Sons.

Cortina, L. M., Magley, V. J., Williams, J. H., & Langhout, R. D. (2001). Incivility in the workplace: Incidence and impact. *Journal of Occupational Health Psychology*, *6*(1), 64–80. https://doi.org/10.1037/1076-8998.6.1.64

Côté, S. (2011). How social class shapes thoughts and actions in organizations. *Research in Organizational Behavior*, *31*, 43–71. https://doi.org/10.1016/j.riob.2011.09.004

Crenshaw, K. (1989). Demarginalizing the intersection of race and sex: A black feminist critique of antidiscrimination doctrine, feminist theory and anti-racist politics. *University of Chicago Legal Forum*, *1989*(1), Article 8. http://chicagounbound.uchicago.edu/uclf/vol1989/iss1/.

Crenshaw, K. (1990). Mapping the margins: Intersectionality, identity politics, and violence against women of color. *Stan. L. Rev.*, *43*, 1241.

Crenshaw, K. (1991). Race, gender, and sexual harassment. *Columbia Law School*, *65*, 1467.

Cuadraz, G. H., & Uttal, L. (1999). Intersectionality and in-depth interviews: Methodological strategies for analyzing race, class, and gender. *Race, Gender & Class*, 156–186.

Daneshvary, N., Waddoups, C. J., & Wimmer, B. S. (2008). Educational attainment and the lesbian wage premium. *Journal of Labor Research*, *29*(4), 365–379.

Davis, A. Y. (1981). *Women, race & class*(1st ed.). Vintage Books.

Derous, E., Ryan, A. M., & Serlie, A. W. (2015). Double jeopardy upon resume screening: When Achmed is less employable than Aisha. *Personnel Psychology*, *68*(3), 659–696. https://doi.org/10.1111/peps.12078

Devos, T., & Banaji, M. R. (2005). American = White? *Journal of Personality and Social Psychology*, *88*(3), 447–466. https://doi.org/10.1037/0022-3514.88.3.447

Eagly, A. H., & Karau, S. J. (2002). Role congruity theory of prejudice toward female leaders. *Psychological Review, 109*(3), 573–598. doi:10.1037/0033-295X.109.3.573

Eagly, A. H., & Kite, M. E. (1987). Are stereotypes of nationalities applied to both women and men? *Journal of Personality and Social Psychology, 53*(3), 451–462. https://doi.org/10.1037/0022-3514.53.3.451

Ellemers, N. (2018). Gender stereotypes. *Annual Review of Psychology, 69*, 275–298. https://doi.org/10.1146/annurev-psych-122216-011719

Epstein, C. F. (1973). Black and female: The double whammy. *Psychology Today, 89*, 57–61

Fiske, S. T., Cuddy, A. J. C., Glick, P., & Xu, J. (2002). A model of (often mixed) stereotype content: Competence and warmth respectively follow from perceived status and competition. *Journal of Personality and Social Psychology, 82*(6), 878–902. https://doi.org/10.1037/0022-3514.82.6.878

Freeman, J. B., Johnson, K. L., Ambady, N., & Rule, N. O. (2010). Sexual orientation perception involves gendered facial cues. *Personality and Social Psychology Bulletin, 36*(10), 1318–1331. https://doi.org/10.1177/0146167210378755

Freeman, J. B., Penner, A. M., Saperstein, A., Scheutz, M., & Ambady, N. (2011). Looking the part: Social status cues shape race perception. *PloS One, 6*(9), e25107. https://doi.org/10.1371/journal.pone.0025107

Galinsky, A. D., Hall, E. V., & Cuddy, A. J. C. (2013). Gendered races: Implications for interracial marriage, leadership selection, and athletic participation. *Psychological Science, 24*(4), 498–506. https://doi.org/10.1177/0956797612457783

Ghavami, N., & Peplau, L. A. (2013). An intersectional analysis of gender and ethnic stereotypes: Testing three hypotheses. *Psychology of Women Quarterly, 37*(1), 113–127. https://doi.org/10.1177/0361684312464203

Glick, P., & Fiske, S. T. (2001). An ambivalent alliance: Hostile and benevolent sexism as complementary justifications for gender inequality. *American Psychologist, 56*(2), 109–118. https://doi.org/10.1037/0003-066X.56.2.109

Goff, P. A., Thomas, M. A., & Jackson, M. C. (2008). "Ain't i a woman? ": Towards an intersectional approach to person perception and group-based harms. *Sex Roles, 59*(5), 392–403. https://doi.org/10.1007/s11199-008-9505-4

Gould, E., & Wilson, V. (2020). Black workers face two of the most lethal preexisting conditions for coronavirus—racism and economic inequality. *Economic Policy Institute*. https://www.epi.org/publication/black-workers-covid/

Gould, E., Perez, D., & Wilson, V. (2020). Latinx workers—particularly women—face devastating job losses in the COVID-19 recession. *Economic Policy Institute*. https://www.epi.org/publication/latinx-workers-covid/

Hall, E. V., Galinsky, A. D., & Phillips, K. W. (2015). Gender profiling: A gendered race perspective on person-position fit. *Personality and Social Psychology Bulletin, 41*(6), 853–868. https://doi.org/10.1177/0146167215580779

Hall, E. V., Hall, A. V., Galinsky, A. D., & Phillips, K. W. (2019). MOSAIC: A model of stereotyping through associated and intersectional categories. *The Academy of Management Review, 44*(3), 643–672. https://doi.org/10.5465/amr.2017.0109

Hallett, H. (2015). Intersectionality and serious mental illness—A case study and recommendations for practice. *Women & Therapy, 38*(1–2), 156–174. https://doi.org/10.1080/02703149.2014.978232

Hayes, J. A., Chun-Kennedy, C., Edens, A., & Locke, B. D. (2011). Do double minority students face double jeopardy? Testing minority stress theory. *Journal of College Counseling*, *14*(2), 117–126. https://doi.org/10.1002/j.2161-1882.2011. tb00267.x

Hebl, M., Cheng, S. K., & Ng, L. C. (2020). Modern discrimination in organizations. *Annual Review of Organizational Psychology and Organizational Behavior*, *7*, 257–282. https://doi.org/10.1146/annurev-orgpsych-012119-044948

Heilman, M. (1983). Sex bias in work settings: The lack of fit model. *Research in Organizational Behavior*, *5*, 269–298.

Hilton, J. L., & Von Hippel, W. (1996). Stereotypes. *Annual review of psychology*, *47*(1), 237–271.

Johnson, K. L., Freeman, J. B., & Pauker, K. (2012). Race is gendered: How covarying phenotypes and stereotypes bias sex categorization. *Journal of Personality and Social Psychology*, *102*(1), 116–131. https://doi.org/10.1037/a0025335

Kang, S. K., Chasteen, A. L., Cadieux, J., Cary, L. A., & Syeda, M. (2014). Comparing young and older adults' perceptions of conflicting stereotypes and multiply-categorizable individuals. *Psychology and Aging*, *29*(3), 469–481. https://doi.org/10.1037/a0037551

King, D. K. (1988). Multiple jeopardy, multiple consciousness: The context of a Black feminist ideology. *Signs: Journal of Women in Culture and Society*, *14*(1), 42–72. https://doi.org/10.1086/494491

King, E. B., Huffman, A. H., & Peddie, C. I. (2013). LGBT parents and the workplace. In A. E. Goldberg & K. R. Allen (Eds.), *LGBT-parent families* (pp. 225–237). Springer.

Kite, M. E., & Deaux, K. (1987). Gender belief systems: Homosexuality and the implicit inversion theory. *Psychology of Women Quarterly*, *11*(1), 83–96. https://doi.org/10.1111/j.1471-6402.1987.tb00776.x

Kite, M. E., Deaux, K., & Haines, E. L. (2008). *Gender stereotypes*. In F. L. Denmark & M. A. Paludi (Eds.), *Women's psychology. Psychology of women: A handbook of issues and theories* (pp. 205–236). Praeger Publishers/Greenwood Publishing Group.

Klawitter, M. (2015). Meta-analysis of the effects of sexual orientation on earnings. *Industrial Relations: A Journal of Economy and Society*, *54*(1), 4–32. https://doi.org/10.1111/irel.12075

Klonoff, E. A., Landrine, H., & Scott, J. (1995). *Double jeopardy: Ethnicity and gender in health research*. In H. Landrine (Ed.), *Bringing cultural diversity to feminist psychology: Theory, research, and practice* (pp. 335–360). American Psychological Association. https://doi.org/10.1037/10501-014

Koenig, A.M., & Eagly, A.H. (2014). Evidence for the social role theory of stereotype content: Observations of groups' roles shape stereotypes. *Journal of Personality and Social Psychology*, *107*(3), 371–392. https://doi.org/10.1037/a0037215

Kohler-Hausmann, I. (2018). Eddie Murphy and the dangers of counterfactual causal thinking about detecting racial discrimination. *Northwestern University Law Review*, *113*, 1163.

Labor force characteristics by race and ethnicity. (2019). [Bureau of Labor Statistics]. https://www.bls.gov/opub/reports/race-and-ethnicity/2019/home.htm

Lincoln, A. E., & Allen, M. P. (2004). Double jeopardy in Hollywood: Age and gender in the careers of film actors, 1926–1999. *Sociological Forum, 19*(4), 611–631. https://doi.org/10.1007/s11206-004-0698-1

Livingston, R. W., & Pearce, N. A. (2009). The Teddy-Bear effect: Does having a baby face benefit black chief executive officers? *Psychological Science, 20*(10), 1229–1236. https://doi.org/10.1111/j.1467-9280.2009.02431.x

Livingston, R. W., Rosette, A. S., & Washington, E. F. (2012). Can an agentic Black woman get ahead? The impact of race and interpersonal dominance on perceptions of female leaders. *Psychological Science, 23*(4), 354–358. https://doi.org/10.1177/0956797611428079

Lord, R. G., Foti, R. J., & De Vader, C. L. (1984). A test of leadership categorization theory: Internal structure, information processing, and leadership perceptions. *Organizational Behavior and Human Performance, 34*(3), 343–378. https://doi.org/10.1016/0030-5073(84)90043-6

Lord, R. G., & Maher, K. J. (1993). *Leadership and information processing: Linking perceptions and performance*. Routledge.

Ma, A. (2020). *The motivation-influence-ability (MIA) model of agency for gender and leadership* [Unpublished doctoral dissertation]. Duke University.

Martin, A. E., North, M. S., & Phillips, K. W. (2019). Intersectional escape: Older women elude agentic prescriptions more than older men. *Personality and Social Psychology Bulletin, 45*(3), 342–359. https://doi.org/10.1177/0146167218784895

Martin, S. R., & Côté, S. (2019). Social class transitioners: Their cultural abilities and organizational importance. *The Academy of Management Review, 44*(3), 618–642. https://doi.org/10.5465/amr.2017.0065

McCall, L. (2001). Sources of racial wage inequality in metropolitan labor markets: Racial, ethnic, and gender differences. *American Sociological Review, 66*(4), 520–541. https://doi.org/10.2307/3088921

McCord, M. A., Joseph, D. L., Dhanani, L. Y., & Beus, J. M. (2018). A meta-analysis of sex and race differences in perceived workplace mistreatment. *Journal of Applied Psychology, 103*(2), 137–163. https://doi.org/10.1037/apl0000250

McGee, E. O. (2020). The agony of stereotyping holds Black women back. *Nature Human Behavior.* https://doi.org/10.1038/s41562-020-01001-8

Mervis, C. B., & Rosch, E. (1981). Categorization of natural objects. *Annual review of psychology, 32*(1), 89–115.

Meyer, I. H. (2010). Identity, stress, and resilience in lesbians, gay men, and bisexuals of color. *The Counseling Psychologist, 38*(3), 442–454. https://doi.org/10.1177/0011000009351601

Nash, J. C. (2008). Re-Thinking Intersectionality. *Feminist Review, 89*(1), 1–15. https://doi.org/10.1057/fr.2008.4

Navarrete, C. D., McDonald, M. M., Molina, L. E., & Sidanius, J. (2010). Prejudice at the nexus of race and gender: An outgroup male target hypothesis. *Journal of Personality and Social Psychology, 98*(6), 933–945. https://doi.org/10.1037/a0017931

Niemann, Y. F., Jennings, L., Rozelle, R. M., Baxter, J. C., & Sullivan, E. (1994). Use of free responses and cluster analysis to determine stereotypes of eight groups. *Personality and Social Psychology Bulletin, 20*(4), 379–390. https://doi.org/10.1177/0146167294204005

Nkomo, S. M., & Cox, T. (1989). Gender differences in the upward mobility of black managers: Double whammy or double advantage?. *Sex Roles, 21*(11–12), 825–839. https://doi.org/10.1007/BF00289811

Operario, D., & Fiske, S. T. (2001). Ethnic identity moderates perceptions of prejudice: Judgments of personal versus group discrimination and subtle versus blatant bias. *Personality and Social Psychology Bulletin, 27*(5), 550–561.

Petsko, C. D., & Bodenhausen, G. V. (2019). Racial stereotyping of gay men: Can a minority sexual orientation erase race? *Journal of Experimental Social Psychology, 83*, 37–54. https://doi.org/10.1016/j.jesp.2019.03.002

Phelan, J. E., & Rudman, L. A. (2010). Prejudice toward female leaders: Backlash effects and women's impression management dilemma. *Social and Personality Psychology Compass, 4*(10), 807–820. https://doi.org/10.1111/j.1751-9004.2010.00306.x

Plant, E. A., Goplen, J., & Kunstman, J. W. (2011). Selective Responses to Threat: The roles of race and gender in decisions to shoot. *Personality and Social Psychology Bulletin, 37*(9), 1274–1281. https://doi.org/10.1177/0146167211408617

Purdie-Vaughns, V., & Eibach, R. P. (2008). Intersectional invisibility: The distinctive advantages and disadvantages of multiple subordinate-group identities. *Sex Roles, 59*(5-6), 377–391. https://doi.org/10.1007/s11199-008-9424-4

Roberson, Q. M. (2019). Diversity in the workplace: A review, synthesis, and future research agenda. *Annual Review of Organizational Psychology and Organizational Behavior, 6*, 69–88. https://doi.org/10.1146/annurev-orgpsych-012218-015243

Rosch, E., & Mervis, C. B. (1975). Family resemblances: Studies in the internal structure of categories. *Cognitive psychology, 7*(4), 573–605.

Rosette, A. S., de Leon, R. P., Koval, C. Z., & Harrison, D. A. (2018). Intersectionality: Connecting experiences of gender with race at work. *Research in Organizational Behavior, 38*, 1–22. https://doi.org/10.1016/j.riob.2018.12.002

Rosette, A. S., Koval, C. Z., Ma, A., & Livingston, R. (2016). Race matters for women leaders: Intersectional effects on agentic deficiencies and penalties. *The Leadership Quarterly, 27*(3), 429–445. https://doi.org/10.1016/j.leaqua.2016.01.008

Rosette, A. S., Leonardelli, G. J., & Phillips, K. W. (2008). The White standard: Racial bias in leader categorization. *Journal of Applied Psychology, 93*(4), 758–777. https://doi.org/10.1037/0021-9010.93.4.758

Rosette, A. S., & Livingston, R. W. (2012). Failure is not an option for Black women: Effects of organizational performance on leaders with single versus dual-subordinate identities. *Journal of Experimental Social Psychology, 48*(5), 1162–1167. https://doi.org/10.1016/j.jesp.2012.05.002

Rudman, L. A. (1998). Self-promotion as a risk factor for women: The costs and benefits of counterstereotypical impression management. *Journal of Personality and Social Psychology, 74*(3), 629–645. https://doi.org/10.1037/0022-3514.74.3.629

Wilkins, C. L., Chan, J. F., & Kaiser, C. R. (2011). Racial stereotypes and interracial attraction: Phenotypic prototypicality and perceived attractiveness of Asians. *Cultural Diversity and Ethnic Minority Psychology, 17*(4), 427–431. https://doi.org/10.1037/a0024733

Wong, Y. J., & McCullough, K. M. (2021). The intersectional prototypicality model: Understanding the discriminatory experiences of Asian American women and men. *Asian American Journal of Psychology, 12*(2), 87–99. https://doi.org/10.1037/aap0000208

Rudman, L. A., & Glick, P. (1999). Feminized management and backlash toward agentic women: The hidden costs to women of a kinder, gentler image of middle managers. *Journal of Personality and Social Psychology, 77*(5), 1004–1010. https://doi.org/10.1037/0022-3514.77.5.1004

Rudman, L. A., & Glick, P. (2001). Prescriptive gender stereotypes and backlash toward agentic women. *Journal of Social Issues, 57*(4), 743–762. https://doi.org/10.1111/0022-4537.00239

Sayce, S., Berry, D., & Bell, M. P. (2012). Inequality in organizations: Stereotyping, discrimination, and labor law exclusions. *Equality, Diversity and Inclusion: An International Journal.* https://doi.org/10.1108/02610151211209090

Schug, J., Alt, N. P., & Klauer, K. C. (2015). Gendered race prototypes: Evidence for the non-prototypicality of Asian men and Black women. *Journal of Experimental Social Psychology, 56*, 121–125. https://doi.org/10.1016/j.jesp.2014.09.012

Schug, J., Alt, N. P., Lu, P. S., Gosin, M., & Fay, J. L. (2017). Gendered race in mass media: Invisibility of Asian men and Black women in popular magazines. *Psychology of Popular Media Culture, 6*(3), 222–236. http://dx.doi.org/10.1037/ppm0000096

Sesko, A. K., & Biernat, M. (2010). Prototypes of race and gender: The invisibility of Black women. *Journal of Experimental Social Psychology, 46*(2), 356–360. https://doi.org/10.1016/j.jesp.2009.10.016

Settles, I. H. (2006). Use of an intersectional framework to understand Black women's racial and gender identities. *Sex Roles: A Journal of Research, 54*(9-10), 589–601. https://doi.org/10.1007/s11199-006-9029-8

Smith, A. N., Watkins, M. B., Ladge, J. J., & Carlton, P. (2019). Making the invisible visible: Paradoxical effects of intersectional invisibility on the career experiences of executive Black women. *Academy of Management Journal, 62*(6), 1705–1734. https://doi.org/10.5465/amj.2017.1513

Smith, E. L. B., & Nkomo, S. M. (2003). *Our separate ways: Black and White women and the struggle for professional identity.* Harvard Business Press.

Stangor, C., & Lange, J. E. (1994). *Mental representations of social groups: Advances in understanding stereotypes and stereotyping.* Academic Press.

Strom, M. A., Zebrowitz, L. A., Zhang, S., Bronstad, P. M., & Lee, H. K. (2012). Skin and bones: The contribution of skin tone and facial structure to racial prototypicality ratings. *PLoS One, 7*(7), e41193.

Szymanski, D. M., & Stewart, D. N. (2010). Racism and sexism as correlates of African American women's psychological distress. *Sex Roles 63*, 226–238. https://doi.org/10.1007/s11199-010-9788-0

Thomas, E. L., Dovidio, J. F., & West, T. V. (2014). Lost in the categorical shuffle: Evidence for the social non-prototypicality of Black women. *Cultural Diversity and Ethnic Minority Psychology, 20*(3), 370–376. https://doi.org/10.1037/a0035096

Thomsen, C., & Finley, J. (2019). On intersectionality: a review essay. *Hypatia, 34*(1), 155–160. https://doi.org https://doi.org/10.1111/hypa.12450

Turco, C. J. (2010). Cultural foundations of tokenism: Evidence from the leveraged buyout industry. *American Sociological Review, 75*(6), 894–913. https://doi.org/10.1177/0003122410388491

Wilks, D. C., & Neto, F. (2013). Workplace well-being, gender and age: Examining the 'Double Jeopardy' effect. *Social Indicators Research, 114,* 875–890 https://doi.org/10.1007/s11205-012-0177-7

Williams, J. C. (2014). Double jeopardy? An empirical study with implications for the debates over implicit bias and intersectionality, 37 *Harv. J.L. & Gender* 185.

Williams, S. L., & Fredrick, E. G. (2015). One size may not fit all: The need for a more inclusive and intersectional psychological science on stigma. *Sex Roles, 73,* 384–390. https://doi.org/10.1007/s11199-015-0491-z

Women in the Workplace 2020. (2020, October 8). https://www.mckinsey.com/featured-insights/diversity-and-inclusion/women-in-the-workplace

NOTES

1. https://www.bbc.com/news/av/election-us-2020-54696386
2. Although a different body of research has identified and explored the potential of a "double advantage" for multiply subordinated individuals, due to space limitations, we do not take up that conversation here. For further discussion, see Nkomo and Cox (1989).
3. For a fuller discussion on this point, see Wilks and Neto, 2013.
4. At this point in the chapter, one might conclude that we have presented work and arguments suggesting that being rendered "invisible" is perhaps preferable to experiencing double jeopardy. However, this is not what we intend to suggest. Rather, both perspectives highlight their own specific forms of oppression, and the goal is not to argue that one is better than the other. Our goal is to shed light on the conditions under which either double jeopardy or intersectional invisibility is likely to be observed.
5. In distinguishing between perceptions of dominance and competence, we draw upon research suggesting that each of these dimensions is a unique component of agency (e.g., Abele et al., 2008; Koenig & Eagly, 2014; Ma, 2020; Rosette et al., 2016).
6. See Kohler-Hausmann (2018) for a brilliant discussion of why this approach (e.g., examining treatment effects of race) is methodologically problematic and unsound.
7. Similar arguments have been made and discussed at length elsewhere. For example, Berdahl and Moore (2006) write that "Like others before it, this study used measures that were based largely on White women's experiences of

sexual harassment and on minority men's experiences of ethnic harassment. These measures may omit experiences unique to minority women and thereby underestimate harassment against them" (p. 433). See also Carter-Sowell and Zimmerman (2015).

8. For a notable example of how stereotypes and experiences are shaped by cultural context and fit, see Turco (2010).

9. https://www.washingtonpost.com/politics/i-am-who-i-am-kamala-harris-daughter-of-indian-and-jamaican-immigrants-defines-herself-simply-as-american/2019/02/02/0b278536-24b7-11e9-ad53-824486280311_story.html

CHAPTER 11

RACIAL AND GENDER DIVERSITY IN ARTIFICIAL INTELLIGENCE PROGRAMMING AND ITS IMPACT ON END USER EXPERIENCES

A Conceptual Model

MaQueba Massey
Jackson State University

Quinetta Roberson
Michigan State University

ABSTRACT

While artificial intelligence (AI) has been lauded for its many benefits, including but not limited to intentionality, intelligence, and adaptability, both practical and scholarly research suggests that such benefits may only be available to members of specific demographic groups. This chapter utilizes social categorization theory, value-in-diversity hypothesis, and the categorization elaboration model to explore algorithm bias in AI due to the lack

The Future of Scholarship on Race in Organizations, pp. 259–278
Copyright © 2022 by Information Age Publishing

of racial and gender diversity in AI programming and datasets. We offer a model and call for empirical attention to understanding the mechanisms underlying the effects of racial and gender diversity (or the lack thereof) on customization and end-user experience through an integration of the information technology and diversity literature. In addition, we offer directions for future practice to enhance both diversity in the AI field as well as consistency in end-user experiences with the technology.

> *"The diversity problem is not just about women. It's about gender, race, and most fundamentally, about power. It affects how AI companies work, what products get built, who they are designed to serve, and who benefits from their development."*

(West et al., 2019, p. 5)

Characterized as machines, technologies, or systems that mimic human intelligence to perform a variety of tasks, artificial intelligence (AI) has received increasing scholarly and practical attention. With benefits that include cost reduction, operational efficiency, new market entry, and a capacity for sustained competitive advantage (see Ransbotham et al., 2017), AI's adoption has expanded across industries. From a research perspective, the benefits of AI for improved problem-solving and decision-making offer opportunities for empirical studies as well as theoretical development (von Krogh, 2018). As advances in AI over the last several decades have enabled breakthroughs across nearly every sector of society (National Science Foundation, 2019), the consideration of AI as a source of sustained competitive advantage is rampant among researchers and practitioners alike.

Despite the advantages of AI, it is not without its flaws. As data and technologies are still evolving, there are limitations to algorithmic performances (Chui et al., 2018). Specifically, with constraints due to available information and techniques, there are imperfections in the choices, outcomes, and predictions that are made. For example, research shows challenges associated with the capacity of AI for accurately differentiating, categorizing, and ranking information (West et al., 2019). Recently, these challenges have been shown to be particularly pronounced when dealing with demographic data, such as facial and image recognition applications, evaluating people in hiring contexts, or assessing crime-related risks (see Daugherty et al., 2019). As such, AI systems have been described as systems of discrimination that mirror and perpetuate the cognitive biases present in human decision-making (West et al., 2019).

While several explanations for inequities in AI processing across demographic groups have been offered, they primarily derive from the human-technology interface where AI systems are developed (Daugherty et al., 2019). As AI systems reflect their creators' values, processing discrepancies have primarily been attributed to a lack of gender and racial diversity within tech companies and those responsible for designing such systems (National Science Board, 2018; West et al., 2019). Yet, while we have data on the representation of different demographic groups within AI and related fields, we have little insight into how diversity (or a lack thereof) influences AI programming. Further, while anecdotal evidence of discrimination from AI systems is available, limited attention has been given to the resultant downstream effects on those who utilize such systems. As a result, our abilities to understand the mechanisms underlying the relationship between diversity and algorithmic bias, offer recommendations for addressing such bias, and improve the end-user outcomes are constrained.

This chapter theoretically examines the relationship between racial and gender diversity in AI development and the end-user experience. Using the categorization-elaboration model (van Knippenberg & van Ginkel, 2010), which explains the mechanisms underlying the positive and negative effects of diversity in work teams, we articulate the processes through which racial and gender diversity may influence AI logic—specifically, image recognition and natural language processing features (see Figure 11.1). In addition, we describe the subsequent impact of such programming outcomes on an application or device performance from the end-users point of view. Based on our proposed framework, we offer directions for future research in this area and recommendations for creating AI environments that are more inclusive of demographic diversity and AI systems unbound by algorithmic bias. Overall, our goal is to advance an understanding of diversity within a context in which it has been relatively ignored and to spur research on a topic that has widespread practical implications.

ARTIFICIAL INTELLIGENCE (AI) PROGRAMMING

Organizational research suggests that AI can be categorized into three systems based on capability—process automation, cognitive insight, and cognitive engagement (Davenport & Ronanki, 2018). Process automation systems use robotic technologies to automate physical and digital business processes. Cognitive insight systems represent machine-learning applications that perform analytic functions to detect, interpret, and model patterns in large datasets. Cognitive engagement systems use natural language processing to communicate with and support employees and customers. With the ultimate goal of streamlining internal business processes, the end-user of process automatic systems is the organization. In contrast, cognitive insight and engagement systems are intended to enhance existing product and service functionality and performance, create new products and services, and optimize marketing and sales processes (Davenport & Ronanki, 2018). Because the end-user for these latter systems are consumer markets, we

Figure 11.1

Conceptual Model for How Racial Diversity Influences Customization and the End-User Experience in Artificial Intelligence

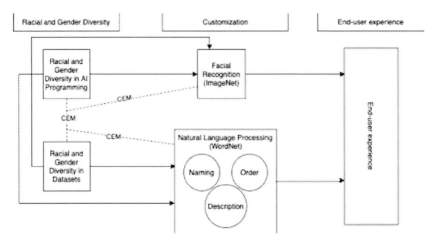

*CEM – categorization elaboration model.

limit the scope of our analysis and discussion to AI developed to provide insight and engagement capabilities.

To deliver a quality experience to end-users, AI relies upon a system of computational logic. Specifically, with algorithms that identify objects and their functions, the relationships between them, and probabilities of accuracy, AI systems produce declarative models of how the world works and use feedback to learn about and refine such models (Nilsson, 1991). Because programmers develop artificial neural networks, association rules, decision trees, and other components of such algorithms (García et al., 2017), these logics are particularly susceptible to human biases. As such, processes to analyze user characteristics, preferences, and behavior may be constrained; thus, diminishing end-user customization and engagement. In the following sections, we discuss customization elements that may be most influenced by human preconceptions and values, especially those stemming from diversity. Consistent with Figure 1, we discuss how customization can occur in facial recognition and natural language processing and the impacts on the end-user experience.

Customization is considered the fulfillment of customers' wants and needs in the product development process (Simpson, 2004). Customization transforms the functional requirements of a product based on the customer and engineers' concerns (Tseng et al., 2017). Because customers' needs are variable and subjective, personalization will likely impact end-user experiences. While functional requirements of AI systems may be customized, we contend that facial recognition and natural language processing may be particularly open to personalization given their reliance upon customers' features. As such, we expect them to influence how end users interface with products and subsequent product success. We discuss these components of customization—facial recognition and natural language processing—and their effects on the end-user experience in the sections below. Therefore, the next two sections will discuss facial recognition and natural language processing to clarify the impact of customization on end-user experiences.

Facial Recognition

Facial recognition technology, a form of biometric security using process automation and cognitive insight, is designed to recognize and learn from digital image patterns (Andrejevic & Selwyn, 2020). Such technologies use automated software to detect facial shapes and features and computationally compare the data with those in image databases. ImageNet, developed around 2009, is an image database that contains over 14 million images, making it one of the largest and most widely used databases in the industry. Despite the database size, research suggests that the images of women and members of ethnic minority groups lack relative to the population's diversity (Yang et al., 2020). As such, image searches within ImageNet have been shown to produce biased results (Celis & Keswani, 2019; Kay et al., 2015). For example, because ImageNet and similar datasets are standardized systems that use facial shape and feature recognition algorithms, such systems have been shown to be more accurate for certain demographic groups (Noble, 2018). In particular, search and recognition have been shown to be problematic among people with darker skin colors (see Andrejevic & Selwyn, 2020). As such, underrepresented groups are often misidentified, and searches for related images can sometimes produce offensive results based on comparisons to animals, inanimate objects, or character costumes (Yang et al., 2020).

Natural Language Processing

Within AI, natural language processing technology using process automation and cognitive engagement is intended to extract meaning from text (Nadkarni et al., 2011). In effect, algorithms are used to identify words or phrases and the relationships between these parts of speech in order to develop semantic rules. WordNet, developed in the mid-1980s, is an extensive lexical database that groups words into concepts based on meaning (Deng et al., 2009). Similar to a thesaurus, such concepts are used for information retrieval and sensemaking. Further, WordNet is the semantic network used to annotate images in ImageNet.

Research highlights computational biases in components of natural language processing (see Leavy, 2018). Specifically, naming, ordering, and descriptive components of word or text databases have been shown to reflect different outputs dependent upon demographic group membership (Leavy, 2018; Yang et al., 2020). Naming refers to categorizing groups of words or images and often reflects the valence associated with a concept. For example, research has shown differences in terminology used to describe people based on gender, race, and sexual orientation with more favorable terms reserved for majority group members (see Bhopal & Donaldson, 1998; Sigelman & Tuch, 1997). Ordering refers to the sequencing of the information, which typically suggests the predominance of the listed information first (Leavy, 2018). Not surprisingly, demographic groups with higher social statuses, such as men and whites, are often listed first in text databases and used to establish the comparative standard for other groups. Similarly, descriptions or how groups are portrayed in text databases also reflect power and status differentials. In particular, variability in the descriptors used to characterize certain groups reflects assumptions about those groups' members (see Allen, 2012).

End-User Experience

Based on the relationship between racial and gender data and how the lack of data could impact customization in terms of facial recognition and natural language processing, we believe this relationship also influences end-user experiences. Mahmood and colleagues (2000) emphasize key drivers of users' satisfaction with information technology: (1) user background, (2) perceived benefits, and (3) organizational support. While user background occurs at the individual level of analysis and captures user-related characteristics and organizational support is more reflective of an organization's readiness to use the technology, the remaining factor—perceived benefits—resides at the user interface and the technology itself. More specifically, the perceived benefits of an information technology system are posited to derive from user expectations of the system, ease of use, and perceived usefulness (Davis, 1989). As these factors determine the overall value of a system in terms of the extent to which it supports the user in decision-making (Mahmood et al., 2000), we use them here to evaluate the value of AI systems across demographic groups.

Despite a lack of research examining demographic differences in users' satisfaction with information technology, the information reviewed above regarding biases in AI design elements suggests that differences in user experiences and subsequently in satisfaction with the technology may exist. For example, as facial recognition systems have been shown to have different accuracy rates across demographic groups (Noble, 2018), those with unique facial shapes or features may experience challenges with such technology, such as a failure to be recognized or miscategorization. Beyond the unexpectedness of such experiences, members of visible minority groups may experience obstacles in interfacing with the systems that require them to be recognized, including gaining entry into a workplace or accessing a computer system. Accordingly, both the ease of use and usefulness of such groups' members' technology would be relatively limited. Demographic minority groups may also experience challenges with natural language processing technologies. Similar to facial recognition technologies, difficulties associated with speech recognition may limit the ease of voice queries (e.g., Alexa) or automated customer service systems for those with language differences. With more negative or disaffirming terminology and descriptions of minority groups, others' perceptions and attitudes may also be influenced. These semantics, as well as ordering that establishes power and status differentials between groups, may reinforce such differentials and adversely impact predictive outcomes for minority groups.

While the above experiences and resultant value of AI processing systems have been attributed to a lack of diversity among those responsible for creating such systems, we have limited insight into how such diversity impacts customization and the user experience. Both scholars and practitioners have assumed that more diversity would alter AI systems' design in ways that would reduce the likelihood of these described experiences and enhance user satisfaction with and the usefulness of such systems. However, we must first understand the processes through which diversity may influence customization and user outcomes. We explore these mechanisms in the section below.

HOW DIVERSITY WORKS IN AI

Although diversity is conceptualized as any difference between people that shapes the degree to which we perceive similarities with others (Jackson, 1992), researchers have categorized such differences in ways that create identity distinctions between groups (Mannix & Neale, 2005; Tsui & Gutek, 1999). For example, some researchers categorize diversity attributes based on the extent to which they are perceptible (Jackson et al., 1995). More observable characteristics, such as gender, race, and age, are included in one category, while less observable differences, such as personality, education, and functional background, are included in another. Alternatively, diversity attributes have been grouped according to their job relatedness or the extent to which they are relevant for task performance (Pelled, 1996). Here, the aforementioned differences in gender, race, and age would be considered less job-related than personality, education, and functional background. Given the lack of racial and gender diversity among AI programmers (National Science Board, 2018; West et al., 2019), we concentrate in this chapter on the two observable demographic attributes, as illustrated in the diversity literature. However, we debate the conceptualization of this attribute as comparatively less job-related than other diversity characteristics. More specifically, because programmers' racial and gender identity may influence AI bias while also representing an opportunity for improved problem-solving, we speculate that reconciling these processes may be critical for understanding and enhancing AI customization and the end-user experience. As indicated by the dotted lines in Figure 11.1, we discuss two diversity-related mechanisms—social categorization and information processing—and their potential effects on AI design and outcomes below. We begin our discussion by situating these processes within the current diversity theory.

Categorization-Elaboration Model

Given divergent conclusions from what researchers have considered the pessimistic versus optimistic view of diversity (Mannix & Neale, 2005), researchers have integrated and reconciled the influences of social identity and categorization with those of information processing diverse groups. Specifically, the categorization-elaboration model (van Knippenberg et al., 2004) articulates how intergroup biases stemming from social categorization processes may disrupt the informational exchange processes critical to realizing the value in diversity. While one may conclude that the prevention of such biases is paramount to experiencing diversity's performance advantages, the authors note that doing so is not sufficient for activating the elaboration of knowledge and perspectives derived from diversity. Instead, facilitating individual- and group-level processing of information and the exchange and integration of perspectives and cognitive resources within the group, or information elaboration, are vital for improving innovation, decision quality, and other positive effects of diversity on group performance.

Consistent with the categorization-elaboration model (van Knippenberg et al., 2004), we would expect social categorization processes to inhibit information processing from any diversity currently among AI programmers. Even within the field, women, ethnic minorities, and other underrepresented groups may be seen as outgroup members due to the lack of diversity within AI programming. As such, those in the majority may consider ingroup members to be more valid or trusted sources of information (Turner et al., 1987) and, thus, more likely to rely on ingroup members' ideas and viewpoints. As a result, the voices and contributions of the outgroup may be marginalized. With the marginalization of outgroup members, limited information exchange may impede decision making and innovation, which may influence customer experiences and satisfaction. Further, because information exchange between groups may be limited, diversity's performance benefits may not be realized. Thus, a lack of diversity in AI programming may diminish the end-user experience.

Social Categorization

A considerable amount of diversity research has been framed within the ideas offered by social-psychological theories of intergroup relations, such as social identity and social categorization theories (Tajfel, 1978; Turner, 1985). These theories articulate processes through within individuals make sense of, and locate themselves within, their social environments (Turner et al., 1987), and therefore are helpful for exploring the processes underlying diversity in groups. Social identity theory (Tajfel, 1978) argues that individuals are motivated to enhance their self-concept by seeking a positively-valenced distinctiveness for their in-groups. By engaging in social comparisons, people differentiate between their in-groups and relevant outgroups and evaluate their social identities (Tajfel & Turner, 1986). Self-categorization theory (Turner, 1985) proposes that as specific social categories become salient, there is a qualitative shift in social perception such that people come to view themselves (and others) more in terms of their group memberships than in terms of their identities (Turner et al., 1987). Accordingly, this categorization process accentuates similarities among individuals sharing group memberships and differences among individuals belonging to different identity groups (Turner, 1985).

Research suggests that group identification is a crucial determinant of individuals' proclivity for defining themselves as members of social groups and engaging in intergroup behavior (Tajfel, 1978; Turner et al., 1987). Specifically, group identification motivates individuals to distinguish between their in-groups and other social groups and create a positive group identity (Turner, 1985; Turner et al., 1987). This process of intergroup differentiation tends to favor ingroup members in ways that enhance the value and distinctiveness of the groups, leading to a positive social identity (Tajfel & Turner, 1986). We expect such a process to influence the relationship between AI programmer diversity and customization. Specifically, as identity processes encourage ingroup/outgroup distinctions, AI programmers may distinguish between themselves as a group and others. Through such intergroup differentiation, they may perceive similarity to those with whom they share characteristics and differences from those belonging to other identity groups. Given a lack of gender and race diversity among AI programmers, these demographic categories may further accentuate differentiation. Those considered to be within AI programmers' ingroup may be ascribed higher value and/or status, thereby facilitating a greater focus on meeting the needs and preferences of customers belonging in that group. Applying these processes to AI, we expect that intergroup differentiation along racial dimensions may impact customization. More specifically, given the limited racial diversity within the AI industry, we anticipate that intergroup differentiation may limit the focus on the needs of racial minority groups, thereby reducing their end-user experiences.

The process of depersonalization, or viewing oneself as an archetype of the ingroup (Hogg et al., 1995), may also help to explain how a lack of diversity in AI influences customization outcomes. Through identification with one's social category, people tend to ascribe normative aspects of group membership to everyone in that group rather than view them as a unique individual (Turner et al., 1987). As outgroup members are perceived according to prototypical aspects associated with their social category, depersonalization serves to reaffirm social structures (Hogg et al., 1995). This may also be the case within AI, as AI programmers may come to depersonalize customers into groups despite the diversity in needs and preferences. Programmers may assume similarities with their own needs and preferences; thus, limiting the breadth or scope of customization in products and services and the end-user experience.

Implicit biases, or negative cognitive associations attributed to members of one's outgroups (Payne & Gawronski, 2010), may further exacerbate the relationship between diversity in AI and customization processes. While implicit biases against outgroups may not necessarily emerge, programmers may not make concentrated efforts to create positive identities for other groups. Given a lack of racial diversity among AI programmers (National Science Board, 2018), racial minorities may be unconsciously discounted or negatively depicted in the programming process. As a result, biases in natural language processing components, such as undesirable names or descriptors, may materialize. Such biases may also appear as favoritism towards programmers' ingroups in language ordering within AI systems. Implicit biases have the ability to impact end-user experiences due to the negative cognitive associations that may be present when developing a process in AI. With race not taken into account or negative customization based on race (Jolls & Sunstein, 2006), the experience for minority end-

Information/Decision Processing

In contrast to social-psychological theories of diversity that view differences as social distinctions that encumber intergroup relations, research has also approached the study of diversity through a more constructive lens. Termed the "value-in-diversity" hypothesis (Cox & Blake, 1991), this perspective establishes that categorical dissimilarity also engenders differences in knowledge, skills, and experiences, which exposes the group to a broader range of viewpoints and opinions. With access to a more extensive and varied pool of informational resources, it is assumed that heterogeneous groups are more likely to generate better quality solutions to problems. Also referred to as the information processing perspective on diversity (Williams & O'Reilly, 1998), research provides evidence of such performance advantages, or value, derived from more heterogeneous groups (see Milliken & Martins, 1996; Williams & O'Reilly, 1998).

The "value-in-diversity" hypothesis also suggests that diversity enhances group decision making (Cox et al., 1991). More specifically, this perspective establishes that diversity can create value and benefit for groups because individuals in heterogeneous groups have a broader range of knowledge, skills, and abilities than homogeneous groups (Hoffman, 1959; Hoffman & Maier, 1961). With this larger pool of cognitive resources, diverse groups are assumed to have greater access to a variety of task-relevant information and expertise. Further, diversity in groups may provide access to a more extensive and more varied social network from which to draw additional resources (Ancona & Caldwell, 1992). Research suggests that such diversity in informational resources may also enhance group problem-solving, as different opinions, approaches, and perspectives give rise to task conflict and dissent (Jehn et al., 1999; Pelled et al., 1999). Further, exposure to minority viewpoints may expose and motivate the consideration of more creative alternatives and solutions (Ancona & Caldwell, 1992; Nemeth, 1986). Thus, the "value-in-diversity" perspective predicts that dissimilarity will enhance decision-making quality in groups and organizations.

We expect that information processing may also influence the relationship between AI programmer diversity and customization. As demographic diversity is posited to bring about differences in background, experience, and other knowledge-based resources, we would expect that such diversity in AI programming would expose the field to a broader pool of informational resources that enhance problem-solving decision-making. Yet, without such diversity, we conjecture that associated performance advantages within the field may be constrained. Specifically, by drawing upon a narrower pool of informational resources, AI programming may not experience the benefits of minority viewpoints and/or alternative perspectives; thus, limiting creativity and innovation as well as task conflict (De Dreu & West, 2001). Further, in the absence of dissent and debate, problem-solving may produce less informed and/or optimal outcomes in the field. Because programmers may not have exposure to divergent ideas and opinions, opportunities to deliberate and improve upon their solutions may be more constrained in the absence of diversity. In customization, this lack of information processing may constrain innovations in the design of facial recognition and natural language processing components of AI.

Further, the innovation rate in developing databases and algorithms reflective of societal diversity may proceed more slowly. The lack of demographic diversity and subsequent cognitive perspectives in AI programming may restrain the consideration of potential biases in AI design components and efforts to reduce any biases that may be limited. In summary, we expect that a lack of diversity in AI programming will negatively impact the end-user experience through

DISCUSSION

While research has explored the import and operation of diversity both in general and within specific fields, scholars have given limited attention to racial and gender diversity in AI programming. Yet, practical evidence suggests that such diversity (or a lack thereof) influences AI databases' customization and subsequent end-user experience. In this chapter, we consider the mechanisms through which diversity may impact this experience. Specifically, we discuss constraints on information processing within the field of AI and how social categorization may elicit biases in the design of AI systems. While we attempt to advance a conceptual understanding of diversity in the AI programming field, much is still unclear about its operation and impact. Accordingly, we call for development in both scholarship and practice on the topic in the following section.

Directions for Future Research

Empirical research is needed to explore the influence of diversity on AI programming. For example, experimental studies that manipulate the gender and/or racial composition of programming teams and examine the effects on programming outcomes may provide insight into diversity's performance impact. Consistent with the findings of diversity research, such work can explore whether heterogeneous programming teams out-perform homogeneous teams and in what ways (e.g., creativity, innovation, the number of ideas, etc.). Such designs would also allow the compositional variation of AI programming teams along with various aspects of diversity. Although practical research has mainly focused on the diversity attributes of gender and race (see West et al., 2019), research to explore the effects of both observable characteristics, such as age or physical ability, and non-observable characteristics, such as educational or socioeconomic background, may provide insight into the effects of different types of diversity on programming outcomes. Research that incorporates multiple diversity attributes may also offer an intersectionality perspective and resultant understanding of how aspects of diversity combine to influence customization. Further, with research designs that allow end-users to rate team outputs, we may also gain insight into how programming team diversity may indirectly influence end user perceptions and attitudes.

Research is also needed to investigate the processes through which diversity impacts AI programming. While practical research describes AI as systems of discrimination that reflect bias, power, and other forms of privilege (see West et al., 2019), there is scant empirical evidence to support such claims. Yet, there are indicators within the functional logic of AI systems that highlight inequalities in how different social groups are portrayed within databases. Therefore, future empirical work should explore the socio-psychological processes stemming from diversity (or a lack thereof) in AI. Using tools to detect implicit bias, stereotypes, or other assumptions among AI programmers, researchers might explore how diversity-related perceptions and ideologies emerge within programming components. For example, experimental studies could examine relationships between implicit associations for various social groups and performance on facial recognition or language processing (e.g., naming, ordering, description) tasks. Alternatively, research could examine the likelihood of programmers detecting bias in these AI design components based on diversity-related perceptions and ideologies. On the whole, such work would be useful for demonstrating the link between diversity and programming behavior or performance at the individual level of analysis.

Research examining group-level diversity and programming processes would also be insightful. Consistent with the categorization elaboration model (van Knippenberg et al., 2004), research on diversity within programming teams may shed light on group process variables. For example, studies to explore how team demography influences relational interactions, such as cohesion and conflict, and subsequent performance outcomes may reveal the mechanisms through which diversity influences AI customization. Similarly, research could examine the impact of diversity on information exchange and other decision processes that would drive performance outcomes, such as programming innovation and decision quality. In line with conceptual work, which suggests that diversity might also facilitate the development of dynamic capabilities (see Roberson et al., 2017), research on diversity in AI programming might also explore how the combination and coordination of knowledge-based resources stemming from such diversity enable the development of programming routines that enhance the end-user experience.

It is important to note that field research is also needed to explore the influence of diversity on AI programming. While we have anecdotal evidence of how a lack of gender and racial diversity among programmers may impact end-user experiences in terms of biases and inaccuracies in searches and other technology usages, we have limited practical evidence of such effects. Accordingly, the study of intact programming teams would offer insight into how diversity influences team processes and customization outcomes. Although the breadth of investigation may be constrained by the amount of diversity in the AI field, this research approach would allow the longitudinal study of how team composition changes influence performance outcomes. Researchers might also conduct qualitative studies of the experiences of those in AI programming—particularly members of underrepresented groups—to determine the trickle-down effects to end-users. Importantly, field research in this area would explore the end user experience to understand end-user groups' variability. As practical research suggests different experiences with technology based on demographic membership (e.g., challenges with facial recognition for those with darker skin or less gender-stereotypical facial features, less desirable choice outcomes for applicants with ethnic names, etc.), empirical research on this topic would allow an understanding of the relationship between employee and customer (i.e., end-user) diversity.

Although not discussed explicitly in our model, research may also examine contextual factors that influence the relationships between diversity in AI programming and customization outcomes. For example, individual perceptions, such as authoritarianism, system justification, or other beliefs that support ingroup/group distinctions, may strengthen social categorization processes and hence, the emergence of bias AI programming components. Alternatively, more diversity-supportive beliefs, such as multiculturalism or value for diversity, may inhibit such effects. Workgroup characteristics and ideologies, such as interdependence and climate for inclusion, respectively, may also moderate the effects of diversity in AI on programming outcomes. Future research may also examine the influence of leader support for diversity or human resource interventions, such as diversity or team training, on AI programming processes and outcomes.

Directions for Future Practice

Given the underrepresentation of women and minorities in AI programming, addressing this issue should be a priority within the field. As many companies refer to a "pipeline problem" and attribute a lack of diversity to the absence of qualified job candidates for AI programming roles (see West et al., 2019), there are a variety of staffing initiatives that may increase the number of women and racial minorities in candidate pools. For example, diversifying recruitment sources to include historically black colleges and universities (HBCUs) and other minority-serving institutions, as well as many professional organizations, focused on diversity in technology, such as the Society of Hispanic Professional Engineers and Black Girls Code, may increase applicant diversity. The company's efforts to diversify AI workforces might also be propelled by going back in the pipeline and offering internships and other development programs to high school and college students from underrepresented groups.

Beyond recruitment, certain selection practices might be useful for enhancing the diversity of the AI programming workforce. Notably, because we have some evidence of differences in job search outcomes across demographic groups, companies should audit selection systems to ensure equity. Given what we currently know about potential algorithmic biases in resume software, evaluating random samples of resumes for job roles at different levels may lessen the likelihood of overlooking qualified applicants. Similarly, utilizing objective and/or performance-based criteria to select candidates for shortlists may also be useful for reducing systemic biases in selection systems. When evaluating candidates, ensuring the use of diverse (i.e., gender, race, age, educational background, work experience, etc.) interview panels that have received training and use structured interview approaches may facilitate more inclusive interview processes.

Organizations should also offer programs and resources to facilitate the success of members of underrepresented groups in the AI industry. While 2020 marks the anniversary of women's right to vote in the United States, there are still instances 100 years later in which women continue to be silenced. For example, a prominent AI ethics researcher, Timnit Gebru, was recently fired for voicing concerns regarding Google's lack of progress in hiring women and minorities, as well as biases built into its artificial intelligence technology (Harwell & Tiku, 2020). Described as "dehumanizing" (Harwell & Tifu, 2020), such environments and the treatment of minorities hinder minorities' abilities to raise issues of concern and bring their best selves forward. As such, engagement and retention programs could help make AI work environments more inclusive for programmers and others from diverse backgrounds. While performance management within the AI programming field tends to be based on coding performance, such systems may be leveraged in other ways to facilitate more inclusive customization. For example, beyond coding output, programmers might be evaluated based on analysis and problem-solving capabilities, which may be applied to addressing special topics in the field, such as strategies for debiasing facial recognition and natural language processing. Related to the end-user experience, programmers might be evaluated according to what their code does after production, including whether end-users across demographic groups have positive experiences with the technology. Internal to programming teams, individuals might be evaluated on inclusive behaviors, such as embracing diversity by seeking input from or collaboration with others.

Indeed, training may be useful for driving inclusive customization. Yet, while many companies offer unconscious bias training in an effort to address biases in programming, other learning approaches might be impactful as well. For example, rather than training programmers to recognize their own implicit biases against specific groups, an alternative approach could train them to identify and address biases with databases or algorithms. Alternatively, a design thinking approach that provides programmers with an end-user problem (such as the search or recognition problems identified earlier in this chapter) and encourages programmers to explore and experiment with different solutions may facilitate skill development in the areas of innovation and problem-solving while maintaining a focus on consistency of end-user experience across all demographic groups. Additional skill-building initiatives that enhance collaboration and interpersonal effectiveness within work teams may help to drive further diversity, equity, and inclusion within the field of AI programming.

The lack of diversity among AI programmers likely becomes a lack of diversity within leadership in the field. Therefore, practices to develop diverse leadership pools (both current and future) might be necessary. Similar to the staffing guidance offered above, objective and/or performance-based criteria should be used to identify high-potential employees and leaders. In addition, opportunities to engage in career development programs designed to enhance employees' knowledge, skills, and abilities in the interest of career enhancement and mobility should be consistently available to programmers across all demographic groups. As research has shown, targeted development programs, such as internships and career tracks for racial minorities, to be associated with the increased representation of African American, Hispanic, Asian, and Native American employees in management ranks (see Roberson et al., 2020), such programs may be useful for doing so within the field of AI. Other targeted initiatives, such as networking and mentoring programs, may also address workplace inequality and amplify the effects of diversity in AI programming.

CONCLUSION

Despite practical interest in the lack of racial diversity in artificial intelligence programming, the evolution of theory and research in this area has not kept pace. To theorize on how racial diversity influences AI customization and the end-user experience, we use social categorization theories, the value-in-diversity hypothesis, and the categorization elaboration model to articulate the mechanisms underlying these relationships. In doing so, we offer a model and call for future research in this area to address bias and the performance effects on the development of AI products and services. In addition, we provide a guide for practitioners to address under-representation issues in the industry and the subsequent capability of technology firms. Overall, we endeavor to combine theory and research in the diversity and AI literature to advance our understanding of how difference can lead to performance benefits within programming but how these opportunities may be missed without sufficient attention to address the absence of such difference within the field.

REFERENCES

Allen, Q. (2012). They think minority means lesser than. *Urban Education, 48*, 171–197.

Ancona, D. G., & Caldwell, D. F. (1992). Bridging the boundary: External activity and performance in organizational teams. *Administrative Science Quarterly, 37*(4), 634–665. https://doi.org/10.2307/2393475

Andrejevic, M., & Selwyn, N. (2020). Facial recognition technology in schools: Critical questions and concerns. *Learning, Media and Technology, 45*, 115–128. https://doi.org/10.1080/17439884.2020.1686014

Bhopal, R., & Donaldson, L. (1998). White, European, Western, Caucasian, or what? Inappropriate labeling in research on race, ethnicity, and health. *American Journal of Public Health, 88*(9), 1303–1307. https://doi.org/10.2105/AJPH.88.9.1303

Celis, E. L., & Keswani, V. (2019). *Implicit diversity in image summarization.* https://arxiv.org/abs/1901.10265

Chui, M., Manyika, J., & Schwartz, D. (2018). The real-world potential and limitations of artificial intelligence. *The McKinsey Quarterly.* https://proxy.library.upenn.edu/login?url=https://www.proquest.com/docview/237189890 9?accoaccou=14707

Cox, T. H., Jr. & Blake, S. (1991). Managing cultural diversity: Implications for organizational competitiveness. *Academy of Management Executive, 5*, 45–56.

Cox, T. H., Lobel, S., & McLeod, P. (1991). Effects of ethnic group cultural differences on cooperative and competitive behavior on a group task. *Academy of Management Journal, 34*, 827–847.

Daugherty, P. R., Wilson, H. J., & Chowdhury, R. (2019). Using artificial intelligence to promote diversity. *MIT Sloan Management Review, 60*(2), 1. https://proxy. library.upenn.edu/login?url=https://www.proquest.com/docview/216159413 3?accountid=14707

Davenport, T. H., & Ronanki, R. (2018). Artificial intelligence for the real world. *Harvard Business Review, 96*, 108-116.

Davis, F. D. (1989). Perceived usefulness, perceived ease of use, and user acceptance of information technology. *MIS Quarterly: Management Information Systems, 13*(3), 319– 339. https://doi.org/10.2307/249008

De Dreu, C. K. W., & West, M. A. (2001). Minority dissent and team innovation: The importance of participation in decision making. *Journal of Applied Psychology.* https://doi.org/10.1037/0021-9010.86.6.1191

Deng, J., Dong, W., Socher, R., Li, L., Li, K., & Fei-Fei, L. (2010). ImageNet: Constructing a large-scale image database. *Journal of Vision, 9*(8), 1037–1037. https://doi.org/10.1167/9.8.1037

García, C. G., Núñez-Valdez, E. R., García-Díaz, V., Bustelo, C. P. G., & Lovelle, J. M. C. (2017). A review of artificial intelligence in the internet of things. *International Journal of Interactive Multimedia and Artificial Intelligence, 4*, 7–10.

Harwell, D., & Tiku, N. (2020). *Google's star AI ethics researcher, one of a few black women in the field, says she was fired for a critical email.* https://www.washingtonpost. com/technology/2020/12/03/timnit-gebru-google-fired/

Hoffman, L. R. (1959). Homogeneity of member personality and its effects on group problem solving. *Journal of Abnormal and Social Psychology, 58*, 27–32.

Hoffman, L. R., & Maier, N. R. F. (1961). Quality and acceptance of problem solutions by members of homogeneous and heterogeneous groups. *Journal of Abnormal Social Psychology. 62*, 401–407.

Hogg, M. a., Terry, D. J., & White, K. M. (1995). A tale of two theories: A critical comparison of identity theory with social identity theory. *Social Psychology Quarterly. 58*(4), 255– 269. http://www.jstor.org/stabl

Jackson, S. E. (1992). Team composition in organizational settings: Issues in managing an increasingly diverse workforce. S. Worchel, W. Wood, & J. Simpson (Eds.), *Group process and productivity* (pp. 138–141). SAGE.

Jackson, S. E., May, K. A., & Whitney, K. (1995). Understanding the dynamics of diversity in decision-making teams. In R. A. Guzzo & E. Salas (Eds.), *Team decision making effectiveness in organizations* (pp. 204–261). Jossey-Bass.

Jehn, K. A., Northcraft, G. B., & Neale, M. A. (1999). Why differences make a difference: A field study of diversity, conflict, and performance in workgroups. *Administrative Science Quarterly, 44*, 741–763.

Jolls, C., & Sunstein, C. R. (2006). The law of implicit bias. *California Law Review,* 969–9960.

Kay, M., Matuszek, C., & Munson, S.A. (2015). Unequal representation and gender stereotypes in image search results for occupations. *In Proceedings of the 33rd Annual ACM Conference on Human Factors in Computing Systems. ACM,* 3819–3828.

Leavy, S. (2018). [ACM Press the 1st International Workshop—Gothenburg, Sweden (2018.05.28-2018.05.28)]. *Proceedings of the 1st International Workshop on Gender Equality in Software Engineering—GE '18—Gender bias in artificial intelligence, 14–16*. https://doi.org/10.1145/3195570.3195580

Mahmood, M., Burn, J., Gemoets, L. & Jacquez, C. (2000). Variables affecting information technology end-user satisfaction: A meta-analysis of the empirical literature, International *Journal of Human-Computer Studies 52*, 751–771.

Mannix, E., & Neale, M. A. (2005). What differences make a difference? The promise and reality of diverse teams in organizations. *Psychological Science in the Public Interest, 6*, 31–55.

Milliken, F. J., & Martins, L. L. (1996). Searching for Common Threads: Understanding the multiple effects of diversity in organizational groups, *Academy of Management Stable, 21*(2), 402–433. https://www.jstor.org/stable/258667

Nadkarni, P. M., Ohno-Machado, L., & Chapman, W. W. (2011). Natural language processing: An introduction. *Journal of the American Medical Informatics Association, 18*, 544–551. https://doi.org/10.1136/amiajnl-2011-000464

National Science Board. (2018). *Report: Science & engineering indicators.* https://www.nsf.gov/statistics/2018/nsb20181/

National Science Foundation. (2019). *Fact sheet: Advancing AI research and workforce.* https://nsf.gov/news/factsheets/Factsheet_AI.pdf

Nemeth, C. (1986). Differential contributions of majority and minority influence. *Psychological Review, 93*, 23–32.

Nilsson, N. J. (1991). Logic and artificial intelligence. *Artificial Intelligence, 47*, 31–56.

Noble, S. (2018). *Algorithms of oppression.* New York University Press.

Payne, B. K., & Gawronski, B. (2010). A history of implicit social cognition: Where is it coming from? Where is it now? Where is it going? In B. Gawronski & B. K. Payne (Eds.), *Handbook of implicit social cognition* (pp. 1–14). Guilford.

Pelled, L. (1996). Demographic diversity, conflict, and workgroup outcomes: An intervening process theory. *Organization Science, 7*, 615–631.

Pelled, L. H., Eisenhardt, K. M., & Xin, K. R. (1999). Exploring the black box: An analysis of workgroup diversity, conflict, and performance. *Administrative Science Quarterly, 44*, 1–28.

Ransbotham, S., Kiron, D., Gerbert, P., & Reeves, M. (2017). Reshaping business with artificial intelligence: Closing the gap between ambition and action. *MIT Sloan Management Review, 59*(1). https://proxy.library.upenn.edu/login?url=https://www.proquest.com/docview/195037403 0?accountid=14707

Roberson, Q., Holmes, O., & Perry, J. L. (2017). Transforming research on diversity and firm performance: A dynamic capabilities perspective. *Academy of Management Annals, 11*(1), 189–216. https://doi.org/10.5465/annals.2014.0019

Roberson, Q. M., King, E. B., & Hebl, M. (2020). Designing more effective practices to address workplace inequality. *Behavioral Science and Policy, 6*(1), 39–49.

Sigelman, L., & Tuch, S. (1997). Metastereotypes: Blacks' perceptions of whites' stereotypes of blacks. *The Public Opinion Quarterly, 61*, 87-101. Retrieved December 6, 2020, from http://www.jstor.org/stable/2749513

Simpson, T.W. (2004). "Product platform design and customization: Status and promise." Artificial intelligence for engineering design. *Analysis and Manufacturing, 18*(1), 3–20 https://doi.org/10.1017/S0890060404040028

Tajfel, H. (1978). Social categorization, social identity and social comparison. In H. Tajfel (Ed.), *Differentiation between Social Groups: Studies in the Social Psychology of Intergroup Relations* (pp. 61–76). Academic Press.

Tajfel, H., & Turner, J. C. (1986). The social identity theory of intergroup behavior. In J. T. Jost & J. Sidanius (Eds.), *Political psychology: Key readings* (pp. 276–293). Psychology Press. https://doi.org/10.4324/9780203505984-16

Tseng, M., Wang, Y., Jiao, R. J. (2017). Mass customization. In L. Laperrière & G. Reinhart (Eds.), *CIRP Encyclopedia of production engineering*. Springer. https://doi.org/10.1007/978-3- 642-35950-7_16701-3

Tsui, A. S. & Gutek, B. A. (1999). *Demographic differences in organizations: Current research and future directions.* Lexington Press.

Turner, J. C. (1985). Social categorization and the self-concept: A social-cognitive theory of group behavior. In E. J. Lawler (Ed.), *Advances in group processes: Theory and research* (Vol. 2, pp. 77–122). JAI Press.

Turner, J. C., Hogg, M. A., Oakes, P. J., Reicher, S. D., & Wetherell, M. S. (1987). *Rediscovering the social group: A self-categorization theory.* Basil Blackwell.

Van Knippenberg, D., De Dreu, C. K. W., & Homan, A. C. (2004). Workgroup diversity and group performance: An integrative model and research agenda. *Journal of Applied Psychology, 89*, 1008–1022.

Van Knippenberg, D., & van Ginkel, W. P. (2010). *The* categorization-elaboration model of workgroup diversity: Wielding the double-edged sword. In R. J. Crisp (Ed.), *Social issues and interventions: The psychology of social and cultural diversity* (pp. 257–280). Wiley Blackwell. https://doi.org/10.1002/9781444325447.ch11

Von Krogh, G. (2018). Guidepost: Artificial intelligence in organizations: New opportunities for phenomenon-based theorizing. *Academy of Management Discoveries, 4*, 404-409.

West, S. M., Whittaker, M., & Crawford, K. (2019). *Discriminating systems: Gender, race, and power in AI.* AI Now Institute. https://ainowinstitute.org/discriminatingsystems.html

Williams, K., & O'Reilly, C. (1998). Forty years of diversity research: A review. In J. A. Chatman & L. Kray (Eds.), *Research in organizational behavior*. Elsevier.

Yang, K., Qinami, K., Fei-Fei, L., Deng, J., & Russakovsky, O. (2019). Towards fairer datasets: Filtering and balancing the distribution of the people subtree in the ImageNet hierarchy. *ArXiv*, 547–558.

ABOUT THE AUTHORS

EDITORS

Eden B. King is the Lynette S. Autrey Professor of Industrial-Organizational Psychology at Rice University. She is pursuing a program of research that aims to make work better for everyone. This research—which has yielded over 100 scholarly products and has been featured in outlets such as the *New York Times*, *Good Morning America*, and *Harvard Business Review*—addresses three primary themes: (1) current manifestations of discrimination and barriers to work-life balance in organizations, (2) consequences of such challenges for its targets and their workplaces, and (3) individual and organizational strategies for reducing discrimination and increasing support for families. In addition to her scholarship, Dr. King has partnered with organizations to improve diversity climate, increase fairness in selection systems, and to design and implement diversity training programs.

Quinetta M. Roberson is the John A. Hannah Distinguished Professor of Management and Psychology at Michigan State University. Prior to her current position, she was an endowed chair at Villanova University and a tenured professor at Cornell University. She has also been a visiting scholar at universities on every continent, except for Antarctica, and served an appointment as Program Director of the Science of Organizations at the National Science Foundation (NSF). She currently serves as President of the Academy of Management (AOM) for 2020–2021. Professor Roberson's research interests focus on developing organizational capability and enhancing effectiveness through the strategic management of people, particularly diverse work teams. Her research has appeared in such journals as the *Academy of Management Journal, Academy of Management Review, Academy of Management Annals, Journal of Applied Psychology, Organizational Behavior and Human Decision Processes, Organizational Research Methods* and *Personnel Psychology*. Professor Roberson was an Associate Editor at the *Journal of Applied Psychology* (2008–2014), and edited a *Handbook of Diversity in the Workplace* published by Oxford Press. Professor Roberson has over 20 years of experience teaching courses and workshops globally on leadership, talent management and diversity.

Mikki Hebl is the Martha and Henry Malcolm Lovett Professor of Psychology and Professor of Management at Rice University, where she has been for more than 20 years. She graduated with her BA from Smith College and her PhD at Dartmouth College. She is an applied psychologist whose research focuses on workplace discrimination and remediation. Her particular area of expertise is in the area of gender discrimination. She has published over 125 articles, received 20 teaching awards, been awarded major NIH and NSF funded grants, and recently received both the lifetime award for Gender and Diversity in Organizations at the Academy of Management (2014) and the national Cherry Professor of the Year Award (2016).

AUTHORS

Richard Burgess is a fourth year PhD Candidate in Organizational Behavior at University of North Carolina's Kenan-Flagler Business School. His research broadly focuses on leadership, team dynamics, and identity. Prior to UNC-Chapel Hill, he received his Bachelor of Science in civil engineering from the Massachusetts Institute of Technology and both an MBA and Master of Science in Public Policy & Management from Carnegie Mellon University.

James T. Carter is a PhD Candidate in the Management Division at Columbia Business School. He uses multiple research methodologies—both quantitative and qualitative—to uncover barriers and pathways to diversity and inclusion. In using experimental, field, and interview data, his research spans both the individual and organizational level, with a particular emphasis on discrimination, social identity, and inequality.

Cydney H. Dupree: Cydney Dupree is a social psychologist who studies stereotyping and inequality. She uses experiments, and field studies across labs, workplaces, and social media to reveal the stereotypes that maintain inequality—and the strategies people use to reverse stereotypes. She earned her doctorate in psychology and social policy from Princeton University.

Ngoc S. Duong, M.S. (he/they) is currently a PhD candidate at the Florida Institute of Technology. Their research interests include applying the multilevel and emergence perspectives to better understand various aspects of Diversity, Equity, and Inclusion (DEI) and interpersonal conflict at work. Specifically, they are interested in how interpersonal conflict can serve as the foundation to DEI-related issues. Outside of academic work, they are also involved and interested in supporting nonprofit organizations.

Sydney N. Green obtained a BS in psychology from Kent State University in 2018, an MA in I/O psychology in 2021, and is a doctoral candidate in I/O psychology at Louisiana State University. Her research interests center around identifying and reducing subtle forms of discriminatory treatment in the workplace and improving the occupational well-being of all marginalized populations.

Gino J. Howard is a doctoral candidate in I/O psychology at Louisiana State University. He received his bachelor's degree in psychology with a concentration in I/O, and a master's degree in I/O psychology at California State University, San Bernardino. His research interests broadly include occupational health psychology and understanding the workplace experience of marginalized populations, work-nonwork domains, and workaholism.

Amber Kea-Edwards is a Clinical Assistant Professor of Management in the College of Business, University of Alabama in Huntsville. She earned her MA in organizational behavior from Claremont Graduate University and a bachelor's degree in Psychology from Winston-Salem State University. She is currently completing her PhD in organizational behavior from Claremont Graduate University. During doctoral studies at Claremont Graduate University, she has presented at both national and international conferences and has a publication in the *Journal of Leadership and Organizational Studies*. She is the recipient of several fellowships and awards for her research on racially inclusive leadership development including the Jenness Hannigan research fellowship.

Michael W. Kraus, Psychologist, studies how inequality fundamentally shapes the dynamics of human social interactions. His current research explores the behaviors and emotional states that maintain and perpetuate economic and racial inequality in society.

MaQueba Massey is a current doctoral student in the Management department of Jackson State University's College of Business where she has taught Principles of Management and Entrepreneurship. Aside from teaching, MaQueba developed research interests in topics related to blockchain technology, smart contracts, diversity and inclusion, and financial inclusion. MaQueba earned her undergraduate and graduate degree in accounting and finance, respectively.

Emily Moore is a PhD candidate at the Gordon S. Lang School of Business and Economics, University of Guelph. Her research interests include women's workplace experiences and workplace equity, diversity and inclusion. She has a Master of Business Administration and a Bachelor of Environmental Studies.

Kalan Norris is a fourth-year doctoral candidate in the Organization and Human Resources Department at the University at Buffalo School of Management. His research and teaching specializes in the areas of organizational behavior, leadership, diversity and inclusion, within-group differences, and research methods. Kalan's research is published in the *Journal of Leadership and Organizational Studies*. He is a PhD Project/ Baruch College Research Fellow, a William H. Hastie Research Fellow, and a recipient of UB's School of Management Rising Star Award. He received his Master of Science in Industrial/Organizational Psychology from Valdosta State University, and his Bachelor of Science in Psychology from the University of Central Florida.

Anju Philip is a PhD candidate at the Gordon S. Lang School of Business and Economics, University of Guelph. She conducts research on the work-life experiences of intersectional communities. She has a Master of Business Administration and Bachelor of Technology in Electronics and Communication Engineering.

Rebecca Ponce de Leon is a PhD candidate in the Management and Organizations department at Duke's Fuqua School of Business. Her research is grounded in the desire to understand the mechanisms that hinder progress toward equality and diversity in organizations and society. In one line of work, she focuses on how social categories, like race and gender, influence stereotypes, prototypes, and attitudes about employees and affect behavior in the workplace. Her second stream of research examines how motivations related to people's identities and ideological beliefs impact biases relevant to organizational life.

Lori Ramirez, MBA, is a business faculty member at the University of Houston–Downtown and a doctoral student at Creighton University. She is the owner of Red Ride Cycling Studio and Inspire Fitness Training Center, boutique fitness studios that bring specialized health and fitness services to underrepresented communities. She is also the cofounder of Beyond Great Inc., a nonprofit organization offering leadership workshops and training to young girls. She holds a Master of Business Administration in Leadership and focuses on research examining diversity in the workplace, the influence of society on organizational behavior, and workplace relationships.

Becky Reichard is an Associate Professor at Claremont Graduate University. She directs LeAD Labs (https://research.cgu.edu/lead-labs/), whose purpose is to advance and align the research and practice of leader development. LeAD Labs serves leaders at all levels of for-profit, non-profit, and community organizations and specializes in the development of new leaders, women, BIPOC, and LGBTQ+ individuals. Professor Reichard has over 45 publications and 100 speaking engagements on leader development. She earned a doctorate in Management from the University of Nebraska-Lincoln and a bachelor's degree in Psychology from Missouri Western State University and is a Clinical Assistant Professor of Management in the College of Business, University of Alabama in Huntsville. She earned her MA in organizational behavior from Claremont Graduate University and a bachelor's degree in Psychology from Winston-Salem State University. She is currently completing her PhD in organizational behavior from Claremont Graduate University. During doctoral studies at Claremont Graduate University, she has presented at both national and international conferences and has a publication in the *Journal of Leadership and Organizational Studies*. She is the recipient of several fellowships and awards for her research on racially inclusive leadership development including the Jenness Hannigan research fellowship.

Quinetta Roberson is the John A. Hannah Distinguished Professor of Management and Psychology. Beyond having held tenured faculty positions at Villanova University and Cornell University, she has been a visiting scholar at universities on six continents, and served as a program director at the National Science Foundation (NSF). Dr. Roberson has published over 40 scholarly journal articles and book chapters, edited a *Handbook of Diversity in the Workplace*, and served as an associate editor at the *Journal* *of Applied Psychology.* She also has over 20 years of global experience with teaching courses, facilitating workshops, and advising organizations on how to drive performance through diversity, inclusive cultures, and equitable work systems, which is informed by her research and corporate experience as a financial analyst. Dr. Roberson earned her PhD in organizational behavior from the University of Maryland, and holds undergraduate and graduate degrees in finance.

Enrica N. Ruggs, PhD, is an associate professor of management in the C.T. Bauer College of Business at the University of Houston. She received her PhD in Industrial-Organizational Psychology from Rice University, her MS degree from St. Mary's University, and her bachelor's degrees (BA and BS) from Prairie View A&M University. In her research she examines individual, organizational, and societal factors that influence inequity in the workplace. Her work focuses on the manifestation of subtle forms of discrimination and mistreatment toward employees with stigmatized identities, the outcomes of these behaviors, and strategies that individuals and organizations can engage in to combat and reduce discrimination. Additionally, she examines the experiences of minority employees to understand factors that influence job attitudes and psychological well-being. Dr. Ruggs has received funding for her work from the National Science Foundation. Her research has been published in academic outlets such as *Journal of Applied Psychology* and *Journal of Management*, and it has been featured in popular media outlets such as the *New York Times*, *U.S. News & World Report, Business Insider,* and *Fortune.* She is a member of several professional associations including the Academy of Management, the Society of Industrial and Organizational Psychology, and Southern Management Association.

Anmol Sachdeva is a doctorate student at Hofstra University pursuing her PhD in Applied Organizational Psychology. Her research interests include studying systemic racism, implicit bias in the workplace, while also focusing on various DEI (diversity, equity, and inclusion) issues. She has actively been involved in designing virtual assessment centers for various corporate organizations for both selections as well as development purposes.

Nicholas Salter is an Assistant Professor of Industrial-Organizational Psychology at Hofstra University. He is the director of the Workplace Inclusion, Leadership, and Diversity (WILD lab) where he and his team study the holistic experiences (positive and negative) of underrepresented and minoritized employees in the workplace. He is particularly interested in how leadership interplays with diversity, equity, and inclusion.

Rachel Williamson Smith is an Assistant Professor of Management at Georgia Southern University. Her research examines (1) the experiences of individuals from diverse backgrounds in the context of the work environment and the importance of diversity for organizations, and (2) both employee well-being (e.g., mindfulness, work engagement) and employee ill-being (e.g., work-family conflict, workaholism).

Hannah Perkins Stark, a Louisiana native, earned her BS in Psychology from LSU in 2020 and is currently pursuing a PhD in IO Psychology at LSU. Her research interests include the work-family interface, employee well-being, and research methods.

Karoline Summerville, MA, is a doctoral candidate in the Organizational Science program at the University of North Carolina at Charlotte. Her research details the causal mechanisms through which macro-level factors influence micro-level outcomes. Her work centers on the dynamics of intersectionality to provide a nuanced understanding of how people from diverse backgrounds experience organizational cultures, policies, and practices in varying ways in terms of advantage and disadvantage. To accomplish this task, she uses a series of methods and techniques— including qualitative research, experimental vignettes, social network analysis, natural language processing and machine learning to reveal the interactive and multilevel nature of diversity at work. Her research has been published in academic outlets such as *Journal of Applied Psychology*, *Leadership Quarterly*, and *Industrial Organizational Psychology*.

Brittany Torrez is a fourth year doctoral student in Organizational Behavior at the Yale School of Management. She employs multiple methodologies to further the study of diversity, equity, and inclusion in organizations. Her current research examines the psychological processes and organizational practices that reproduce racial inequality in the workplace.

Horatio D. Traylor is a PhD student in the Department of Management & Leadership at Bauer College of Business. Prior to joining Bauer, Traylor earned his BS in Psychology from Louisiana State University.

Sarah Singletary Walker, PhD, earned a bachelor's degree in Psychology from Dillard University and a PhD in Industrial/Organizational Psychology from Rice University. Her training in Industrial/Organizational Psychology provides her specific expertise in diversity, recruitment, selection, training, testing and measurement. She is the Vice President of the Division of Equity, Diversity, and Inclusion at Creighton University and is also a Full Professor in the Heider College of Business at Creighton. Her research interests include examining the experiences of marginalized individuals (e.g., racioethnic minorities, pregnant women, LGBTQIA, older workers) at work with a specific focus on individual and organizational-level strategies for creating more equitable workplaces.

Catherine Warren is an Industrial/Organizational Psychology PhD candidate at the Florida Institute of Technology, and a member of the Institute of Culture, Collaboration, and Management (ICCM). Her streams of research include teams, inclusion, and diversity in the workplace.

Shana M. Yearwod is a PhD candidate in Social-Organizational Psychology at Teachers College, Columbia University. Her research seeks to understand how Black women's participation in the labor force is shaped by sociohistorical factors, as well as modern-day stereotypes. She is also a diversity, equity, and inclusion strategist and facilitator, working with leaders and teams to increase awareness, strengthen relationships, and create systems-level change in organizations.

Printed in the United States
by Baker & Taylor Publisher Services